Medieval Lowestoft

Medieval Lowestoft

The Origins and Growth of a Suffolk Coastal Community

David Butcher

THE BOYDELL PRESS

First published 2016
The Boydell Press, Woodbridge

ISBN 978 1 78327 149 8

The Boydell Press is an imprint of Boydell & Brewer Ltd
PO Box 9, Woodbridge, Suffolk IP12 3DF, UK
and of Boydell & Brewer Inc.
668 Mt Hope Avenue, Rochester, NY 14620–2731, USA
website: www.boydellandbrewer.com

A catalogue record for this book is available
from the British Library

To Hluda – 'The Loud One' – whose name remains spoken in the land of his adoption

Contents

Illustrations

Plates

All photographs are by the author unless otherwise stated.

Maps

Tables

Abbreviations

AHR	*Agricultural History Review*
al.	*alias*, otherwise
AS	Anglo-Saxon
ASu.	Archdeaconry of Suffolk (re the proving of wills)
bis	Twice
BL	British Library
CCR	*Calendar of Close Rolls*
CoCR	*Calendar of Charter Rolls*
CFR	*Calendar of Fine Rolls*
CIM	*Calendar of Inquisitions Miscellaneous*
CPR	*Calendar of Patent Rolls*
CSPD	*Calendar of State Papers Domestic*
CSPF	*Calendar of State Papers Foreign*
EHR	*Economic History Review*
Gr	Greek
Heb	Hebrew
Is.	Island(s)
L	Latin
LA&LHS	Lowestoft Archaeological and Local History Society
LPFD	*Letters and Papers, Foreign and Domestic*
M	membrane (an individual part of a rolled-up document, stitched to others))
MCL	Magdalen College Library
ME	Middle English
NAHRG	Norfolk Archaeological and Historical Research Group
NCC	Norwich Consistory Court (re the proving of wills)
NRO	Norfolk Record Office
NRS	Norfolk Record Society
ob.	*obiit* (died)
OE	Old English
OFr	Old French

OHG	Old High German
ON	Old Norse
PCC	Prerogative Court of Canterbury (re the proving of wills)
PRME	*Parliament Rolls of Medieval England*
PSIA	*Proceedings of the Suffolk Institute of Archaeology*
rot	*rotulus* (a rolled-up document)
SA	Sudbury Archdeaconry (re the proving of wills)
SGB	Suffolk Green Books
SRO(I)	Suffolk Record Office (Ipswich)
SRO(L)	Suffolk Record Office (Lowestoft)
SRS	Suffolk Records Society
TNA	The National Archives, Kew
VCH	*Victoria County History*

A note on dating, transcription, currency, weights and measures, and references

All dates given are new style, with the year taken as beginning on 1 January, not 25 March. Personal names are reproduced both in the original spelling used and in modern format, depending on context and author's intentions, while original passages of prose quoted have modernised spelling with the original grammatical forms retained. Earlier names used for Lowestoft's streets and roadways are italicised. Currency values are given in the pre-decimal format of £ s d (pounds, shillings and pence), with twelve pence to the shilling and twenty shillings to the pound. Weights and measures are also pre-decimal, using the old, long-established Imperial system and with explanations provided in context. For the sake of consistency, all volume numbers of books and periodicals have been given in Arabic numerals.

Acknowledgements

Much of the preparatory work carried out for this volume has by its very nature been a solitary exercise, but I am also indebted to a number of people who have assisted me in various ways over the years. Long before any idea had formed of producing a written account of Lowestoft's medieval past, Brenda Parry-Jones (archivist at Magdalen College, Oxford) was very helpful in supplying photocopies of surviving documentation relating to the manor of Akethorpe. The late Peter Northeast helped to convert a classical Latin background into one with a medieval focus, particularly where legal abbreviations and the like were concerned – to say nothing of the intricacies of Gothic script! His generous support in providing details of Lowestoft testators' bequests will always be valued and to be able to respond with a return of information relating to fishing and other maritime practice was always a particular delight.

A debt of gratitude to Ivan Bunn (archival assistant at the Lowestoft branch of the Suffolk Record Office) has to be recorded, not only for preparing the maps and certain of the plates used to illustrate the text but also for reading some of the chapters and making constructive comments thereon. We continue to collaborate on matters of mutual interest relating to the town's past. Paul Durbidge has always been a key figure where archaeological matters are concerned and has been an ongoing source of information and support in matters relating to what lies below ground. His work carried out in the local area over many years is of considerable significance in understanding developments in the half-hundreds of Lothingland and Mutford. Michael Soanes, the writer's friend and long-time instructor in medieval religious practice, offered valuable advice relating to the town's clergy – though there is considerable difference of opinion when it comes to the legacy of the English Reformation, with any personal difficulties being resolved by regarding its effects as a matter of interpretation! Another productive working relationship has been with John Bussey, whose interest in the Lowestoft porcelain factory's Good Cross Chapel pattern led to a successful collaboration on its origins some years ago.

Among other valued contributions has been that made by my wife, Ann, who has once again used her expertise to format the photographic images used as illustrations – and thanks are due for her patience and attention to detail. A debt of gratitude is also due to volunteers at the Lowestoft Heritage Workshop Centre, where Leslie Parfitt, particularly, and Chris Whiting have been willing to carry out the printing of manuscript copies of the book prior to its publication. The Centre functions as part of the Lowestoft Civic Society and I am appreciative of the interest taken in my work by the organisation's chairman, John Stannard, and of the support shown in a number of local history projects of mutual interest that have taken place over the years.

Nor should the influence of the University of East Anglia in my development as an historian be overlooked. It was the late A. Hassell Smith who initially brought focus and specific purpose to a long-standing interest in the history of Norfolk and Suffolk and helped to foster the skills necessary to synthesise intention and research into coherent historical expression. The time spent studying for a part-time MPhil degree in the Centre of East Anglian Studies under his tutelage during the mid–late 1980s was both challenging and enjoyable. A little later on, from about 1990 to 2004, an extensive period as part-time tutor in the UEA's Continuing Studies Department, teaching adult evening classes on the Certificate in English Local History course at Lowestoft College of Further Education, added further to the range of skills acquired. Both department heads, the late Chris Barringer and his successor, Adam Longcroft, were always helpful and supportive.

Special reference must also be made to the interest and assistance of Professor Mark Bailey, whose perceptive and helpful peer review of the initial text was instrumental in broadening the scope of the book and placing it in a wider context. Sincere thanks are due to him for the trouble he took in appraising the text and making suggestions for further reading and for guidance in improving accuracy of expression where it was needed in both text and glossary. Any mistakes to be found remain, of course, the fault of the writer.

Finally, thanks are due to staff at The Boydell Press for their assistance and encouragement. Rob Kinsey, Rohais Haughton and Nick Bingham were helpful and attentive in matters of a technical nature once the work had reached manuscript stage, while Caroline Palmer showed great interest in the project from the start and was supportive of the writer in the book's creation – particularly during its later stages.

Preface

With the history of Lowestoft during the early modern period having been duly explored and a study produced (*Lowestoft 1550–1750*), it is time to turn to the town's medieval antecedents. The previous volume was a carefully integrated piece of work based on a wide range of source material collected over many years and closely interconnected and cross-referenced, wherever possible, to produce an intricate picture of a local society at a crucial point in its evolution.[1] Such a statement is not possible for earlier phases of the town's past, because the necessary variety of documentary sources with which to create a rich and complex reconstruction of life at the time does not exist. So this volume presents a series of individual studies of specific areas of human activity which helped to form the community of Lowestoft as it was at the time, with certain of them (particularly within the maritime context) having the capacity to influence later developments.

However, it also needs to be said that this book does not consist solely of a series of 'stand-alone' chapters each of which addresses a discrete aspect of Lowestoft's medieval past. A certain degree of linkage is possible (particularly with reference to the local topography), whereby a sense of the township's growth and development is able to be grasped. Two key documents assist the process – the Domesday Survey (1086) and the Lothingland Hundred Roll (1274) – and their respective collections of data not only reveal features of Lowestoft's physical and economic being but also provide information regarding social structure. Other useful and relevant medieval sources include the Patent Rolls, Close Rolls and Fine Rolls, whose published calendars are instructive in a variety of ways, shedding light on different aspects of community activity.

It is worth pointing out that Lowestoft, as it is seen today, is very much the product of mid–late nineteenth-century development brought about by the builder/contractor/entrepreneur Samuel Morton Peto, who purchased the

[1] Published in 2008, by The Boydell Press.

ailing harbour works in 1844 and established rail links with Norwich (1847) and Ipswich (1859), thereby creating a major boost to maritime enterprise based on fishing and cross-North Sea trade. The 1831 census shows the town with a population of 4,238; by 1911, it had grown to 37,886. The twentieth century generally saw a continuation of growth (a process that is ongoing), in terms of both population and urban spread, and the town has for many years been Suffolk's second largest community (after Ipswich), with a population currently in excess of 70,000 – this allowing for a certain degree of inflation caused by the absorption of four neighbouring parishes: Gunton, Kirkley, Oulton Broad and Pakefield.[2] In the case of the first-named place, the process of integration is a matter of wheels coming full circle, since Gunton was a twelfth-century creation formed partly from the parish to the north of it, Corton, and partly from Lowestoft itself.

It is a matter mainly of opinion and guesswork as to how the present-day Lowestoft urban unit will continue its development in both economic and social terms. The 1980s and 1990s, particularly, saw the loss of major industries in the town, together with the jobs these provided. Two long-established shipyards shut down, as did two important food-processing factories; a company which fabricated bus-bodies on the chassis-frames closed its doors and a major television manufacturing enterprise changed hands, resulting in a large reduction in its labour force (it, too, eventually ceased to function); a works which made doors and windows for the building industry (importing large quantities of softwood timber) first reduced the scale of its operation, then closed down; and, perhaps most poignantly of all, the mid-water trawling fleet completely disappeared, leaving only a handful of inshore vessels working and the fish market a vestige of its former self.

Light engineering has continued to operate, a wide variety of local service industries has developed and the North Sea gas fields have kept supply and standby vessels employed. However, the overall pattern of the last thirty years has been one of industrial decline – and even the long-established seaside holiday trade no longer draws in the number of visitors that it once did. There seems to be a certain degree of optimism, in some quarters, that renewable energy (in the form of North Sea wind farms, producing electricity) may help to provide some kind of economic recovery in the number of jobs created by both constructing and servicing the turbines, but this new activity's overall effect is not able as yet to be fully ascertained. The future of Lowestoft, therefore, is as much a matter of asking questions as giving answers – a process not so very different, in essence, as that involved in creating an assessment of its

[2] The 2011 Census figure for Lowestoft was 70,945. The two previous ones, 2001 and 1991, showed 68,340 and 62,907.

past. Whether or not the attempt to present a cogent account of the town's early history has succeeded will have to be left to the individual responses of the people who read the pages which follow.

One further statement which needs to be made is that I am not a medievalist. In attempting to create a 'prequel' to the account of Lowestoft's development during the early modern period I am aware that some points of the volume may fall short of the degree of detail and breadth of context required by specialists. Having made this *apologia*, I also hope that the work will be found acceptable at its own level and will make a useful contribution to the debate regarding the essence of small towns – especially those in a maritime environment. The sources available to enable a partial recreation of Lowestoft's earlier past have been investigated as thoroughly as possible and I have tried to present a clear and logically constructed account of the community's growth and development over a period of some 800–900 years.

– 1 –

The settlement's roots

Anglo-Saxon origins

In attempting to reach any sense of when, how and where the earliest hub of settlement (constituting what might be termed 'proto-Lowestoft') was formed, the investigator is handicapped by the limited amount of archaeological evidence concerning the parish at large. Important and significant finds of Lower Paleolithic flint artefacts which came to light at Pakefield (three to four miles away, south by west) during 2001–2 gave an indication of the presence of hominids in the local area some 700,000 years ago, during the Gunz-Mindel interglacial period, when Britain was an integral part of the European land-mass.[1] These flakes and cores are currently among the earliest signs of human activity found anywhere north of the Alps, but their discovery does not contribute anything to the study of Lowestoft's early founding and development because of their remoteness in time from the period of recorded history. A huge leap forward is therefore required to reach a point where any sense of the town's beginnings can be arrived at – and, before that is attempted, it is necessary to consider (if only in a cursory manner) the settlement's presence in its local geographical area.

Reference has already been made to the comparative paucity of known archaeological discoveries in the parish of Lowestoft itself – a fact which is alluded to in a report concerning the archaeology of the Suffolk coastal zone prepared by two members of the county's specialist unit.[2] One contributory

[1] Three local amateur archaeologists, Paul Durbidge, Robert Mutch and Adrian Charlton, were instrumental in making initial discoveries at a cliff-base location before the site became the focus of wider professional interest, establishing it as one of international importance. See P. Durbidge, 'The earliest humans in northern Europe: artefacts from the Cromer Forest Bed Formations at Pakefield, Suffolk', in LA&LHS *Annual Report*, 38 (Lowestoft, 2006), pp. 21–5.
[2] C. Good and J. Plouviez, *Archaeological Service Report: The Archaeology of the Suffolk Coast* (Bury St Edmunds, 2007), pp. 35–6.

cause is the town's remoteness (being in the extreme north-eastern corner of Suffolk) from the county archaeological service, located in Ipswich and Bury St Edmunds, which has led to a marked under-recording of amateur finds. However, the overriding reason for the dearth of information lies in the rapid expansion of the town during the second half of the nineteenth century and practically the whole of the twentieth. Most of Lowestoft's available land is now built over and much of the construction took place before there was sufficient awareness of the need to investigate particular areas of land ahead of their development. It is, therefore, largely a matter of conjecture as to what might have been missed as the roadways were put down and the houses went up, and the best hints are largely to be found in sporadic finds made on allotments and in gardens, consisting mainly of flint tools dating from the late Neolithic and early Bronze Age periods, as well as occasional sherds of Roman and Anglo-Saxon pottery.

In a wider context, the area to the north of Lowestoft, forming what was later to become the Half-hundred of Lothingland (of which Lowestoft eventually became the main town), has much the same kind of evidence for human habitation – some of it of considerable, in terms of quantity and topographical extent. Of the present-day communities known to the writer, Blundeston, Corton, Hopton, Lound and Somerleyton have all yielded material of the kind cited at the end of the previous paragraph, with cropmarks evident in aerial photographs adding further to a sense of a settlement pattern that shows human activity dating back as much as 4,000–5,000 years, and perhaps further.[3] There are also pronounced signs of a later co-axial field system stretching from Lowestoft itself to the northernmost limits of Lothingland, in Belton and Burgh Castle, which has been interpreted as late Iron Age or Roman in date.[4] Pioneering work carried out by John Peterson, of the University of East Anglia, has further suggested that this may be the result of *centuriation* (the planned setting-out of land for varying purposes – including agriculture – using a grid system) practised during Roman times, though without attaching any approximate date.[5]

[3] Archaeological distinctions in Lothingland have unfortunately become blurred since the transfer, in 1974, of five and a half northern parishes to Norfolk (Belton, Bradwell, Burgh Castle, Fritton, part-Herringfleet and Hopton). This administrative exercise, deriving from the Local Government Act passed during Edward Heath's premiership, has led to an artificial divide in the recording of the history of Lothingland. Realistically, in terms of its physical geography, the area annexed remains part of Suffolk.

[4] Good and Plouviez, *Suffolk Coast*, p. 37.

[5] J. Peterson, 'Possible extension of Roman centuriation to Lothingland (Norfolk/Suffolk)', in NAHRG *Annual Report*, 17 (Norwich, 2008), pp. 57–60.

Regarding specific Roman presence in Lowestoft itself, it is difficult to make any detailed comment, but one particular part of the town is still known as *Roman Hill* (as a result of finds made there during the late nineteenth and early twentieth centuries). It is located to the west of the present-day town centre on ground that reaches about fifty feet above sea level and may be taken as roughly centring on the Ethel Road area (TM59 545934). The silver coins, the pottery sherds and the bronze fragment from a statue found hereabouts have been variously referred to in previous publications and may well suggest some kind of settlement.[6] In the absence of detailed investigation of the location and the proper recording and dating of artefacts no informed comment is able to be made, but it does seem likely that there was some kind of occupation of this particular part of modern Lowestoft in Roman times – though over how long a period of time, and of what kind, cannot even be guessed at. As is so often the case with references to the finding of archaeological material in previous eras, the sense of the human activity revealed thereby is both fascinating and frustrating at the same time.

During the late third century the southern North Sea and English Channel coasts became exposed to raids by members of tribes native to the Frisian Islands and adjacent parts of the European mainland. The response to these barbarian incursions was a defensive chain of nine major forts (named in the *Notitia Dignitatum*) and interposing installations to guard what was known as the *Saxon Shore*. It began at *Branodunum* (Brancaster), on the Wash, and ended at *Portus Adurni* (Portchester), on the Solent. Lothingland had its own guardian presence at *Gariannonum* (Burgh Castle), built c. AD 270–90 and occupied by Stablesian cavalrymen from the Adriatic area. It was erected to protect what might be termed a 'soft under-belly' created by the presence of a large, shallow estuary (later to be known as *Breydon Water*) into which the waters of the rivers Yare, Bure and Waveney emptied and which, in the absence of the coastal sandbar that was to form later and allow Great Yarmouth to develop,[7] provided an ideal entry point and landing place for shallow-draught vessels of the type used by the Frisians and Saxons. Much of this stretch of water would have taken the form of coastal mudflats at low tide – and not just around the edges – being analogous, perhaps, with the Essex marshes of today. But at high-tide, and probably mid-water as well, it would have provided convenient access to the higher, settled land which surrounded it.

[6] M.L. Powell, *Lowestoft Through the Ages* (Lowestoft, 1950), pp. 32–6 contains useful summarised information concerning the artefacts and their general location.

[7] The formation of this feature was probably greatly assisted by the drop in sea levels which occurred during the late Anglo-Saxon period.

All sides of the estuarine area would have given good opportunities for raiding activity, the perpetrators being able to steal produce, livestock, tools and domestic artefacts from the agricultural communities there. It is likely that the Lothingland area was already well known to Anglo-Saxon invaders by the time that Rome withdrew its legions from Britain in AD 410; following the imperial departure, they came in increasing numbers to settle in eastern and southern England. It is not possible to say at what point during the fifth or sixth centuries the Lowestoft area was first occupied by the newcomers (or whether, in fact, it was as late as the seventh century), but place-name analysis provides some clues as to possible origins, at least as far as ethnic links are concerned.

The name Lowestoft means 'the homestead of Hloðvér', deriving from a combination of an Old Norse personal name and '*toft*', which could also have a Nordic derivation. This might seem to suggest Scandinavian beginnings, dating back to either the mid-ninth or the late tenth/early eleventh centuries, but another explanation also offers itself. The island of Lothingland, on which Lowestoft is situated (and which is, indeed, surrounded by water on all sides), has a name which translates as 'the land of the people of Hlud', deriving from Anglo-Saxon elements: the personal name *Hlud* (meaning 'loud one'), the suffix *-ing* (meaning 'the descendants of') and *land* (meaning 'area' or 'estate'). The Latinised version of the name used in the Domesday Survey (1086) is *Ludingalanda* – a form that would seem to be adhering to an earlier one than that of *Lothingland* itself (which suggests Scandinavian influence in the use of *th* to replace the letter *d*) – and it is interesting to note that *Ludingland* was a spelling which continued in use in various kinds of documentation long after William I's audit of the country had been carried out.

There is no doubting the pronounced Nordic influence in the place-names of Lothingland generally, half of which are either wholly or partly Scandinavian in origin. However, rather than the area being one of primary Scandinavian settlement, it is much more likely to be an example of an Anglo-Saxon homeland that was taken over and reshaped by incomers. If this theory can find acceptance, then *Lowestoft* could easily have had its form changed from *Hluda's toft* to *Hloðver's* (or *Hlothver's*) *toft* – the latter word also being found as an Old English term, thus making it one that was not exclusively Scandinavian. The question can then be asked: 'Who was Hluda?' And there is, of course, no definitive answer. All that can be arrived at is a sense of some tribal leader, or family head, whose presence and personality were defined by the sound of his voice.[8]

[8] An identical patronym is in evidence, also, in the name of the Broadland parish of Ludham, in East Norfolk.

'The Loud One'! What kind of image is created by the description? One of authority, perhaps, and of dominant character. The man was certainly important enough in his own time to give his name to the wider locality in which he settled, and it has survived down to the present day. Even the area to the south of what is now the Lowestoft inner harbour and the stretch of water forming the broad at Oulton seems to have once been thought of as associated with him, because Domesday entries for the Half-hundred of Mutford are classified as relating to *Ludinga H.* (Lothing Hundred). Hluda's influence, therefore, seems to have spread across a well-defined natural boundary into another district – though without the permanence associated with Lothingland (or Ludingland) itself. Both half-hundreds remained as largely autonomous units (though sharing a six-monthly hundred court) until formally united as one, in 1763, for purposes of Poor Law administration.[9]

With the one-time existence of the man Hluda having now been established, it is time to consider where he might have founded his *toft*, or homestead. The Lowestoft locality offered easy access from the sea, with sheltered inshore reaches lying between a wide beach and the outlying sandbanks, and with inland access provided on the cliff-face by surface-water channels grooved into the soft glacial deposits.[10] Even more advantageous to incomers from across the North Sea was the presence of a low shingle bank at the southern end of the beach, separating a large freshwater lagoon from the ocean itself and offering a safe haven for the craft in which they had sailed – including a possible 'arm' of water, or inlet, leading northwards from it at the bottom end of what is now Rotterdam Road.[11] Lake Lothing, as it later became known, lay on an east–west alignment at the bottom of a gentle, south-facing acclivity,

[9] The *tourn*, as it is referred to in late sixteenth-century and early seventeenth-century documentation, was held during April/May and October in a building close to the present-day *Commodore* public house, in Commodore Road, Oulton Broad – this particular location being the traditional meeting-point of the two half-hundreds, long known as *Mutford Bridge* (earlier, *Motforth Bregge*). The first element derives from OE *mōtford*, meaning 'the ford at which moots were held', and the second from OE *brycg* – the 'bridge', in this case, referring to the reinforced earthern causeway that once crossed the meeting-point of Lake Lothing and Oulton's freshwater mere.

[10] These were later engineered into a series of managed footways and cart tracks known as *scores* (from ON *skora*, meaning 'to cut' or 'to incise'), and they remain a notable landscape feature today.

[11] The stretch of impounded water may once have been a pre-glacial outlet of the River Waveney and the shingle bar itself was periodically carried away by surge tides before being reinstated by the natural process of *longshore drift* and human restorative intervention. When it was breached in 1830, during the construction of Lowestoft Harbour, a causeway of oak logs was found beneath it, leading to speculation that this feature may have dated from Roman times and have been part of a coastal road linking the shore-fort of *Garrianonum* and its companion to the south at Walton (Felixstowe). See Powell, *Lowestoft*, p. 32.

the land dropping from 100 feet or so at the northern extremity to sea level at the edge of the mere.[12] The surface soils (as in practically the whole of the parish, as it was later to become) were light and sandy, resulting in little substantial tree cover and large areas of heath, and any existing areas of cultivated land would have been relatively easy to work compared with heavier clays and loams (Plate 1).

Plate 1. The Lake Lothing inlet site, at the meeting-point of Rotterdam Road, Denmark Road and Peto Way. Cranes associated with Lowestoft's inner harbour works are clearly visible in the distance. Rotterdam Road is the highway shown in the immediate foreground and runs on the north–south alignment of the former inlet.

It has been observed that many small towns in England, during the Anglo-Saxon period, had their origins in one or other of four types of previously established centre:[13] Roman towns and forts, high-status secular strongholds and royal vills, hundredal and other local administrative centres, and cathedrals and monastic establishments. Lowestoft can claim no such precedents. It had its origins on a favoured piece of land easily approached from the sea, which had seen occupation of some kind just to the east during Roman times and earlier human activity in the area generally going back to the Neolithic

[12] A manorial roll of 1618 refers to it as *The Fresh Water* or *The Great Water* (the sides of it having been widened by peat-digging throughout the later medieval period). See SRO(L), 194/A10/73.
[13] J. Blair, 'Small towns 600–1270', in D.M. Palliser (ed.), *The Cambridge Urban History of Britain* (Cambridge, 2000), vol. 1, p. 250.

period. Thus, particular aspects of local topography seem to have been the key factor in a settlement of some kind being established, though there is no way of knowing whether or not an existing population was present in the area at the time that Hluda and his followers arrived.

A site somewhere on the slope described above would have been a suitable place to build either an individual homestead or a small settlement. The area offered a relatively sheltered, well-drained environment, with land suitable to the growing of crops of various kinds and with tracts of heath available for the gathering of bracken for animal bedding, the rough grazing of livestock, the cutting of gorse and thorn for firewood and the taking of small timber (birch and thorn) for building repairs and fuel.[14] Pockets of clay were present in places, which would have provided the material for daub, and oak, elm, beech and hazel were almost certainly available relatively near at hand for the structural framing of houses and the infill of the walls. The lagoon itself would have provided reed and sedge for thatching; peat was able to be dug from around its margins (becoming even more accessible when sea levels dropped during the late Anglo-Saxon period); and it sustained coarse fish and wildfowl that could be taken for food. Supplies of drinking water were also to be had in a number of places where the light topsoil thinned sufficiently for springs to well up from the ground above the underlying, impervious clay.

Having taken account of the basic advantages for human habitation offered by the sloping ground above Lake Lothing, an attempt must be made to decide upon a likely location for Hluda's settlement. After due consideration of the basic configuration of local landforms and the long-established trackways that these produced, the writer is inclined to place it somewhere in the north-eastern corner of the Lowestoft municipal cemetery, close to the roundabout where Normanston Drive, Rotterdam Road and St Peter's Street converge (TM59 541936; Plate 2), as shown on Map 1. This site, due north of the inlet mentioned above, remained in continuous habitation and use until the township relocated to a cliff-side location during the first half of the fourteenth century. Unfortunately, the development of this particular part of the parish during the later nineteenth and early twentieth centuries destroyed its potential archaeological value, and any finds that might have manifested themselves either went unnoticed or were ignored. It would have been advantageous to have had evidence of early Anglo-Saxon settlement, but in its absence informed conjecture will have to suffice.

[14] M. Bailey, *Medieval Suffolk* (Woodbridge, 2007), pp. 96–8, has pertinent things to say about the importance of heath in the medieval rural economy.

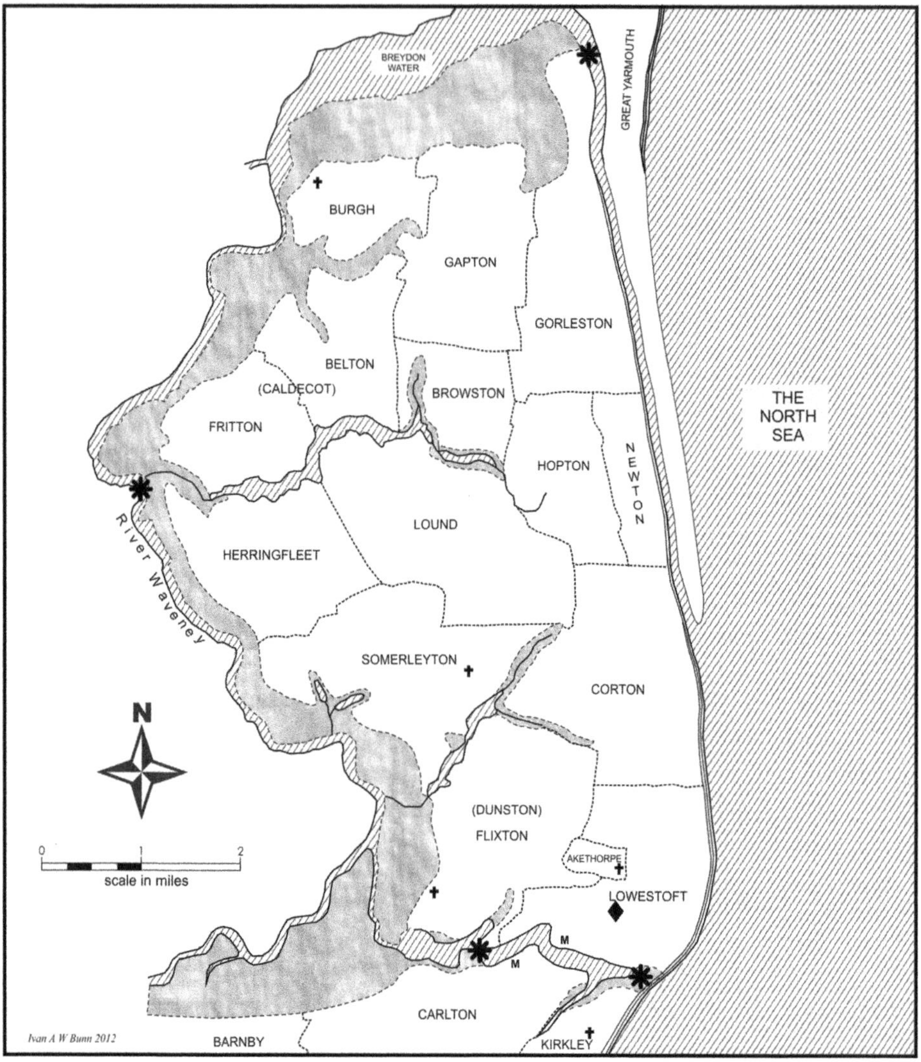

Map 1. Lothingland Half-hundred at Domesday.

Notes:

- Crosses represent churches referred to (directly or indirectly) in the Survey.
- Asterisks show the four fording-places or crossing-points providing access to, and egress from, the Island of Lothingland. The bridges eventually built across them were a much later feature.
- The areas represented in light grey shading are the tidal mudflats alongside the River Waveney and the main inland stretches of marsh. Lakes, rivers and the sea are shown in diagonal hatching.

- Approximate boundaries for the communities are defined by dotted lines. Caldecot and Dunston are shown in their respective locations, but are bracketed because of insufficient information regarding their limits.
- The letter M indicates the position of two former burial mounds.
- The sandbar on which Great Yarmouth was founded (the result of the drop in sea levels during late Anglo-Saxon times and of longshore drift bringing eroded material from much further up the Norfolk coast) grew progressively southwards in spit form until well into the fourteenth century. During the Anglo-Saxon era, it gradually closed off the mouth of the estuary of Roman times and, by impeding the outflow of the rivers Yare, Bure and Waveney to the sea, made possible the gradual reclamation of the area known today as Halvergate Marshes.
- The inlet leading from Lake Lothing to Lowestoft's first site is not shown, owing to lack of information regarding its size and the problem of scaling it correctly. It may well have undergone silting up and drainage by Domesday.

Plate 2. The Normanston Drive – Rotterdam Road – St Peter's Street roundabout looking northwards towards St Margaret's Church. The original township's site was located a little to the south-south-west.

One reference that may be of significance is to be found in the manor roll of 1618, which lists every building and piece of land in the parish. By the time that the document was drawn up the land along the northern edge of Lake Lothing had been parcelled up into strips providing managed rough grazing, or *bruery*, for livestock. In the section of the document dealing with this particular area the Latin text informs the reader that a man named William Willes held a half-acre strip with a mound situated thereon (*cum Monte sup eand*). The approximate location of this feature is now occupied by the Peto Way roundabout, providing access to various parts of the North Quay Retail Park (it may have been even further down towards the water, where the railway runs). It was complemented by another mound located on the other side of Lake Lothing, three-quarters of a mile away to the south-west, at the end of Stanley Road, on land that had once been part of the great East Heath in Carlton Colville.

Both of these tumuli (for that is almost certainly what they were) have been long removed by the later development of the ground on which they stood. The shape of them is not known, and it is possible that they might have dated from the Bronze Age. However, their location close to water, on heathland and above normal flooding level suggests that they could have been ship-burials of the early Anglo-Saxon period.[15] The mound on the south side of Lake Lothing must have been an imposing structure, as the local children who played on it at the end of the nineteenth century and the beginning of the twentieth referred to it as 'The King's Hill'.[16] It is conceivable that the name might have derived from the old nursery rhyme, 'I'm the King of the Castle'; it is also within the bounds of possibility that it might have been a vestigial folk-memory, passed down in local lore for more than a millennium. Speculation is all that the modern observer is left with.

There is, however, no need to speculate as to the presence of early Anglo-Saxon settlement, which was discovered on Bloodmoor Hill in an area that was later to accommodate the parish boundary between Gisleham and Carlton Colville (TM48 520896). The site, at which one vill and a number of cemetery areas have been excavated, has been dated to the late sixth or early

[15] In 1830, a buried boat, still largely intact, was discovered on the southern edge of Fritton Lake, five miles or more north-north-west of the Lowestoft mound, on Ashby Warren (approximate location: TG40 484001). It is generally referred to as 'the Ashby Dell boat', but at the time it was committed to the ground (sixth or seventh century) the parish of Ashby did not exist – and did not, in fact, emerge as an entity in its own right until the twelfth century.
[16] The writer was given this information by his friend and collaborator in the study of local history, Ivan Bunn, who had received it during a conversation with an elderly lady during the 1970s.

seventh century.[17] It is adjudged to be one of the most important early Anglo-Saxon sites found in Suffolk. A team from the Cambridge Archaeological Unit worked there from 1998 to 2001 and discovered a number of interesting features – among them, burials showing an east–west alignment and with associated grave goods (thus showing an intermingling of Christian custom with established pagan traditions). A community of similar type and date could well have been in existence three miles or so away to the north-north-east, in the location identified as that where Lowestoft had its origins. But there is no means of establishing proof; the proposition has to be accepted (or not) on the conjectural evidence offered.

One topographical feature relating to Lowestoft which is beyond objection is the proximity of an *outlier* connected with it, known as Akethorpe. This small community is recorded in Domesday and there is a good deal of thirteenth- and fourteenth-century documentation relating to it. It was situated half a mile to the north and north-west of its larger neighbour, on higher ground, and the name suggests later development. The first element derives from the Old English word *āc*, meaning 'oak', while the second one is either the Old English or Scandinavian *Þorp* or *Þrop*, meaning 'farm' or 'hamlet' (depending on context). The place-name derivation is topographically sound, as Akethorpe's location was on heavier soil than that of Lowestoft, at about 100 feet above sea level, and the clay content suits the growth of oaks more than does the lighter land fifty feet lower down the slope. Its position is clearly shown in Map 1 and, in the light of the information contained there, it is now time to turn to what Domesday reveals about Lowestoft (and the communities to the north of it), 400 years or more after it was founded.

Domesday data and analysis

The purpose of William I's great survey of 1086 has long been debated. Was it simply a tax enquiry, enabling the monarch to know the value of geldable (taxable) land outside his own personal estate, or demesne?[18] Or was it a survey of the economic state of the country, logging differences between the England of Edward the Confessor and the country, as it was, twenty years after the Conquest? Did it have political intent, in revealing the fealty between lord and underling, thereby enabling judgements to be made as to individual loyalties in times of potential rebellion and invasion? Was it a means of assessing the ability of regions to support the quartering and provisioning of troops,

[17] Good and Plouviez, *Suffolk Coast*, p. 38.

[18] D. Roffe, *Decoding Domesday* (Woodbridge, 2007), pp. 231 and 237, argues that it was.

if required? Or was it, in its sheer scope and scale, an audit of the whole nation, embodying all four of the intentions outlined and perhaps others as well? A definitive answer may not be crucial to the local historian of today, because the importance of the information lies not only in what it can tell us of the past but also the manner in which it can enhance our understanding of what may still be seen around us. The five tables which follow (previously published in the writer's The Island of Lothingland: a Domesday and Hundred Roll Handbook) present the Domesday assessment of Lothingland as a whole, enabling Lowestoft to be seen in its local context.

Table 1. Lothingland manors, holdings and outliers (pp. 283a, 283b, 284a, 284b, 294a, 336a, 381a, 445a).

Community	Estates	Values
Akethorp(e)	1 manor (80 acres)*	10s
Belton	**1 *outlier* (120 acres)**, 1 holding (90 acres)	-; 10s (10s)
Browston	1 manor (40 acres), 1 holding (30 acres), 1 manor (60 acres), 1 holding (30 acres), 1 holding (80 acres)	5s; 2s; 5s (5s); 3s; 6s(6s)
Burgh [Castle]	1 manor (480 acres – inc. a church, with 11 acres)	106s (100s)
Caldecot	1 manor (120 acres)	8s (10s)
Corton	1 manor (240 acres), 1 holding (80 acres)	20s (20s); 10s (10s)
Dunston	1 holding (15 acres), 1 manor (45 acres)	30d; 3s (10s)
Earetuna	1 holding (40 acres)	4s (4s)
Flixton	1 manor (360 acres), 1 holding (360 acres), 1 manor (240 acres), 1 holding (5 acres), 1 manor (120 acres + church)	30s (30s); 40s (40s); 30s (30s); 10d; 20s (20s)
Fritton	1 manor (240 acres), 1 holding (60 acres), 1 holding (80 acres), 1 holding (30 acres)	20s (20s) 5s (5s); 10s (10s); 3s;
Gapton	1 manor (240 acres), 1 manor (60 acres), 1 manor (60 acres), 1 holding (40 acres), 1 holding (30 acres)	60s (60s); 5s; 4s; 4s; 2s
Gorleston	**1 manor (600 acres)**, **1 holding (90 acres)**, 1 holding (120 acres)	-; -; 16s (20s)
Herringfleet	1 manor (120 acres)	4s (4s)
Hopton	1 manor (80 acres), 1 manor (60 acres), 1 holding (80 acres)	5s (5s); 5s (5s); 10s (10s);
Lound	**1 *outlier* (240 acres)**, 1 manor (180 acres), 1 holding (120), 1 manor (120 acres), 1 holding (40 acres)	-; 20s (10s); 10s (10s); 10s (10s); 5s
Lowestoft	**1 *outlier* (450 acres)**	-
Newton	1 holding (30 acres)	3s

Table 1 *cont.*

Community	Estates	Values
Somerleyton	**1 holding (90 acres)**, 1 manor (240 acres), 1 holding (40 acres), 1 manor (40 acres)*, 1 holding (20 acres + church), 1 holding (30 acres)	-; 20s (20s); 3s; 5s; 3s; 2s
	22 manors, 3 *outliers* (each part of the manor of the half-hundred) and 24 holdings (2 of them part of the manor of the half-hundred) – making 49 estates in all. *Priest named.	**Total values:** £27 9s 4d (1066, £27 6s 4d). 6 exemptions (-).
	Earetuna is a misrepresentation of **Karetuna (Corton).**	

Notes:

- Tax values shown thus () are those of 1066. All values given represent annual payments due to the Crown from the area's lesser manors and its unmanorialised tenants. Lands not used for the direct supply of an overlord's household were often referred to as *warland* and were liable for a range of payments in the form of rents and services. The word has its origins in the OE *wara* ('defence') – a specific use of the noun referring to military obligations connected with particular pieces of non-seigneurial (non-manorial) land. It is now generally accepted that these payments were made in cash (Roffe, *Domesday*, p. 243). The main purpose of the Domesday Survey itself was probably to ascertain the nature and value of the taxable service due to the Crown (Roffe, *Domesday*, p. 315).
- The areas of land recorded are those under cultivation.
- The hyphen is used to indicate values that are not given. They all relate to estates (shown in bold font) that formed the seigneurial estate of the manor of Lothingland Half-hundred (centred on Gorleston) and these constituted what was known as *inland* – land that was directly under the control of the manorial lord and exempt from paying tax. Inland consisted of estates specifically used for the supply and maintenance of the lord's household and they are shown here in bold font. A detailed explanation of inland and warland may be found in R. Faith, *The English Peasantry and the Growth of Lordship* (Leicester, 1997), Chapters 2, 3, 4 and 5.
- The unassessed estates shown in bold font thus constituted the personal estate of the half-hundred's lord, as opposed to his jurisdictional reach (which encompassed the district as a whole). Thus, the Half-hundred of Lothingland has to be seen and understood in two different contexts: a specific unit of land (composed of different holdings) forming a seigneurial estate and a wider area of legal and fiscal administration.
- The Domesday text used was the Suffolk volume, parts 1 and 2 (ed. A. Rumble), in the Phillimore facsimile series. The page numbers at the head of the table, and those which follow, are those of the original Domesday folios.

Table 2. Land, livestock and other assets (pp. 283a, 283b, 284a, 284b, 294a, 336a, 381a, 445a).

Community	Arable (acres)	Meadow (acres)	Wood	Teams (8 oxen a team)	Horses	Cattle	Sheep	Pigs	Varia
Akethorp(e)	80	1	5 pigs	1½	0	0	48	3	
Belton	210	0	0	2½ (5)	1	0	160	0	
Browston	240	0	10 pigs	4	2	4	70	14	3 goats
Burgh [Castle]	480	10	0	5 (7)	3	6	160	17	3 salt-pans
Caldecot	120	0	0	½ (1)	0	0	0	0	
Corton	320	0	3 pigs	6 (7)	2	5	50	12	
Dunston	60	½	4 pigs	½	0	0	0	0	
Earetuna	40	0	0	½	0	0	0	0	
Flixton	1085	13	28 pigs	17½ (25)	2	6	200	21	20 goats, ½ mill
Fritton	410	0	20 pigs	5 (6½)	2	8	160	16	3 goats, 3 hives (1 salt-pan)
Gapton	430	4½	0	5½ (6½)	1	7	110	9	
Gorleston	810	10	8 pigs	11 (16½)	0 (2)	0 (5)	300	0	3 salt-pans
Herringfleet	120	0	10 pigs	0 (1½)	0	0	0	0	
Hopton	220	0	20 pigs	4 (5)	2	9	129	16	3 hives
Lound	700	3	112 pigs	7½ (9)	3	10	110	27	2 hives
Lowestoft	450	5	8 pigs	5 (7)	0	8 (14)	160	11	
Newton	30	0	0	½	0	0	0	0	
Somerleyton	460	1	34 pigs	4½ (5)	3	4	63	11	
	6265 [+10?]	48 [+1?]	262 pigs	81 (109)	21 (23)	67(78)	1720	157	26 goats, 8 hives, 6 (7) salt-pans, ½ mill

Notes:

- Note that *Earetuna* is a misrepresentation of Karetuna (Corton).
- Note also that Burgh had a church endowed with ten acres of arable land and one acre of meadow. It is not specified whether this was a separate holding or part of the manor (probably the latter). Both areas of land are indicated by being placed in square brackets beneath the half-hundred totals.
- The figures shown thus () refer to the year 1066, showing what the situation had been twenty years before.

Table 3. Place-name derivation and population (283a, 283b, 284a, 284b, 294a, 336a, 381a, 445a).

Derivation	Community	Freemen	Villans	Bordars	Slaves
Anglo-Scandinavian	**Akethorp(e)** (*Aketorp*)	1	0	3	0
Anglo-Scandinavian	**Belton** (*Beletuna*)	3	1	4	1
Old English	**Browston** (*Brockestuna*)	6	0	3	0
Old English	**Burgh** [**Castle**] (*Burch*)	0	10	5	0 (2)
Old English	**Caldecot** (*Caldecotan*)	0 (1)	0	3 (1)	0
Anglo-Scandinavian	**Corton** (*Karetuna*)	16	0	5 (6)	0
Old English	**Dunston** (*Dun[e]stuna*)	2	0	½	0
(Probable misrepresentation)	***Earetuna***	1	0	0	0
Anglo-Scandinavian	**Flixton** (*Flixtuna*)	25	4	34 (39)	4
Anglo-Scandinavian	**Fritton** (*Fridetuna*)	6	2(4)	3	3
Old English	**Gapton** (*Gabbatuna*)	5	2 (3)	4 (3)	0
Old English	**Gorleston** (*Gorlestuna*)	24	12 (20)	5	4 (5)
Anglo-Scandinavian	**Herringfleet** (*Herlingaflet*)	1	2	1	0
Old English	**Hopton** (*Ho.tuna*)	10	0	2	1
Scandinavian	**Lound** (*Lunda*)	9	2	10	2
Scandinavian	**Lowestoft** (*Lothu Wistoft*)	0	3 (5)	10	3 (5)
Old English	**Newton** (*Neutuna*)	1	0	0	0
Anglo-Scandinavian	**Somerleyton** (*Sumerledetuna*)	8	4	6 (5)	0
		118 (119)	42 (55)	98½ (100½)	18 (23)

Notes:

- Domesday forms are shown in brackets. Note that Earetuna – implied as a Latinised form of Southtown by W.A. Copinger, *The Manors of Suffolk*, vol. 5 (1905), p. 66 – is a misrepresentation of Karetuna (Corton).
- The Akethorp(e) freeman was a priest; so was one of the Somerleyton freemen.
- Twenty-four Yarmouth fishermen belonged to the manor of Gorleston, but are not included in the figures above.
- The figures shown thus () refer to the year 1066.
- If the men listed are regarded as family heads, a multiplier of 4.75 may be applied to each of them to estimate notional population numbers.
- Freemen constituted c. 43 per cent of the recorded male population. The proportion was even higher in the neighbouring half-hundred of Mutford, being c. 70 per cent. The figure for Suffolk as a whole was c. 45 per cent.
- Classification of the four categories of men recorded may be summarised, or generalised, thus: *freemen* held their land, outside of the local predominant manor usually, in return for geld payments and specified services (often wide-ranging) and could often dispose of it without encumbrance; *villans* (*villeins*) were the highest level of workers (often with specialist skills) tied to a manor, with consequent amounts of land allotted to them for subsistence and, possibly, surplus; *bordars* formed a

'middling' tier of workers, often responsible for all kinds of quasi-domestic tasks and allotted smallholdings on which to maintain themselves and their families; *slaves* were the lowest level, assisting with menial but necessary tasks (e.g. ploughing, muck-spreading) and given accommodation either in-house or in the humblest type of cot – the latter not necessarily having land attached.

- *Villan* (villein), in being a post-Conquest, Norman classification, or term, is extremely difficult to give a precise meaning to because of the diverse types of worker it seems to have described.
- The likely explanation for a ½-bordar being attached to one of the Dunston estates probably lies in the man's labour services. Perhaps half his working week was devoted to his freeman master, the other half to his own land.

The first thing that needs to be said is that, at the time of Domesday, Gorleston was the hub of the Lothingland manor, with its 600 acres of arable land conforming to the size of holding reckoned to be sufficient for the maintenance of a greater thane (*thegn*) and his household.[19] Gyrth Godwinson (younger brother of Harold) had been lord of Lothingland prior to the Norman invasion and, having also fallen at Hastings, his lands became part of King William's personal estate. Earl Gyrth had entrusted the administration of Lothingland to a thegn named Wulfsi (al. Ulsi) – a man who may also have perished at Hastings.[20] After the Conquest, the duties fell upon Roger Bigot (al. Bigod), sheriff of Norfolk and Suffolk, but so extensive were his responsibilities in East Anglia that he would have found someone of lesser rank to supervise the royal manor in Lothingland. In addition to this particular estate (dispersed across the communities of Gorleston, Belton, Lound, Lowestoft and Somerleyton), there were all the other smaller ones formerly held by Anglo-Saxon freemen, named and unnamed, which had come into the possession of Norman overlords – particularly the monarch. The royal connection was the predominant one in Lothingland, as may be seen in Table 4, only seven of the forty-nine holdings being in other hands.

[19] 600 acres was 5 *hides* in area, the hide being 120 acres of arable land. It was later known as the *carucate*.

[20] P. Warner, *The Origins of Suffolk* (Manchester, 1996), p. 194, identifies him as the supervisor of Mutford Half-hundred also.

Table 4. Overlordship and fealty (pp. 283a, 283b, 284a, 284b, 294a, 336a, 381a, 445a).

Community	Estates	Title-holder (1086)	Title-holder (pre-1066)
Akethorp(e)	80 acre manor (+ church?)	King	Aelmer the Priest
Belton	**120 acre *outlier***	**King**	**Earl Gyrth** (no freemen attached)
	90 acre holding	King	3 freemen
Browston	40 acre manor	King	Ulfketel
	30 acre holding	King	1 freeman (under Ulfketel)
	60 acre manor	King	Brother
	30 acre holding	King	Godwin
	80 acre holding	King	2 freemen
Burgh [Castle]	480 acre manor (+ church)	Ralph the Crossbowman	Archishop Stigand (no freemen attached)
Caldecot	120 acre manor	Ralph the Crossbowman	Bondi (under Earl Gyrth)
Corton	240 acre manor	King	Alric (under Earl Gyrth)
	80 acre holding	King	15 freemen (under Alric)
(Earetuna)	40 acre holding	Ralph the Crossbowman	Ketel (under Ulf)
Dunston	15 acre holding	Count Alan of Brittany	Thored
	45 acre manor	Roger Bigod	Ali (under Manni)
Flixton	360 acre manor	King	Hakon (under Earl Gyrth)
	360 acre holding	King	21 freemen (under Hakon)
	240 acre manor	King	Edric
	5 acre holding	King	2 freemen (under Edric)
	120 acre manor (+ church)	Bishop of Thetford	Archishop Stigand (no freemen attached)
Fritton	240 acre manor	King	Godwin (under Earl Gyrth)
	60 acre holding	King	2 freemen (under Godwin)
	80 acre holding	King	2 freemen
	30 acre holding	King	Leofric
Gapton	240 acre manor	King	Wulfsi (no freemen attached)
	60 acre manor	King	Ulf
	60 acre manor	King	Aethelstan
	40 acre holding	King	Sprotwulf
	30 acre holding	King	Wulfnoth
Gorleston	**600 acre manor**	**King**	**Earl Gyrth** (no freemen attached)
	90 acre holding	**King**	**Earl Gyrth** (20 freemen)
	120 acre holding	King	4 freemen
Herringfleet	120 acre manor	King	Wulfsi
Hopton	80 acre manor	King	Thorgar (under Earl Gyrth)
	60 acre manor	King	Siric (under Earl Gyrth)
	80 acre holding	King	8 freemen (under Thorgar and Siric)

Table 4 *cont.*

Community	Estates	Title-holder (1086)	Title-holder (pre-1066)
Lound	**240 acre *outlier***	**King**	**Earl Gyrth** (no freemen attached)
	180 acre manor	King	Alric (under Earl Gyrth)
	120 acre holding	King	4 freemen (under Alric)
	120 acre manor	King	Wulfsi (under Earl Gyrth)
	40 acre holding	King	3 freemen (under Wulfsi)
Lowestoft	**450 acre outlier**	**King**	**Earl Gyrth** (no freemen attached)
Newton	30 acre holding	King	1 freeman
Somerleyton	**90 acre holding**	**King**	**Earl Gyrth** (no freemen attached)
	240 acre manor	King	Ulf (under Earl Gyrth)
	40 acre holding	King	5 freemen (under Ulf)
	40 acre manor	King	Wihtred the Priest
	20 acre holding (+church)	King	[Wihtred the Priest?]
	30 acre holding	Ralph the Crossbowman	Alwold (under Earl Gyrth)

Notes:

- As was made clear in the third note to Table 1, the holdings in bold font formed the Lothingland manorial *demesne*.
- Following the Norman victory at Hastings, there was widespread dispossession of Anglo-Saxon tenants throughout the country, both in terms of the families of men killed in the battle and also of those individuals who had survived the slaughter or who had not even taken part.

In spite of the profound change(s) in who controlled the holding of land, the basic business of working the soil remained essentially the same, with both seigneurial (manorial) and non-seigneurial estates operated by the peasantry. The four socio-economic levels (freeman, villan, bordar and slave) are identified and explained in the notes to Table 3; the first-named were mainly attached to independent holdings, the other three to manors. Although Gorleston was the seat of power in the half-hundred, its 810 acres of cultivated land and population of c. 200 people did not make it the largest and most populous community. That distinction went to Flixton (later to become a much diminished parish, following the emergence of Oulton), with 1,085 arable acres and a population of over 300 inhabitants. Lowestoft, with 450 acres and a population of c. seventy-five residents, was of much lesser significance in the local scheme of things.[21]

[21] The number of people per community has been calculated using the formula referred to in the fifth note, Table 3.

During the late Anglo-Saxon period, governance of the half-hundred from the hub at Gorleston was assisted by the division of the whole jurisdiction into four geographically arranged leets, or letes, functionally named as North, South, East and West. Belton, Browston, Burgh, Caldecot, Fritton and Gapton made up the first; Akethorpe, Dunston, Flixton and Lowestoft the second; Corton, Gorleston, Hopton and Newton the third; and Herringfleet, Lound and Somerleyton the fourth. The principal purpose of leets was to facilitate the collection of geld, the nationally imposed tax due to the Crown,[22] with hundreds being assessed at £1 and half-hundreds at 10s, and with the basic geld unit being the *hide* (120 acres of cultivated land) – a unit that was to be renamed as 'carucate' after the Norman Conquest. The payment per hide in Lothingland worked out at 2.3 pence, which meant that Lowestoft paid an annual sum of 9d on its 450 acres (Flixton, the largest and most populous community, paid 21d; Gorleston, the manorial hub, contributed 15d).[23] The geld analysis adduced for Lothingland in volume 1 of the *Victoria County History of Suffolk* seems to be based on a post-Conquest reorganisation of the system of leets, with a notional 20d payment due from each of the six areas which existed at the time (Burgh and Gorleston having become autonomous units in their own right).[24] Such basic arithmetic may be over-simplistic.

Further developments in the centuries following Domesday seem to have converted the Anglo-Saxon areas of local taxation into instruments of manorial jurisdiction – and James Campbell is at least one commentator who seems prepared to consider this development as a distinct possibility.[25] The four largest Lothingland manorial leets continued to be known by the cardinal compass points, though changes did occur in the communities that comprised them. Following the various boundary adjustments which took place, North Leet eventually consisted of Belton, Bradwell and Fritton; South Leet was formed from Blundeston, Flixton, Lound and Oulton; East Leet was comprised of Corton, Gunton, Hopton, Lowestoft and Newton; and West Leet was made up from Ashby, Herringfleet and Somerleyton. Burgh and Gorleston retained their separate status and Lowestoft eventually achieved this distinction also, after it had become the dominant township in the half-hundred by the end of the fifteenth century (it did, however, remain nominally part of East Leet,

[22] Warner, *Suffolk*, p. 159.

[23] For the Half-hundred data, as unit, see D. Butcher, *The Island of Lothingland: a Domesday and Hundred Roll Handbook* (Lowestoft, 2012), pp. 14–15.

[24] B.A. Lees, 'Introduction to the Suffolk Domesday', in W. Page (ed.), *VCH Suffolk*, vol. 1 (London, 1911), pp. 361 and 416.

[25] J. Campbell, 'Hundreds and leets: a survey with suggestions', in C. Harper-Bill (ed.), *Medieval East Anglia* (Woodbridge, 2005), p. 159.

despite having its own discrete court).[26] Remarkably, the Lothingland leet courts survived well into the eighteenth century as instruments of manorial administration and the surviving records of their proceedings have not escaped attention.[27]

Returning to the time of Domesday, part of the hub manor's means of controlling its subordinate estates may possibly be seen in its having three *outliers*,[28] at Belton (120 cultivated acres), Lound (240 acres) and Lowestoft (450 acres) – and their geographical locations in the half-hundred are interesting. Not only did they serve as agricultural suppliers to the manor itself, they also seem to have functioned as extensions of its influence through being placed in a loosely spaced alignment (see Map 1) on a north-by-west/south-by-east axis that ran roughly across the middle of the half-hundred itself. This arrangement is unlikely to have been accidental and almost certainly dated from Anglo-Saxon times.[29] It demonstrates something of the well-ordered local organisation of land use and management, as well as serving as a microcosm of the efficient national administration which the Normans usurped and shaped for their own purposes. Table 5 shows the overall pattern of landholding in Lothingland Half-hundred, with the various estates recorded in terms of arable acreage, peasant workforce, number of plough-teams (eight oxen to the team), status as manors or non-manorial holdings and the various overlords.

Table 5. The pattern of landholding.

Community	Estates	Personnel and Plough-teams	Status	Overlord
Akethorp(e)	80 acre manor (church?)	1 freeman (priest), 3 bordars, 1½ teams (1d+½t)	*Seigneurial*	The king
Belton	**120 acre *outlier***	**1 villan, 4 bordars, 1 slave, 1½ teams (1d+½t)**	**Seigneurial**	**The king**
	90 acre holding	3 freemen, 1 team	Free	The king
Browston	40 acre manor	1 freeman, ½ team	Free	The king
	30 acre holding (sub m.)	1 freeman	Free	The king
	60 acre manor	1 freeman, 2 bordars, 1½ teams (1d+½t)	*Seigneurial*	The king
	30 acre holding	1 freeman, ½ team	Free	The king
	80 acre holding	2 freemen, 1 bordar, 1½ teams	Free, + bond	The king

[26] Its jurors attended the swearing of the homage, but took little further part in the business.
[27] Campbell, 'Hundreds and leets', p. 165.
[28] The Latin word used in the Domesday text is *beruita*, meaning 'berwick' (from OE *berewica*) or 'grange'. There was also a fourth holding, at Somerleyton, which was not termed an 'outlier'.
[29] In fact, it goes back further: to the Roman co-axial field pattern, which observes the same orientation.

Table 5 *cont.*

Community	Estates	Personnel and Plough-teams	Status	Overlord
Burgh [Castle]	480 acre manor (inc. 11 acre holding and church)	10 villans, 5 smallholders, 5 teams (2d+3t)	Seigneurial	Ralph the Crossbowman
Caldecot	120 acre manor	3 bordars, ½ team (d)	Seigneurial	Ralph the Crossbowman
Corton	240 acre manor	1 freeman, 5 bordars, 3 teams (2d+1t)	*Seigneurial?*	The king
	80 acre holding	15 freemen, 3 teams	Free	The king
Dunston	15 acre holding	1 freeman	Free	Count Alan
	45 acre manor	1 freeman, ½ bordar, ½ team (d)	*Seigneurial*	Roger Bigod
Earetuna	40 acre holding	1 freeman, ½ team	Free	Ralph the Crossbowman
Flixton	360 acre manor	1 freeman, 2 villans, 14 bordars, 4 slaves, 4 teams (2d+2t)	*Seigneurial*	The king
	360 acre holding (sub m.)	21 freemen, 6 bordars, 8 teams	Free, + bond	The king
	240 acre manor	1 freeman, 2 villans, 6 bordars, 3½ teams (2d+1½t)	*Seigneurial*	The king
	5 acre holding (sub m.)	2 freemen	Free	The king
	120 acre holding and 1 church	8 bordars, 2 teams (d)	*Seigneurial*	Bishop of Thetford
Fritton	240 acre manor	1 freeman, 2 villans, 2 bordars, 3 slaves, 3 teams (2d+1t)	*Seigneurial*	The king
	60 acre holding (sub m.)	2 freemen, 1 team	Free	The king
	80 acre holding	2 freemen, 1 bordar, 1 team	Free, + bond	The king
	30 acre holding	1 freeman	Free	The king
Gapton	240 acre manor	1 freeman, 2 villans, 2 bordars, 3 teams (2d+1t)	*Seigneurial*	The king
	60 acre manor	1 freeman, 1 bordar, 1 team (d)	*Seigneurial*	The king
	60 acre manor	1 freeman, ½ team	Free	The king
	40 acre holding	1 freeman, 1 bordar, 1 team	Free, + bond	The king
	30 acre holding	1 freeman	Free	The king
Gorleston	**600 acre manor**	**12 villans, 5 bordars, 4 slaves, 4 teams (1d+3t)**	**Seigneurial**	**The king**
	90 acre holding (sub m.)	**20 freemen, 5 teams**	**Seigneurial**	**The king**
	120 acre holding	4 freemen, 2 teams	Free	The king
Herringfleet	120 acre manor	1 freeman, 2 villans, 1 bordar	*Seigneurial*	The king
Hopton	80 acre manor	1 freeman, 1 bordar, 1 team (d)	*Seigneurial*	The king
	60 acre manor	1 freeman, 1 bordar, 1 slave, 1 team (d)	*Seigneurial*	The king
	80 acre holding (sub ms.)	8 freemen, 2 teams	Free	The king
Lound	**240 acre *outlier***	**4 bordars, 2 slaves, 1½ teams (1d+½t)**	**Seigneurial**	**The king**
	180 acre manor	1 freeman, 2 villans, 3 bordars, 2 teams (1d+1t)	*Seigneurial*	The king
	120 acre holding (sub m.)	4 freemen, 1½ teams	Free	The king
	120 acre manor	1 freeman, 3 bordars, 2 teams (d)	*Seigneurial*	The king
	40 acre holding (sub m.)	3 freemen, ½ team	Free	The king

Table 5 *cont.*

Community	Estates	Personnel and Plough-teams	Status	Overlord
Lowestoft	**450 acre *outlier***	**3 villans, 10 bordars, 3 slaves, 5 teams (2d+3t)**	**Seigneurial**	**The king**
Newton	30 acre holding	1 freeman, ½ team	Free	The king
Somerleyton	**90 acre holding**	**?**	**Seigneurial**	**The king**
	240 acre manor	1 freeman, 4 villans, 4 bordars, 2½ teams (2d+½t)	*Seigneurial*	The king
	40 acre holding (sub m.)	5 freemen, 1 team	Free	The king
	40 acre manor (church?)	1 freeman (priest), 2 bordars, 1 team	*Seigneurial*	The king
	20 acre holding and church	[Freeman-priest?]	?	The king
	30 acre holding	1 freeman	Free	Ralph the Crossbowman

Notes:

- The half-hundred manor's estates are indicated in bold font.
- Entries show demesne teams first (d) and tenants' second (t), where applicable. Teams on manors which have no specific reference to ownership/control of the oxen are presumed to represent a demesne asset.
- Holdings subordinate to manors are indicated thus (sub m.), immediately below the parent estate.
- Seigneurial structure was of two kinds. The paramount manor of Gorleston (with its three outliers and two associated freemen's estate) and the much smaller unit at Caldecot had been under the control of Earl Gyrth and the manors of Burgh and Flixton Church under the jurisdiction of Archbishop Stigand (presumably, all with stewards). After the Conquest Gorleston was Crown Estate, Burgh and Caldecot were held by Ralph the Crossbowman, and Flixton Church by the bishop of Thetford. All other manors were held by freemen (owing allegiance to the king, as overlord and successor to Gyrth) and have their seigneurial status (if such it was) indicated in italic font.
- The occasional references to '+ bond' indicate non-manorial estates where freemen had the labour service of bordars.
- The holders of estates without plough-teams must have negotiated the tilling of their land with neighbours who had the necessary equipment and who would have made a charge of some kind for their services.

Turning specifically to Lowestoft now, it is time to look at its economic and social structure insofar as the Domesday Survey allows this to be done.[30]

[30] Anyone wishing to study Lothingland Half-hundred in greater detail should consult Butcher, *The Island of Lothingland*, published by (and available at) the Lowestoft Heritage Workshop Centre, Wilde's Score.

The text cites the area of arable land as *4 carucates less 30 acres* (*1111.car træ.xxx. ac min*) – in other words, 450 acres, as previously mentioned. Table 2 reveals that it had five acres of meadow (used primarily for the cutting of hay) and woodland sufficient to sustain eight pigs – one of the lower estimates to be found in the half-hundred. It had five teams of oxen, used for ploughing (two belonging to the lord of the half-hundred and three to the tenants), eight cattle, 160 sheep and eleven pigs.[31] With the exception of the tenants' plough-teams (and even these may have been a manorial asset), all of these animals were the property of the lord. It was not part of Domesday's purpose to record the personal livestock of the peasantry – who, in Lowestoft's case, consisted of the three villans, ten bordars and three slaves referred to earlier.

The township's *outlier*, Akethorpe, also has to be taken into consideration when attempting to create a picture of life at the time. At its nearest point it was only half a mile away to the north, and its estate consisted of a manor held by a freeman-priest called Aelmer. The name identifies him as an Anglo-Saxon and he worked his holding with the assistance of three bordars. He may well have been married,[32] meaning that he and his workers were part of a population of about twenty people, which, when added to Lowestoft's seventy-five or so, gives a total loosely in the range of ninety to a hundred souls. The Akethorpe manor consisted of eighty acres of arable land, one acre of meadow, woodland sufficient for five pigs, one and a half plough teams (in other words, twelve oxen), forty-eight sheep and three pigs. Aelmer and his workforce may have lived somewhere on the manor; it is equally possible (given the short distance between the two holdings) that they had cottages in the Lowestoft township.

The presence of a priest locally means almost certainly that there was a place of worship as well. Churches usually feature in the Domesday Survey only if they had an endowment of land to make them taxable and three are listed for Lothingland: Burgh (11 acres), Flixton (120 acres) and Somerleyton (20 acres).[33] The church at Akethorpe was probably a small, unendowed wooden building standing at the eastern extremity of the manor, half a mile up the hill due north of the Lowestoft township. It was soon to become the parish church for

[31] With Domesday woodland's area being assessed for its capacity to sustain pigs, the dominant tree species must have been *oak* and *beech*. It is noticeable that there are examples of estates where the number of pigs kept was less than the feeding potential offered by the area of woodland present, where it was more than the estimated capacity (Lowestoft had eleven), and also where pigs were reared in the absence of woodland. The 'rule of thumb' means of assessment can probably be interpreted as one pig = one acre of woodland (hence, Lowestoft had eight acres).

[32] Celibacy for the clergy (long recommended as an ideal) was not made obligatory until AD 1139, at the second Lateran Council, during the papacy of Innocent II.

[33] The church of St Michael, Flixton (which later became St Michael, Oulton), was one of the ten richest in Suffolk.

Lowestoft, dedicated to St Margaret[34] – one of four foundations in Lothingland granted by Henry I to St Bartholomew's Priory, Smithfield (the others being All Saints, Belton, St Andrew's, Gorleston, and the church of St Nicholas, Little Yarmouth).[35] After Lowestoft had relocated to a cliff-side site 200 or more years later it was further removed from its church, leading eventually to speculation as to possible reasons for the separation – none of which has included the adoption of a building which had once belonged to a smaller neighbour.

The whole of Lothingland was essentially rural in nature at the time of Domesday. Even the focal point of its manor, Gorleston, was nothing more than a village. Only three communities in the whole of east Norfolk and north-east Suffolk have been identified as being urban or proto-urban in character – Yarmouth, Beccles and Bungay – with the middle one of the trio owing much of its local growth and importance to the direct interest and encouragement of the Abbey of St Edmund, Bury.[36] All three were located in nearby hundreds (East Flegg and Wangford, respectively), but there was a long way for any of the Lothingland settlements to go before any of them took on an urban character in the way of size, social and economic complexity, or some degree of autonomy in the running of civic affairs. And, in achieving such concomitants, there had to be certain conditions in place to allow such development to take place. It was Lowestoft, of course, which eventually became the dominant presence in the half-hundred – a story that will unfold as the narrative continues.

The Domesday record, in stating that Lowestoft's area of cultivated land totalled 450 acres, also shows that it was 75 per cent of the total of the 600 or more acres revealed in the 1618 manor roll – which means that 150 acres had been put under the plough during the interim. This was probably achieved by clearing and ploughing up areas of heath, which were extensive in different parts of the parish and of some importance in the manorial economy. Reference has been made earlier to their value in providing a range of materials

[34] The dedication may have been a renaming of the post-Conquest period, as Margaret of Antioch seems to have had an appeal for some members of the Norman military elite. There are, for instance, five churches dedicated to her in north-east Suffolk and nine in south-east Norfolk – all of them in parishes where Roger Bigot had control of lands, either in his own right or as surrogate for the king.

[35] Little Yarmouth was the northernmost part of Gorleston and was later renamed Southtown – this reflecting its position relative to that of Great Yarmouth itself, though situated on the other side of the river. No church is referred to in Domesday, nor any priest mentioned, and with Henry I dying in 1135 the foundation must have been made at some point between 1086 and that particular year. Likewise with the churches at Belton and Gorleston. At a later date, the chapel of Northville (also a sector of northern Gorleston) was added to the other benefices.

[36] B. Brodt, 'East Anglia', in D.M. Palliser (ed.), *The Cambridge Urban History of Britain*, vol. 1 (Cambridge, 2000), pp. 643–5.

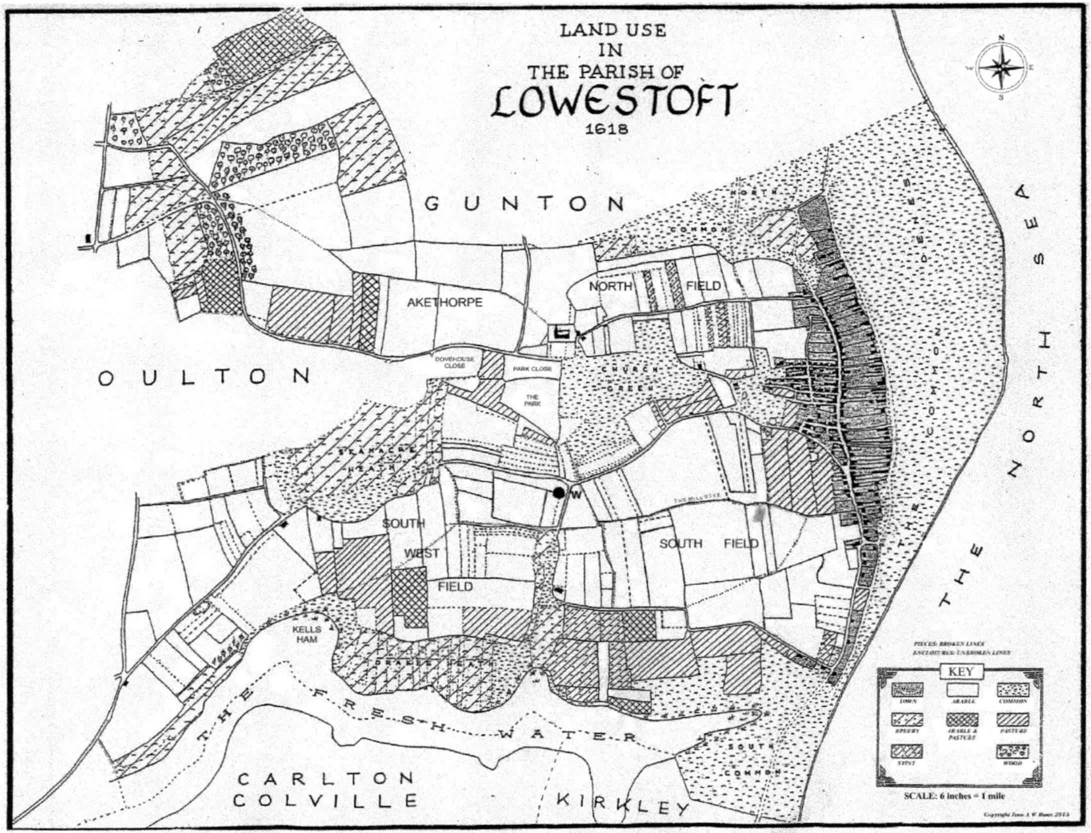

Map 2. Lowestoft parish land use in 1618. The map shows an interim landscape, in operation between the medieval three-field system and the later, fully enclosed, rectilinear field pattern evident on the tithe map of 1842.

Key:

- Solid lines: enclosed areas
- Broken lines: unenclosed spaces
- Solid circle: the site of the Anglo-Saxon and medieval settlement – the centre of population, until the township was moved to a cliff-top location after c. 1300.
- W: the community's windmill.

Notes to Map 2:

- The inlet referred to earlier (on p. 5), leading northwards from the main stretch of water forming Lake Lothing, is discernible as the 'neck' of common land separating the South and South-West Fields. It probably served originally as the means of access used to reach the site chosen to found a settlement, but its exact size is not known. The single building complex shown immediately to the east of it was a farmstead known as Smithmarsh.

and uses – not the least of which was rough grazing for livestock. This helps to explain the number of sheep kept in the parish, and in Akethorpe as well for that matter, as it, too, had a large area of heath. The animals' movement would have been controlled, but they would have spent much of the year grazing on the scrub vegetation so common along the Suffolk coast.

The manor roll also gives a valuable insight into the organisation of the arable farming carried out in Lowestoft, plainly showing the use of the classic open-field system so widespread in much of lowland England. Map 2 shows that, as in so many other communities, there were three common fields set out in strips, a number of which were still in evidence in 1618, even though a great deal of enclosure had taken place during the later medieval period. Akethorpe, too, must have had some means of resting part of its cultivated land every third year, but this does not manifest itself in the document. Lowestoft's three fields are named in the roll as The North Field, The South Field and The South West Field – prosaic descriptions, to be sure, but ones which are accurate in topographical terms.[37] The township itself, probably arranged as a cluster of cottages and hovels with a surrounding fence (as much for the safekeeping of livestock as for the protection of the inhabitants), was situated near the meeting point of the South and South West fields (Plate 3), which were both much larger than the northernmost one. By the time that William I's commissioners conducted their enquiry, it may well have been on this site for the best part of 400 years or more.

There is much debate as to the origins of the three-field system and its development into the fully fledged model of the Middle Ages, with its distinctive regional variations, but it can be accepted as a method of cultivation adopted by the Anglo-Saxons and in widespread use by the time of Domesday. The fields would have grown mainly cereal crops and legumes (peas and beans), and in Lowestoft's case the light soils would have been suited to barley, rye and oats. Akethorpe, on the other hand, with its heavier ground above the 75-

[37] The first-named space has been perpetuated in the name of a local school built on part of its former location: Northfield St Nicholas Primary School.

and 100-foot contour lines, would have been more suited to the production of wheat. The vegetables which formed a major part of the peasant diet would have been mainly grown in plots close to the houses. Life expectancy at the time was around forty years or so, and the Lowestoft tenants, at the time of Domesday, were effectively as much a part of the lord's manorial stock as the crops and animals themselves because they were tied to the land and were the chattels of their master. Born into servitude, they laboured in working the soil as custom and the seasons dictated – and, when their lives were done, their bodies became part of the element they had tended.

Plate 3. The Normanston Cemetery entrance, marked by the building on the left-hand side of the image and with the traffic roundabout referred to in Plate 2 occupying the middle ground. This particular feature is, near enough, the meeting point of the South and South-West common fields.

– 2 –

Post-Domesday developments

Hundred Roll information

The Lothingland Hundred Roll of 1274–5 was one small part of a country-wide survey ordered by Edward I to enquire into the extent of the transfer of royal demesne into private hands and to investigate the abuse of office by local administrators.[1] The long reign of his father, Henry III, had seen considerable erosion of the Crown Estate and Edward wished to reassert royal authority wherever possible and increase revenues. He had been on campaign abroad, serving in the Seventh (and last) Crusade, when his father died in 1272, and it was a further two years before he reached England to take up his crown. The overriding compulsion to carry out this audit was the new king's intention to bring discipline and order to the royal finances and to ascertain the annual value of the rents due from his estates. In Lothingland's case, the evidence required was collected by an appointed jury of six local men (John of Ashby, Nicholas of Fritton, William of Yarmouth, William Assheman, John of Belton and William Manekyn), working under the direction of the county sheriff.[2] They drew upon their own specialist knowledge of local tenancy, and that of people known to them, and the combination of personal memory and documented proof of title (wherever this existed) produced an impressive record of landholding and community affairs.

Nationally, the enquiry process itself began in mid-November 1274 and

[1] S. Raban, *A Second Domesday? The Hundred Rolls of 1279–80* (Oxford, 2004), pp. 21–3.
[2] The names of these men are interesting, showing as they do an intermediate stage in the development of what later became known as surnames. The four individuals named after their places of residence were likely to have been major (if not the main) landholders in each community; the other two are identified by other associations: a topographical reference to ash trees and a personal physical characteristic ('little man').

finished four months later,[3] and the evidence for Lothingland available to us now was produced either from the original documentation or from the early nineteenth-century printed version. It was published posthumously, in 1902, by Lord John Hervey of Ickworth.[4] The results create a most interesting study of the area, both topographically and socially, although Lowestoft's part is limited in extent by its having remained under what seems to have been tighter control for most of the time since Domesday. There had been less selling-off of this part of the royal estate in Lothingland than was evident in other places and there had, of course, been no part of its cultivated area in the hands of freemen (as was the case in much of the rest of the jurisdiction). Hence, it does not feature in the main body of the text (which deals with the tenure of alienated former Crown Estate), but it does have a valuable early section of its own focused on the township, which enables an assessment to be made of changes that had taken place over the previous two centuries. In the wider context of Lothingland itself there had been profound changes in the local pattern of settlement, with five Domesday communities ceasing to exist as entities in their own right and six new ones appearing. Map 3 shows these developments.

The township of Lowestoft was still located in the same part of the parish as at the time of Map 1, but its move to a cliff-side location was not far off, probably beginning within the next twenty years or so. The Hundred Roll document begins with a statement of how the Manor of Lothingland, with an annual value of £70, had passed from the hands of the king (Henry III) into those of Lady Dervorgille de Balliol in exchange for lands belonging to her in Cheshire – probably to assist royal control of the Welsh border area. This transaction had been carried out in December 1237 and the title remained in de Balliol family control until 1294.[5] After this introduction, a statement then follows that there were two townships in the manor, Gorleston and Lowestoft, which perhaps gives a hint that Lowestoft had grown in importance from being a mere outlier to the hub manor, as recorded in Domesday.[6]

[3] Raban, *Second Domesday?* pp. 23–4.

[4] J.W.N. Hervey, *The Hundred Rolls and Extracts Therefrom: Made by Authority, Second Edward I, County of Suffolk: Lothingland* (Ipswich, 1902). The original document may be found at TNA, SC5/Suff/Chap/4; a printed copy of the Latin text is present in W. Illingworth (ed.), *Rotuli Hundredorum* (London, 1818), vol. 2, pp. 160–71. In addition to Lothingland, it covers Babergh, Blything, Carlford, Risbridge, Samford and Wangford hundreds and the liberty of St Edmundsbury.

[5] Dervorgille de Balliol was one of the great women of the thirteenth century. She and her husband, John de Balliol of Barnard Castle, were the parents of John de Balliol the younger, who became king of Scotland in 1291, with Edward I supporting him in his claim against his cousin, Robert Bruce. When de Balliol formed an anti-English alliance with Philip IV of France in 1294 Edward confiscated all his English lands. The manor of Lothingland, along with other titles, eventually passed to the king's nephew, John de Dreux, earl of Richmond.

[6] Rather than give copious page references to distract the reader, the Hundred Roll information

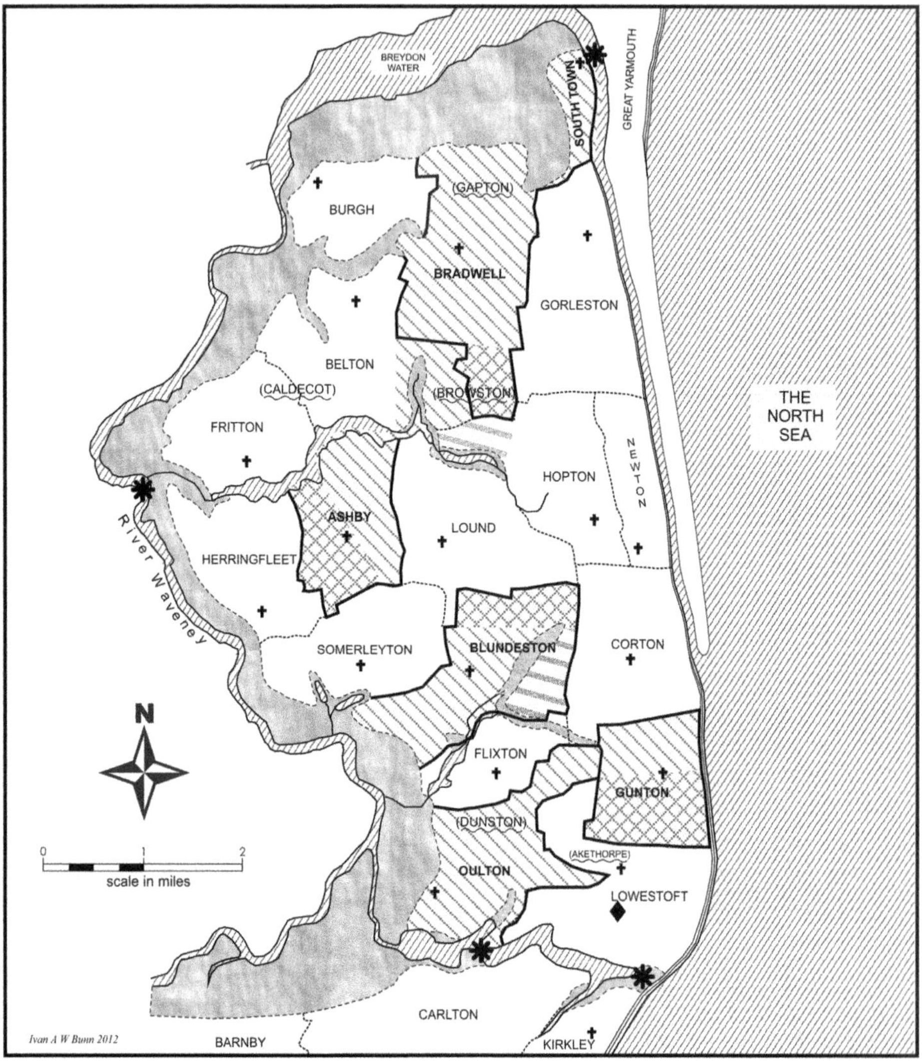

Map 3. Lothingland Half-hundred in 1274.

Notes:

- Crosses indicate parish churches (founding dates unknown). On the evidence of Fritton's apsidal chancel and Herringfleet's Saxo-Norman round tower, some of the buildings probably date originally from the late eleventh century. The ruined church of St Andrew, Flixton, which was built to serve a parish greatly reduced in size, also shows Norman characteristics in the herringbone brickwork of its nave walls. St Michael's, Oulton (formerly Flixton), is an impressive follow-up to its Anglo-Saxon predecessor, being of Norman tripartite construction with a square central tower.

- Norman influence may also be seen in the round towers of Belton, Bradwell, Burgh Castle, Gunton (north and south doorways also) and Lound, while Ashby has a Norman round 'stump', with the rest of the tower being of later (probably fifteenth-century) octagonal construction, with angles quoined in brick. The sum total of church construction during the post-Conquest period suggests considerable activity, as communities old and new gained churches for the first time and as existing buildings were updated and remodelled.
- Church founding and building (three recorded at Domesday; eighteen in existence a century or so later) needs to be seen not only as the spread of organised religion in terms of the Christian faith but also as a means of exerting social and moral control over local populations. Personal elevation and influence in the community may also have been a motivating factor in raising the buildings on the part of the founders of churches.
- Crossing-places are indicated as in Map 1 – as are tidal mudflats, areas of inland marsh and stretches of water.
- Dotted lines indicate parish boundaries, as previously, and are probably still best regarded as approximate.
- Six new parishes (Ashby, Blundeston, Bradwell, Gunton, Oulton and Southtown) have their boundaries shown by thickened lines and their names given in bold font. Contrasting types of shading indicate the land they developed from, formerly located in what then became adjoining communities. Part of Browston was taken to form Bradwell; two other sectors were incorporated, respectively, into Belton and Hopton.
- Akethorp(e), Browston, Caldecot, Dunston and Gapton are bracketed and underlined in the locations they occupied within the parishes which had subsumed them.
- The sand-spit formed by the combination of longshore drift and outward flow of the River Yare is shown as having reached further south than on Map 1, reflecting the passage of time during which the new parishes had formed (the documentary evidence suggests that all of them were well established by c. 1200). The length and width of the spit on all five maps is approximate only, owing to a lack of specific topographical data.

Next is a description of the demesne in each place: arable land once held by Henry III but now in the tenure of Devorgille de Balliol (leased to the tenants at 6d per acre). Gorleston had sixty-six acres (thirteen holdings, with three shared, in the hands of eighteen tenants – annual value, £1 13s 0d) and Lowestoft seventy-three (twenty-five holdings, with four shared, in the hands of twenty-five tenants – annual value, £1 16s 6d).[7] As well as these lands, there were two larger areas (one in each township) held in *villeinage*, meaning

relating to the Gorleston and Lowestoft townships is to be found in Hervey, *Hundred Rolls*, pp. 3–11, 54–63 (Gorleston alone) and 66–7. The original Latin text is placed on the left-hand page of the book, with a transcription facing it on the right.

[7] The stated total is 73; if the individual holdings are added up, 71¾ is arrived at.

that the peasantry worked them for themselves in return for rent payments to the lord (demesne work having once been compulsory and without payment). Gorleston had 258 acres (twenty holdings, five shared, in the hands of twenty-four named tenants and others not named) and Lowestoft 289¼ acres (twenty-six holdings, none shared, twenty-five tenants, with one man occupying two holdings), yielding respective annual rents of £1 2s 4¼d and £1 0s 10d – which works out at a charge of just over 1d per acre. If both types of land are added together, Gorleston had 324 acres of cultivated manorial land (plus a further 120 in the Northville common field) and Lowestoft 362¼ – noticeably different from the 600 and 450 acres recorded at Domesday.

Either the missing acreages had gone out of cultivation or the land had changed tenure (further holdings, described on p. 39, have still to be considered). By the time that the Lowestoft manorial survey, previously cited, was drawn up in 1618, practically the whole of the farmland in the parish was freehold, so perhaps the latter explanation is the correct one. Nineteen of the Gorleston villeinage plots are described as messuages, implying that a dwelling was attached, but there is no reference to housing of any kind in the Lowestoft description. In fact, what are referred to in the Hundred Roll as the areas of land held in villeinage had become known as chief tenements (or *chieves*) by 1618. These had increased in number to twenty-eight (from twenty-six), with fourteen of them split into half-chieves (to make an overall total of thirty-five holdings), but at least sixteen of them were still referred to by the names of the people who are mentioned as occupying them in the Hundred Roll. The manor roll further reveals that, far from having the original villeinage plot size of twelve acres, the chieves had become reduced to small areas of land of between one-eighth and one-half of an acre, which were equitably spaced throughout the three former common fields and whose holders were responsible for the collection of lord's rents on the surrounding twelve or thirteen acres.

This suggests that the basic structure of villein tenure in Gorleston and Lowestoft would have resulted in the former community having a township of linear type, determined by nineteen of the twenty holdings having a cottage attached, whereas the latter would have had a nucleated area of settlement.[8] In fifteen cases in Gorleston the size of plot was the classic twelve acres (one-tenth of a hide), with the remaining five being four and a half, twenty-four (an amalgamation of two single ones), eight and a half, six (half-size) and thirty-five – these latter ones being departures from the original scheme and

[8] R. Faith, *The English Peasantry and the Growth of Lordship* (Leicester, 1997), p. 229. Figure 27 (which shows the layout of a community in Co. Durham) probably shared basic similarities with the configuration of Gorleston: regular plots laid out on either side of the street.

the result of both the subdivision and blocking-up of land. Interestingly, two of them are described as each having lost three acres to coastal erosion, which would seem to indicate the possible effect of rising sea levels at this time – a process which continued well into the fourteenth century and eventually led (with the possible help of storm surges) to the flooding of the extensive peat diggings in south-east Norfolk long known as The Broads.

With Lowestoft's villein lands dispersed throughout the three common fields, their various holders presumably lived in a tightly-built township located close to the meeting-point of the two largest ones. Fourteen of the twenty-six holdings were twelve acres in area, one was twenty-four, two were eighteen, one was fifteen, one was ten, one was eight, three were six, two were four and one was two and a quarter. Again, these twelve departures from the norm must have resulted from land exchanges at some point, though it is a moot point as to how the quarter-acre (a rood) crept into the process – unless it was a single cultivated strip. The tenants themselves had increased considerably in number overall from the sixteen listed in Domesday (three villans, ten bordars and three slaves), and their status had changed also. Bordar and slave were terms no longer used and most of the peasantry was simply classified as being of villein status – this form of the word replacing the earlier version. Levels of wealth and standing varied considerably among villeins, but one factor in their lives was constant: they were still tied to the manor on which they lived and were the chattels of their lord.

Table 6. Lowestoft landholders (Hundred Roll) – acreage occupied.

Name	**Demesne**	**Details (demesne)**	**Villeinage**	**Total**
Adam the Deacon	3¾			3¾
Adam the Deacon	6	Shared with John, s. of Odo		6^{s}
Alan Kadiman			12	12
Alice Thomas	1½	Sister of Richard Thomas		1½
Christiana Eylested	1¼			1¼
Edmund ?	?½			?½
Henry Adam	4	Shared with Robert Eylested		4^{s}
Henry Adam	6			6
Henry ?	2			2
Henry Aleyn			12	12
Henry Austin			4	4
*Henry Justice			12	12
*Henry Man			12	12
Henry Man			12	12
*Henry Ringebell			12	12

Table 6 *cont.*

Name	Demesne	Details (demesne)	Villeinage	Total
John Catherine	1			1
John Fellawe			12	12
*John Jerald			12	12
John Mariot			15	15
John Mariot	3			3
John the Deacon	1¼			1¼
John, s. of Joceus	1			1
*John, s. of Odo	6	Shared with Adam the Deacon		6^{s}
John, s. of Odo	1½	Shared with Margaret, d. of Elina		1½^{s}
*Jordan of the Moor			12	12
Margaret, d. of Elina	1½	Shared with John, s. of Odo		1½^{s}
Nicholas le Ray	¼			¼
Prior of Bromholm	7			7
*Richard Burt			18	18
Richard Dun	2	Shared with Seman le Cherrent	6	8^{s}
*Richard Pipewell			4	4
Richard of Pissewell	2			2
*Richard Thurkild			12	12
*Richard of the Woodhouse	6			6
Richard, s. of John Gode	5		18	23
Richard, s. of John Gode	½			½
Richard Thomas	4		8	12
*Richard Walter(s)	½		6	6½
Robert Eylefled			12	12
Robert Eylested	4	Shared with Henry Adam		4^{s}
Robert, s. of Bele	3¾		2¼	6
*Seman Carpenter			10	10
Seman le Cherrent	2	Shared with Richard Dun		2^{s}
*Seman the Deacon			12	12
*Thomas Haenyld			12	12
Thomas Monk			12	12
*Thomas of the Cliff			6	6
William of Weston	5			5
*William Reynald	3		24	27
41 tenants	25 holdings		26 holdings	

Notes:

- The total acreage of demesne land adds up to 71¾ acres (as stated in fn. 7 above), which is 1¼ short of the total of 73stated in the Hundred Roll. This may be at least partly accounted for by the missing element in the sixth row of the table, where the tenant's name is also incomplete.

- Four surnames (Eylefled/Eylested and Pipewell/Pissewell) were almost certainly variants of two actual names, with variations in the original text (or misreadings of it) being responsible for the differences. The tenant Richard Walter(s) is found listed with both forms of the surname used.
- The symbols s. and d. stand for son and daughter; the [s] represents shared holdings.
- An asterisk indicates a tenant whose surname was still being used to identify a chief tenement over 300 years later (in fact, right into the early nineteenth century). There are sixteen examples to be seen, as referred to previously in the text (p. 32).

The list of Lowestoft tenantry shown in Table 6 contains eight examples of people who held both demesne and villein-tenure land (Richard Dun, Richard Gode, Richard Pipewell, Richard Thomas, Richard Walters, Robert Bele, Robert Eylested and William Reynald), but there were no such parallels in Gorleston. The two sets of tenants there were discrete. The combined numbers of named landholders in each community were close: forty-one in Lowestoft and forty-two in Gorleston (plus a handful of unnamed ones in the latter). If the great majority were residents, then the men among them may be tentatively treated as family heads (they may not all have been married) and used to work out population numbers. This means removing three women from the Lowestoft demesne tenants and two male outsiders (the prior of Bromholm and William of Weston),[9] leaving a total of thirty-seven. For Gorleston, two women need to be omitted from the demesne list, as well as two men from Corton, while three further women and three male outsiders require removal from the villeinage land.[10] This produces a total of thirty-two. However, neither community can have the respective populations of c. 175 and 150 that the use of the multiplier of 4.75 (previously cited) would attribute to them, because the Hundred Roll reveals a substantial number of inhabitants in each place who held tenements other than the strips laid out in the common fields and the villeinage plots (in Gorleston's case) located elsewhere.

There were 154 of them altogether in Gorleston, making a total of 196 named tenants in all. After thirty-six women, two religious institutions, the bailiff of Lothingland, a collection of tenants from outside the manor (treated as a composite body) and twenty-four men bearing the name of other

[9] The prior of Bromholm was head of the Cluniac foundation at Bacton, on the north Norfolk coast; William of Weston came from a parish near Beccles.

[10] These men came from Enges (a small community on the northern boundary of Bradwell), Reston (a satellite on Gorleston's southern boundary with Hopton) and Norwich.

local communities (e.g. John of Belton) have been removed, that still leaves 132 adult males and a possible population of c. 630 people. The figure is undoubtedly inflated to a degree, because not all of these men would have been married or, if they were, had children. But even if a 20 per cent reduction is applied by way of compensation, that still leaves around 500. A notional Domesday population for Gorleston works out at about 200 (Flixton was the most populous settlement at 300 or more), so the community had certainly grown in size during the two centuries since Domesday.

What of Lowestoft? The number of tenants of one kind or another referred to in the Hundred Roll comes to sixty-eight – a much smaller total than Gorleston's. After seven women, two religious houses (Bromholm Priory and Langley Abbey), the bailiff of Lothingland, the county sheriff of Suffolk (Roger de Coleville), the vicar of Lowestoft and two outsiders (William of Weston and Alan de Wymendhale) are removed, the figure stands at fifty-five.[11] When multiplied by 4.75, this produces a total of about 260 people (c. 210 if a 20 per cent corrective reduction is applied). Either total is considerably higher than the seventy-five or so of Domesday, even if Domesday Akethorpe's fourteen people are added on to bring the total up to about ninety. Lowestoft, like the hub of the half-hundred manor further to the north, had more than doubled its population during the intervening 200 years, even if with a notably lower total.

One key factor in Gorleston's expansion, in terms of both physical extent and number of inhabitants, is a development not matched in Lowestoft. Put simply, it resulted from the selling of villeinage land for house-building (with the lord's knowledge or indifference). Seventeen of the twenty tenements had dwelling plots hived off and conveyed to new tenants (some intensively developed, others less so), with the number of units created thereby totalling about fifty-three and occupying 110 acres of land. The layout of the township must have changed radically because of this large increase in the housing stock, which presumably resulted from demographic and economic demand. Scrutiny of the new tenants' names suggests that a number of them were related to the holders of the land, but others seem to have had no obvious connection to the area. Much of the Hundred Roll information, given the nature of the enquiry into misuse of the Crown Estate, is retrospective (sometimes going back over a considerable number of years), but the sense conveyed of the

[11] Wymendhale (or Wymundhal) was a Domesday community integrated into the parish of Kirkley in the years following the Survey. Its dominant family had extensive landholdings and Alan de Wymendhale was lord of the manor of Kirkley and Gisleham in Mutford Half-hundred and of Brampton in Blything Hundred.

increase in Gorleston's house-building (many of the units were described as cottage tenements) is that it was comparatively recent.

Given that the purpose of this book is to scrutinise Lowestoft's medieval development, Gorleston's expansion cannot be investigated any further. It would seem that the large-scale transfer of villeinage land must have stemmed, in part at least, from a contemporary need, but it was undoubtedly assisted also by weak control caused by the manor having an absentee lord. Lowestoft was in the same situation, but there was no obvious equivalent alienation of manorial land.[12] The township's general layout and arrangement was different from that of Gorleston, with the house plots grouped closely together and not aligned regularly along a street. Any expansion required could be accommodated on the edges of the nucleated settlement, without radical alteration of its basic configuration. Increasing population numbers and a flourishing land market during the mid–late thirteenth century would have created the opportunity to build, and the Hundred Roll is unequivocal in stating that Gorleston's expansion had taken place during the de Balliol family's tenancy of the half-hundred – with or without its knowledge (the bailiff being a key figure in either case).

Further information regarding Lowestoft's topography and economy is contained in the Hundred Roll's details relating to tenants other than the ones holding demesne and villeinage land. The great majority of these people were obviously residents of the community and their sundry diverse holdings help to create a sense of the local environment and life at the time. The details relating to the great majority of them constitute the final section of the Hundred Roll data, which appears to have been almost an afterthought – a tidying-up exercise relating to material which should either have been included earlier in the account or which perhaps was not seen as being relevant at that particular stage. Whatever the case, the information revealed makes a valuable contribution to creating a picture of Lowestoft as it was at the time. Table 7 presents the facts.

[12] Fourteen of the Gorleston *villeinage plots* are described as having *tofts* incorporated, which identifies them as what would today be described as *smallholdings*. With sufficient cultivated land for community need being available in the common fields, the tenants probably saw an opportunity to capitalise on available assets and convert land adjacent to their dwellings into house-plots.

Table 7. Lowestoft landholders (additional to demesne and villeinage).

Name	Holding	Rent	Comments
Abbot of Langley	5 acre turbary	5s	Shared with Thomas Thurkild
*Adam the Deacon	1 acre of marsh	4d	Held of the king
Alan de Wymendhale	¼ acre of meadow	½d	Held of the king?
Alice Rustert	1 cottage	½d	Held of the king
Bailiff of Lothingland	2 acres of meadow	3s 4d	Named *The King's Meadow* and once held of him
*Henry Adams	1 acre of marsh	4d	Held of the king
Henry the Miller	½ acre	6d	Shared with William Gosenol and held of the king
John Bonde	9 acres of wood	10s	Formerly held of the king
John Sefrey	¼ acre	½d	Held of the king
Lena of the Lone house	1 cottage	1d	Held of the king
Lena Wyard	3 acres	8d	Held of the king
Margaret of the Stonegate	3 acres	4d	Held of the king?
Nicholas, son of Sewall	6 acres	10d	Held of the king?
Robert Eywald	3 acres	4d	Held of the king
Robert le Shirreve	1 acre	4d	Held of the king?
Robert le Shirreve	¼ acre	1d	Part of 1 acre, formerly held of the king
Robert the Smith	4 acres	4d	Held of the king
Robert Weyn	⅛ acre	2d	Formerly part of 1 acre held by the king
Roger de Coleville	1 piece of heath	-	Known as *Hulteshill*; no rent paid
Roger of the Bridge	Right of crossing	4s	Fording-point at Mutford Bridge
Symon Bacon	5 acres	9d	Held of the king
Thomas, nephew of the Dean	2 cottages	1d	Held of the king
*Thomas Haenyld	1 cottage	1½d	Formerly part of 1 acre held of the king
Thomas of Oulton	3 acres	6d	Held of the king? One fowl also part of the rent
Thomas Storck	1 cottage	2d	Part of 1 acre formerly held of the king
Thomas Thurkild	5 acre turbary	5s	Shared with the abbot of Langley
Vicar of Lowestoft	1 house	6d	Formerly part of 1 acre held of the king
William Gode	¼ acre of common	½d	Held of the king?
William Gosenol	½ acre	6d	Shared with Henry the Miller and held of the king
William Piledhil	5 acres	6d	Held of the king?
*William Reynald	2 acres of herbage	12d	Formerly held of the king
*William Reynald	2 acres of marsh	1d	Formerly held of the king

Notes:

- Use of an asterisk against a name indicates a tenant who also held either demesne or villeinage land, or both.
- The references to acreage alone apply to land that was under cultivation.
- All references to the king are retrospective, because Henry III had demised Lothingland Manor to Dervorgille de Balliol in 1237. There is sometimes a specific statement that certain holdings had once been held of (from) the king, with such tenure implied on other occasions. The latter references are those bearing a question mark.
- The value of the rents of these holdings adds up to £1 16s 0½d.

This assemblage of information contributes to an understanding of the developing Lowestoft community. First, it reveals a total of just over thirty-three acres of cultivated land situated somewhere in the common fields which, if added to the combined figure of 362¼ acres of demesne and villeinage soil, brings the total to 395¼ – which then has to be increased to 421 (closer to the Domesday total of 450) by the addition of 25¾ acres of glebe land (see Chapter 6). Two of the very small pieces of land (the quarter-acre holdings) were probably single strips somewhere in the common fields and their rental value would seem to suggest, perhaps, a general payment of 4d per acre for agricultural use. However, this rental value does not seem to have applied universally and a holding's worth must sometimes have been assessed using criteria which may not be immediately obvious to the investigator of today. The highest value of all is that attached to Robert Weyn's one-eighth of an acre piece, because the annual rent of 2d paid on it works out at 1s 4d per acre. This suggests that the land had been converted to domestic or trade use (or both combined, with house and workshop), with a much higher return for the lord deriving from the increased rental value.

The half-acre held by Henry the Miller and his associate, William Gosenol, with its rent-payment of 6d, may well have been the plot of land on which the township's windmill stood. This structure was located very close to the dwellings (being a stone's throw due east of them), on a high point which still has its distinctive topographical form today, even though completely built over with houses – the modern road which traverses it is known, tellingly, as Hill Road (Plate 4). Its elevated nature provided a suitable site for a post-mill to operate successfully, being roughly in the middle of the three-field system and sufficiently raised to catch even light winds. It was a location which was eventually to cause its downfall (literally!), because it was completely wrecked in a gale in 1608 and not replaced, the centre of population having moved away to a cliff-top site over 250 years before. In case it might be thought

Plate 4. The site of the original windmill. This view, looking up the pronounced gradient of Hill Road, shows where the mill once stood at the top of the slope.

that the windmill site sounds rather oversized, it is worth noting that it was customary to have a generous space around such a facility for the movement of carts, the placing of ancillary buildings and even to allow the miller to grow crops of his own. The mill itself may well have been a demesne asset originally, with payment made to the lord for its use, but its operation seems to have passed into private hands at some point for a fixed annual rent.

In the five references to the acre of land which had once been held by the king, it is also revealed that the parcelling-up of this particular piece of soil had been carried out by John de Balliol's bailiff – de Balliol perhaps having assumed control of his wife's estates or simply been given precedence by the Hundred Roll jurors. The ground must have been situated close to the township (probably as part of the cultivated area of the South-West Field) and its subsequent uses suggest a very modest extension of it. Robert le Shirreve presumably carried on cropping his quarter-acre with its rent equivalent of 4d an acre, and Robert Weyn's one-eighth of an acre holding has already been commented on.[13] The other three components, however, relate to dwellings,

[13] The former man's name would seem to suggest elevated ancestry, with its reference to the office of sheriff. It is possible that he came from important Anglo-Saxon stock, forced downwards in the social order after the Norman Conquest.

with two modest units (the cots) and a more substantial one: the vicar of Lowestoft's house (so termed in the Hundred Roll).[14] The rental values of 1½d, 2d and 6d give a sense of the relative size not only of the living space but perhaps of plot size as well, with the clergyman's messuage possibly being about three-eighths of an acre in area, compared with an eighth or so for each of the other two. The total rental value of 1s 0½d per annum clearly shows, even in the late twelfth century, that developed land yielded a higher financial return than that devoted to agriculture.

The other four dwellings referred to (all cottages) would also have been of comparatively modest proportions, and mainly located in the township, although the name of at least one of the tenants, Lena of the Lone House, is interesting in suggesting a woman who lived in a dwelling of some kind that was removed from the main concentration of houses and was distinctive by its isolation. The rent of 1d suggests that it may have been a larger structure that that of Alice Rustert, whose home carried half that annual value – as did the two cottages belonging to Thomas, nephew of the Dean – but the difference in payment was probably due to the size of plot on which the buildings stood. The society of the time was founded on the holding of land and the money generated from rents, and therefore the size of a house plot was probably more important than the building that stood on it.

Thomas's name is an interesting one, because it has nothing to do with an uncle who was a high-ranking churchman. The word dean, in this case, derives from the medieval Latin word *decanus* (rooted in the classical Latin *decem*), meaning ten, and it refers to a man alternatively known as a headborough: someone who was of standing in an Anglo-Saxon community and was held responsible for the good behaviour of his tithing-group. The system of frankpledge, as it was known, arranged all males over the age of twelve years into groups of ten (and occasionally twelve), with each member of a group being responsible for the good behaviour of the others. The designated head of each group had to account for its conduct at the annual hundred court held by the county sheriff. This was a system of social control that carried on right through into the early modern period, with manorial leet courts increasingly used to review standards of good conduct.[15]

There are five other surnames (the modern term, used for convenience) in Table 7 which may also assist an understanding of the Lowestoft community as it was developing during the second half of the thirteenth century. Robert

[14] At a later period the vicarage house was situated at the south-western corner of the churchyard, with the clergyman farming his own area of glebe land next to it.

[15] Lowestoft's leet court was active well into the eighteenth century. See D. Butcher, *Lowestoft, 1550–1750* (Woodbridge, 2008), pp. 254–64.

the Smith made tools and accessories for a range of activities (particularly agricultural ones) and carried out essential repairs where needed, and Robert Weyn (wain) may have been involved in making carts. Roger of the Bridge supervised the crossing of the causeway at the meeting point of Lake Lothing and Oulton's mere (giving assistance where necessary) and may well have lived in a house close by. He would have levied a charge for his services and some of the income generated went to paying the lord of the manor an annual rent of 4s for the privilege of operation. Alice Rustert may have been engaged in harvesting heath materials (such as gorse and bracken) for fuel or other purposes – an occupation noted as one carried out by women.[16] Margaret of the Stonegate must have lived somewhere in the south-western extremity of the parish, at the bottom end (east side) of what is now called Gorleston Road – a stretch of highway formerly known as *Steyngate Way* and (on the evidence of its name) once part of a Roman road.

Table 6 also contains names that have either occupational or topographical significance. Taken alphabetically by forename (the manner in which both tables are arranged), the first to be noted is Alan Kadiman. The first element of his surname derives from the Middle English word *cade*, meaning 'cask', so he may possibly have been a cooper by trade. Wooden barrels would have been used both to store and transport fish, as well as a large range of wet and dry goods, so a specialist tradesman (as with the smith) would have been required for both manufacture and repair. Seman Carpenter is another artisan whose name reveals his calling and, in a world where wood was used for the construction of houses and boats, for the making of agricultural equipment and tools and also for the production of domestic utensils, his skills would have been in constant demand.

Henry Justice may have been some kind of local legal officer (or was descended from a man, or men, who had exercised such a function), but what his duties may have been cannot be guessed at. John the Deacon and Seman the Deacon give no such problems of identification, as deacon was a variant of the word dean (noted above) and the two men were therefore also headboroughs of the manor. Three topographical references remain. Jordan of the Moor may well have been one of the minority of people living outside the township, because the chief tenement named after him was (according to the 1618 manor roll) situated on arable land located on the northern edge of the South-West Field, in the area now occupied by a recreational skate-park and a large traffic roundabout linking Normanston Drive, Peto Way and Fir Lane.[17]

[16] Bailey, *Suffolk*, p. 159.
[17] D. Butcher (ed.), *The Lowestoft Manor Roll of 1618* (Lowestoft, 2004), p. 89 – a Heritage Workshop Centre publication.

Plate 5. The Normanston Park recreation ground. This substantial open area is the remaining undeveloped part of the former South-West Field. The field as a whole is shown in the 1618 manor roll to have had vestiges of strips set within the overall pattern of later enclosure (see Map 2).

This had once been part of the extensive area of heath known as *Skamacre* – and moor is, of course, a word deriving from OE *mōr*, meaning 'waste land' or 'marsh' (Plate 5).

Richard of the Woodhouse's dwelling is unable to be as readily located – though the chief tenement bearing his name was situated in the northern half of the North Field, next to the roadway which divided it (*Church Way*, later renamed St Margaret's Road) and not far from the parish church.[18] His surname is unlikely to have specifically referred to the build of his residence, because nearly all the houses of the peasantry were constructed of timber and wattle-and-daub. It is more likely to have been a description of its location, close to an area of woodland. Lowestoft had very little of this particular resource and it was almost all located in the extreme north-western sector of the parish, on the higher, heavier land adjacent to the manor of Akethorpe and in the area now occupied by the Pound Farm Estate and the area north of Somerleyton Road. Thomas of the Cliff is somewhat easier to locate. He seems to have given his name to *Clifton's Half-chieve*, which stood in the built-

[18] Butcher, *Manor Roll*, p. 49.

up area of the later medieval township, after it had moved from the earlier original site, and was located on land to the north of *West Lane* (later *Swan Lane*, today's Mariner's Street).[19] His dwelling was probably located there as well (another of the parish's outlying homesteads) and its approximate position today would be adjacent to (or even underneath!) Jubilee Way.

Before leaving the commentary deriving from Tables 6 and 7, it is necessary to consider the six types of land referred to in the latter, other than that devoted to agriculture. Taken collectively, they have a good deal to say about the rural economy of the time – especially the keeping of livestock and its general management. Meadow was mainly reserved for the growing of hay (fed to horses), with livestock being turned out to graze on the aftermath after it had been harvested. *The King's Meadow*, as it is referred to, may once have been part of the demesne, and its relatively high rental value (3s 4d) suggests land of good quality – perhaps capable, even at that period in history, of producing two tons of hay from the two-acre area. Alan de Wymendhale's quarter-acre plot (or strip), on the other hand, may well have been of lower fertility, which would account for the much lower rental-charge.

William Reynald's two acres of herbage (*herbagium* in the Hundred Roll document) would have been grassland, but of a type intended primarily for direct grazing rather the growing of hay. Even so, its value in sustaining livestock is reflected in the relatively high rent of 6d per annum, and it may well have been used for feeding horses. Reynald held thirty-one acres of land altogether (three demesne, twenty-four villeinage, two herbage and two marsh), which made him the most substantial occupier of the time – a man who would almost certainly have kept horses. The reference to the herbage having once been held of the king would, again, seem to suggest that it was former demesne that had been disposed of at some point. Reynald's two acres of marsh (yet again, apparently once part of the lord's personal estate) would also have been used for grazing – primarily during the spring, summer and autumn – and it was not the only piece of such land in use.

Adam the Deacon (yet another headborough in the community) and Henry Adams each held an acre of marsh. But whereas Reynald paid only a halfpenny per acre in rent, they paid 4d. This was either because their areas of marsh were of better grazing quality or, more likely, because they were still under the lord's control. Land of any kind that had been demised into private ownership, having been disposed of for a capital sum, then usually carried a lesser rental value. The total area of the four acres of marsh would have been situated in the area known later as *Smithmarsh* (an extension of *Drake's Heath*): what today forms the southern section of Rotterdam Road

[19] Butcher, *Manor Roll*, p. 69.

(with land situated to the eastern side of it), from the Norwich Road junction down to the roundabout where it joins Denmark Road and Peto Way, with railway land lying to the south of that.[20] This particular part of Lowestoft was only just above sea level and was boggy in character for a very long time. An examination of Map 2 enables the reader to see that it was, in fact, the vestigial remains of the Lake Lothing inlet or 'arm' (referred to on p. 5) in which Lowestoft's first Anglo-Saxon settlers may have berthed their boats and to the north of which Hluda's township was founded. As a specific comment on the rents recorded in Table 7, it is worth saying that these were a much more convenient form of income for a manorial lord (especially an absentee) than labour services and gave the tenants greater flexibility and freedom of action in managing their holdings as they wanted.

The last type of grazing land referred to in Table 7 is heath (or common),[21] the value of which as a resource for the post-Roman incomers was discussed in Chapter 1. Often referred to in old documentation as waste, it was anything but, having a wide variety of uses. Lowestoft had seven areas of it (six of them large and one small), which the 1618 manor roll identifies as *The Common Denes*, *The North Common*, *Goose* (or *Fair*) *Green*, *Church Green*, *Skamacre Heath*, *Drake's Heath* and *The South Common*.[22] Leaving out *The Denes*, which constituted the scrub-grown beach area above high-water mark, there were c. 205 acres of heathland above cliff-level out of a total 1,275. This represents about 16 per cent of the land, and it would have been more extensive 300 years before – perhaps as much as 30 per cent or more. The manor roll records about 600 acres of arable land, which is 150 more than the Domesday total and over 200 more than the figure based on Hundred Roll data (see p. 39). Much of this 'new' land would have been husbanded from areas previously given over to heath. And another factor to be taken into consideration is the land on which the relocated township grew up: around sixty acres in area and once part of the manorial waste itself.

There is a view that animals were allowed to roam unchecked over heathland. This was not always the case; the grazing was sometimes controlled by being set out in strips, with marker-posts, within which the individual

[20] The manor roll, previously cited, refers to it as *Seethmarsh*, a name possibly deriving from the pools of water located there in places (or even from the edge of Lake Lothing itself, which it adjoined) and the visual effect conveyed when these were disturbed by the wind. See Butcher, *Manor Roll*, p. 106.

[21] 'Common' in the sense that it was available for all local people to use, but only if they observed the manorial rules concerning its management and paid the appropriate fees (*fines*) for the materials consumed. See Bailey, *Suffolk*, pp. 96–8 (previously cited), regarding the importance of heath in the county's medieval economy.

[22] Five of these are named in Map 2 (p. 25) – the only exception being the smallest, *Goose Green*, which was located on the immediate western edge of the relocated town.

holders fenced their sheep or tethered larger animals such as cattle. Such practices produced a type of managed heathland known as bruery. This kind of management was common practice by the time of the Lowestoft manor roll, with the whole of the *Drake's Heath* area parcelled up and with *Skamacre* arranged in much larger sections, but there is no obvious indication in the Hundred Roll of how the Lowestoft heathland was used. It is simply referred to as a type of usable ground and left at that. One of the two references, however – William Gode's quarter-acre of common – may, because of the small size of the area held, be referring to a strip or piece (the latter being of square or rectangular shape, but not elongated). *Hulteshill*, held by Roger de Coleville, is even described as a piece and was probably located on the higher ground above *Drake's Heath* and *Smithmarsh*, in the area occupied today by Norfolk Street and Kent Road (Plate 6). Its acquisition by the man named may not have been legal.

Plate 6. Kent Road: a view taken at its junction with Rotterdam Road. The steep rise in the ground hereabouts is clearly visible, leading up to the one-time area of heathland known as Hulteshill.

Another holding whose occupation may also have resulted from malpractice of some kind (to be elaborated upon later) was the nine acres of wood held by John Bonde. The relatively high rent of more than 1s an acre reflects the value of woodland in the medieval rural economy, simply because the material was needed for such a wide variety of purposes. The area recorded in the Hundred Roll was almost certainly located in the extreme north-western sector of the parish, referred to above in connection with the dwelling-place of Richard of the Woodhouse, and it is not inconceivable that this man was the custodian of the resource and responsible for its management (which would have included the practice of coppicing). The species growing there would have been native hardwoods, such as oak, beech, ash, hornbeam and hazel, all with different qualities and specific uses for both the standard trees and the underwood.[23]

The final type of land featuring in Table 7 is turbary: an area given over to the digging of peat. The five acres referred to are still identifiable because the land eventually flooded and became known as *Leathes Ham* (*Kells Ham* in the manor roll) after the family that once lived in a large house on the adjoining land.[24] It is the stretch of water north of the railway line (which had to be embanked in order to cross it) at the bottom of Normanston Park – a mere that acts as an extension of Lake Lothing, almost, and which is an important haven for water-birds of all kinds (Plate 7). Its medieval origins serve to further our understanding of community activity at the time, as peat was widely used as a domestic fuel and the location of this particular facility was only half a mile or so away from the main area of settlement itself.

It is possible that the abbot of Langley (head of a Premonstratensian house about twelve miles away, near Loddon, in south Norfolk) took a proportion of the turves dug for use in his own establishment, but the passage by road via Beccles would have been longer and more time-consuming than the crow's-flight distance, and there must have been deposits of peat, given the neighbouring marshland environment, much closer to the abbey itself. The likelihood is (considering the way that religious houses invested in land located at some distance from where they were situated) that the institution had acquired a stake in the Lowestoft turbary to make money from the sale of its end product. Whether or not it was an original stakeholder (to use a modern term) cannot be known, nor can the length of time Thomas Thurkild had been involved, but it was obviously profitable for both parties to share the relatively high annual rent of 5s and make money from exploitation of the

[23] *Underwood* was the term used in a managed woodland environment for the smaller *arisings* deriving from *coppicing* the different species. *Timber* referred to the trunks of the larger, *standard* trees grown for constructional work of different kinds. For further information, see Oliver Rackham's formative work *Woodlands* (London, 2006), as well as other of his publications.

[24] The word *ham* is from OE *ham(m)* or *hom(m)*, meaning 'land enclosed by water' or even 'water-meadow'. It later broadened its meaning to refer to ground that was damp or marshy in character and located anywhere near water. The area to the east of Durban Road, adjacent to Fen Park in Kirkley, was always known as 'The Ham'.

Plate 7. Leathes Ham. This picture was taken about ten years ago and gives a good impression of the flooded area of the medieval peat diggings.

resource. Thurkild's surname would seem to indicate that his ancestors were of Scandinavian origins, because its two elements derive from the Old Norse *Thor* (god of thunder) and *ketill*, meaning 'a cauldron' or 'cooking vessel'. A relative, Richard, held twelve acres of villeinage land which, along with the turbary interest, might seem to suggest that the family was among the more substantial ones in Lowestoft at the time.[25] People's names have a good deal of information to reveal concerning their predecessors' socio-economic and ethnic origins, and a study of the Lowestoft tenants' Christian names and surnames is to be found in Appendix 1.

Thomas Thurkild, however, may not have had a direct residential connection with Lowestoft. A man of that name had been a Great Yarmouth port bailiff in 1269 and he might possibly have been the same person as the one holding the turbary rights referred to above.[26] A study of the Lothingland Hundred Roll shows that a number of people belonging to families in the upper echelons of local society had property interests in diverse places

[25] A man named Richard Thirkyld (*sic*) also held two and a half strips in the common field at Gorleston, known as *Northtown Field*. It may well have been the same person.

[26] There were four bailiffs elected annually to hold office and they were the men responsible for seeing that the town's civic order was maintained and its affairs run honestly and efficiently.

throughout the Island, and Thurkild could have been one of them. Furthermore, there was a great deal of dispute, lasting for practically the whole of the thirteenth century, between Great Yarmouth and the leading landholders in Lothingland concerning trading rights – the former wishing to maintain its dominance in both fishing and general maritime traffic and the latter trying to assert their own legitimate interests. It is noticeable that a handful of the Yarmouth governing elite had holdings in Lothingland that were too small to have been of any economic significance (Thurkild's was not one of them) and one possible reason for holding them may have been to give the occupiers an insider's view of any economic activity on the Island that might have been prejudicial to Yarmouth's own interests.

The trouble had begun in 1208, in which year King John had granted Great Yarmouth a charter giving it borough status and trading autonomy in its local area. Three years later, in 1211, he granted a market charter to the manor of Lothingland, allowing its citizens trading rights on the Suffolk side of the river dividing it from the Norfolk town (the market place was originally located somewhere at the northern end of Gorleston, close to the water). The awarding of the latter privilege was bound to have caused contention, and disputes immediately arose between the two parties as to which goods could and could not be legitimately handled on their respective wharfs. The matter of herrings proved a particularly thorny issue and, when Lowestoft eventually became the leading community in Lothingland, it became the focus of Yarmouth's attention and commercial opposition. The disputes continued until final legal resolution (in Lowestoft's favour) in 1662, with minor 'rumblings' continuing into the early eighteenth century.

Legal mutterings of a different kind are to be found in the Hundred Roll, in the form of complaints made by the Lothingland jurors concerning the conduct of the officials responsible for the governance of the Island. The three main culprits are all referred to in Table 7 (John Bonde, Richard Foxton and Roger de Coleville) and, while none of them lived in Lowestoft, they would all have had an influence on it to a certain degree. Foxton was the bailiff (or steward) of the Manor of Lothingland at the time the Hundred Roll was compiled, and Bonde had been his predecessor. De Coleville was an influential local knight living in the parish of Carlton, in Mutford Half-hundred (the family's long association with the place eventually led to it being called Carlton Colville) – a man who had been sheriff of Suffolk in 1266–7. All of them had obviously overstepped the mark where their duties were concerned, with Bonde being the worst offender.

Table 7 makes a number of references to lands that had once been part of the royal estate with the expression *formerly held of the king*. This is a convenient modern paraphrase of the facts variously worded in the Hundred Roll text.

It is possible that the holdings in question had been legally demised to the occupants by Lothingland bailiffs acting on behalf of either the monarch or (more probably) the de Balliol family – after the latter had assumed control of the manor – but there is more than a hint of malpractice in the evidence noted by the royal commissioners compiling the roll. Taken in sequence from the document, there has to be some suspicion that William Reynald had acquired his two-acre piece of herbage from Richard Foxton without the authority of the lord, with Foxton getting some kind of pay-off for his actions, while it looks as if his father had done the same thing with an earlier bailiff, Roger Fitzosbert (of Somerleyton), regarding the two-acre marsh holding. Reynald, as was pointed out earlier, was the largest holder of land in Lowestoft and may therefore have been the community's 'main man'. As such, he would have had regular contact with the manorial supervisor and they might well have used this acquaintance to their mutual advantage.

Roger de Coleville's area of heathland is the next holding to feature. He had probably done some kind of deal with Foxton to acquire it, with the non-payment of rent being his reward for having paid the latter its purchase price. He is described as holding the property *in severalty*, which means that there were no common rights attached to it – giving him sole use of the assets. John Bonde's nine-acre wood follows – a valuable resource and, given his track record (reproduced later), one that may have been illegally acquired when he himself was half-hundred bailiff. His successor, Richard Foxton, had probably used his own tenure of the position to appropriate the two-acre *King's Meadow* and the roll is specific in saying that the facility 'remains to the use of the Bailiff of Lothingland', thereby giving no room for doubt as to who had occupancy and control of it.

The final set of transfers the validity of which may have been in doubt are the five small transactions, listed together and previously referred to (pp. 40–1), which follow the details given concerning the Lowestoft villeinage tenants and their holdings. They were all connected with an acre of land, which had been parcelled up into building plots and one other small tenement. Thomas Haenild and Thomas Storck had cottages built, and the parish's vicar a house, while Robert Weyn finished up with a holding one-eighth of an acre in size and Robert Shirreve one of a quarter-acre. These last two had widely varying rental values (1s 4d and 4d per acre, respectively), probably showing the difference between developed land and that used for agriculture.

Before leaving the matter of possible administrative malpractice, it is worth considering the three people named, because there is further information relating to all of them at the time that the Hundred Roll was drawn up. No excuse is made for going into these men's wrongdoings, because such misdemeanour reflects the society of the time and, while they may not have been residents of Lowestoft, they were part of the socio-economic fabric of the area in which that community was located and typical (Bonde, especially) of the way in which some men were able to rise in the world. They also represent the structure of local government, in that de Coleville was involved at the higher, county (or shire) level, while Foxton and Bonde functioned within the hundred or half-hundred – this being the component that, added to a number of others, made up the shire. And at the bottom level was the parish, a collection of which (usually observing natural landforms and boundaries) formed the hundred – with men such as William Reynald, Adam the Deacon and Seman the Deacon (plus the local priest) acting as civic leaders.

Richard Foxton's first recorded aberration, other than his activity in Lowestoft, is the failure to arrest Henry Carman, who was presented at the hundred court for the crime of theft and evaded apprehension by offering his servant, David Kel, in his place. Foxton accepted a bribe of 3s and allowed Carman to enjoy the right of frankpledge. He also took the sum of 4s from Alneta of Oulton when she was indicted for theft and allowed her to go free, without bail. Further bribery came from Henry, son of the clerk of Oulton (probably not a parish clerk at this time, but someone in minor orders in the church), who paid 4s for his restoration to frankpledge when under indictment for the receipt of stolen goods, and from Galfrey (Geoffrey) Nockdam, who handed over 6s 8d to avoid arrest for receiving sheaves of barley (estimated at two bushels of grain) stolen at night. Then there was the matter of the rape of Sybil Galle by John Cruke, with the offender paying Foxton 4s to escape from the consequences of his actions. Finally, with the help of his servant, Henry Fiket, he was said to have beaten Stephen of Carlton in the matter of a pig worth 12d (belonging to the victim), which he claimed to be requisitioning on behalf of the king.[27] Stephen had contested the claim and sought legal redress, naming guarantors to support his case. Foxton had refused to acknowledge this due process and gaoled him for eight days at Gorleston, whereupon Stephen had taken his case to the justices in Westminster (probably to the Court of Common Pleas).

De Coleville was of higher social status than Foxton and had obviously upset a number of Lothingland's freeholders in the year he had served as county sheriff (1266–7). There are no fewer than sixty-four complaints recorded in the roll, spread across the half-hundred, of how he had requisitioned barley for supply of the king's household and his own (forty-five of the former and nineteen of the latter) and had not paid for it. Mixed in with these charges are seven relating to malt and nine to the taking of herrings (cured ones, almost certainly) – both commodities being for royal use. Henry III and

[27] The Carlton referred to was a Lothingland settlement, not the one in Mutford Half-hundred.

his court were lodged at Bury St Edmunds on 7–18 February 1267 (probably at the abbey),[28] and part of de Coleville's duties would have been to help provision this large assembly of people. It would have been easy for him to requisition foodstuffs in his home area and he obviously took the opportunity to supply himself as well as the Crown. There is no readily accessible record to show whether or nor Mutford Half-hundred (where he lived) was similarly treated, but it has been recorded that de Colville and his assistant (possibly John Bonde) had been accredited at the Exchequer with funds for securing and conveying victuals.[29] Obviously, the money had not reached the suppliers!

A further charge against de Coleville was that he had taken a 40s bribe from William of Enges and Henry of Hobland to restore them to view of frankpledge when charged with the death of Robert de la Grenehore. This restoration of civic and legal rectitude to men suspected of murder was a serious matter under the law, but the outcome of the matter is not known. In his own half-hundred he was accused of constructing an illegal fish-trap in the *Kirkley Stream*, which ran into Lake Lothing on the opposite side of the water to the Lowestoft township, on a south by east bearing.[30] Later information concerning the man shows that he must have ridden out these local storms, because on 5 July 1277 he was given royal protection for one year, under the clause *volumus*, for going to Wales on the king's service (almost certainly to take part in Edward I's wars against the Welsh).[31] This particular privilege gave the bearer immunity from legal cases during the period of absence and de Coleville was awarded it again on 2 November 1281 when going overseas on royal business.[32]

John Bonde was of lower social status than de Coleville, and was therefore much more involved with what may be termed the grass-roots level of local affairs. It is not known from what economic base he started, but he obviously used his time of office as bailiff (steward) of Lothingland to amass both real estate and money by dishonest practice. It has already been seen that he was the occupier of a nine-acre wood in Lowestoft, but the Hundred Roll reveals further that he also held the following list of properties located in the Island: a share of a quarter-acre free tenement in Carlton; a twelve-acre messuage in Ashby (some of it sub-let); a two-acre free tenement in Dunston (some of it sub-let); a four-acre free tenement in Dunston (some of it sub-let); a one and a quarter acre free tenement in Corton (some of it sub-let); a twelve-acre

[28] A.E. Stamp (ed.), *CCR, Henry III*, vol. 13 (London, 1938), pp. 289–95.
[29] H.M. Cam, *The Hundred and the Hundred Rolls* (London, 1930 and 1963), p. 101.
[30] A.I. Suckling, *The History and Antiquities of the County of Suffolk*, vol. 1 (London, 1846), p. 238.
[31] H.C. Maxwell Lyte (ed.), *CPR, Edward I*, vol. 1 (London, 1892), p. 217.
[32] Maxwell Lyte, *CPR, Edward I*, vol. 1, p. 462.

messuage in Gorleston; eight pieces of the demised villeinage land referred to on p. 36 (one of quarter of an acre, two of half an acre, one of three-quarters of an acre, one of one acre, two of one and a half acres, and one of six acres, which was shared), four of them without rent-payments; a quarter-acre plot (no rent paid) once held directly from the Crown; and a half-share of one strip in the common field named *Northtown*. Given that many of the Gorleston villeinage sales had been to create house plots, it is likely that Bonde was aiming to do the same. He may well have lived on the twelve-acre messuage he held in the town, because at least four other residents shared his surname – thereby giving the impression of a family group being concentrated there.

His misdemeanours while in office were many and varied. While serving as bailiff of the half-hundred he had made two encroachments (each one acre in size) on marshland and meadow in Gorleston. Both areas formed part of the commonage of the local villein tenants and their exclusive use of the ground is specifically referred to. He had also accepted a payment of 15s from Thomas the Tailor of Oulton for aiding the latter after his arrest for the murder of a person unnamed (his clerk, Henry Assheman, had also received 4s in this matter, as well as the gift of a mule worth 4s). A further charge stated that he had not allowed a surrogate for Symon of Dunston (probably because of the latter's illness or infirmity) in the matter of carrying the rod of office and issuing court summonses to the hundred-court – duties, or obligations, which accompanied the holding of Symon's free tenement – until Symon himself had paid him the sum of 6s 8d. He had also accepted an annual payment of 3½d from Thomas of Denton for restoring the frankpledge status of that man's son, Adam, after he had been arrested for the murder of Henry Kempe.

Misappropriation of tax payments (with the collusion of the clerk, Henry Assheman) was evident in the collection of money due to the Crown, totalling 100s and more, from Geoffrey le Poer, John of Belton and others, which had then not been paid over. Further cases of bribery, on top of those already mentioned, came in the form of accepting sums of 18d and 12d from Nicholas Maryot and Richard, son of Ralph, for freeing them from jury service at assize sessions – the former man being exempted twice and the latter once. And Bonde had also been complicit in Henry Assheman receiving a payment of 12d from Richard Maynard for similar evasion of legal duty. Finally, while serving as coroner for Lothingland – the post being held in tandem with that of bailiff – he had taken no action in the matter of the murder of a local man in Oulton by John, son of Symon (who had then taken sanctuary in the church), until he had received a payment of 6s 8d from the township.

Such, then, was the conduct of at least some local government officials (responsible for the good governance of the half-hundred and the good behaviour of its inhabitants) in the world of the late thirteenth century, as

Lowestoft moved from its position as manorial outlier, or grange, to one of primacy in Lothingland Half-hundred.

Manorial changes

As was noted earlier, Lowestoft's appearance in the Hundred Roll of 1274 is limited in scale by virtue of the document being mainly concerned with Lothingland's free tenements (held without encumbrance, but liable to payment of annual rent to the Crown) and because there had been less selling-off of land held in villeinage than had been the case in Gorleston. Map 4 shows the general layout of parishes in the half-hundred, together with the various small settlements (some of which have been mentioned in previous paragraphs, either as places in their own right or as part of people's names). The location of the Lowestoft township at the time has been omitted in order to present the whole Lothingland jurisdiction as an entity in its own right, without drawing attention to any one particular community. It is interesting to note that some of the names of the lesser settlements (all of them post-Domesday) are still in use today, with Boyton, Claydon and Wheatcroft being the best examples.

In terms of its status and administration during the thirteenth century, one extremely important element in the development of Lowestoft tends to pass almost unnoticed: that of being made a manor in its own right. The fact is declared in the *Liber Feodorum*, where, in information recorded for the year 1212, it is stated that Beccles was royal demesne and belonged to the manor of Lowestoft.[33] The reference to Beccles must be connected in some way to Domesday information, where it is revealed that the Crown held a quarter-share of the town's market (the rest of it being in the tenure and control of the abbey at Bury St Edmunds). This specific clause is included in the data relating to Lothingland Half-hundred – and so, with the king being lord of the manor there, the market privilege must be seen as part of its assets. What the *Liber Feodorum* meant exactly in declaring that Beccles *belonged* to the manor of Lowestoft is not clear, but some element of control is implied and this probably related to the share of the market rather than to the whole community. What matters most, in any consideration of Lowestoft's development, is that it is described as a manor – as opposed to an outlier – and the implication is one of growing half-hundredal influence and increasing

[33] H. C. Maxwell Lyte (ed.), *Liber Feodorum*, vol. 1 (London, 1920), p. 134. *The Book of Fees*, to give its name in translation, is a collection of information from the first half of the thirteenth century giving all kinds of details concerning English manors, particularly in relation to the lords and their service obligations.

self-autonomy. Interestingly (and frustratingly), the Hundred Roll makes no reference to the town's elevation, which had probably resulted from the administrative subdivision of the Lothingland estate.

In his masterly overview of the county, Mark Bailey has summarised the pattern of landholding in Suffolk as one characterised by weak manorial structure, with the average vill split between a number of manors and with the average lord working his own demesne and being moderately wealthy on the proceeds.[34] Lowestoft did not observe all of these norms. It certainly functioned under weak manorial control through not having a resident lord – but, in being created from an established outlier, it became a single-manor parish in its own right and not one divided into a number of discrete estates. Its tenants constituted a very small part of the 20 per cent of the county's villein workforce (as opposed to the 80 per cent enjoying free tenancy), but in being under the control of a bailiff rather than a lord they had greater freedom of action to organise their landholdings in the way they wanted and to work co-operatively if it suited them. As long as the rents were paid over, it is unlikely that the bailiff would have been particularly concerned about the fine details of agricultural practice, and he may even have helped the tenants to do what they wanted. It would also appear that, with the service due to the lord consisting mainly of cash payments, Lowestoft's workforce was less restricted in personal terms and had greater freedom of action than was the case on manors where the peasantry was more strictly supervised and controlled.

There is further evidence of increasing influence on Lowestoft's part to be found elsewhere in the Hundred Roll (in the section recording privileges relating to Lothingland manor), where it is revealed that the township had a gaol and stocks, in addition to those located in Gorleston.[35] It would seem, therefore, that at some point the manorial steward, or bailiff, had decided that dual control of the estate was desirable and (with the approval of the monarch) had given the biggest of the three Domesday outliers a share in its administration. This was not only sound in principle, with regard to the decentralisation of the manor's control and the provision of a better overview of events in the local area. It was also geographically appropriate in providing two centres of power at opposite ends of the jurisdiction: Gorleston to the

[34] Bailey, *Suffolk*, p. 290.

[35] The Lowestoft tithe map of 1842 (NRO, TA 658) shows three arable fields, numbered 118, 119 and 120 and named as *First*, *Second* and *Third Dungeon Piece*. In the middle of the last one is a piece of pasture land simply named *Dungeon*. The name does not feature in the 1618 manor roll, but it could be a reference to the siting of the gaol, bridging the centuries. All the land is located in the area of the Newson's Meadow housing development, with the western extremity of *Dungeon* touching onto what is now Rotterdam Road. The prison would therefore have stood less than 400 yards from the township.

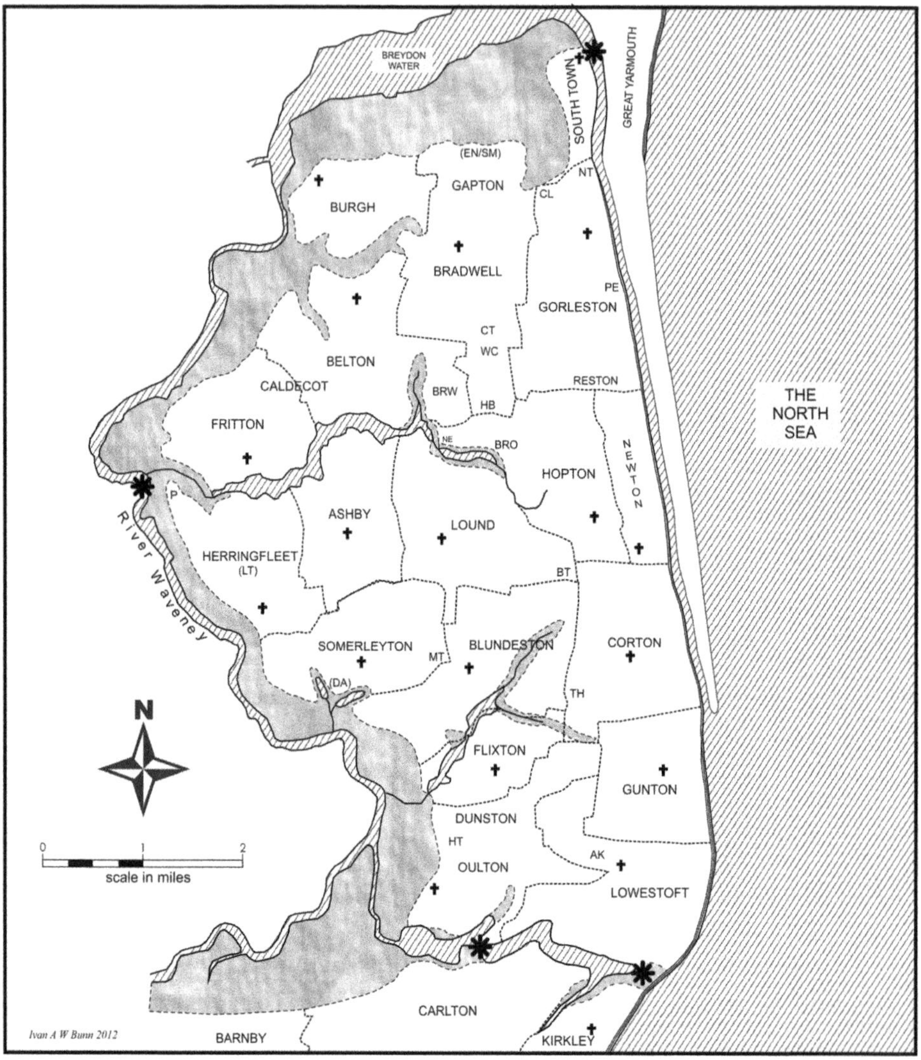

Map 4. Hundred Roll parishes and lesser settlements.

Notes:

- Key to lesser settlements: AK = Akethorp, BT = Boyton, BRO = Brotherton, BRW = Browston, CT = Carlton, CL = Claydon, DA = The Dale, EN = Enges, HB = Hobland, HT = Houton, LT = Lanthorp, MT = Manthorp, NE = The Nes(s), NT = Northtown, PE = Peneston, SM = Smallmoor, TH = Thorpe, WC = Wheatcroft.
- P = St Olave's Priory, Herringfleet (Augustinian canons) – founded c. 1216 by Roger Fitzosbert. The Augustinian friary of Southtown/Little Yarmouth, with its (later) famous library, wasn't established until c. 1310.

- Parish churches, crossing-places, tidal mudflats, areas of inland marsh, stretches of water and parish boundaries are all indicated as previously. Owing to the silting-up process and man's intervention, there had been conversion of the flats into grazing marsh in a number of areas (particularly Gorleston) – reclamation that was to continue until well into the early modern period.
- Names of most lesser settlements are placed in their locations in the different parishes except for the four whose exact position is not known, which are shown in brackets. Enges and Smallmoor were definitely located somewhere at the northern end of Gapton-Bradwell and The Dale in the vicinity of either of the two Somerleyton peat diggings (these being later known as Wicker Well and Summer Water), but Lanthorp is not able to be placed in any specific part of Herringfleet (hence its abbreviation being placed beneath the parish-name).
- Although Bradwell and Oulton parishes were well established by 1274, both Gapton and Dunston (though absorbed) still seem to have had some kind of local autonomy and status.
- Parish church dedications are as follows: All Saints (Belton), St Andrew (Flixton and Gorleston), St Bartholomew (Corton), St Edmund (Fritton), St John the Baptist (Lound), St Margaret (Herringfleet, Hopton and Lowestoft), St Mary (Ashby, Blundeston, Newton and Somerleyton), St Michael (Oulton), St Nicholas (Bradwell and Southtown), St Peter (Gunton), St Peter and St Paul (Burgh).
- The three Domesday churches recorded have early dedications: Blundeston St Mary (previously Somerleyton), Burgh St Peter and St Paul and Oulton St Michael (previously Flixton). St Mary, as the mother of Christ, was venerated from very early on in the western church's history; Saints Peter and Paul were its two formative founding figures; and St Michael, the archangel, was the symbolic 'soldier of the faith'. Lowestoft St Margaret (previously Akethorpe) was probably a renaming of the post-Conquest period – perhaps associated with Roger Bigot (or Bigod), sheriff of Norfolk and Suffolk and controller of the royal estates, who seems to have had an affinity with the saint and may have adopted her as his religious patroness.
- The sand-spit guiding the passage of the River Yare into the sea was to reach its maximum length southwards by the middle of the fourteenth century, finishing at a point more or less opposite Gunton church. Coastal erosion (itself partly the result of a rise in sea levels) thereafter began to remove it, before eventually abrading the cliff-line itself and leading, ultimately, to the disappearance of Newton.

north-east and Lowestoft in the south-east. Both townships had also long held the right of free warren, conferred upon them by royal grant – a privilege which entitled the holder to hunt and take game from land held of the monarch. As all land in the country was, by feudal theory, held in this manner, it simply gave licence to the person or persons named to hunt over the particular area referred to in the grant. In the case of a township being named, it meant that the demesne tenants had the right to do so.

Other details relating to specific rights and privileges appertaining to the manor of Lothingland are worth recording at this point. Firstly, its annually held court (effectively a leet, but a hundred court also because of the area covered) had once adjudged upon *de vetito namio* pleas. These were legal cases concerning the distraint of goods or property made legally or illegally, but the practice seems to have ceased before the reign of Edward I (probably when Henry III demised the manor to Dervorgille de Balliol in 1237). The right of wreck of the sea was another manorial perquisite, whereby the lord could claim half the value of any item retrieved from the shallows or washed up on the shore, with the other half going to the finder. This may have been another reason for giving Lowestoft privileges on a par with those of Gorleston. With townships placed at either end of the local coastline, better scrutiny of wreck could be exercised, with less chance of finders taking for themselves the whole value of what had been found.

The right to hold the annual view of frankpledge, whereby the good conduct of the half-hundred's inhabitants was considered, was also part of the manorial responsibility to maintain good order within its boundaries.[36] So was the yearly assize of bread and ale, which aimed at maintaining the retail price and quality of both products (staples of diet in the medieval world) in terms of the ingredients used. There was to be no dishonest practice in the production and sale of these commodities, such as the adulteration of flour with meal made from dried peas or beans and the watering down of ale after it had been brewed. Most threatening of all where would-be malefactors were concerned was the manor's right of execution for criminal offences, referred to as liberty of the gallows, with hanging probably able to be carried out in both Gorleston and Lowestoft.

The grant of a market to the half-hundred in the year 1211 has already been mentioned (p. 49). It was an important privilege, but fraught with difficulty from the start. Located on low-lying land close to the river, somewhere in the northern part of Gorleston, the market space proved liable to tidal flooding and, at some point between 1212 and 1226 (while William de Longspée, earl of Salisbury, held title to Lothingland, having rented it from the Crown), it was changed to a different site and the market day moved from Sunday to Thursday.[37] The new location must still have been at Gorleston's northern end, because the 1274 Hundred Roll records that the inhabitants of Little Yarmouth (later called Southtown) had encroached upon it, to the extent of thirty feet on all sides, and built houses on the land. Of the seven encroach-

[36] The word *frankpledge* derived from a medieval French mistranslation of OE *friÞborh*: 'peace-pledge'.
[37] De Longspée's tenancy is recorded in *Liber Feodorum*, 1, p. 139, and confirmed by the *CFR, Henry III*, C60/22 (Arts and Humanties Research Council, online resource: www.finerollshenry3.org).

ments reported, this was the first and the most significant in terms of both the location and the infringement of manorial rights.[38]

Another difficulty regarding Lothingland's commercial activities is to be found in the jurors' attestation that, when the manor was conveyed to Dervorgille de Balliol (in 1237, for a rental to the Crown of £70 p.a.), the value would have been £10 more if the estate had 'liberty of the water and other things' that it had enjoyed during the reigns of John and Henry III. It was said that the burgesses of Great Yarmouth were now in occupation of the water (i.e. the river which separated that town from Gorleston) – a take-over that had occurred when Roger Fitzosbert (lord of Somerleyton) leased the manor from the Crown for a three-year period in 1226 (following William de Longspée's death) at an annual rent of £80. After his tenancy, the title was then transferred to 'the men of Lothingland' (leading, but unnamed, freeholders on the Island) in 1230 for the sum of £70 annually.[39]

The jurors were in no doubt as to the effect of Great Yarmouth's infringement of the Lothingland manor's rights, and their words may be used to sum up local feelings concerning the matter nearly fifty years after it had first occurred:

> the burgesses of Great Yarmouth, in the time of King Henry, father of the now King, have appropriated to their own use the water which is divided between the County of Norfolk and the County of Suffolk, and of the which water the moiety [half] had regard to the manor of Lothingland in the time of King John and his ancestors, Kings of England.[40] And this appropriation of the water aforesaid is to the damage of the lord King and his manor of Lothingland in the extent of 10 pounds a year, and this appropriation was made in the time of King Henry, father of the now lord King, when Roger Fitz Osbert held the manor to farm [i.e. rented it]. Now the said bailiffs of Great Yarmouth take custom of ships and nets from the marshes, viz. Stonere, Fulholm and Buterdish, which are upon the demesne of the lord King in Lothingland.

The last reference, to collection of customs payments on marshland at Gorleston, shows the Yarmouth civic leaders exceeding their authority. According

[38] The most singular was Warin Blench's occupation of a plot, in Little Yarmouth, on which the *royal trebuchet* had stood (this referring to the manorial ducking stool rather than a military siege engine). House-building on the Lothingland market place itself may have resulted in a further move to the southern end of Gorleston's main street and would seem to suggest that the trading facility was in a weak economic state. See Appendix 5.

[39] Arts and Humanities Research Council, *CFR, Henry III*, C60/24, C60/29 and C60/30 record these transfers.

[40] In other words, Yarmouth had control of the dividing river to its halfway point, with Lothingland having identical jurisdiction on its own side. See Hervey, *Hundred Rolls*, pp. 72 and 73.

to another part of the Hundred Roll, there were seven such areas altogether (the name of one of them, *Cobbeholm*, has survived down to the present day) and, with *holm* meaning 'island', they demonstrate the progressive reclamation of usable land, by drainage, from the progressive silting-up of the former estuarine area which had been such a feature of the local landscape in Roman times. In plain terms, the jurors' evidence shows that Yarmouth officials were taking customs payments from ships anchored on the Suffolk side of the river, as well as imposing tolls for the privilege of spreading out herring nets (to dry and be cleaned) – on land, of course, which was situated in Suffolk and was part of Lothingland manor's territory.

The roots of this action lay back in the time that Roger Fitzosbert had held the Lothingland title. He claimed to have the right to collect certain customs duties (relating to vessels belonging to Lothingland owners) in Great Yarmouth – an authority contested by the Norfolk town's civic heads. An enquiry was ordered by Henry III in 1228, headed up by four royal justices (Martin de Pateshall, Walter de Evermewe, Fulk de Banignard and Hamo de Stanhoe), to enquire into all matters of local dispute.[41] The outcome of this was to declare Yarmouth's primacy in matters of local trade and maritime activity, but to allow lesser (unimportant) goods and victuals to be unloaded on the Suffolk side of the river. This particular compromise became the source of dispute between the two parties, especially in the matter of herrings landed during the autumn season (29 September to 11 November). Were the fish Yarmouth's staple product, over which it had exclusive control, or were they simply a foodstuff able to be traded freely and without encumbrance? The matter was one which caused considerable contention. It seems likely that at least some of 'the men of Lothingland' did seek to provoke the ruling elite in Great Yarmouth by claiming rights they did not have. And this, in turn, resulted in the Yarmouth men resorting to illegal tactics themselves, even to the point (according to the Hundred Roll jurors) of confiscating goods and chattels belonging to their neighbours (i.e. people who lived in Lothingland) for the payment of debts without due legal process. This kind of action, it was claimed, was even taken in cases where the debts had not been incurred by Lothingland people themselves and where they were acting as guarantors for others.

Much will be made, in a later chapter, of the economic rivalry between Lowestoft and Great Yarmouth, but it is important to set the scene in advance. It did not just start in the middle of the fourteenth century; the roots of

[41] A.W. Ecclestone, *Henry Manship's Great Yarmouth* (Great Yarmouth, 1971), p. 95. The writer was drawing upon the work of Yarmouth's legendary antiquarian (a lawyer by training), who died in 1625.

dispute went back well over a hundred years earlier, before Lowestoft began to emerge as the dominant community in the Half-hundred of Lothingland. Certain steps along the way towards its eventual supremacy have already been mentioned (notably, the granting of manorial status and the apparently equal share received in the government of the half-hundred, along with Gorleston). Another development came in 1306. Reference has already been made to the confiscation, by Edward I, of all de Balliol family lands in England because John de Balliol the Younger (as king of Scotland) had formed an alliance with Philip IV of France in the year 1294. Twelve years later Edward conferred a number of these estates on his nephew, John de Dreux, earl of Richmond, including the manors of Lothingland and Lowestoft.

It may have been the holding of these two particular titles by yet another absentee lord that assisted what seems to have been the merging of the Lothingland and Lowestoft estates – not into a single consolidated unit but into more of a duality of tenure, whereby one manor was held in tandem with the other. On 15 November 1308 de Dreux (under his alias of John de Brittany) received a royal grant entitling Lowestoft – not Lothingland – to stage a weekly market (Wednesday) and an annual fair, the latter to be held on the vigil of St Margaret – the feast itself (20 July) and six days following.[42] Thus was the patroness of the parish church (formerly the church of Akethorpe) given extra significance as a figure in the town's development. It is not known whether or not the venue (or venues) for these events was located within the area occupied by the original settlement, but it is interesting to note that the dual privilege of market and fair was made at a time when the township had begun to relocate itself to a cliff-side site (see below). There is no doubt that the grant was of key importance in allowing Lowestoft to grow in importance within both the Lothingland area and the neighbouring Mutford Half-hundred. It was probably made in recognition of the place's increasing influence locally and may even have played a part in the relocation itself; the possible lack of a suitable location in, or near, the old township site on which to stage both market and fair may have been a factor in causing the centre of population to move.

[42] C.G. Crump and R.D. Trimmer (eds), *CoCR*, vol. 3 (London, 1908), p. 123. Bailey, *Suffolk*, p. 119, comments on how lords of the manor often acquired rights of market and fair simultaneously and how the latter were often held during religious festivals with local connections. The grant of an eight-day fair to Lowestoft, rather than the usual three- or four-day one, suggests either perceived potential in the town's economic fortunes or a genuine increase in trading activity at the time.

The 1327 Lay Subsidy

The national tax levied in 1327 to raise revenue for the Crown came at a troubled time for the country, for this was the year in which Edward II was deposed by his wife, Isabella, and her lover, Roger Mortimer, earl of March – ostensibly in favour of the future Edward III, who was fourteen years old at the time. It was also a time of conflict with Scotland, with an army from north of the border making an incursion into England and engaging with English forces near Stanhope, in County Durham. The tax collected per head of population, on those able to afford it, was set at one-twentieth of the value of movable goods worth 5s or more and twenty-nine of Lowestoft's citizens were found liable for payment (Table 8).[43]

Table 8. Contributors to the 1327 Lay Subsidy.

Name	Amount	Name	Amount
Emma le Monner	9d	Richard Jakelin [Jacklin]	16d
*John Howlot [Howlett]	10d	John of Baldiswelle [Bawdeswell]	8d
*Warin Howlot [Howlett]	20d	*Reginald Reynald [Reynolds]	2s
John Aleyn [Allen]	9d	Geoffrey the Channdler [Chandler]	8d
John Coyt	10d	Peter the Blobbere	16d
Robert Elflet [Eylested]	10d	*Henry Dekne [Deacon]	8d
*John Gerald	10d	Robert of Derom [Dereham]	10d
Andrew Botild	12d	Reginald of Brundale [Brundall]	20d
*John Ode	10d	*Edmund of Akethorpe	10d
Edmund Wyard [Wyatt]	10d	*William Dekne [Deacon]	10d
Thomas Gilly	8d	*Thomas Dekne [Deacon]	8d
Matilda Elys [Ellis]	20d	*Richard Ode	12d
*Robert Haghenild [Haenyld]	12d	William Grym [Grimes]	18d
*Thomas of Eston [Easton]	8d	John, son of Sarre [Sarah]	18d
William Wyard [Wyatt]	10d		
		Total:	£1 9s 6d

Notes:

- An asterisk indicates surnames that were still being used to identify manorial chief tenements throughout the early modern period. Eight family connections are noted here, five of which (Gerald, Ode, Hagenhild, Reynald and Dekne) appear in Table 6. Howlot, Eston and Akethorpe are new additions.

[43] S.H.A. Hervey, *Suffolk in 1327*, SGB 9 (Woodbridge, 1906), p. 95. There were a number of subsidies levied between c. 1280 and 1334, but that of 1327 provides a particularly comprehensive national record.

- The tenants underlined have surnames which are also to be found in Tables 6 and 7.
- Square brackets enclose common modern spellings of names.
- With a lowest payment per head of 8d and a highest one of 2s (24d), the value of movable goods assessed ranged from 13s 4d to £2.

Comment will be made in Chapter 3 concerning the total amount of tax paid by the Lowestoft populace relative to that raised in neighbouring communities. The main use of the data at this stage will be to investigate possible changes in the nature of the town's society in the fifty years since the Hundred Roll enquiry was carried out. One noticeable feature, when the surnames in Table 8 are set against those recorded in Tables 6 and 7, is the small number of families that appear to have continued living in the parish. The only ones occurring in both sources are Aleyn, Elflet/Eylested, Gerald/Jerald, Ode, Haghenild/Haenyld, Wyard, Reynald and Dekne/Deacon – with a member of the Reynalds (significantly, perhaps) being the highest taxpayer, just as an ancestor had been the largest holder of land. However, it has to be borne in mind that two different kinds of criteria are in operation regarding the nature of the material presented. The Hundred Roll records people who held land and (where appropriate) the rents paid thereon; the Subsidy shows the tax paid on personal possessions and stock-in-trade worth a capital sum of 5s or more. Therefore, it should not be assumed that a large turnover of population must have taken place in Lowestoft between 1274 and 1327, because land held both in demesne and in villeinage did not necessarily mean that the occupiers were wealthy – especially where smaller acreages were concerned.

Then there is the matter of members of the villein class being tied to the manor on which they lived. An absentee lord (especially one as remote as John de Dreux) may have resulted in less tight control of the tenants than would have been the case under a resident one, although the steward's supervision would not necessarily have allowed the workforce to enjoy freedom of movement to any great degree. And, in any case, it is unclear what conditions might promote such mobility in the first place. The breakdown of manorial structure and the national labour shortage resulting from the Black Death were still a generation away. Most of the Lowestoft tenants probably had no need to move elsewhere and there would be little, if anything, to be gained from doing so. They had their various landholdings, large or small, and the means of maintaining themselves and their families thereby, in addition to any other sources of income available to them through involvement in maritime activity or through having practical skills of use to the community as a whole.

Having said that, some degree of inward movement is detectable. Twelve of the taxpayers named in Table 8 (belonging to the family groups mentioned above) were obviously connected with people listed earlier, in Tables 6 and

7. What, then, of the seventeen who seem to have had no previous links? Personal connections, in some cases, cannot be ruled out, but nor can they be presumed to have existed. In three cases the surnames are encountered in other Lothingland communities in the 1274 Hundred Roll: le Monner (rendered as le Muner) in Gorleston, Elys (or Eleys) in Gunton and Eston in Oulton, while the name Botild is to be found in fourteenth-century documentation relating to Gisleham and Mutford.[44] At any point during the intervening fifty years a member of these families could have migrated to Lowestoft and joined its population – not to become part of the peasantry, but to live by some trade or occupation that was useful to the community.

Other incomers are indicated by having names relating either to a previous place of residence or to their family group's original home. There are three such places, all in Norfolk: Bawdeswell, Dereham (probably East Dereham) and Brundall. What had brought them to Lowestoft and made them residents there? Again, the likelihood is that they were part of an emerging class of people involved in trade of one kind or another, rather than being of the level of society that was tied to the land. Two of the names recorded shed particular light on themselves and their community. Geoffrey the Chandler may be indicative of a developing community increasing its range of activities and skills, in that he was probably a candle-maker rather than someone engaged in the sale of grocery items, candles being a more expensive and effective means of indoor illumination than tallow rush-lights. Peter the Blobber was not nearly so fortunate; his name would seem to suggest either that he had thick, protruding lips and a spluttering manner of speech or that he was an indiscreet chatterbox – neither of which is a particularly flattering image.

John and Warin Howlot, John Coyt, Thomas Gilly, Richard Jakelin, William Gryme and John, son of Sarah, cannot easily be categorised by name alone, but they too had come into Lowestoft for particular reasons and become part of its social structure. Again, their presence among the community's taxpayers would seem to suggest that they were not of villein status, but had means of livelihood other than simply tilling the soil, and therefore reflect a society diversifying from agriculture alone to a more complex economy. Edmund of Akethorpe, of course, was a local person and a member of the family which held title to Lowestoft's Domesday outlier – long integrated by now into its larger neighbour's parochial structure, but still an independent manor at this time.

[44] The name Eston (especially as it is preceded by 'of') probably refers to the parish of origin, located immediately to the north of Southwold. Alternatively spelled as Easton, it eventually became known as Easton Bavents – the second element deriving from the de Bavent family, lords of the manor there during the thirteenth and fourteenth centuries.

Akethorpe

Before leaving this appraisal of Lowestoft's structure during the 200 years following Domesday, it is necessary to give some attention to its smaller neighbour – not only because of the latter's integration within the adjacent, larger community, but because it has surviving documentation of a kind not available for Lowestoft itself. This consists largely of fourteenth- and fifteenth-century account rolls and rentals appertaining to its manor and, while these records are mainly concerned with the money generated for the holder of the title from the renting-out of demesne lands, they also have the ability to reveal changes in agricultural practice. Essentially, Lowestoft was a one-manor parish, but it did have a small part of its total area in the hands of another lord.

As has already been seen, at Domesday Akethorpe was a small, independent manor held by an Anglo-Saxon priest named Aelmer. There is little documentation concerning it in the two centuries following, but it does feature fleetingly in land disputes between interested parties. In 1205–6 Agnes, Margaret and Wulviva, daughters of Selida, were involved in a case versus Stephen, son of Benedict, while twenty or more years later, in 1227–8, Geoffrey, son of Osbert, and his wife, Edith, were in opposition to Stephen de Steingat[45] – the last name of all being recognisable as also belonging to one of the Lowestoft landholders listed in Table 7 (Margaret of the Stonegate). Then, in late April 1240, Richard of Akethorpe is found in dispute with Stephen of Akethorpe and his brother John.[46]

This last-named case would seem to refer to a family group bearing the name of the community in which they were probably the dominant landholders, and holders also of the manorial title, following on at some point from Aelmer. The 1274 Hundred Roll refers to later members, Mabel and her son Robert, who jointly held twenty acres of arable land and pieces of heath totalling forty acres. A further seven acres of arable were held by the prior of Herringfleet and the rest of the estate (acreage not specified) by other unnamed people.[47] The rent payable to the Crown on this holding was 10s 4d, which was very close indeed to the sum of 10s payable on the Domesday manor, and so it is possible that the two areas under discussion were one and the same.

The Domesday estate had eighty acres of arable land, one acre of meadow and five acres of wood; the Hundred Roll estate, twenty-seven acres of

[45] W. Rye (ed.), *A Calendar of the Feet of Fines for Suffolk* (Ipswich, 1900), pp. 13 and 27.
[46] E.J. Gallagher, *The Civil Pleas of the Suffolk Eyre of 1240*, SRS 52 (Woodbridge, 2009), p. 7.
[47] Hervey, *Hundred Rolls*, pp. 36 and 37.

arable (including Herringfleet Priory's seven) and forty acres of heath, plus an unspecified amount of arable held by unnamed tenants. Domesday does not record heath, or waste, but the two arable totals of eighty acres and twenty-seven-plus may not have been very far apart if the acreage held by the unnamed occupiers added up to anything substantial. Certainly, the de Akethorpe family connection had been quite a long one, because the Hundred Roll jurors testified that in the time of King Richard I (1189–99) William of Akethorpe had held the estate. Furthermore, there were two other Akethorpe holdings referred to in the roll: a split one formed of land in both Akethorpe and Corton (total area unknown), valued at 4s 4d a year, and another in Akethorpe itself (area also unknown) worth 2s 8d.[48] Both of these lesser holdings could easily have been composed partly of land once belonging to the Domesday manor of Akethorpe, which had been alienated at some stage prior to the Hundred Roll enquiry.

Robert of Akethorpe is detectable in other records as being involved in property disputes – probably with his brother, Richard (of Akethorpe). The latter paid over the sum of 13s 4d (one mark) in July 1254 to have a case of *mort d'ancestor* heard in the presence of a royal justice named William le Breton – this showing that he believed he had been illegally dispossessed of land due to him by inheritance.[49] Less than two years later, in March 1256, he paid 6s 8d for an assize of novel disseisin to be held before the same judge, which means that he was bringing a case to court concerning land from which he had (in his opinion) been wrongly dispossessed. Robert of Akethorpe reciprocated this action at exactly the same time.[50]

Fourteen years later, in January and July 1270, Robert of Akethorpe (who seems to have prevailed in the family dispute) twice paid the sum of 6s 8d (half a mark, in the terminology of the time) for writs of *ad terminum*, which shows that he was seeking to recover possession of two different properties from tenants whose occupancy had exceeded the term agreed.[51] There was a great deal of litigation during the late medieval period relating to the holding and occupation of land, which speaks both of its importance in the medieval economy and of the social status that accompanied its possession – especially if it was a manor, with the accompanying privileges of lordship.

It is doubtful, given the comparatively small size, that the Akethorpe estate had its agriculture organised on a three-field system, as was the case in Lowestoft – though the 1618 manor roll certainly suggests the survival of strips at

[48] Possibly thirteen acres and eight acres respectively, if a rent of 4d per acre was paid.
[49] Arts and Humanities Research Council, *CFR, Henry III*, C60/51.
[50] Arts and Humanities Research Council, *CFR, Henry III*, C60/53.
[51] Arts and Humanities Research Council, *CFR, Henry III*, C60/ 67.

one point along *Oxemere Lane* (now Oulton Road) (see Map 2). By that time the size of the manor had increased to ninety-nine acres, sixty-eight of which were arable land, nineteen were down to grass, and twelve were managed woodland. There may also have been areas consisting of bruery and heath located in the adjacent parish of Gunton. Domesday shows that Akethorpe's livestock mainly consisted of sheep, of which there were forty-eight (there were also twelve oxen for ploughing and three pigs), which would have been at least partly grazed on such land. A damaged indenture of the mid-fifteenth century contains a reference to foldage and commonage, but that is all that can be read.[52] According to the Hundred Roll the Lowestoft tenants paid their lord of the manor 6s 8d a year for foldage (i.e. the obligation to graze their sheep at night on demesne land that had either had a crop taken from it or was being rested on the three-year rotation cycle). Thus, the tenants were paying for their animals' feed while giving the lord the benefit of the manure produced – though he (or she) had to provide a sheep-fold (made of hurdles) for impounding the animals during the nocturnal hours.

Arable practice, in terms of the way that fields were arranged, changed considerably throughout parts of lowland England during the late medieval period, and this is mirrored in both Akethorpe and Lowestoft. The manor roll clearly shows that much of the land had been enclosed by 1618 and, with both estates taken together, the proportion is as follows: excluding five open areas of common or waste (*The Denes*, *North Common*, *Church Green*, *South Common* and the much smaller *Goose Green*), 68 per cent of all the land used for agriculture or animal husbandry was fenced. Of the different categories of land use, 73 per cent of arable soil, 92 per cent of the meadow, pasture and stintland and 31 per cent of the bruery – the last named being located at *Skamacre Heath*, *Drakes Heath* and *Smithmarsh* – were fenced. The very high percentage of grassland that was hedged round should come as no surprise, given the need to keep livestock confined. Nor is it remarkable that so much of the managed heathland should have remained unfenced, in view of its traditionally open nature. However, the fact that three-quarters of the arable had been enclosed by 1618 shows just how far the move away from open-field agriculture had progressed.

The old system, however, is still clearly visible in Map 2 (p. 25) – especially in the smallest of the three Lowestoft open fields, *The North Field*. Here, the relatively level nature of the land enabled the strips to be set out on a north–south alignment, with an average (and traditional) strip length of about a furlong (220 yards) observed on either side of the *Church Way* track (now St Margaret's Road), leading from the late medieval town site to the parish

[52] MCL, FP 54.

church. Before the relocation of the town, what became the roadway had probably been a central baulk (unploughed ridge), running east–west and dividing the two sets of furrows. The two larger fields, *The South* and *The South-West*, would have had similar divisions, creating workable sections within them and giving the ploughmen reference points when operating their teams. Again, surviving strips are recognisable in a number of places, with some (east of *Skamacre Heath* and south of *Church Green*) showing a rough east–west alignment to take account of the sloping ground and prevent the soil washing down the incline in heavy rainfall. With the single-furrow ploughs of the time being able to draw a furrow of perhaps six to nine inches' width, the classic one-acre strip of 220 yards length by twenty-two yards width (4,840 square yards = one acre) would have been made up of about 100 furrows. It was always reckoned at one time that the English ploughman could till an acre a day (a target more likely to have been achieved on light land rather than clay). If this were true, then he would have walked twelve and a half miles to do it! Lesser areas accomplished would have meant lesser distances covered, but there is no doubt as to the arduous nature of the work and the physical effort involved.

The animals used to pull ploughs during the Anglo-Saxon period were usually oxen (castrated male cattle), but in the centuries following Domesday horses began to feature more and more – until, by the beginning of the sixteenth century, they were the favoured creature for the work. To a certain degree, the preference for one over the other was an economic equation: oxen were easier and cheaper to feed than horses and had slaughter-value as meat and leather, while horses covered the ground with more facility and had greater versatility for other types of haulage work. It is a matter of conjecture, therefore, as to which were employed in working the Lowestoft and Akethorpe land during the Middle Ages, and a combination of the two is probably the answer, with horses assuming growing importance in the era following the ravages of the Black Death.[53]

Periodic reference has been made thus far to the three-field system of agriculture, but it is a term which is both misleading and simplistic. The writer has a basic knowledge of medieval farming practice, but he has no desire to become deeply engaged in the more specialist aspects of crop regimes and livestock management. At the same time, Lowestoft (together with Akethorpe) relied on arable production and animal husbandry to produce at

[53] B.M.S. Campbell, *English Seigniorial Agriculture, 1250–1450* (Cambridge, 2006), p. 122, notes this development in east Norfolk, particularly in areas of light soil. Bailey, *Suffolk*, p. 80, notes the pronounced presence of horses in the county as a feature dating back to the late thirteenth century.

least some of the food consumed by its population and to provide materials for certain of its industries (notably, brewing and leather manufacture). Farming was still of sufficient importance locally in the early modern period to provide a safety net for the community; when the maritime economy (particularly fishing) underwent a period of severe difficulty during the first half of the seventeenth century the townspeople were able to fall back on the land to sustain themselves.[54] Therefore, it is important that some attempt is made to discuss any specific features of Lowestoft's agriculture that are able to be detected.

The major impediment to detailed analysis is the absence of any surviving manorial documentation – especially court rolls, in which the misdemeanours of the tenants (notably, their infringement of the rules governing land management) often reveal a great deal of information regarding changes in farming practice. In being located in the far north-eastern corner of Suffolk, Lowestoft sat on the coastal Sandlings belt – a broad stretch of light soils characterised by heathland, which is still much in evidence today in a number of places – and what has become known as the 'sheep–corn' farming regime.[55] Described in very broad terms, this involved growing barley, rye or oats as arable crops on light soils (wherever they prevailed), with sheep feeding on the harvest aftermath and subsequent fallows and manuring the land as they did so. Following the demographic, social and economic dislocation caused by the Black Death, it has been observed that, of the seven main types of farming detectable in medieval England, sheep–corn husbandry increased in scale most of all.[56]

On the slender evidence available (notably, local soil type and the reference to foldage on p. 67, above), there is no reason to believe that Lowestoft's farming regime was not of the sheep–corn type. Light land was suitable for sheep-rearing (especially where there was much heath and rough pasture) and for the culture of barley – the low nitrogen content producing grain that was well suited for brewing[57] – and the parish met these requirements fully. Both sheep and cattle have been adjudged the most versatile of farm animals in their ability to yield the greatest variety of useful products,[58] but Lowestoft had comparatively little land suitable for supporting the latter in substantial numbers and even the eighteenth-century tithe accounts do not show significant beast-keeping as part

[54] Butcher, *Lowestoft*, p. 64.

[55] B.M.S. Campbell, K.C. Bartley and J.P. Power, 'The demesne-farming systems of post Black Death England: a classification', AHR, 44/2 (1996), p. 164.

[56] Campbell et al., 'Demesne-farming systems', p. 177. See also pp. 142–3 (especially Table 4) for the seven basic farming types.

[57] Campbell et al., 'Demesne-farming systems', pp. 154 and 155.

[58] Campbell, *Seigniorial Agriculture*, p. 103.

of local husbandry.[59] In conjunction with the probate data available from c. 1560–1730, the picture is very much one of a secondary interest on the part of farmers, as well as of merchants, craftsmen and mariners.

Sheep themselves seem to have been to have been of minor importance in the Lowestoft economy during the early modern period,[60] but, while there is no way of ascertaining their overall significance during medieval times, it is likely that numbers were considerably higher. The Domesday count of 160 for Lowestoft and forty-eight for Akethorpe is suggestive of this, but for how long the situation prevailed is not known. It is possible that, as the town developed a more specialist maritime function from the early fourteenth century onwards, its pattern of husbandry changed because an increased number of men involved in fishing and seaborne trade meant that fewer hands were available to be engaged in farming. Additionally, the cumulative engrossment and enclosure of land within the common fields would have substantially reduced the number of sheep able to be kept.

In terms of the field system itself, the three basic arable units are plain to see in Map 2, with residual survival of open strips aligned on either a north–south or an east–west axis. There are also extensive areas of land where the strips had obviously been engrossed at some stage and amalgamated into larger, mainly rectangular, enclosed areas. This is likely to have been the result of the cumulative piecemeal enclosure process noted by Mark Bailey as occurring in central and east Suffolk during the late medieval period, especially in areas of weak manorial control (a feature of Lowestoft previously referred to, caused by its having an absentee lord), where tenant initiative for self-advancement was more likely to be possible.[61] Given its function as an outlier to the Lothingland hub-manor before becoming a manor in its own right, and given the absence of manorial documentation relating to its administration, it is not possible to ascertain definitively whether Lowestoft had what Bailey describes as an irregular field system or a more tightly controlled one.

The former type (with its partially regulated cropping practice) is identifiable by being mainly located in areas of poor soil – which Lowestoft, and some of Akethorpe, had – and having a field pattern less regular and regimented than the classic Midland tripartite one.[62] The number and shape of fields could vary; the tenants' holdings were dispersed; marker-posts and stones defined individual boundaries, sometimes with interposing hedges;

[59] Butcher, *Lowestoft*, pp. 213 and 214.
[60] Butcher, *Lowestoft*, p. 215.
[61] M. Bailey, 'The form, function and evolution of irregular field systems in Suffolk, c. 1300 to c. 1550', *AHR*, 57/1 (2009), pp. 27, 28 and 33.
[62] Bailey, *Suffolk*, p. 102.

and the individual parcels of arable land were arranged in plots or pieces (L. *pecia*) of often about half an acre in area. The Lowestoft manor roll of 1618 records ninety-eight such parcels totalling 340 acres in all, which produces an average size of one and a half acres.[63] Other points of comparison include the cropping regime of barley, rye and oats, with sheep as the dominant livestock species, folded nocturnally on the post-harvest fallows and grazing the nearby areas of permanent pasture (usually heath) during the day.[64] Owing to the absence of appropriate records, it is not possible to ascertain whether or not there was communal control of cropping procedures and patterns, so as to create compact blocks of fallow to facilitate folding, but it is likely that the people involved in both crop and animal husbandry co-operated with each other in order to achieve the best and most profitable results.

Earlier in this chapter details were given of Lowestoft's (and Gorleston's) manorial structure, in terms of the respective amounts of demesne and villeinage land present in each community, as revealed in the 1274 Hundred Roll (pp. 31–9). Changes in the pattern of landholding during the two centuries separating Domesday and Edward I's enquiry seem to have significantly reduced the amount of demesne in each community – a process facilitated by the remoteness of the Crown (and then the de Balliol family) as holder of the Lothingland Half-hundred's title. Lowestoft is accredited with seventy-three acres (it had become sixty-eight by the time the manor roll of 1618 was drawn up), with a further 289¼ held in villeinage by twenty-five tenants. As an outlier of the hub manor during the late Anglo-Saxon period and at Domesday, the community had had its agricultural system set out originally in the classic three-field pattern (as reflected visually in Map 2) with the main object of servicing the hub itself. Changes during the twelfth and thirteenth centuries may have caused subsequent internal modifications to this structure, to produce what Mark Bailey has defined as an 'irregular common field system with partially regulated cropping'.[65]

Weak lordship was a key factor in the process of change, and one not solely caused by the remoteness of the holder of the title (successively, the Crown, the de Balliol family and the earl of Richmond). Much of the degrading of the original, tightly organised procedures of field management has already been alluded to earlier in this chapter with reference to the venality and opportunism of local officials – particularly bailiffs of the half-hundred – as they sold off parts of the demesne and colluded with tenants in various kinds

[63] D. Butcher, 'The development of pre-industrial Lowestoft, 1560–1730' (unpub. MPhil thesis, Univ. East Anglia, 1991), p. 303.
[64] Bailey, 'Form, function and evolution', pp. 19 and 21, and Bailey, *Suffolk*, p. 105.
[65] Bailey, *Suffolk*, p. 105.

of irregularity. Such abuse must have continued apace after the disruption caused by the Black Death and, by the early seventeenth century, practically the whole of the community's agricultural land (960 acres out of c. 1,000) was held by freehold tenure.[66] It was a state of affairs far removed from what had prevailed 300–400 years earlier.

Taking into account the factor of an absentee lord, changes in the layout and management of the land must also have been influenced by the tenantry itself. The twenty-five men named in Table 6 (p. 33) as holders of the villeinage land in 1274 effectively had control (under the eye of the bailiff) of the parish's agriculture, and their residual influence is demonstrated by the use throughout the early modern period of sixteen of their surnames to identify the Lowestoft manorial chief tenements. Villein tenure itself has been identified as being relatively uncommon in Suffolk during the thirteenth century (with no more than 20 per cent of the peasantry involved), but higher rates are detectable on the Bury Abbey estates in the west of the county and in parts of the east.[67] In Lowestoft 60 per cent of its main body of tenants held land under villeinage procedure(s) and, with the demesne farmed out among a further twenty-seven men (eight of whom also had villeinage parcels), there was no strong central control of the community's agriculture. Thus, the labour dues and food-rents customarily owed to the lord (especially a resident one) had been largely commuted to cash payments, imposing a far less onerous form of service on the tenants and giving them de facto status approaching that enjoyed by freemen.

As long as the rents due to the lord were paid over it is unlikely that the bailiff would have agonised unduly about how the tenants were managing the land – and it is conceivable, in any case, that a far-distant lord may not even have known the true annual value of his Lowestoft estate. It was this kind of remoteness and lack of detailed knowledge that encouraged the type of behaviour recorded earlier (pp. 49–53), and there seems little doubt that collusion between tenants and officers was seen as being of mutual advantage. It has been said that any tenant holding ten or more acres of land during the period 1200–1349 was well placed to benefit from the high price of agricultural produce.[68] Towards the end of the thirteenth century Lowestoft had half of its main workforce (twenty-one out of a total of forty-one) in this category. And it may well have been that the wealth accrued by these men and their successors was one of the factors in the community's growth in economic power and social confidence during the late thirteenth and early fourteenth

[66] Butcher, *Lowestoft*, p. 131.
[67] Bailey, *Suffolk*, p. 50.
[68] Bailey, *Suffolk*, p. 59.

centuries – to the point where it was able (with other contributory factors taken into account) to move itself to a cliff-top location, a development that is the subject of the next chapter.

One effect of Lowestoft's earlier system of land management, and of the progressive changes made to it, is that the parish was much enclosed by 1618.[69] The figures cited earlier (p. 67) include Akethorpe in the reckoning because the manor roll treated the estate as if it were part of the Lowestoft totality and no longer a separate seigneurial holding. And this was indeed the case: the lands had been in the control of Magdalen College, Oxford, since the late 1470s, but without manorial status. How this came about has yet to be considered; of more immediate importance is the fact that extant documentation relating to Akethorpe manor (as it still was at the time) shows that a good deal of enclosure had taken place. A demesne account roll and rental of 1438–9 make reference to two arable enclosures (sized seven and three and a half acres respectively), two that were a combination of arable and pasture (sized thirty and a half and sixteen acres respectively) and one that had neither size nor use referred to (Table 9).[70] Four of them are also named: *Sty Close* (three and a half acres), *Akethorpe Close* (thirty and a half), *Dunnes Close* (sixteen) and *Yelvertons Close* (no size given) – the last two perhaps bearing the names of former tenants. In addition to these particular areas were four unfenced pieces – with the word 'piece' being used in isolation from any additional information suggesting that the land was arable, which it almost certainly was. Their sizes are given as seven acres, two and three-quarters (two holdings combined) and one. The last was referred to as *Browne's Pightle*, again suggesting an earlier occupant.

Table 9. Akethorpe account roll and rental details (1438–9).

Name	**Holding**	**Details**	**Rent**
Simon Bochere	Site of Akethorpe manor, with two adjacent enclosures. Also, enclosures called Akethorpe Close and Stys Close	First two enclosures sized 7 acres; the other two, 30½ acres and 3½ acres. Leased for 7 years and in second year of term	55s 4d
Richard Key Simon Russell William Leverych	An enclosure called Yelvertons	Holding accompanied by 5 acres of heath situated in Gunton. Leased for 7 years and in second year of term	43s 4d

[69] A feature of Suffolk generally. See J. Thirsk, *The Agrarian History of England and Wales*, vol. 4 (Cambridge, 1967), p. 203.
[70] MCL, 73/4 and 151/19.

Table 9 *cont.*

Name	Holding	Details	Rent
Henry Steyngate	A piece of arable land, to the south of Yelvertons	7 acres in size. Leased for 7 years and in second year of term	8s
William Veyse	Two pieces of land, to the east of Akethorpe Close	2¾ acres in size. Leased for 7 years and in second year of term	2s 6d
John Steyngate	An enclosure called Dunnes	16 acres in size and in second year of 7-year term	40s
Edmund Boyton	A pightle called Browne's Pightle	1 acre in size and in second year of term	2s
John Parkyn	An alder carr	1 acre in size and in second year of term	4s 8d

Depending on the area of arable land in the two mixed-use enclosures (which was likely to have been more extensive than the pasture), and taking into account that the size of *Yelverton's Close* is not specified, the total area of cultivated ground may not have been radically different from the sixty-eight acres of the manor roll. And there are other features of Akethorpe manor revealed in the earlier documentation that are not to be found later on and which are able to cast further light on the management and practice of rural economy in the middle of the fifteenth century. One is the reference to a one-acre area of alder carr, whose occupant was allowed to have the underwood growing there (to be cut at reasonable intervals, so as to conserve it), but was forbidden to cut down the trees themselves.[71] Then there are the instructions given to the holder of the largest proportion of the estate, which required him to fence off the enclosures he held with ditch and thorn (blackthorn) at his own expense and to cut the thorn whenever necessary.

The introduction to the account roll states that the manorial bailiff, Robert Andrew, was £38 3s 4d in arrears to the lord on the previous year's accounts. With an annual rental value of £7 15s 10d deriving from the Akethorpe lands (suggesting substantial increases in charges per acre since the time of the Hundred Roll), it would seem that a rolling debt had been incurred, possibly by Andrew being neglectful in his duties or even using the money himself, or by his being unable to get it from the tenants, in the first place, during a

[71] Alder grows in damp conditions and its wood is resistant to rotting. It was used for posts and piling, and it also produced high-grade charcoal, later to be used in the manufacture of gunpowder.

time of agricultural depression.[72] Perhaps the most interesting piece of information in the whole document is to be found in the description of Simon Bochere's holding, where it states that he was in occupancy of 'the site of the manor of Akethorphalle with two large enclosures adjoining containing about seven acres of land by estimation, with a barn and granary built thereon'.[73] This suggests that a manor house had once been present, but was no longer in existence – the result, perhaps, of unfavourable economic conditions or change of title (or both).

On the opposite side of what is now Oulton Road (formerly *Oxemere Lane*), and to the west of Rotterdam Road, was a group of fields some of which also had names suggestive of the one-time presence of a manor house (Plate 8). The area today is occupied by post-war housing development forming the Harp's Close Road/Larch Road/Lilac Drive/Bramble Green/Magnolia Court/Mimosa Walk/Northgate complex, situated in what the 1618 manor roll refers to as *The Park Field* and *Ringbell and Shelton*. This block of land was situated between *Church Green* to the east and *Skamacre Heath* to the west and was obviously primarily arable in nature (with some pasture-land included), reclaimed originally from the heathland on either side (see Map 2). The name *Park* is significant because it identifies the location as having been fenced off at some stage to form the surrounds of a manor house.

Within this particular collection of fields the arable enclosure located in the north-eastern corner (and lying to the south-west of the parish church) was known as *Park Close*, while the one immediately to the south of it was *The Park*. In today's terms, the location is due west of Rotterdam Road, where it joins the traffic roundabout linking it with Church Road, Oulton Road and Hollingsworth Road. The space is occupied by houses on Larch Road, Bramble Green, Gorse Green, Viburnum Green, Jasmine Green and Broom Road. Immediately to the west were two pasture enclosures: a regularly shaped one of two acres and a larger, irregularly shaped one abutting it to the south (now occupied by Harp's Close Road, Lilac Drive and the top end of Northgate). The former belonged to Magdalen College, Oxford, and therefore had a link in some way with Akethorpe; it was located in close proximity, anyway. Standing next to these two areas of pasture (and with only its north-eastern corner shown in Map 2, as the bulk of it was located in Oulton parish) was an arable enclosure called *Dovehouse Close*. The land is now built over by Evans Drive,

[72] Bailey, *Suffolk*, pp. 231–2, notes the difficulty of rent collection during the late fourteenth and the first half of the fifteenth century, with deteriorating economic conditions leading to cash-flow problems and giving tenants the excuse to plead poverty. Elsewhere, on p. 283, the term 'Great Slump' is used of the mid-fifteenth century itself.

[73] It is not clear, from the wording, whether the two enclosures were seven acres in area individually or collectively.

Plate 8. The northern end of Rotterdam Road (west side). The area shown represents part of the area once referred to as The Park Field, which was itself subdivided into two enclosures: Park Close and The Park.

June Avenue and Olive Court, but the earlier name for it again has associations with a manor house, in that dove-houses were used to keep pigeons as a source of winter food for wealthy households.

The three names *Park Close*, *The Park* and *Dovehouse Close*, when taken together, do not act as proof-positive exactly, but they are strongly suggestive of the presence of a manor house in the vicinity at some time. It could have been Lowestoft's (conveniently close to the parish church and sufficiently removed from the centre of population), constructed at some point after the town had gained manorial status either late in the twelfth century or early in the thirteenth. But there is an objection to this: Lowestoft never had a resident lord and it is doubtful whether a manorial residence and appurtenances would have been built for a steward. So, was the house that of the lord of Akethorpe at some stage? This seems to be the likelihood. With the manor being a small one, it is conceivable that land may have been leased (or even purchased) in an adjacent estate for the construction of a dwelling and outbuildings simply to avoid taking up ground belonging to the main estate, thereby avoiding loss of revenue. Both the account roll and rental cited above demonstrate that the estate was farmed out to different tenants, and this may well have been the case for a considerable period of time, depending on when it was exactly that the de Akethorpe family had either disposed of the property or been forced to give it up.

One interesting feature of the manor's lands is that the two-acre pasture enclosure of regular shape mentioned above was the only property listed in the 1618 manor roll as belonging to the Akethorpe estate on the south side of *Oxemere Lane*. Was it a vestige, therefore, of other land which once been located there? Or had it been acquired to extend the manor's holdings? The roll also refers to a two-acre meadow, known as *Alder Carr Meadow*, lying immediately to the west of it and located in the parish of Oulton (held by John Utber, one of Lowestoft's leading townsmen). Was this, therefore, the area where John Parkyn's one-acre carr (see Table 8) had been situated and which, having been drained, was given a new purpose? None of these questions can be answered definitively, but they serve to create the sense of a flexible local landscape that changed hands and use frequently as the years went by.

As a final word, it is necessary to consider how the manor of Akethorpe came into the possession of an Oxford college. Magdalen had been founded in 1458 by William Waynflete, bishop of Winchester and chancellor of England (until his dismissal from the latter post in July 1460). He was also co-executor of Sir John Fastolf, one of the country's leading soldiers of the early fifteenth century. Descended from a long-established Great Yarmouth ruling family, Fastolf had built a castle for himself – using his considerable financial resources deriving from family fortunes established by his father, Alexander, and his uncle, Hugh, from an advantageous marriage into the Scrope family, and from money made by the ransoming of high-ranking French prisoners captured during campaigns in the Hundred Years War – during the 1430s and 1440s at nearby Caister, where he eventually lived in comfortable retirement. Fastolf died, widowed and childless, in 1459 (in his eightieth year) and among his many bequests was provision to found a chantry college at Caister for seven priests, financed by lands including the manor of Akethorpe, purchased in March 1426 for the sum of £136 13s 4d.[74] His lawyer, John Paston I, a man who had become increasingly indispensable to him during his declining years, was his chief executor also and has been suspected of manipulating Fastolf's last will and testament to his own advantage (he was certainly the main beneficiary). The Caister bequest was never implemented and, after Paston died in May 1466, the endowment was eventually diverted to Magdalen twelve years later (Waynflete was instrumental), being used to finance seven

[74] The acquisition of Akethorpe is to be found in 'Aspects of the Career of Sir John Fastolf, 1380–1459', Table 1, p. 7. This unpublished paper (1982) by Anthony Smith of Pembroke College, Oxford, was later published as Chapter 9 in R.E. Archer and S. Walker (eds), *Rulers and Ruled in Late Medieval England* (London, 1995), pp. 137–53. The book shows that Fastolf spent £12,628 between 1415 and 1445 on buying up land in East Anglia – much of it in Lothingland Half-hundred (p. 137). Papers in the possession of Magdalen College, Oxford, were an important source in tracing his activities.

scholars there.[75] It is still being used, indirectly, on the college website as a means of publicising the importance of legacies in helping to fund university education. Anyone making a bequest is invited to join The Fastolf Society and attend an annual lunch.

Following Fastolf's death there was a long wrangle over the validity of his will and the Paston family incurred the enmity of powerful people claiming an interest in his extensive landholdings. Akethorpe featured in evidence given to the effect that John Russe, its steward at the time and an associate of John Paston I (he was also collector of customs in the port of Great Yarmouth, a town bailiff there and its MP), had been promised title to the manor at a preferential price in return for attesting that he had been present at Fastolf's death and that the making of his will had been legally carried out.[76] It is not within the compass of this study to go any further into the matter, but it is interesting that this one small estate should have played an important part in the legal complexities which followed the death of Fastolf and which feature so prominently in *The Paston Letters.*

Under Magdalen College's stewardship Akethorpe was well managed and eventually grew in size. It has already been shown how it was ninety-nine acres in area at the time of the 1618 manor roll, and the Lowestoft tithe accounts reveal it as being only half an acre larger in 1720, when it was rented from the College by a merchant named John Jex.[77] A complete change in the layout and size of the fields had occurred during the following century as agricultural improvements took effect, and by the 1840s the estate had grown to 174 acres (including former dole-land), thirty-four of them located in Gunton.[78] When it eventually came to be sold in 1955, to a Lowestoft building company, Warnes Brothers, Akethorpe had remained in the hands of Magdalen College for nearly 500 years – though no longer functioning as a manor, simply as a rented estate. The firm still uses the former *College Farm* complex as its headquarters and the Magdalen crest is visible on the front of the farmhouse, on a date tablet for 1892 – the year that the dwelling was built (Plate 9). Thus is so much of past centuries encapsulated in one small piece of stone.

[75] W.A. Copinger, *The Manors of Suffolk*, vol. 5 (Manchester, 1909), p. 56. H.C. Maxwell Lyte (gen. ed.), *CPR, Edward IV, Edward V and Richard III (1476–85)*, p. 143, shows that the transfer was officially sanctioned on 12 February 1479.

[76] C. Richmond, *The Paston Family in the Fifteenth Century: Fastolf's Will* (Cambridge, 1996), pp. 129–33.

[77] NRO, PD 589/80. These records also show that there were an additional forty acres of *dole-land* for grazing, twenty-three and a half of which lay in neighbouring Gunton.

[78] MCL, Akethorpe terrier (1843).

Plate 9. College Farm. This late nineteenth-century building once served as the main dwelling of the former Magdalen College estate. The date tablet is clearly visible below the middle window on the first floor.

– 3 –

The relocation of the township

Reasons for the move

It is perhaps unwise to single out any one particular event in the life of a community over a period of about 1,500 years as being the crucial or formative one (other than its founding), but there is a good case for doing so where Lowestoft is concerned. The town's change of location, from its original site to one slightly less than a mile to the east-north-east, was of key importance in its subsequent development, as this allowed it to take advantage of both the land-based and maritime opportunities that were available to it. The cliff-top position was bleaker and more exposed to the elements than its predecessor, but it gave the local people greater flexibility in more conveniently pursuing a range of economic activities based on the products of land and sea.

Both the Domesday Survey (1086) and the Hundred Roll enquiry (1274) give the sense of a place founded on, or grounded in, agriculture – and there is no doubt that the soil was instrumental in feeding the population and providing it with a range of materials with which to make many of the necessary utensils and tools required to maintain a basic standard of living. Yet the ocean was only a short distance away and it, too, was capable of both providing food and creating a highway on which all kinds of goods and commodities could be conveyed both inwards and outwards. Herrings shoaled close to shore in both the autumn and the spring, and would certainly have been netted by small boats working off the local beach – and other species too, both pelagic and demersal, would have been caught by either net or line at other times.

There is no direct reference to fish or fishing in the Domesday information relating to Lowestoft, though Gorleston is recorded as having twenty-four fishermen who worked in Great Yarmouth but belonged to the Lothingland manor. And there is ample evidence for the catching of herrings locally to be found in data relating to Mutford Half-hundred. A number of its manors (both coastal and inland) paid herring rents of varying value to the lord, Hugh de Montfort, who probably took quantities of salted fish to supply his household.[1] Further down the coast, Southwold paid an annual toll of 25,000 fish to the Abbey of Bury St Edmunds, while the inland town of Beccles was levied at 60,000 to the same institution. With something like 800–1,000 fish per barrel, it can be seen that catches were small in scale compared with later times, but the potential was there to increase the scope of the operation for markets at home and abroad.

Nothing has been found in any documentation to prove that Lowestoft changed its location from the original one (shown previously in Maps 1 and 3, pp. 8 and 30) as a result of specific maritime considerations. However, it would have made sense for the community to relocate to the position shown in Map 5 so as to be more conveniently situated for the pursuit of sea-related activities. It is evident, as was made clear in the previous chapter, that Great Yarmouth was sensitive regarding the economic aspirations of its Lothingland neighbours and determined to maintain what it saw as its primacy in local maritime trade. Gorleston, on its own doorstep, was the community most likely to have been seen as a threat initially, but, as Lowestoft emerged as a significant force in the governing structure of Lothingland, it too would have come under Yarmouth's scrutiny.

Other than the need to occupy a more suitable site for the pursuit of fishing and maritime trade, it is also possible that the grant of a market and fair to the town in 1308 had a part to play in its relocation. The point has previously been made (p. 61) that there may not have been a suitable site in, or near, the established township on which to stage the two events, and so a new venue would have been needed. It is also possible that rising sea levels at this time, together with periodic catastrophic tidal surges occurring c. 1275–1340 (both of which may have combined to cause flooding of peat diggings in south Norfolk, creating The Broads), had caused the inlet on Lake Lothing, previously referred to (pp. 5 and 45), to revert to an earlier state, thus causing inconvenience near the centre of population, with increasingly saturated land to the south of it. It would have made sense to seek somewhere better drained, which offered fresh opportunities for expansion of the community in both economic and demographic terms.

[1] Beckton (in Pakefield), Carlton, Gisleham, Hornes (in either Carlton or Rushmere), Kessingland, Kirkley, Rothenhall (between Pakefield and Kessingland), Rushmere and Wimundhall (in Kirkley) all had estates paying herring dues of modest value. So did Stoven, in Blything Hundred, as well as Weston, Willingham, Worlingham and *Hatheburgfield* (in North Cove) in Wangford Hundred.

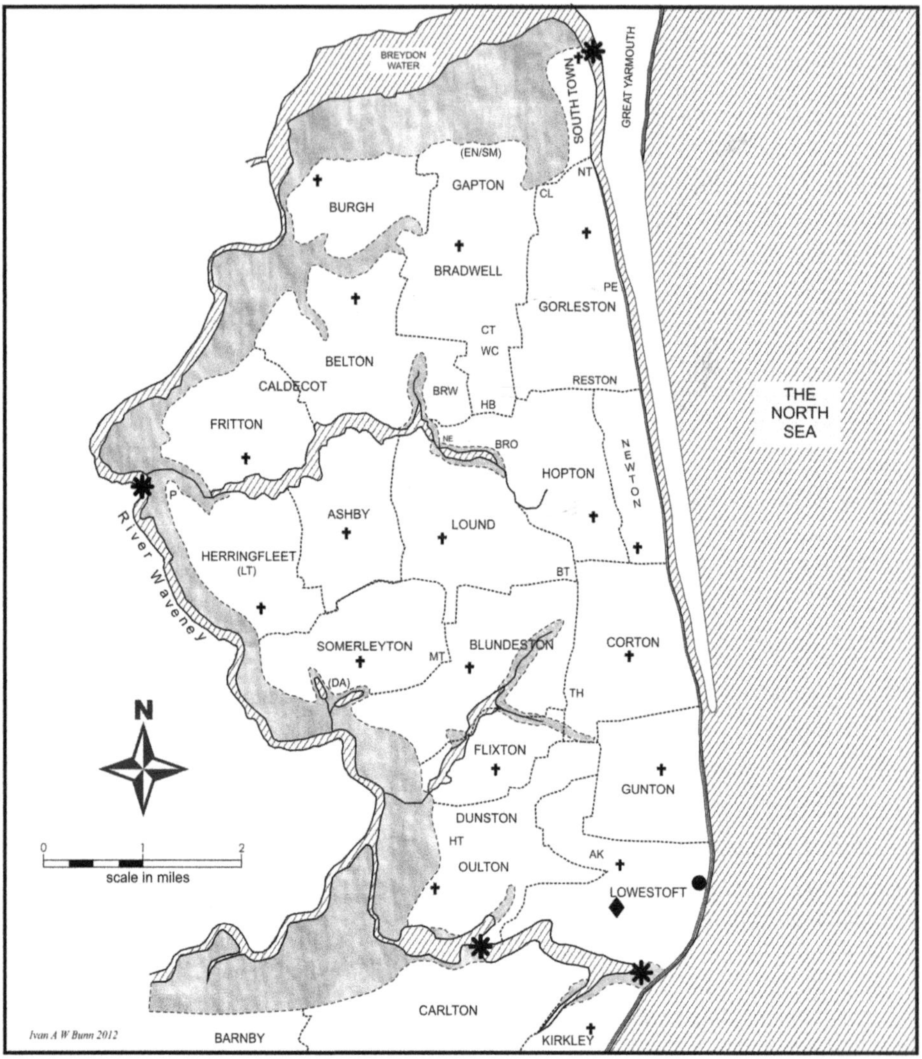

Map 5. Lothingland Half-hundred in the fourteenth century.

Notes:

- All topographical features previously commented on regarding this base-map continue to apply.
- Lowestoft's original location is indicated, as before, with the new one represented by a solid circle.
- Lesser settlements are represented by initials (see Map 4, p. 56, for key).

A further factor worthy of consideration is the increase in the size of Lowestoft's population during the twelfth and thirteenth centuries. This was demonstrated as accurately as possible, on the information available, in the previous chapter (p. 36) and the estimate of c. 200–250 people may have been sufficiently high in number (if true) to create the need for a different location in which to provide adequate space for an expanding number of inhabitants and dwelling-houses. This would have been particularly the case if the original township site was constrained in its ability to grow larger because of its position at the meeting point of the two larger common fields, with trackways to the north, east and south of it. Intrusion into arable land would not have been welcome and there was no structured linear layout, as at Gorleston, to allow (even encourage, perhaps) the spread of cottages and outbuildings. What has been termed 'rural congestion' had reached a peak countrywide by the beginning of the fourteenth century (set against a backdrop of poor harvests during the first two decades), which therefore places Lowestoft in a national context at the time it relocated itself.[2]

Furthermore, an increasing population would have eventually needed economic activity beyond mere subsistence and local service to enable it to flourish. The sea offered the best chance of being able to do this; so, if the town was to expand, it would have to do it somewhere else. And, in any case, a process of proto-urbanisation may already have begun in what had been an essentially rural community. There is slender evidence that Lowestoft may have been changing in nature by the end of the thirteenth century and the earlier part of the fourteenth. The Hundred Roll data (Tables 6 and 7, pp. 33 and 38), for instance, reveal personal names that refer to or imply specific areas of occupation: metal fabrication, wood-working, milling, peat-digging, making casks, building carts and the cutting of furze, bracken and scrub. Obviously, all of them relate to the land in one way or another, but they were not exclusive to the practice of husbandry and had relevance to areas of activity other than agriculture. Fifty years later the 1327 Subsidy information (Table 8, p. 62) reveals the presence of someone involved in supplying the luxury end of the domestic market (a candlemaker), as well as a certain degree of inward population migration from both close at hand and further afield – a feature associated with urban development of the time.[3]

At the same time as this modestly increasing diversity in land-based activity was developing, a range of occupations associated with the sea would also already have emerged. The autumn herring season would have been the prime area of interest, with the catching and processing of fish (the latter

[2] Campbell et al., 'Demesne-farming systems', p. 131.
[3] Bailey, *Suffolk*, p. 161.

involving the community's women to a certain degree) of some significance in the local economy. Added to this would have been the necessary ancillary tasks which serviced and underpinned the fishing operation itself, particularly the manufacture and maintenance of nets and the construction of vessels in which to put to sea. The former area would almost certainly have made use of female labour, while the latter would have extended the range of work available to men with wood- and metal-working skills. Cartage would also have been required to move the freshly caught fish from the shoreline to the inland location of the township – unless, of course, curing facilities had already been established in the beach area itself.

The new site

It is clear from details to be found in a series of court baron extracts relating to the streets and buildings of the early eighteenth-century town that it had originally grown up on what had been coastal heathland. The term 'a messuage (or cottage) from the waste of the lord' is periodically encountered in the description of individual plots, leaving the reader in no doubt as to their origins.[4] The light, sandy topsoil would have been covered naturally in bracken, gorse, thorn and scrub birch, and the area (like others of its kind in the parish) would have been used for the rough grazing of livestock and the exploitation of useful materials. It must at one time have been a cliff-top stretch linking *The North Common* and its southern counterpart, with both *The North Field* and *The South Field* making major intrusions into it as some of this marginal land was put under the plough (see Map 2, p. 25). It may not have been of the most fertile nature, but it was easily workable and capable of growing a range of crops.

The edge of this cliff-top area was the site chosen on which to relocate the community of Lowestoft, and it had a number of features to commend it (Plate 10). It was close to the beach and therefore able to offer convenience of operation where fishing and other maritime pursuits were concerned. Access was made possible by a number of deeply cut rainwater drainage channels in the cliff-face (*scores*), which could be used as footways, and much of the beach's surface was covered in low shrubbery and scrub grass, enabling it to

[4] The document cited is a near-complete sequence of transfer, from c. 1600 onwards, relating to every *copyhold tenement* in the town (c. 85 per cent of the houses and ancillary buildings). It was compiled by the Revd John Tanner (vicar of the parish 1708–59) between 1720 and 1725 – his position as local priest and *chief tenant* of the manor giving him access to the records – and it is a primary source of inestimable value. See SRO(L), 454/2.

be traversed more easily than either sand or shingle. The light nature of the cliff-top's surface soil meant that it drained easily – a process that was aided by a slope in the land, falling from north to south (with a lesser drop from west to east) – and the clay layer beneath acted as a moisture-trap, which could be accessed by the sinking of wells to provide supplies of water. Admittedly, the bulk of the arable farmland was now further away than it had formerly been, but this in itself may suggest a recognition that the town's future lay more with the sea than with the land and that maritime pursuits would increasingly become the community's defining feature.

There was at least one overriding advantage to the lord of the manor in sanctioning relocation of the township around the year 1300. Whether it was Edward I or his successor, John de Dreux, is not known (it could have been either), but it must surely have been brought to either man's attention by the steward, or bailiff. And he, in turn, would have been responding to the wishes of the people (or, at least, to those of their leaders, the manorial chief tenants) in requesting such a major change. And there is no denying that there was money in it for the lord. The area of heathland chosen for the new site would have brought in a certain return, in its undeveloped state, in the form of fees charged for grazing rights and the taking of materials. But it would not have amounted to much. Turning the ground over to building houses would have raised cash from the initial sale of the land, with an ongoing and regular income assured from having the different properties regulated by a form of customary tenure whereby an annual rent was paid to the lord (based on the size of the dwelling and its plot) and an entry fine levied on each new tenant as he or she took over the messuage.

The best guess as to the purchase of the land in the first place is that the wealthier members of the community, such as William Reynald and his like, pooled their resources and carried it out with the assistance of the manor's steward, buying as much ground as was needed and leaving future acquisition(s) to take place as required. The 1618 manor roll reveals that the 203 copyhold properties in town (149 of which were houses) yielded an annual return of £4 14s 10½d, while the forty-five freehold dwellings produced c. £1 5s 0d and the farmland (also freehold) £7 19s 2d – a grand total of c. £14.[5] These individual sums and the overall amount would have been larger than their fourteenth-century counterparts because the town had grown in size (both with regard to physical extent and the number of people), but they serve to illustrate the point made in the previous

[5] Butcher, *Lowestoft*, pp. 19 and 201 fn. 2. Formal copyhold tenure developed during the mid–late sixteenth century from older medieval customary procedures before becoming codified under common law practice.

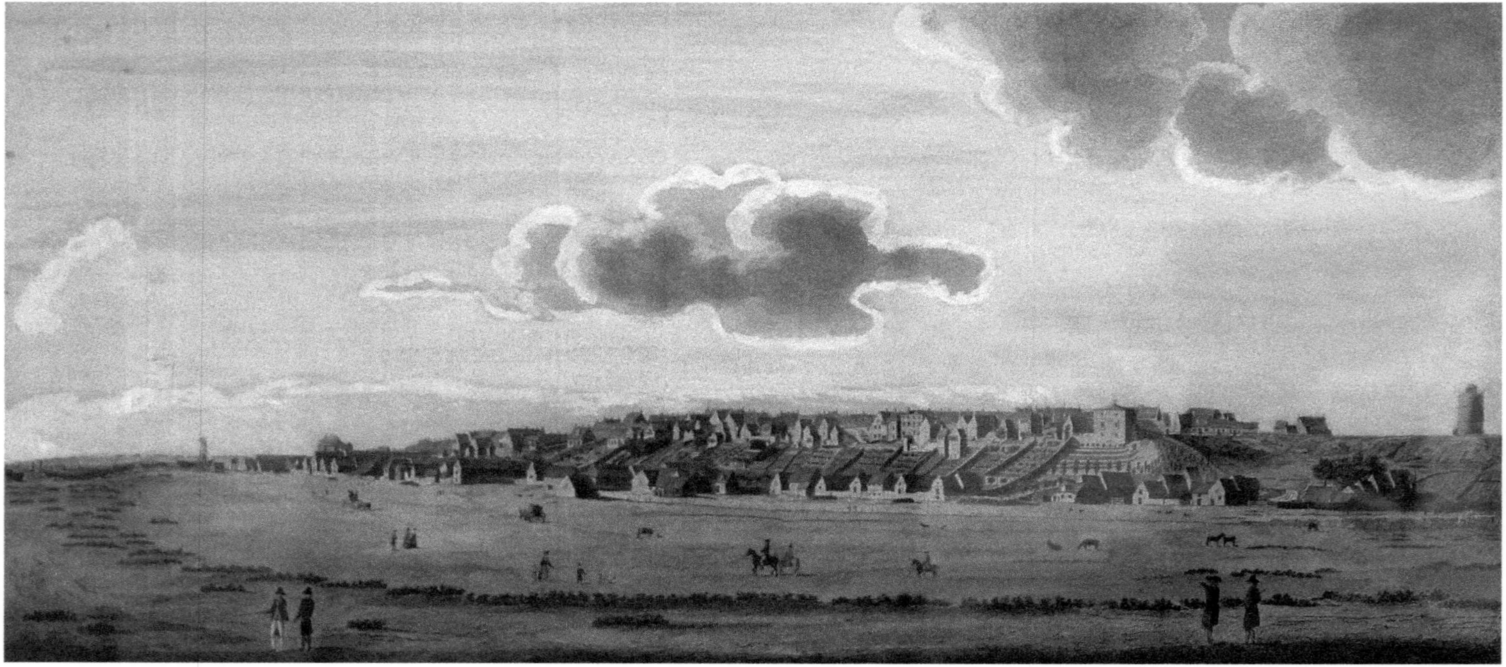

Plate 10. A late eighteenth-century panoramic view of the town. This typical topographical print of 1790 (coloured in its original form, but shown in monochrome here) admirably demonstrates Lowestoft's cliff-top location. The original ink-and-wash view was executed by Richard Powles, leading illustrator at the town's porcelain factory. The engraving made from it was published by J. Harris, of Cornhill, London, who also retailed Thomas Rowlandson's work.

paragraph regarding the benefits of property development as a generator of income for manorial lords.

The observation has been made that the majority of late medieval English towns were seigneurial foundations (not royal boroughs) and that, despite the absence of formal grants of self-government, the citizens enjoyed more autonomy than might at first be apparent.[6] This was true of Lowestoft in both instances. Its relocation must have had approval from the manorial lord, via the agency of the steward or bailiff, and its inhabitants certainly had a good deal of self-determination in the conduct of local affairs – largely because of the lord being an absentee, whose prime interest lay in receiving the annual income yielded by his estate, not in taking any direct part in its administration. Hence, the major influence in shaping the town's development rested with the chief tenants of the manor, whose origins as holders of villein tenements (as revealed in the 1274 Hundred Roll) gradually evolved from a purely agricultural function to one of civic leadership and urban activity. It is possible (even likely) that the ties of villeinage in Lowestoft had never been particularly strong and that the disappearance of serfdom, noted as occurring throughout Suffolk during the fifteenth century,[7] never applied to the town because of this very factor.

The physical layout of the town at the time of the manor roll is revealed in Map 6 and a few general remarks may be helpful, especially if comparisons are made with Map 2 (p. 25). It is immediately apparent that the relocated community was placed (as was stated above) between *The North Common* and *The South Common*, with a surviving remnant of waste named *Goose Green* on its western perimeter. This last-named area would once have joined up with *Church Green*, which would itself have linked to *Skamacre Heath*. During the Anglo-Saxon period arable land was progressively reclaimed from the dominant heath and it can be plainly seen how *The North Field*, *The South Field* and *The South West Field* are all edged by waste of one kind or another – thereby revealing their origins. In all likelihood, the two areas of the town made up of freehold dwellings (referred to in passing above regarding their annual rental value) were of later origin than the rest of the built-up area.

The main collection of houses (copyhold tenure in 1618, but villein tenements at an earlier time) stood on former heath, but the two smaller, freehold ones were built on land once used for agriculture. The first of these was known as *West Lands* and stood to the north of *Swan Lane* (now Mariners Street) in what had obviously once been part of the easterly section of *The North Field*.

[6] S.H. Rigby and E. Ewan, 'Government, power and authority, 1300–1540', in D.M. Palliser (ed.), *The Cambridge Urban History of Britain* (Cambridge, 2000), vol. 1, pp. 293–4.
[7] Bailey, *Suffolk*, pp. 193–201.

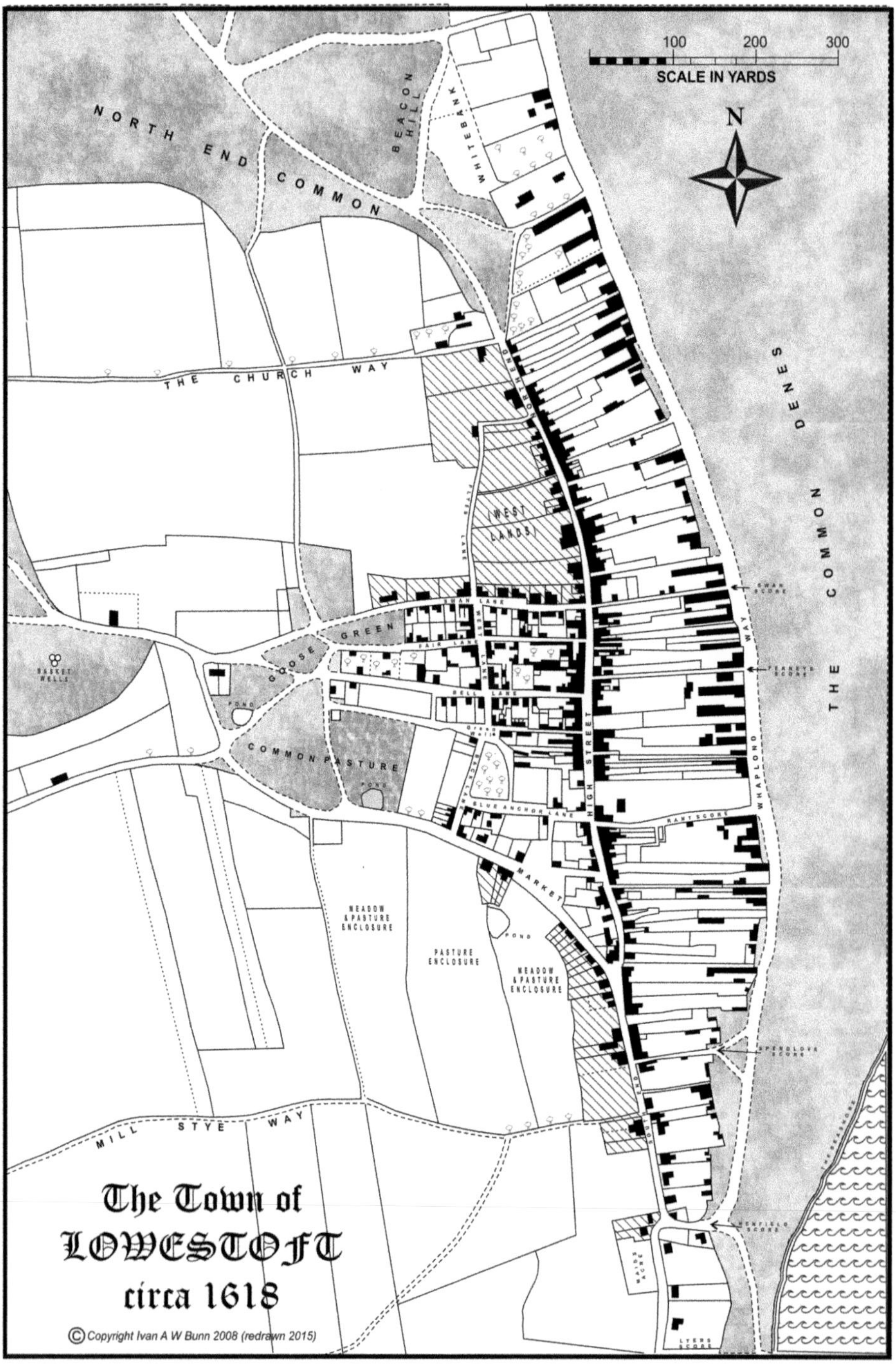

Map 6. The town of Lowestoft in 1618.

Notes to Map 6:

- The diagonal shading used on the two areas of land to the west of the High Street, at its northern and southern ends, indicates the two parts of town where the houses were held by freehold tenure.
- Vestiges of medieval open-field strips are discernible to the north and south of Mill Stye Way.

The second was located to the south of the market place and abutted onto land lying mainly to the north of the *Mill Stye* trackway – ground which had once formed part of *The South Field*. The land consisted mainly of three feeding enclosures (sixteen and a half acres in area), with arable land on the other side of the track, the areas of pasture almost certainly having been sown at some point to provide grazing for the townspeople's livestock and for that brought to be traded at the Wednesday market.[8]

To the observer of today, perhaps the most important aspect of Lowestoft's shift to a new location is that it provides an example of early fourteenth-century town-planning. Archaeological work carried out at varying times between 2000 and 2004, to the rear of Nos 74, 75, 76, 77–79 and 80 High Street, produced a number of medieval potsherds the earliest of which dated from c. 1300.[9] This would seem to serve as an indication that the move from the earlier site began in earnest at about this time, establishing the community in its new location. By the time that the Black Death struck during 1348–9 there is evidence to suggest that the new town had been completed (see p. 97). In the aftermath of the disaster, as rural populations in Suffolk (and elsewhere) diminished and as village communities underwent a period of dilapidation and retraction,[10] it is perhaps worth speculating on the effect on Lowestoft. Did the town, as part of its recovery, exercise any kind of 'pull' on people from adjacent parishes, drawing them in to start new lives in an environment more conducive to personal advancement than the one they had left?

The sinuous alignment of the *High Street* (a name still in use today) followed the line of the cliff, dropping some fifty feet from north to south over a total length of c. 1000 yards. Halfway along, a gridiron of five smaller

[8] When the houses numbered 75–83 Arnold Street were built, some years ago, a pump was in action for a number of weeks draining the site. The spring(s) which fed the large pond opposite the market place were still active (though no longer visible) and the site had to be specially prepared before construction above ground could take place.
[9] P. Durbidge, 'A second limited excavation in the grounds of the John Wilde School, Lowestoft', LA&LHS *Annual Report*, 37 (Lowestoft, 2005), pp. 30–31.
[10] Bailey, *Suffolk*, pp. 235–9.

cross-lanes extended westwards towards *Goose Green*, with another roadway (running parallel to the main thoroughfare) crossing these. At the time of the manor roll (1618) this final road was named in three sections (running south to north) as *Back Lane*, *West Lane* and *Flyes Lane* – the last of these being a reference to an early sixteenth-century townsman, Roger Flye, who held land in the vicinity. The Jubilee Way relief-road of today follows the old route exactly, though with major widening carried out to accommodate the flow of traffic.

The basic principle of residential distribution seems to have been that the wealthier members of the community were placed along the *High Street* (especially on the east side), with the lesser people occupying the smaller plots and houses in the gridiron area. Thus, there was deliberate social and economic differentiation from the start, which may not have been the case in the original township. The manor roll names the five cross-lanes as *Swan Lane*, *Fair Lane–Tylers Lane* (the former being the westward section, the latter the eastward one), *Bell Lane*, *Frary Lane* (to the east of *Green Well*) and *Blue Anchor Lane*. They are the Mariners Street, Dove Street–Compass Street, Crown Street (East and West), Wesleyan Chapel Lane and Dukes Head Street of today. These lesser roadways bore names earlier than the ones cited in 1618, but they have not all been recorded and handed down.

The arrangement of house plots set at right angles to one long main street was typical of many medieval settlements, and the gridiron pattern of the side-street area is also recognisably medieval (arguably a Norman influence being continued). Lowestoft combined the two models because this was what the basic configuration of the local landforms and social considerations dictated, and the result was an interesting one, which allowed for expansion of the community within a prescribed area. No accurate picture of the original construction (other than the street plan) is possible, but it is reasonable to suppose on evidence deriving from surviving seventeenth- and eighteenth-century manorial records that the physical framework of the town remained the same and that the building plots were subdivided as time went on (and some of the larger dwellings tenemented) to accommodate the growing population. Even as late as the 1831 census, when Lowestoft had a population of 4,238 people, it was still largely contained within its medieval limits.

Creating a new town

The primary concern of the local people, at the time they were establishing their new township, must have been how to make the face of the cliff usable. A slope of up to 60 degrees or more, consisting of stratified glacial deposits, did not lend itself to ease of management, and intervention was necessary to create viable house plots along the edge of the cliff and provide easy access to the shoreline. The latter requirement had already been partly met by nature in the form of gulley-ways created by the grooving action of surface water draining down the face. These were known as scores (as previously referred to) and they were conveniently spaced along the length of cliff chosen for the re-siting of the town. Some were suitable for footways, others for use by carts, and their presence became (and remains) one of the distinctive features of Lowestoft's urban topography. Their function was improved, with the passage of time, by the building of retaining walls along their sides, the levelling and consolidation of their surfaces and, in the case of those used as footways, the introduction of steps and paving (Plate 11).

The solution adopted to make the cliff-face usable was to terrace it – a considerable undertaking both in terms of scale and of the labour required. No estimate can be made of the time it took, but it was certainly a matter of years rather than months, and it was probably carried out and completed before the house plots were set out and dwellings erected. A great deal of communal organisation and effort (probably spearheaded by the chief tenants) must have

Plate 11. Mariner's Score, as it appeared forty years ago. The building on the right-hand side stood on the site of the town's first highlight (1628) and was eventually destroyed by fire. The lighthouse site of today was first developed in 1676, on an out-of-town location (as it was then), because of the fire risk to nearby properties posed by its coal-burning predecessor.

gone into the operation, which would have had to be carried out alongside the farming, fishing and other activities by which the inhabitants sustained themselves. And one can only wonder at the amount of labour involved and the sheer commitment of people to see the project through to its conclusion. Investigation of the terraces' structure shows that the overall exercise was not a piecemeal affair, but a planned and co-ordinated one backed by a high level of engineering competence on the part of whoever directed it. The general north–south alignment of the various levels is consistent and unbroken, detectable even where the scores cross the terraces at right-angles, and the landscaping overall (even though much compromised today by neglect and modern interference) still has the capacity to impress.

Altogether, about 1,000 yards of cliff were terraced, probably working from north to south with the downward slope of the land. Three steps were cut into the face over most of the length, diminishing to two and then, finally, to one in the last 300 yards at the southern end, as the ground level sloped downwards to just above sea level. This was effectively the end of what may be termed the built-up area; all that remained to the south of it were three or four houses strung out along the roadway leading to the shingle bank separating Lake Lothing from the sea and carrying the roadway to Kirkley and Pakefield. It is just possible that these dwellings were surviving outliers from the original Anglo-Saxon settlement, which the newly created town almost (but not quite) integrated within itself. And it is also possible (even likely) that the fourteenth-century urban creation was not as long, anyway, as the place revealed in the 1618 manor roll. Given the smaller population of 300 years before, the new town of the time may well have terminated just to the south-south-east of the market place, where the *High Street* was met by a roadway leading out north-westwards (initially) towards the original township. Thus, in today's terms, everything to the south of Herring Fishery Score (or even a little to the north of it) is likely to have been an addition to the initial plan. In fact, even with the terracing having been completed along the initial length of cliff chosen, it is not to say that all the burgage plots were necessarily set out and developed at the same time. There would undoubtedly have been spaces left, to be adopted later.

In terms of practicalities, the work of creating the terraces consisted mainly of digging, levelling and constructing retaining walls to hold back the stratified sands and clays. To start with most of the cliff-top plots were probably roughly the same width, but as the years passed subdivision occurred, leading to many becoming narrower. In the first phase of construction timber may have been used for the retaining walls, but the earliest ones identifiable today (dating from the sixteenth and seventeenth centuries) show a combination of brick and cobbled flint. The latter material was readily available from the beach, while there were pockets of suitable clay for making bricks scattered throughout the parish.

During the summer of 2000, while work was being carried out to the rear of 80 High Street (Plate 12), an interesting discovery was made when a new retaining wall was being built on the first step down from the cliff-top. At the bottom of the trench forming the footing a layer of clay was discovered which had nothing to do with the natural, glacial stratification. It had been introduced deliberately, almost certainly with the intention of making a foundation on which the original retaining wall could sit. The material would almost certainly have been dug from close at hand, reconstituted with water to puddle it and then laid as a base-course. This one discovery may be regarded as slender evidence for claiming it to be the basic method of footing the terrace walls along the whole length of the cliff, but the principle was structurally sound and made good use of a plentiful local resource.

Once constructed, the terraces became an important part of each house plot. The street-level space behind the dwelling formed the backyard, which

Plate 12. Terracing to the rear of 80 High Street. This view shows how the cliff-face was managed and made usable. The new retaining wall referred to is to be seen in the upper half of the image; the building to the reader's left is the headquarters of the Lowestoft Heritage Workshop Centre.

could be used for all kinds of outbuildings and storage facilities and probably had this function from the very beginning. The first terrace-level proper, on the uppermost step cut into the cliff, was a multi-purpose area by the time of the manor roll, often used as a garden, with fruit bushes and trees planted there. It also served as a dumping area for all kinds of domestic waste – something deemed less offensive at the time than would be the case today. The stage or stages below this (depending on the height of the cliff) was/were used mainly for the erection of buildings connected with fishing and other maritime activity: curing houses, net-stores, tackle-sheds, stables and the like. Whether or not these uses were implemented from the earliest days of the new town is not known, but there is a good chance that at least some of them would have been.

The stratification of the local soils has already been referred to with regard to the cliff-face's profile. It played a vital role in providing a source of water for domestic use and industrial purposes (especially brewing and tanning hides for leather). Precipitation filtered down through the light topsoil covering much of the parish, finding its way to an impervious layer of clay. From there, a good deal of it worked its way through to the face of the cliff, following a minor slope of the land from west to east and emerging as a line of springs. All the houses along the top of the cliff had either their own wells or ones that were shared with adjacent properties, and this was largely the case with the dwellings located on the west side of the High Street. However, the smaller houses in the side-street area were not as generously endowed with wells and a number of their inhabitants drew water either from *Green Well* (located at the intersection of *Back Lane* and *West Lane*) or from *Basket Wells* (situated at the eastern extremity of *Church Green*; Plate 13).[11]

Other than the demands created by its inhabitants' domestic requirements, the relocated town had further considerations to take account of. The royal grant of a market and fair in November 1308 to the lord of the manor, John de Dreux, was a crucial one in the town's development, helping it, eventually, to become the dominant community not only in Lothingland Half-hundred but in most of the neighbouring Mutford jurisdiction also. There was no guarantee, however, that the grant of a market *per se* (with or without accompanying fair) was a guarantee of economic success. Within Lothingland itself, apart from the half-hundred market located at Gorleston (awarded 1211), Somerleyton had been granted a market in 1227, Flixton in 1253, Belton the

[11] The name *Basket Wells* derived from the shafts being lined with wicker panels. This particular facility was located close to the boundary of allotments with the children's play-area opposite St Margaret's Community Primary School, on Church Road. The water table was quite close to the surface hereabouts and, when Nos 58 and 60 Winnipeg Road were being built a few years ago, water soon made its presence known.

Plate 13. The location of Basket Wells. The medieval watering place lay just beyond the hedgerow, the land in the foreground serving as a communal drying area known as The Bleach (a children's play-area occupies some of the space today). The building seen in the background is part of the Lowestoft College of Further Education.

right of market and fair in March 1270, and Oulton similar privileges in February 1307. In Mutford Half-hundred Kessingland was awarded a market and fair in October 1251 and Carlton Colville in October 1267.[12] None of these communities developed and prospered in the way that Lowestoft eventually did. Therefore, there must have been factors other than founding-grants alone which enabled certain enterprises to flourish and others to fail. One contributory factor towards the latter outcome, which has been noted, was too close a proximity of markets to each other[13] – and Lothingland and Mutford half-hundreds certainly showed this characteristic in no uncertain manner!

It is possible (perhaps even likely) that a manor with a resident lord, directing his own demesne in the traditional way, may not have produced

[12] In Carlton's case the grant was made to the lord of Carlton Hall manor (as opposed to the manor of Bromholm). Kessingland had four medieval manors and the grant there was made to the lord of the largest of these, which eventually (though not at the time) became known as Stapleton's. For more detailed information on all local manors see Butcher, *The Island of Lothingland*, pp. 141–7, and *Mutford Half-hundred: Domesday Analysis and Medieval Exploration* (Lowestoft, 2013), pp. 39–66 (the latter also a Heritage Workshop Centre publication).
[13] Bailey, *Suffolk*, p. 127.

conditions conducive to the practice of commerce – especially where the introduction of a market was concerned, with its accompanying inconveniences and intrusions. But it has been noted that, in Suffolk, with its absence of boroughs (and their rules and restrictions) and its abundance of market towns, the manorial system was capable of accommodating and stimulating trade with a range of facilitating mechanisms.[14] With the added convenience of a non-resident lord (at least, as far as the tenants, and perhaps even the bailiff, or steward, were concerned), activity beyond merely working the land must have been made easier. The starting-up of a market, if the venture established itself and became successful, was then a means of creating revenue for the landlord and income for the traders themselves – to say nothing of the service provided to the surrounding area from which the market derived its viability. Thus, the initial establishment of the Lowestoft market must have taken place with the support of the manorial lord (John de Dreux), who, in turn, had presumably been persuaded of the venture's success by his bailiff – the latter working in collaboration with the influential chief tenants of the manor (proto-community leaders of their type), who were not only convinced of their town's growing influence and importance but bent on advancing it.

Once the privileges of market and fair had been established, of course, venues for the holding of these events had to be found – something which may not have been possible (as discussed on p. 61) in the original settlement. Scrutiny of the *High Street* even today (with road-widening having taken place at either end during the 1890s) suggests that it was probably sufficiently broad originally between *Swan Lane* and *Blue Anchor Lane* (Mariners Street and Dukes Head Street) to have accommodated market stalls, a usable width of thirty to thirty-five feet being available. Such a location would have established the classic middle-of-town site for a medieval market. However, it must have been realised (even at the time) that the area was not suitable because of the congestion it would have caused on the narrower sections of the roadway, to north and south, and in the cross-lane area also – the latter being particularly restricted for the movement of people and merchandise, especially if horses and carts were present.

The solution was to adopt an edge-of-town location, upwards of half an acre in area, where the new main street met a trackway from the old settlement area running along the northern edge of *The South Field*. This gave not only plenty of space for trading activity but also easy access and egress along both roadways, as well as ample space for livestock on the land opposite. It is noticeable that freehold houses occupy part of this sector of the old common field, but that a gap was left directly in front of the market area, showing that

[14] Bailey, *Suffolk*, p. 142.

the dwellings post-dated the establishment of it. The sowing of grass into what had previously been arable space (with strips on a north–south alignment) to eventually form three separate pasture areas, may well have been carried out early on in the relocation of the town to provide convenient grazing for the inhabitants' livestock as well as for beasts brought to market – and a pond was probably dug at much the same time for watering the animals, taking advantage of a low spot where the spring-line came close to the surface of the ground.

In addition to the main market place, there was a separate area for trading in grain further to the north, between *Tylers Lane* and *Swan Lane*, on the site of the present-day Town Hall. Perhaps this was recognition of the commodity's importance in the medieval economy, whereby its staple role was thought worthy of its being given distinction in its own right. On a practical level also, the number of people buying corn of different types and the transport needed to convey it would have benefited from a separate, dedicated market space, and there were convenient entry and exit routes to the north, west and south. A market cross was set up on the site, close to a chapel-of-ease built for winter worship when the roadways leading westwards to the parish church were befouled with mud. The latter building was licensed in 1350 by William Bateman, bishop of Norwich, which may perhaps indicate that the new town was fully established on its site by then – having been completed by the time that the Black Death brought devastation and disruption during 1348–9.[15] At a later date, both it and the corn cross seem to have undergone reconstruction to create one integrated edifice, which remained in use until 1698, when it underwent major changes to create the predecessor of today's Town Hall (the latter being built in the Italianate style and opened for use in 1860). This particular structure consisted of a triple-arcaded corn-trading area with folding wooden doors fronting the street, with a civic meeting room above and a rearward range housing the chapel-of-ease (Plate 14).

So much for the market areas; but what of the fairstead? The original grant allowed for an eight-day celebration beginning on the vigil of the parish's patron, St Margaret of Antioch (19 July), and this was superseded in December 1445 by a re-grant to the lord (William de la Pole, marquis of Suffolk) allowing two fairs to be held: on the feast day of St Philip and St James (1 May) and on that of St Michael and All Angels (29 September), with three celebratory days on either side of each festival.[16] In both cases,

[15] O.J. Benedictow, *The Black Death, 1346–1353: The Complete History* (Woodbridge, 2004), p. 138, states that the disease reached southern East Anglia (specifically, north Essex and south Suffolk) at the end of 1348.

[16] W.R. Cunningham (ed.), *CoCR*, vol. 6 (London, 1916), p. 59.

Plate 14. The Town Hall: Lowestoft's former civic hub, standing on a site of key importance in the community's overall development and currently no longer used as a centre of local government.

awarding the privilege made no difference to the place where the event was held. A misconception as to the venue (and that of the market) was created in the 1790s by Edmund Gillingwater, the late eighteenth-century historian of Lowestoft, when he wrote that both market and fair were originally held 'below the town' – assuming from this that *The Denes* was the place in question.[17] It would appear from this misunderstanding that, at some point, the Latin phrase *infra villam* ('within the town'), in the wording of the grant, had been mistakenly translated as 'below the town' by applying the classical Latin meaning of the preposition, not that of its medieval successor.

The main market place in the old town part of Lowestoft has not been used for its intended purpose for some considerable time, but it retains something of its original, open nature (though increasingly encroached upon by houses and inns during the eighteenth and nineteenth centuries) through being used as a car park. The fairstead was situated not far from it to the north-west, with the annual (then six-monthly) event being staged on the common land immediately abutting the township on its western edge. This vestige of heathland,

[17] E. Gillingwater, *An Historical Account of the Ancient Town of Lowestoft* (London, 1790), p. 55.

which was obviously an eastwards extension of *Church Green*, was known either as *Fair Green* or *Goose Green*, with the side-street running to and from it bearing the name *Fair Lane* (now Dove Street). The dual use suggested by the two names is an interesting one, with changes of function obviously in operation depending on what was required of the land. Given the way that geese foul any location they inhabit for any length of time, it is to be hoped that they were removed from their pasture well before the fairs were held![18] Another possibility, suggested in some of the manorial documentation, is that the northern sector was the part where the fair was staged and the southern one the portion reserved for grazing geese.

As with the market place, this particular area (called St Margaret's Plain) has remained open in nature and is, in keeping with life's current demands, also used as a car park. The rest of the common pasture, lying south of the fairstead, has long been built over, though a vestige of the old landscape can still be detected. Scrutiny of Map 6 reveals the presence of a pond on the southern boundary of the land's eastern sector, which was obviously put there for the watering of livestock. Indeed, it was known as *The Watering*, and it also served as the site of the town's ducking stool. It was situated at what is now the bottom end of Thurston Road, near to where that particular piece of highway joins the blanked-off section of St Peter's Street, and in spite of the over-layering of concrete and tarmac it is still possible to detect a depression where the pond once stood (Plate 15).

An alternative name for *Fair Lane* found in the 1618 manor roll is *Bier Lane*, which suggests that this was the route by which corpses were once carried to the parish church for burial. The roadway linked directly to a track crossing *Church Green* and conveyance of the dead (largely uncoffined at that time) would have been both direct and expeditious. The other main route to St Margaret's was *Church Way* (now St Margaret's Road), which lay at the northern end of the *High Street* and had obviously once served as a baulk dividing *The North Field* into two major sections. The role of older names in helping to establish the previous use and function of particular areas within an urban (and a rural) landscape has long been recognised, and the last obvious example that can legitimately cited for Lowestoft (within the present context) is *Cross Score*. This was the name once given to the footway Mariner's Score before it became known as *Swan Score* (named after the inn which stood at the top of it, on the southern side) – a reference which must surely have emanated from its proximity to the *Corn Cross*.

[18] A leet court minute of 1582 shows that *Goose Green* was the only area of common where geese were allowed to graze. A fine of 2d a bird was imposed on anyone breaking the ordinance. See SRO(L), 194/A10/4.

Plate 15. The Watering. The occupant of the shop premises shown has changed since the picture was taken, but the building occupies part of the site of the former communal pond.

Regarding the specific functions of the Lowestoft market and fair, it has to be said that (in the absence of any documentary evidence) little is known of the latter's activity – though an informed guess may be allowed to suggest that trading in cured fish might well have taken place (smoked herrings, to begin with, followed by dried, salted cod later on). Much more is known about the weekly Wednesday market, not from medieval sources but from the copious manorial records of the early modern period, particularly the annual leet court minutes. These show the market to have been a neighbourhood affair, serving much of the half-hundreds of Lothingland and Mutford, with a 'pull' also exercised on traders from further afield (especially those involved in the supply of food and drink).[19] There is no reason why its operation during the late medieval period should have been greatly different, except perhaps in the matter of scale, because the town had grown further in size and influence by c. 1600 than had been the case 100 years before. A current discussion on marketing networks in late medieval England focuses on whether small

[19] Butcher, *Lowestoft*, pp. 10, 65 and 259–61. Bailey, *Suffolk*, p. 131, cites medieval market towns as serving agrarian hinterlands of six to eight miles in distance; Lowestoft's area of influence was closer to five to six miles, with Beccles and Great Yarmouth exercising influence to the west-south-west and north, respectively.

towns acted as hubs of supply for larger urban communities in their respective regions or whether they functioned as centres of consumption in their own right.[20] The writer has no hesitation in identifying Lowestoft as belonging to the latter category, with the factor of service to its neighbourhood also being a vital component of its viability.

One particular feature of market conduct during both the medieval and early modern periods was regulation of the trading activity that took place in the interests of the paying customer. Thus there was close supervision of the price of goods and their quality, inspection of weights and measures in the cause of fair dealing, and the attempt (given the perishability of many foodstuffs) to create as hygienic a selling environment as was possible.[21] With Lowestoft being an unchartered town, there was probably never an official clerk of the market to order affairs and to send six-monthly lists of fines for offences committed to the Exchequer – nor any periodic inspection visits by the Royal Clerk of Markets.[22] The town's weekly trading forum functioned under ordinances (or assizes) that were nationally laid down, but were applied by local, manorial process. Thus, its conduct was probably very largely controlled by the annually elected parish constables, ale-founders (or tasters) and searchers and sealers of leather, with an overview exercised by the steward. Any irregularities noted were dealt with by the leet court, which met once a year on the first Saturday in Lent. Such a pattern of administration broadly fits in with what has been observed in Newmarket, another Suffolk community with an absentee lord.[23]

In the absence of any surviving medieval documentation, the best that can be done is turn to what survives from early modern times and express the hope that the procedures recorded matched those of an earlier era (in principle, at least, there is no reason to believe that they would have differed greatly). There is a single volume of leet and court baron minutes for the years 1582–5,[24] but the main sequence of surviving material begins in 1616 and runs through in an almost unbroken sequence until the year 1770, when the leet court seems to have reached the end of its useful working life – holding its last session on 3 March.[25] Property transfers, however, continued to be written up in the court baron proceedings (though with diminishing regularity, as time wore on) right into the twentieth century, with the last entry being made during the 1930s.

[20] Bailey, *Suffolk*, p. 168.
[21] J. Davis, 'Market regulation in fifteenth-century England', in B. Dodds and C. Liddy (eds), *Commercial Activity, Markets and Entrepreneurs in the Middle Ages* (Woodbridge, 2011), p. 81.
[22] Davis, 'Market regulation', pp. 91, 93 and 95–6.
[23] Bailey, *Suffolk*, pp. 142–3.
[24] SRO(L), 194/A10/4.
[25] SRO(L), 194/A10/5–20; Butcher, *Lowestoft*, p. 250.

Details of market and trading offences, collected from a selection of English counties during the fourteenth and fifteenth centuries (1353–1458), show eighteen individual trades or occupations involved in cases of deception or poor quality in the sale of goods: millers, bakers, brewers, fishers, butchers, cooks, poulterers, innkeepers, vintners, chandlers, tanners, shoemakers, tailors, skinners, smiths, spicers, grain-buyers and flour-sellers.[26] Lowestoft was not sufficiently large to have had the whole range of occupations cited (especially at the more luxury-orientated end of commercial activity), but those underlined above all featured in its leet court records at one time or another for varying acts of dishonesty in the retailing of goods.[27] Forestalling (the act of selling wares either before the duly appointed starting hour of market activity or making sale of them on the way to the market itself) is also referred to in the list of national offences. Lowestoft has examples of this practice also, as well as of the offence known as regrating: the selling-on of goods (for profit) on the market where they had been purchased.

Concluding remarks

A physical examination of the town, based on information in the manor roll of 1618 and on the measurement of house frontages carried out as part of research into its past, reveals that about half the dwellings on the *High Street* had plot widths in the range of thirty to fifty feet, with the other half being somewhere between fifteen and twenty-five (some of these latter probably being the result of subdivision at some stage). The wider plots had dwellings fronting the street lengthways, while the narrower ones were gable-end on to it. In the side-street area the individual messuages were generally much smaller, with an average size of about twenty to thirty feet wide by about fifty to sixty long. With the earliest house still standing above ground today on the High Street (No. 36) dating from c. 1480–1500 (Plate 16), and with much refacading of the eighteenth and nineteenth centuries in evidence along the roadway's length, no picture can really be formed of the original urban landscape of the fourteenth century.

Originally, on the east side of the *High Street* (and to a lesser degree, on the west), the plot widths had been larger. What the manor roll shows is the result of two centuries or more of subdivision. The cliff-top burgage plots (which varied in length from 150 to 200 yards) seem to have originally been about forty yards wide, giving them an area of anything between one and a quarter

26 Davis, 'Market regulation', pp. 92–3.
27 Butcher, *Lowestoft*, pp. 259–61.

Plate 16. No. 36 High Street, the oldest house in Lowestoft. The timber framing is of the highest order, both in terms of the quality of material used and of its shaping and embellishment.

and one and three-quarters of an acre. Their size is best demonstrated by the messuage immediately to the north of *Rant Score*, which had not undergone subdivision and was occupied by *The Angel* inn. At something approaching 200 yards in length by an average of slightly more than forty yards in width, the plot's area came to about one and three-quarter acres. Its open, undeveloped nature contrasts strongly with the infill to be seen on either side of it for much of the total length of the cliff.

If attention is focused on the broader scheme of layout, rather than on the infill which progressively followed on from its implementation, it can be seen that the cliff-top was originally set out in about twenty large plots starting at a point opposite the junction of the *High Street* with *Church Way* and running southwards somewhere just to the north of *Spendlove Score* (now Herring Fishery Score). Depending on whether the initial terracing phase stopped at this point or continued to the score itself (see p. 92), there were then up to another seven plots running down to *Henfield Score*. On the west side of the main roadway *The Westlands* seems to have had five or six substantial messuages laid out, followed by others fronting (and meshed in with) the cross-lane area: one plot between *Swan Lane* and *Tyler's Lane* (accommodating the corn cross and the chapel-of-ease), two between *Tyler's Lane* and *Bell Lane*, one between *Bell Lane* and the alleyway leading to *Green Well*, and two between this particular footpath and *Blue Anchor Lane*.

The market place's surrounds were differently configured from the *High Street* area in not being of linear form. There seems to have been a basic arrangement of three oblong plots adjacent to the trading space, which gradually underwent subdivision into smaller holdings. On the opposite side of the roadway the pasture enclosure had been organised in such a way as to allow free movement to and from the market, with a small plot in the north-western corner and three larger ones to the south-east. Finally, there were two further plots to the south of *The Mill Stye* (or *Mill Stye Way*), which may have been of later origin than the other ones discussed.

The main question arising from this overview of proto-urban planning is how far the large plots fronting the main street on its western side originally ran back towards *West Lane*. Was housing for the lesser members of the community planned as part of the layout from the start, or did it occur later for whatever reasons prevailed? Was the town's change of location, in fact, a two-phase process, with the more important members of the community making the move first and the others following on later? Certainly, the people with an interest in fishing and maritime enterprise needed to be nearer the sea in order to operate more effectively. But did the lower levels of the peasantry, whose main concern it was to till and tend the fields, have the same imperative to follow? Nothing can be proved either way, and no doubt the whole of the community was engaged in carrying out the manual work required to construct the new town, but the whole population may not have migrated together.

Scrutiny of both street plan and basic plot arrangement can thus serve to give a skeletal idea of the medieval town, and certain key features (such as market place, corn cross and chapel-of-ease, and the fairstead) may assist in providing reference points. But that is all. It is not possible to recreate the visual aspect of the dwellings and domestic appurtenances of the time. Lowestoft has seventeen houses on the High Street dating wholly, or in part, from before 1600 and the quality of build is sometimes very impressive. But all the construction is late medieval or mid–late sixteenth-century in date (the latter date a trait observed over much of lowland England and referred to as The Great Rebuilding): the replacement of earlier housing stock as the town grew and prospered. The manor roll of 1618 gives a total of 211 houses in the parish, with 194 of them located in the main built-up urban area. They housed a population of c. 1,200–1,300 people at the time – a fall from the 1,500 or so at the end of the sixteenth century because of a serious plague outbreak in 1603 that killed about 300 of the inhabitants and from which the town had not recovered.[28] In either case, the number of residents was considerably in excess of that of the fourteenth century – as was the number of dwellings.

If there is practically nothing of the original relocated town to be seen above ground, other than its street pattern, there are one or two vestiges remaining below the surface. A fine vaulted cellar, dating from the first half of the fourteenth century, has survived beneath No. 160 High Street, its high-quality brickwork being similar to that which can be seen in the undercroft of Herringfleet Priory, seven miles or so to the north-west of Lowestoft. If it was typical of other structures of a similar nature that once existed in the town, then the quality of build generally was very sound. Another surviving medieval vault of later date is to be found further to the south on the other side of the road, at Nos 41–42 High Street (Plate 17). It lies beneath a late Georgian building long since converted to shop premises, and is again of brick construction. There is less head-room than in the first cellar referred to, but the groined ceiling is still impressive – even though it was compromised by work carried out during the 1970s, when the floor above was reinforced to carry chest freezers.[29]

[28] Butcher, *Lowestoft*, pp. 31 and 52.

[29] No. 160 High Street is part of a late nineteenth-century residential terrace. Nos 41–42 occupy the site of what was once *The Swan* inn, one of the town's premier hostelries of the late medieval and early modern periods.

Plate 17. Nos 41–42 High Street. This late eighteenth-century double dwelling encapsulates much of the history of Lowestoft High Street, standing as it does on the site of the medieval Swan Inn at the top end of Mariner's Score (see Plate 11). The roadway's story has been one of constant change and redevelopment, to take account of contemporary needs and demands at any one time.

Other buildings along the High Street also have cellars but, while being of similar dimensions to the two surviving medieval ones, they have largely been reconstructed at some stage (mainly in the nineteenth century). It is apparent that storage space below ground was an important feature of the construction of the larger dwellings, probably from the time that they were first built, and their presence may well indicate a growing involvement in maritime trade on the part of the townspeople. Safe storage of goods, not only for domestic use but also for sale or re-sale, was perhaps becoming part of the town's function as it moved from a mainly agricultural economy to one that was becoming more mercantile in nature.

The most recent opportunity to investigate an early cellar on Lowestoft High Street was unfortunately missed during the construction of a new terrace of houses in Compass Street during 2013. It was known that a filled-in cellar existed under a space that had been used for many years as a car park for people working at the Town Hall, and this was flagged up to both the local District Council and to the archaeological team responsible for digging the site ahead of construction work. Somehow, the advice was either overlooked or ignored and irreparable damage done to a surviving vestige of the town's past. The cellar had once belonged to an inn called *The New White Horse*, which was demolished in 1703 and moved further to the west in order to provide a small overspill market area because the main one was becoming congested (largely because of building encroachment onto it). The fill used to close up the cellar would have been worth investigation in its own right – to say nothing of the structure itself. Something of this nature must not be allowed to happen again.

As a final word on evidence remaining below ground of Lowestoft's development on its new town site, some interesting features were found in 2011 and 2013 on the house plot belonging to the former No. 1 High Street. An exploratory dig and its follow-up on the site, once occupied by a large detached marine residence of the early nineteenth century (pulled down c. 1960), revealed considerable remains of early brick walling dating from the first part of the fourteenth century. The demolished building had stood on the position once taken up by the three most northerly dwellings on the east side of Lowestoft High Street and, although its deep footings had seriously compromised the integrity of the earlier building work, enough of the latter remained to enable some important assessments to be made of what had been constructed. Altogether, and excavating as far as was possible on a north–south alignment, a thirty-five-foot length of wall was exposed, well over nine feet high from the top to the base-level. A little below the ground's surface there was evidence of the top four or five courses of bricks beginning to arch over in what was probably a vaulted cellar's ceiling not unlike the two described above (Plate 18). The wall probably ran on in both directions, but it was not possible to dig further to the north because of the possibility of undermining a footpath, and there were interruptions of the fabric to the south caused by later modifications.

It may have been that this large underground space had originally served all three of the houses which stood above it (with appropriate divisions made within), but it was not possible to reach a positive conclusion because of later interference. What was not in doubt was the quality of the construction, the masonry being of a serpentine nature (to give lateral strength without buttressing), around eighteen inches thick at the bottom and tapering upwards to around fifteen inches, with irregularly coursed header-bond throughout. The inner surface of the wall had been lime-washed at some stage, but it was also calcified over much of its area by the reaction of moisture with the lime mortar used in the brickwork – a feature which might have been caused by damp air within the original cellar areas, by direct contact with soil and infill after the site had been redeveloped, or even by a combination of the two. All the loose bricks able to be retrieved from the courses nearest to the surface

Plate 18. Medieval wall, No. 1 High Street. This image shows part of the masonry exposed during archaeological investigation. The standard of build was impressive, both in terms of the quality of the bricks and the nature of construction.

were typically narrow, with some variation in length and width, and it was noticeable that the fabric (orange-red in colour) had been well fired to give durability below ground.[30]

The people involved in the dig (members of the Lowestoft Archaeological and Local History Society and of the Lowestoft Heritage Workshop Centre) were all impressed with both the scale of the work excavated and the quality of construction. If what was found was typical of the rest of the High Street area, then once again the overall operation of establishing the new town is

[30] For a full description of the dig see P. Durbidge, *A Report on the Limited Excavation on the Site of No. 1 High Street, Lowestoft* (Lowestoft, 2014) (a Heritage Workshop Centre publication).

deserving of the greatest admiration. The amount of work in establishing the cliff-face terracing in the first place has already been commented on; the building which followed is no less worthy of respect. The two surviving cellars and the excavated section of wall just described show brick-making capability of the first order. Was all the expertise present within the parish, both for the preliminary engineering and the subsequent construction work, or were outside sources of labour employed? An answer cannot be easily arrived at and attempting to find one is not really possible. Comment has been made on the increasing use of brick in urban construction in Suffolk during the fifteenth century,[31] but Lowestoft was using it as a major building material in the first half of the fourteenth.

The clay used to make the bricks was probably dug and fired locally, as deposits of the material were available in a number of places. Pockets of chalk to produce the lime needed for mortar were also to be found and there was at least one kiln in operation on the western edge of the town during the early modern period. Information on the use of bricks in medieval Ipswich has purported to show the transition from imported stock from abroad (The Netherlands) to local manufacture during the early fifteenth century,[32] but it is likely that such importation was a top-up to local production, rather than the main source of supply. Data relating to the quantities of imported stock for the years 1396–8 are cited, showing that 41,000 floor-bricks and 42,000 standard ones came into the town, but these numbers are small.[33] It takes something like 10,000 bricks to build a modern two- to three-bedroom terraced house and around 16–18,000 to create a detached three-bedroom dwelling. Even allowing for differences in size between medieval bricks and modern ones, a valid comparison between then and now can be made, and the importation figures cited for Ipswich do not show the construction (or reconstruction) of a town reliant for major building work on overseas sources of brick. The limited amount of material suggests the specific ordering of high-quality stock (for which The Netherlands were renowned) for a particular project or projects.

It is a reasonable supposition that at least some of the first houses built on the cliff-top at Lowestoft were of open hall construction, perhaps aisled in the emerging fashion of the time, cellared beneath, and (given the width of plot available) probably standing broadside on to the road. The smaller dwellings that were eventually built in the side-street area would have been scaled-down versions of their larger counterparts, and all of them would have been built of

[31] Bailey, *Suffolk*, p. 278.
[32] N. Amor, *Late Medieval Ipswich: Trade and Industry* (Woodbridge, 2011), pp. 102–3.
[33] Amor, *Ipswich*, p. 72.

timber frames, with wattle-and-daub panelling infill and thatched roofs. Before upper floors began to be introduced (particularly during the fifteenth century), the larger houses were open to the rafters and arranged in three basic cells or spaces: a service area (including buttery and pantry), a hall (with hearth) and a parlour. A passageway giving access to and egress from the building stood between the service area and the rest of the house (with doors at each end), and there was a doorway leading from it into the hall. Because of the risk of fire, the kitchen was often a separate, detached or lean-to building – though, as time went by, it was increasingly incorporated within the body of the dwelling.

There is no intention, as part of this narrative, to go into the intricacies of medieval house construction and the multiple uses made of the internal spaces. Suffice it to say that, during the 200 or so years following Lowestoft's move to its new site, important changes were made in basic house design whereby the introduction of first-floor rooms and chimney stacks (the two often accompanying each other) brought about increased standards of amenity and comfort, which even filtered down eventually to the lesser members of society. The town's early modern housing accommodation has been thoroughly investigated elsewhere and there is nothing to be gained from repetition.[34]

The only point that can usefully be made is that Lowestoft never had much in the way of its own resources of timber. The manor roll shows only about twenty to twenty-five acres of woodland in the parish (1.5 per cent of the total area) and this would not have been sufficient at any stage to support a large programme of house-building, let alone the construction of fishing vessels and other craft. Supplies of suitable timber would have been available at a price from various local estates (Somerleyton, Mutford and Sotterley being likely sources) and conserving use of the material in dwellings was eventually made possible by adopting the half-timbering method of construction. This meant building the ground-floor walls of rubble and brick and setting a timber-framed upper section onto them. A number of surviving examples are still standing above ground in the town (Plate 19) and they are impressive enough in their own right to give some small sense of its appearance as described by Thomas Howard, the third duke of Norfolk, in May 1545. While conducting a review of coastal defences between Great Yarmouth and Orford, he referred to Lowestoft in the following terms: 'The town is as pretty a town as I know any few on the sea coasts, and as thrifty and honest people in the same, and right well builded.'[35]

[34] See Butcher, *Lowestoft*, pp. 90–128.

[35] J. Gairdner and R.H. Brodie (eds), *LPFD Henry VIII*, vol. 20(i), p. 370.

Plate 19. Nos 102–104 High Street. This half-timbered merchant's house dates from c. 1530 and is seen here as it appeared some forty years ago. The first-floor jetty is plainly visible and the wall-cladding at that level conceals timber studs with herringbone brickwork between.

What he was looking at was probably a long way from what had originally stood along the cliff-top, both in terms of time's passing and of the changes this had brought. And it brings forward the question previously asked regarding the town's relocation, and now repeated once again. How was it done, in terms of both the human effort involved and the financial cost? The latter is particularly mysterious as (in theory, at least) the community was not apparently particularly wealthy in the earlier part of the fourteenth century. The Lay Subsidy of 1327 set out the tax payments due to the Crown from England's inhabitants and it was calculated at a rate of one-twentieth (5 per cent) per person on movable goods worth 5s or more – the minimal payment to be made being one of 3d, therefore. The data compiled for the half-hundreds of

Mutford and Lothingland show Lowestoft to be fourteenth in the list of the twenty-one community payments recorded, with twenty-nine of its inhabitants paying a total of £1 9s 6d. This works out at an average of fractionally over 1s per head.[36] Table 10 presents the overall picture for the two half-hundreds.

Table 10. The 1327 Lay Subsidy (tax paid by local communities).

	No. of people	Amount paid
Community (Mutford)		
Kessingland	73	£4 2s 0d
Mutford	77	£2 7s 6d
Carlton	30	£2 2s 5d
Pakefield and Kirkley	32	£2 1s 3d
Gisleham and part-Rushmere	41	£1 10s 0d
		Total: £13 4s 0d
Community (Lothingland)		
Gorleston and Reston	76	£7 6s 10½d
Southtown	22	£2 13s 6d
Belton	39	£2 6s 4d
Corton	18	£2 2s 6d
Blundeston	28	£1 18s 3d
Somerleyton	24	£1 17s 2d
Oulton and Flixton	22	£1 15s 11d
Bradwell	22	£1 14s 8d
Lowestoft	29	£1 9s 6d
Lound	14	£1 8s 8d
Fritton	12	£1 4s 9d
Hopton	16	£1 4s 6d
Gunton	12	£1 1s 8d
Herringfleet	15	£1 0s 2d
Burgh Castle	10	£0 18s 2d
Ashby	10	£0 16s 0d
		Total: £30 18s 9½d

Notes:

- The listing of communities has been changed from a random sequence to one of descending order of payment made.
- The sums shown have been changed from a predominantly shillings and pence format to the £ s d model.
- Barnby is not included in the figures for Mutford Half-hundred, nor Newton in those for Lothingland. This could possibly show impoverishment in each com-

[36] Hervey, *Suffolk in 1327*, p. 95.

munity, with small populations not reaching the threshold of wealth required for assessment, or it could simply be a matter of clerical error.

A great deal of time could be spent on analysing the many aspects of local society that are to be found in the table's statistics (such as the inhabitants of Lound and Corton paying double or more the rate of tax that Lowestoft's did), but that is not part of the agenda here. The main point for discussion is how a comparatively modest standing in the hierarchy of local communities, in terms of assessed taxable wealth and the amount paid, matches with what was happening in Lowestoft at the time. For it was not just a matter of building a new town; the local population had also started the construction of a very large replacement parish church (see Chapter 6). The money must have come largely from within the community, so why is this not reflected in the figures above – both in terms of the amount of tax paid and the number of people contributing?

The point has been made elsewhere that, with regard to civic poverty, protestations made by communities during the late medieval period concerning their tax burdens do not always equate to personal levels of wealth. Thus, a township was capable of pleading hardship as individual incomes rose.[37] Nothing is known of Lowestoft's official response to the financial demands made on it in 1327, but was there some kind of creative accountancy exercised on its behalf, in acknowledgement of its large and expensive commitments? It seems unlikely that the townspeople would have been able to dupe the officials responsible for collecting the money due, for they would have been locals themselves (as revealed in the previous chapter, with regard to the various kinds of malpractice recorded in the conduct of financial affairs). Therefore, a hidden factor is present somewhere in the data shown. What it was is not known and it is unlikely ever to manifest itself.

[37] Amor, *Ipswich*, pp. 3–4.

– 4 –

Fishing and associated activities

Drift-net fishing

One frustrating feature of both subsistence and commercial fishing during the medieval period is that comparatively little specific documentary information exists regarding the vessels and gear employed in coastal parishes. The sixteenth, seventeenth and eighteenth centuries have much more detailed sources of evidence in probate documents (especially inventories), manorial records and tithe accounts, which may (in the case of fishing gear particularly) allow an insight into previous practice. The basic techniques for catching fish have not essentially changed in centuries, and that includes many of the methods employed today, so it is probably permissible for aspects of capture of the early modern era to be applied to an earlier time period.

There is no doubt that the inhabitants of Lowestoft, from very early on, would have been aware of the sources of food available from the sea. Two pelagic species, herrings and sprats, shoaled relatively close inshore during the autumn and early winter, while the former were also available during the spring – again, at no great distance from land. The late spring–early summer months made mackerel available and demersal fish of different types would have been present all year round, with species taken varying seasonally: broadly speaking, whiting and cod during the autumn and winter, flatfish (e.g. flounders, dabs and soles) during the spring and summer. This is a generalised view of the situation, but it serves to give some idea of the opportunities available to local people of the time.

The Lowestoft fishing industry of the early modern period has been investigated extensively elsewhere and it would be of limited use to repeat the findings here, aside from occasional cross-references where useful.[1] The main

[1] D. Butcher, *The Ocean's Gift* (Norwich, 1995); D. Butcher, 'The herring fisheries in the

purpose of this chapter is to consider the role of maritime pursuits as influences in Lowestoft's medieval economy and to acknowledge the advantages of relocating the town to a cliff-top position. As was discussed in the opening pages of the previous chapter, sea-based enterprise was probably not the only consideration in making the move from the original township's site, but it is likely to have been an important one – perhaps, even, the most significant.

As far as fishing is concerned, the main period of activity along the East Anglian coast was the autumn herring season – an enterprise that lasted from the late Anglo-Saxon period into the 1960s, when a combination of factors (including over-exploitation of the stocks) brought it to a close. Numbers of herrings have increased in the southern North Sea since intensive fishing for them ceased, but whether or not a viable fishery will ever again be established remains to be seen. At the time that Lowestoft was establishing itself as a new planned town, the fish resource was probably already an important staple in the community's diet, and one with the capacity also to satisfy demand from further afield. Fish of all kinds, both marine and freshwater, were needed in large quantities to satisfy the religious requirements of the Roman Catholic church and (in the educated strata of society, at least) to maintain the balance of the humours in the body.[2] The market, therefore, was both local and national (and international, in the case of herring and cod), and there was money to be made from supplying it.

The scale of Lowestoft's medieval fishing activity cannot be estimated because no specific records concerning it have survived (if, indeed, they ever existed) – unlike, for instance, the early fifteenth-century Dunwich bailiffs' accounts.[3] It is only possible to present certain aspects of it, based on peripheral evidence and on the principle that an established industry of the early modern period must have had well-founded antecedents. In the case of herring catching, there is also the concern shown by the civic authorities of Great Yarmouth, particularly during the fourteenth century, that its six-week autumn fair (29 September to 11 November) would be adversely affected by an emerging local rival perhaps even more threatening than its immediate neighbours to the north and south: Caister and Gorleston. The Norfolk port's defence of its trading privileges will be considered later in this chapter, but the perceived commercial threat from Lowestoft must have had

early modern period: Lowestoft as microcosm', in D.J. Starkey, C. Reid and N. Ashcroft (eds), *England's Sea Fisheries* (London, 2000), pp. 54–63; Butcher, *Lowestoft*, pp. 161–85.

[2] C.W. Woolgar, 'Take this penance now and afterwards the fare will improve: seafood and late medieval diet', in D.J. Starkey, C. Reid and N. Ashcroft (eds), *England's Sea Fisheries* (London, 2000), pp. 36–7.

[3] M. Bailey (ed.), *The Bailiffs' Minute Book of Dunwich, 1404–1430*, SRS 34 (Woodbridge, 1992).

some basis and the catching and processing of herrings was obviously of key significance.

Capturing the fish was largely a matter of taking advantage of a behavioural characteristic of the species, whereby the shoals rose from the seabed at dusk to swim in the upper levels of the ocean, feeding on the zooplankton to be found there. Thus, it was largely a night-time exercise, though daytime shoaling close to the surface was not unknown. The presence of herring was indicated in a number of ways that became familiar to fishermen and were eventually incorporated into the collective folk-memory associated with the industry. Feeding activity by gulls was one sign; the colour of the water another (especially if oil globules were visible). Then there was the matter of knowing how to work the tides in order to achieve the best results, and how to assess the favourable nature (or otherwise) of weather conditions.[4] Success in any fishing enterprise was the result of close observation of the workings of nature and of the experience gained from finding out which practices were effective and which were not – and herring-catching was no exception.

The time-honoured method of taking the species was by drift net, a series of which (joined end to end) were paid out over the side of the boat and allowed to float in the upper levels of the sea rather like a series of tennis nets fixed together – though with much smaller meshes! The operating vessel drifted along with the tide, its gear streaming out ahead of it, with periodic inspection of the nearest net carried out in order to monitor the number of fish being caught. Alternatively, the crew might cast the boat off from the fleet of nets and row the craft up and down it to ascertain the success of the operation. This particular practice of checking catch-levels at intervals remained in use throughout the whole period of herring-catching. Hauling of the first net and 'looking on' was particularly associated with both sailing luggers and steam drifters of the nineteenth and twentieth centuries, while rowing up and down has remained in use with longshore craft right down to the present day.

The drift nets themselves were known as flews and their meshes were made of hemp or linen twine, with each individual mesh being about an inch square. Both fibres would have been available from local sources (not specifically Lowestoft itself so much as the surrounding parishes in both Lothingland and Mutford) and it is interesting to note that the term lints was used to describe both herring and mackerel nets well into the twentieth century – even though

[4] South-westerly winds, for instance, were reckoned to be beneficial for catching herrings, whereas easterly ones were bad because they had the effect of drawing the fish away from land out into deeper water.

Egyptian cotton had long superseded earlier materials.[5] The nets would have been made by family groups involved in fishing, and probate inventories of the early modern era which refer to twyning wheels (when these were in the possession of fishermen) show that hemp or flax fibre was being spun into twine for making nets and lines.

The nets of this period were about twenty yards long and of variable depth, according to the depth of the water fished. There is no compelling reason to believe that medieval gear would have varied greatly from what was being used 400 or 500 years later. Therefore, the six scores, nine scores and twelve scores so frequently encountered in both inventories and wills of Tudor and Stuart times may well have had earlier counterparts. The specific terminology used is a reference to the vertical dimensions of the nets described, as drift-net size was always expressed in terms of scores (twenties) of meshes depth. The nine scores seem to have been the ones most commonly used and would have been fifteen feet (180 inches) deep.

Each individual net consisted of four separate knitted sections known as ranns, and these were laced together, the topmost and lowest being made of thicker twine than the middle ones and known respectively as the hoddy and the deepyne. The four sections of mesh were then secured to a framework of hemp cord in order to give each net its required shape, and in such a way as to make the meshes form the required diamond configuration able to catch the herrings effectively by the gills when they rose from the seabed. The nets used for each fishing trip were laced together down the sides and secured at the top to a thick hempen rope known as the warrope (later, warp), hanging down in the water under the weight of the twine from which they were made as it became saturated. The warrope itself was held up, near the surface of the sea, by small wooden casks acting as floats. This basic catching method remained in use up until the end of North Sea drift-net fishing during the 1960s (Plate 20), though the development of lighter, more efficient cotton nets during the first half of the nineteenth century meant that the warp had to be transferred from the top of the gear to the bottom in order to weight the nets down effectively and get them to hang correctly in the water.

It is known from an unpublished source of c. 1800 that the three-masted Lowestoft fishing craft of the time (known as great boats) worked about 100 nets per vessel, meaning an overall length of 2,000 yards – or just over a mile.[6]

[5] The 1618 manor roll shows that there were a handful of small hemp-lands within the built-up area of Lowestoft itself, one of which is still perpetuated in the name The Hemplands, this roadway being located at the northern end of town, between Park Road and Jubilee Way, abutting onto Osborne Street and the end of Melbourne Road.

[6] I. Gillingwater, *A History of Lowestoft and Lothingland*, vol. 3 (c. 1800), p. 175.

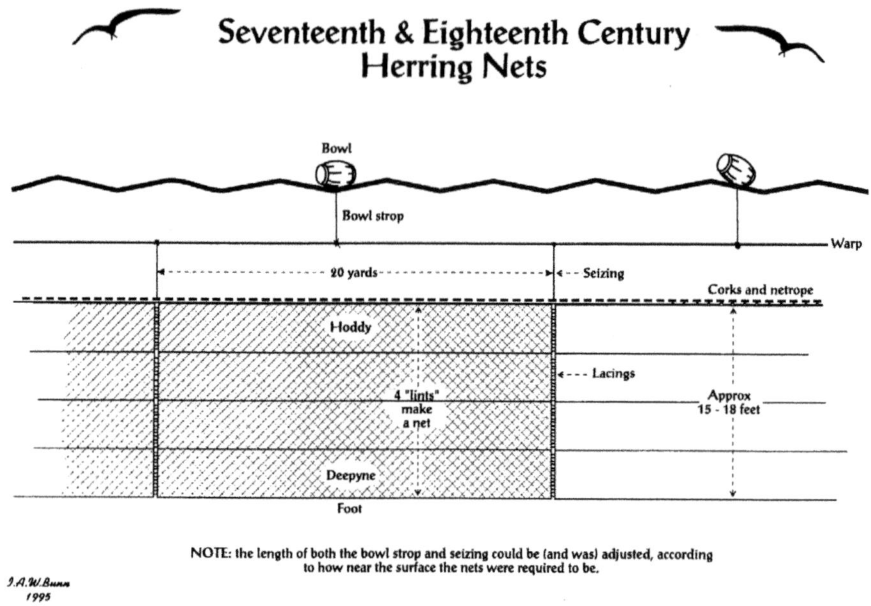

Plate 20. Seventeenth-/eighteenth-century drift nets. This type of gear remained in use well into the nineteenth century, until cotton replaced hemp twine. The extent to which cork floats were used on the headline during medieval times is not known, but they became widely used during the seventeenth and eighteenth centuries as the use of glass bottles (with their corks) to store and retail wine increased.

The medieval fishing effort would have been much smaller in scale, in terms both of the vessels used and of the amount of gear they carried. A great boat was probably in the range of fifty to sixty feet long, with a crew of ten men, whereas the typical vessel of 400–500 years earlier would have been nearer to twelve or fifteen feet in length, with just a single mast stepped amidships. Oars, also, would have been used for propulsion and the crew would have consisted of three to four men (boats of this kind were still in operation during the first half of the eighteenth century and are referred to in the parish tithe records). When not engaged in fishing, such craft would have been used for offloading cargo from larger trading vessels lying offshore and for conveying goods outwards to them. A royal inquisition of 1336 (the year before the Hundred Years War officially began), which sought to collect details of ships suitable for military transports, recorded twenty-one vessels owned in the Holkham–Wells area of the north Norfolk coast. Two of them had a carrying capacity of twenty tons

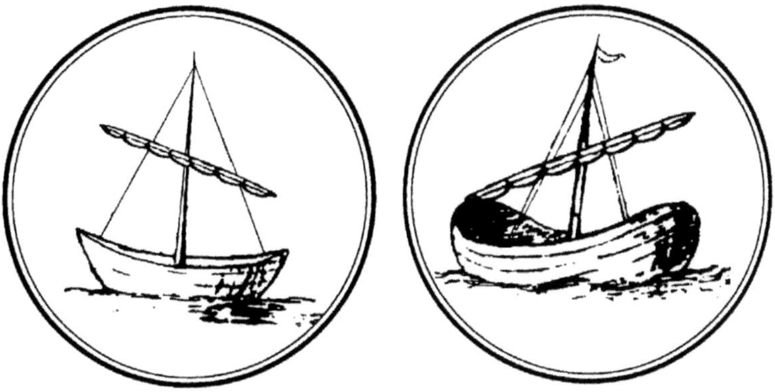

Plate 21. Late sixteenth-century small craft. These computer-enhanced images derive from the same source as that used in Plate 22. The vessels, having a single mast stepped amidships (one which may have been removable) and no deck, would have been propelled by sail or oars. Used for either fishing or ferrying goods, they were handy and versatile, and larger versions (with decking) would have been involved in coastal and overseas trade.

(*tuns*), the rest were rated at about twelve.[7] It is possible that Lowestoft had craft of similar size, but there is no documentary evidence available.

Even though the fishing operation was smaller in scale than that conducted during the early modern period, this does not mean that it was insignificant. The boats used would have been capable of either working close in to land or going out beyond the off-lying sandbanks into deeper water. And while they may not have carried any more than about fifteen to twenty nets (the number is not known for certain), this would still have produced a considerable quantity of fish in even a moderate season. The first three decades of the eighteenth century show an average of about a dozen small boats (Plate 21) working directly off the beach during the autumn herring season (loosely defined as October to mid-December), with between fifteen and twenty of the larger vessels operating further out from land – a total employment number of 200 or so men and boys.[8] There are no statistics available for medieval times and all comment on this period must therefore remain generalised.

One great advantage attaching to the small craft used in drift-net fishing during the fourteenth and fifteenth centuries is their comparative ease

[7] M. Kowaleski, 'The shipmaster as entrepreneur in medieval England', in B. Dodds and C.D. Liddy (eds), *Commercial Activity, Markets and Entrepreneurs in the Middle Ages* (Woodbridge, 2011), p. 166.

[8] Butcher, *Lowestoft*, p. 193.

of handling compared with larger vessels. The shoreline was their home, for they were built there above high-water mark and pulled up above it and left beached when not in use. Larger vessels, once constructed, had to anchor in the shallows and take their chance on what wind and tide might do to them. Admittedly, Lowestoft offered a haven between the outlying sandbanks and the shoreline itself (particularly giving shelter from westerly and north-westerly gales) – but there were other times, with the wind in the east, when conditions could be difficult for ships lying at anchor. Small vessels were also handier in the practice of fishing itself and there were economies of scale in what they did, through their being less expensive to operate and maintain. On the evidence provided by the parish tithe records of the early eighteenth century, they were often more cost-effective than their larger counterparts.

Two other species of fish caught by drift-net were mackerel and sprats – the former requiring a larger mesh than herrings and the latter a smaller one. Mackerel were taken in the late spring and early summer and the fishery would have been limited in scale by the boats employed not being able to sail far from shore in order to catch them. During the early modern period Lowestoft's great boats worked off the north Norfolk coast for the first part of the season, but this would probably not have been the case in medieval times, because an earlier equivalent of this type of vessel had not been developed. Such fish as were caught would have needed to be landed quickly (because of their perishable nature) and consumed within two or three days, which means that they were probably eaten mainly in the immediate local area, with some perhaps conveyed to local inland market towns, such as Beccles and Bungay, or even to Norwich, with its important Friday fish market.

Sprats (often referred to at the time as sparlings or sperlings) were caught during the winter, following on from the herring harvest, but they never assumed the importance in Lowestoft that they did further south along the Suffolk coast. Late medieval records show the significance of sprats in the maritime economies of Southwold, Dunwich, Aldeburgh and Orford, but Lowestoft never involved itself with the species to the same degree. There is little doubt that the fish would have been caught and consumed, because of their palatability and nutritional value, but they never became the object of capture and processing in the way that they did in the other four communities mentioned – or even, for that matter, in Kessingland, which was situated closer to Lowestoft and might therefore be expected to show similarities.

Herrings were thus undoubtedly the town's main commercial priority and those caught in the autumn, making their way southwards towards spawning grounds in the Dover Straits, were in prime condition: full of milt (sperm) and roe (eggs) and with a fat content that was no more than 7 per cent of average body weight – this latter being generally in the range of four to five ounces.[9] The fish caught during the summer were much more oily and perishable, while the spring variety were recovering from spawning (known as spents or shotten herrings), which had reduced their weight and made the flesh less palatable. The only thing to be said in favour of them was that they provided a source of food which was there for the taking at a time when pelagic species generally were scarce.

The processing of herrings was already well established by the time that Lowestoft was relocating itself onto the cliff-top. The herring rents referred to in the Domesday Survey, paid by estates in Mutford Half-hundred to their lord, Hugh de Montfort (p. 81), would have been fish preserved by some kind of salting process, with added drying – either by direct exposure to the air or by being smoked above slow-burning fires. White or pickled herrings were probably not available at this time, being the result of a curing method developed in Skånia, in southern Sweden, towards the end of the thirteenth century.[10] This involved removing the gills and gut, after a neat incision had been made in the throat of the fish, and then packing them in barrels (in layers, or tiers, set at right-angles to each other) with a sprinkling of salt on each layer. Great Yarmouth produced large quantities of them during late medieval and early modern times, but Lowestoft did not go in for them to the same extent.

Its own particular speciality was the red herring – a fish that was left ungutted, dry-salted in heaps on the ground for two or three days, with periodic rousing (or turning) and reheaping, and was then smoked above slow, controlled fires for anything between a week and a month, depending on the strength of the cure required.[11] At some stage, brining the herrings in vats was adopted by curers as an alternative to the earlier preparatory method (which continued to be used as well) – but this practice still involved the use of salt, which was perhaps the most important ingredient in the preservation of all kinds of foodstuffs until the introduction of refrigeration. Its main property was to act as an agent for drawing water from the tissues of whatever was being preserved, this being an essential part of slowing down the natural process of decay, and its value in the pre-industrial world cannot truly be understood by anyone who did not live in such times. It is now known how medically harmful excessive consumption of salt can be; but people living in earlier times had no choice but to use it.

[9] W.C. Hodgson, *The Herring and Its Fishery* (London, 1957), pp. 110–11.

[10] R.W. Unger, 'The Netherlands herring fishery in the late Middle Ages: the false legend of Willem Beukels of Biervliet', *Viator*, 9 (1978), pp. 335–56.

[11] Autumn herrings were feeding only very lightly, prior to spawning, and the gut was able to be left in if they were to be *redded*.

Domesday makes reference to seven salt-works in Lothingland (three at Burgh Castle, three at Gorleston and one at Fritton, which had gone out of use), but none are mentioned in connection with Mutford Half-hundred, even though herrings were being cured there to supply Hugh de Montfort's household. It is just possible that some salt manufacture went unrecorded, if it was an intermittent rather than a full-time operation – but, as always, the Survey leaves the reader with as many questions as answers. It might be thought, given the two communities' proximity to Great Yarmouth, with its important autumn herring fair, that the salt produced at Burgh and Gorleston went to service the curing operation in that town. However, both places were part of the Lothingland area and it was seen in Chapter 2 how commercial rivalry with Yarmouth caused strained relationships between the two entities for much of the thirteenth and fourteenth centuries.

In any case, Yarmouth would have had access to nearby supplies of salt because Caister, immediately to the north of it, had forty-five salt-works recorded at Domesday. The term *salin(ar)ia* (abbreviated to *sal* or *saline*) indicates production, but gives no clue as to method: either filtration and evaporation of sea water in open-air, clay-lined pans or the boiling-down of the brine in containers made of lead or iron (or a combination of both processes). Given the close manorial ties between Gorleston and Lowestoft, it is possible that salt from the former community found its way to the latter, which may even have produced low-grade material of its own along the tide-line as time and opportunity offered (especially from late spring until early autumn). The extent of the fishing operation at Gorleston is not known and it is perhaps significant that the only fishermen referred to in connection with it in Domesday are the twenty-four said to have belonged to Yarmouth.

That town itself is almost completely lacking in information relating to its economic function and structure and its Domesday entry is the least detailed, by far, of all the identifiable urban centres in Norfolk and Suffolk. All that is revealed is the presence of seventy burgesses among its population and the composite rental values of it and three adjacent hundreds (East Flegg, West Flegg and either Walsham or Happing). It is probable, of course, that some of the burgesses referred to had interests in fishing (especially the autumn herring season), but it was likely to have been in the handling, processing and sale of fish rather than in going to sea and catching them. Even at Domesday, the majority of people coming to the town during the autumn were probably from other locations along the east and south coasts of England, as well as from north-western France and the Low Countries.

Lowestoft's sources of salt, then, is a matter which cannot be definitively resolved. Local supplies alone would not have been sufficient to service the increasing levels of fish-curing activity that seem to have been occurring during the late medieval period and stocks must have been imported from outside. Early modern evidence shows that quantities of both grey salt and white salt were being held by Lowestoft merchants (the former being a coarser variety, which was refined by boiling and evaporation to produce the latter), while bay salt was being brought in from the Nantes area of south-western France – importation which may also have occurred in earlier times.[12] Other possible sources were The Netherlands, Lincolnshire and Cheshire. Refinement of the product, both locally produced and imported, was probably carried out in Lowestoft, with the heat required to raise the temperature of the brine achieved by burning peat dug from around the edges of Lake Lothing. Even as late as the beginning of the seventeenth century, a man named John Browne is described as a flag-graver (peat-digger) in his wife's burial registration of 17 February 1605.

The other key requirement in curing herrings, apart from salt, was wood. Large amounts of ash and oak were used in making clapboards (barrel-staves) and in providing the billets needed to fuel the curing-house fires. Ash was the favoured type for both purposes because it was less dense than oak (thereby producing lighter casks) and it burned less acridly, but less of it was grown and therefore oak became more commonly used. Lowestoft's lack of timber resources has already been referred to, and most of the material required must have been produced by coppicing in managed woodlands within, say, a day's travel of the town. During the sixteenth and seventeenth centuries oak barrel-staves were brought in from the Sussex Weald and from ports along the Baltic coastline, and this may also have been done in earlier times. Once again, however, there is no firm evidence.

The curing process for producing red herrings, after the initial salting had been carried out and the fish washed and drained, was to thread them through mouth and gill-opening onto slender seasoned hazel rods about four feet in length (again, produced by coppicing). These speets, as they were termed (a variant of 'spits'), were then lodged on a series of wooden racks set within the fish-house(s). Once all the speets of herring were in place, slow fires of billet-wood (short, thick rods) were lit on the floor and kept smouldering for the required length of time.[13] The smoking process (or drying, as it was called)

[12] Bay salt was the term used for a product of reasonable quality (but not the finest) from the Bay of Bourgneuf. By the late sixteenth century the term had become generic, describing any salt produced in coastal areas abutting onto the Bay of Biscay. For a detailed explanation of the English medieval salt trade, see A.R. Bridbury, *England and the Salt Trade in the Later Middle Ages* (Oxford, 1955).

[13] The slow nature of the firing suggests the wood used may have been *green* rather than *seasoned*, which would have produced more smoke than flame and been easier to control. It is likely that the billets would have been stripped of bark, as an extract from it (after steeping in water) was used to tan leather and preserve fishing gear.

was not continuous, however; the fires were extinguished every six or seven days and the oil in the herrings allowed to exude for a day or two – a process which prevented them from becoming desiccated and unpalatable and which was usually referred to as sweating. At the end of the curing time they were packed in casks of around thirty-two gallons' capacity (each containing about 800–1,000 fish), ready for shipment. Smaller quantities for local use were packed into rectangular wicker cases known as cades – a term also used for the quantity of 500–600 cured fish contained therein.

The fish-houses were of distinctive build and may be seen represented (as they appeared at the time) in a diagrammatic view of the town produced in c. 1580 (Plate 22).[14] The medieval equivalents would probably have been smaller and may well have had walls constructed of timber and daub rather than brick (a working wooden smokehouse in the back streets of Kirkley survived into the 1970s). It is also possible that the tiled roofs of the early modern period were preceded by shingles (tiles are specifically referred to in the will of John Waynflete Snr in 1460).[15] The most notable feature is what may appear to be windows, but which are in fact smoke and air vents (probably louvred or shuttered to moderate the effect of the wind) and which were an essential part of the buildings' function.

Generally speaking, fish-houses were longer than they were wide (a characteristic not represented in the picture, but something in the range of twenty to thirty feet by ten to twelve) and during the time in question were probably no more than fifteen to twenty feet high. The wooden drying racks set horizontally along the inner face of the longer walls were paralleled by a matching series fixed to lines of spaced vertical posts set in the building's interior and stretching from floor to roof – and it was across these spars (set about four feet apart) that the speets of salted herring were placed to cure by smoking. The fish-houses were loaded from the top downwards and the men (or women) doing the work used the inner racks as ladders to assist them in their task. A space about head-high was left at the bottom to enable the fires to function effectively, and the door was kept shut while the smoking process was taking place. The flooring material used was beaten loam and clay, sometimes mixed with lime, but in more recent times this was superseded by floor-bricks of different kinds and eventually (in the larger commercial fish-houses) even by concrete.

[14] The illustration is taken from a map of the local coastline stretching from Gorleston to Pakefield, a copy of which was long held in the Lowestoft Library local studies collection and provided the picture seen here: now SRO(L) 368. The original document itself was acquired by the British Library in 1973 (Add. Mss 56070).

[15] NRO, NCC 136 Betyns. He lived in Southwold and held a High Street dwelling in Lowestoft (now Nos 61 and 62).

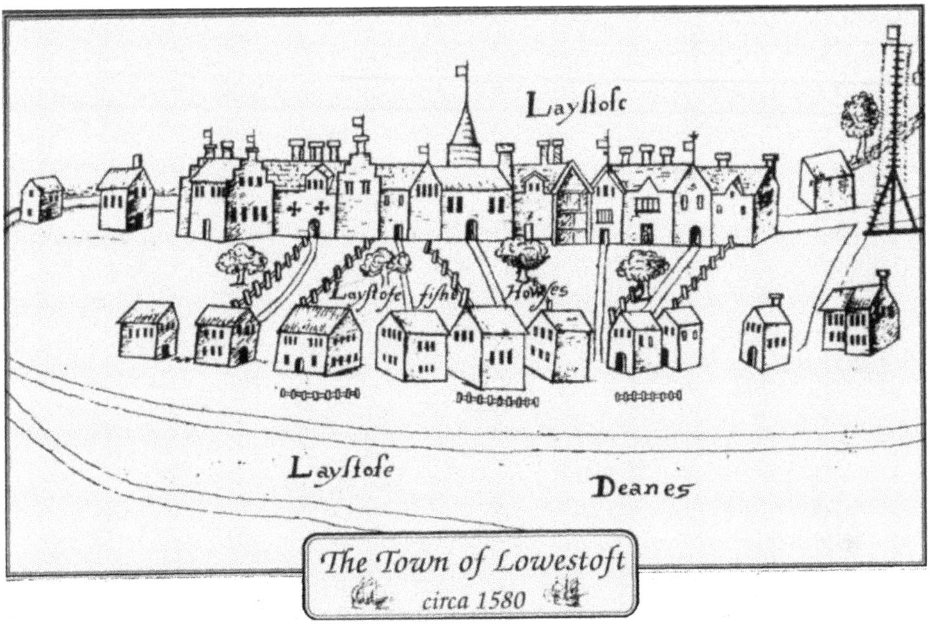

Plate 22. A diagrammatic view of the town in c. 1580. This stylised, military-looking vignette gives no indication of the cliff's terracing, but shows the curing premises in a line at its base. The ladder-like structure on the right-hand extremity represents a beacon erected in 1550 to warn of coastal attack.

Edmund Gillingwater, in his late eighteenth-century history of the town, gives a good account of the curing of red herrings and was in no doubt as to the superiority of Lowestoft's product over that of Great Yarmouth.[16] He attributed this to the location of the fish-houses at the foot of the cliff, which allowed free passage of air to assist the curing process – whereas Yarmouth's equivalent buildings were hemmed in among the townspeople's dwellings, in very narrow streets, which prevented good air circulation. Apart from any benefits to be had in creating a better product, the separation of curing premises from living accommodation must have benefited the local residents, who would not have had to tolerate the concentrated wood-smoke in the air they had to breathe!

Another factor relevant in the proximity of fish-houses and dwellings was the fire-risk – especially to thatched roofs. Even though there was a considerable distance between the source and the affected area, Lowestoft's worst recorded fire, on 10 March 1645, originated in a fish-house just to the south

[16] Gillingwater, *Lowestoft*, pp. 95–8.

of the present-day Lighthouse Score and spread in a southerly direction on a strong northerly breeze typical of the time of year.[17] This carried the sparks from the source of the blaze across all the other fish-houses, as far as Rant Score, igniting them on the way. Then there seems to have been a change of wind direction, to the east or south-east, because the fire moved up onto the middle part of the High Street and destroyed a number of houses and work-premises on either side of the roadway. Apart from the obvious danger of open fires (even though slow-burning), the potential hazard of fish-curing premises was increased by the build-up of fish-oil and soot on the inside of the walls, eventually leading to a tar-like accretion that was potentially (and actually) combustible.[18]

With the town's fish-curing premises located at the foot of the cliff, below the dwelling-houses situated above, the question arises as to which were constructed first. Did the fish-houses follow on from the terracing of the cliff-face and setting-out of building plots, or were they already in place when the township moved? The latter possibility deserves serious consideration. Handling and processing herrings close to where they were landed made more sense than moving them inland to the site of the original settlement, where there was limited space to accommodate curing facilities and where a return journey to the beach would have been needed for any maritime transportation of the product. Fourteenth-century documentation shows that local red herrings were an important commercial commodity, something which almost certainly had its roots in the previous 100 years. And, as fishing and general seaborne trade expanded, it was logical to relocate the community to where such vital activity was taking place.

Such references as occur in national records relate mainly to Great Yarmouth – for example, the wreck of a French vessel bound for Bayonne, loaded with red herrings, which foundered near Lowestoft during a storm in January 1362.[19] A royal mandate was granted to the sheriffs of Suffolk and Norfolk to investigate the complaint made by the merchant who had sold the fish (John de Tryton), and by the four French buyers, that most of the cargo had been washed ashore and removed by local men. The investigators had the task of

[17] D. Butcher and I. Bunn, *Lowestoft Burning: The Fire of 1645* (Lowestoft, 2003), p. 5 (a Lowestoft Heritage Workshop Centre publication).

[18] Another fire of similar origins to that of 1645, but of much more limited extent (12 November 1717), is recorded in Gillingwater, *Lowestoft*, p. 63, using a contemporary report by the parish's vicar, John Tanner, as the source. It started in a fish-house at the back of what is now No. 58 High Street, and spread to similar buildings both north and south at Nos 55 and 56–7 and Nos 59–60. Luckily for the town as a whole, this was the only damage done. See also Butcher and Bunn, *Lowestoft Burning*, pp. 14–15.

[19] H.C. Maxwell Lyte (gen. ed.), *CPR, Edward III*, vol. 12 (London, 1912), p. 136.

establishing whether or not the goods could be classed as wreck and, if not, to carry out retrieval of the merchandise and see it returned to the rightful owners. It was one of many cases to appear in the Calendar of Patent Rolls during the fourteenth and fifteenth centuries concerning the legitimate (or illegal) acquisition of shipwrecked cargoes.

In theory, most (if not all) of Lowestoft's exports consisting of major foodstuffs and wool products should probably either have been shipped out of Yarmouth itself (having been given clearance) or have undergone scrutiny by its officers before leaving home waters. Observance of this procedure seems to have been extremely lax and early fifteenth-century returns for the port of Southampton show that cargoes of red herrings were being received from Lowestoft during the 1420s and 1430s.[20] They were also reaching the town from Yarmouth, but the years cited do not show arrivals from both places in the same twelve-month period. This may have been the result of variable trading patterns and fluctuations in the demand for cured fish; it might also have been a case of Lowestoft craftily slipping in to fill a gap in the market when its rival could not supply what was required. Direct commercial links with the capital are suggested by a London fishmonger, John Ingram, having tenancy of a customary fish-house in Lowestoft, which is referred to in his will of October 1441.[21]

Lining

The other main type of fishing practised in Lowestoft, in addition to drift-netting, was the method known as lining. This was carried out largely during the winter and spring, probably for cod and whiting during the former season and for rays (especially thornbacks) during the latter. Hand-operated draw nets (a type of seine) were also possibly worked along the shoreline for flatfish, and anything else that offered itself, during the summer and early autumn, but there is no firm evidence that this kind of fishing was in operation and the practice must therefore be conjectural (it was certainly well-established by the early modern period). Lining, however, was certainly done, being one of the most ancient means of fishing known to man: a baited hook, weighted down in the water and secured to the end of a hand-held line. What could be more basic and elemental?

[20] Woolgar, 'Seafood and late medieval diet', in D.J. Starkey, C. Reid and N. Ashcroft (eds), *England's Sea Fisheries* (London, 2000), p. 41.
[21] R.R. Sharpe (ed.), *Calendar of Wills Proved and Enrolled in the Court of Hustings, London*, part 2 (London, 1890), Roll 170 (52), p. 498.

Again, as with drift-netting, there is no written evidence known to the writer as to the specific size of the gear – but, given that it would have been carried out in small vessels close to shore and in relatively shallow waters, the hand-lines would have been of no great length. They would have been made of hemp twine, with a barbed iron hook tied to one end through an eye; the bait was secured to the hook and the line weighted down to lie on the seabed. By the late medieval period some of the hooks had been modified to incorporate a swivel at the end where the line was tied to prevent twisting round as the gear was hauled – a feature of particular use when handling large fish (especially cod) in deep water.[22] A sophisticated development of this kind would probably not have been required in the inshore reaches off Lowestoft, and the fishing operation itself would have been small in scale and perhaps comparable (in terms of the number of vessels and men involved) to the longshore activity of later times.

The catches taken by lining, being relatively small-scale, would probably have been consumed within the local area, serving to feed the Lowestoft population itself and inland communities within the proverbial day's travel of the town. Demersal fish were always gutted as the first step in processing, in order to remove the most perishable and contaminative parts, and this was followed by either dry-salting or brining, depending on what was to be done with them. If practice in early modern times is anything to go by, much (if not most) of a day's catch was sold directly on the beach to interested parties, who would then deal with what they had purchased in whatever way suited them. But, in due course, a type of lining was practised by some of the townsmen that was different in scale and location from anything which had preceded it.

It was carried out on what became known as the northern voyages, concentrated (loosely speaking) on Faeroe and Iceland – particularly the latter. At one time or another, vessels from Lynn, Wells, Blakeney and the Glaven ports, Cromer, Great Yarmouth, Lowestoft, Southwold, Walberswick, Dunwich, Aldeburgh, Orford, Woodbridge and Orwell Haven (Ipswich) were all involved, though not necessarily concurrently. It is not possible to give a precise date for the start of this fishery, but it was probably the result of English east coast ports (Scarborough particularly, in the first instance) working progressively further and further northwards in pursuit of cod. This species, because of the size it could attain, its comparative ease of curing and the many possible ways of preparing it for the table, had become one of the great European staples by the late medieval period. Exploitation of the southern

[22] M. Kowaleski, 'Fishing and fisheries in the Middle Ages: the western fisheries', in D.J. Starkey, C. Reid and N. Ashcroft (eds), *England's Sea Fisheries* (London, 2000), p. 27.

North Sea stocks by a number of interested nations eventually led to their craft moving to more and more distant locations in order to catch it.

In 1397 Iceland passed from the strict economic control of Norway to the looser jurisdiction of Denmark. The latter country declared a trade monopoly with its new territory, but then did nothing positive in the way of enforcing this and conducting any commercial traffic.[23] The particular time at which Iceland changed hands coincided with the disastrous aftermath of the volcanic eruption of Mount Hekla in 1389 and it is likely that the island's population might even have welcomed the arrival of foreigners to fish its waters and bring it trading opportunities. It is generally thought that East Anglian and other English vessels began to work off Iceland in the early fifteenth century, with 1408 sometimes cited as the year in which the voyages began.[24] The venture may well have started earlier than this, but attaching a precise date to it does not matter a great deal.

A decline in the herring and sprat fisheries along part of the Suffolk coast to the south of Lowestoft has been detected at this time, with Dunwich, Sizewell and Thorpeness cited as the communities affected.[25] There is no data available for Lowestoft, but the start of the northern voyages obviously occurred at a time of difficulty for some fishing stations and must have had an alleviating effect on their economies. Lining for cod in distant waters was not a one-sided activity and the outward leg of the voyage saw at least some of the East Anglian vessels taking various commodities with them to exchange for dried cod prepared by the Icelanders themselves. An upturn in the trade has been noted in the port of Ipswich at the end of the fifteenth century, and one particular ship's master carried woollen cloth, knitted caps, honey, linen and pig-iron northwards, leaving home at the end of April and returning in late August with a cargo of dried cod and wadmal cloth – a coarse, hard-wearing woollen material produced by the Icelanders themselves.[26] It is possible that this voyage was a trading one only, with no fishing carried out as part of the venture.

In Lowestoft's case (and, probably, in all of the other English fishing-stations involved), participation in the northern voyages meant using a completely different kind of craft from the type used in inshore lining. Broadly speaking, it had to be much larger, decked over and able to provide both living accommodation for the crew and storage space for the equipment used and the catches

[23] M. Kurlansky, *Cod* (London, 1998), p. 147.
[24] W. Childs, 'Fishing and fisheries in the Middle Ages: the eastern fisheries', in D.J. Starkey, C. Reid and N. Ashcroft (eds), *England's Sea Fisheries* (London, 2000), p. 22.
[25] Bailey, *Suffolk*, p. 277.
[26] Amor, *Ipswich*, p. 188.

of fish taken. Until the end of the seventeenth and the beginning of the eighteenth centuries (in Lowestoft's case, at least), when separate types of vessel were developed, fishing and trading craft were interchangeable, converting from one operation to the other as season and commercial opportunity dictated.[27] The barks, cogs, doggers and farkosts encountered in late medieval documentation were all stoutly built vessels with one or two square-rigged masts and with raised decks fore and aft, able to fish distant waters and perform other maritime activity as and when needed.[28] Lowestoft would have had to develop and build such craft for itself, down on the shoreline, just as it had contrived to do with its smaller boats, though whether or not specialist labour was brought in from outside to assist in the task must remain conjectural. Once constructed and pulled down into the water, the boats would have had to anchor up in the shallows, being too large to beach when not in use.

The 1618 manor roll shows that specialist shipbuilding took place at the southern end of the cliff where the ground began to drop away pronouncedly southwards, down towards beach level. Two or three main families were involved (particularly the Barnards) and the topography hereabouts lent itself to the activity, mainly because the lesser gradients resulted in the two southernmost scores, *Henfield* and *Lyers*, being much easier to use for the transporting of heavy materials (especially timber). Another thing in its favour was that the area was roughly aligned with the shingle bank separating Lake Lothing from the sea, a natural feature which served also to carry a roadway southwards to Kirkley and Pakefield and to other places further removed.

Reference to *The Denes*, as an area of common or waste, has already been made, but it served a number of other purposes as well. Until Lowestoft's harbour was built in 1827–30 (of limited size, at first), it functioned as an open-air wharf for all kinds of inward and outward merchandise (including fresh and processed fish); small craft were pulled up above the tide-line and beached; various kinds of associated equipment were left there; and fishing gear was mended and given preservative treatment against the detrimental effects of long exposure to salt water. Ropes, lines and nets were all periodically soaked in a tanning agent made from steeping oak or ash bark in water, and then spread out to dry on *The Denes* – some of the scrub vegetation which grew there even helping to keep the equipment up above the ground so that it could drain freely and benefit from the circulation of air.[29] At a much later

[27] Butcher, *Lowestoft*, pp. 163–4.

[28] For a compendium of medieval and early modern fishing terms see D. Butcher, *Rigged for River and Sea* (Hull, 2008).

[29] The term *barking*, to describe the preservation of herring nets, remained in use well into the twentieth century, even though bark had long ceased to be used, having been replaced by a solution of *cutch* (the gum of the tropical tree *Acacia catechu*) and boiling water.

date lines of posts with crossbars attached were erected to perform this task and some of the late nineteenth-/early twentieth-century ones can still be seen *in situ* at the northern end. They remained in use right into the 1970s for trawl gear.

Not a great deal is known about the part of Lowestoft's late medieval lining activity in the northern voyages, other than the fact that it was certainly involved from the mid–late fifteenth century onwards, if not earlier. The fishery, although profitable, tended to be a somewhat fragmentary affair because of a number of contributory factors. European enmities and conflicts tended to influence whether or not vessels sailed north; owners and masters may well have had their craft committed to other pursuits at the time of year that the fishing took place (broadly speaking, March–June); bad weather could easily disrupt planned activity; and, during the Hundred Years War period, there was always the chance that the monarch might require larger fishing and trading vessels for the transport of men and materials to France. Thus, the Iceland fishery did not observe a regular pattern, year by year, and the number of vessels involved tended to fluctuate.

The one constant factor was the method of fishing employed, a much larger-scale version of what was practised close to land in home waters. Again, as with drift-netting, very little written evidence of what was done is available, but a good late seventeenth-century source is able to provide a detailed insight and may (given the way that basic fishing techniques remain unchanged over long periods of time) be describing what took place over 200 years before.[30] The hand-lines used were ninety fathoms in length (540 feet), with a lead sinker six to seven pounds in weight attached to the end of them. Secured above this was a short iron bar known as a chop-stick, to each end of which was attached a length of line (a snood, or snud) bearing a baited hook – the bait itself consisting, almost certainly, of small cod and other unvalued species cut up into pieces.

The length of line reflected the considerable depth of water fished, but there were also occasions (beginning probably during the late fifteenth/early sixteenth century) when Englishmen fishermen worked closer to land, in shallower reaches, and employed longlines: a continuous length of lines tied end to end, weighted down onto the seabed, with snudded hooks set about nine feet apart alternating along the master-line. Such gear could be up to a mile or more in length and was unpopular with the native Icelanders, who believed that it was too efficient a means of capture and would result in depleted stocks. Whether or not the Lowestoft vessels employed this technique at any time is not known.

[30] J. Collins, *Salt and Fishery, a Discourse Thereof* (London, 1682), pp. 106–7.

Once the cod or ling (the other main species sought) had been hooked – this manifesting itself by a pull on the line being felt by the hands of the operator – it was hauled to the surface and brought inboard. It was then decapitated, gutted, split open, boned and rubbed with salt in a wooden trough. Following this treatment, it was sent down into the hold, where it joined its fellows in special compartments, all of them being laid head to tail in tiers with a further sprinkling of salt on each layer as the level built up. All the livers removed in the gutting process were kept and salted down in wooden casks, to be reduced (by boiling) to train oil when the vessel reached home.[31] This product was traditionally used to fuel oil-lamps and to dress leather once it had been tanned. Again, the processing described here is sixteenth- and seventeenth-century practice, but it may well have been close to what had been done in earlier times on the Iceland voyage.

The salting and drying carried out on board was often not the end of the matter regarding preparation of the fish for use or sale. Once a vessel had reached its home port the catch was unloaded and put ashore for further curative treatment (in Lowestoft's case, using the smaller inshore craft as ferry boats). The cod and ling were washed and partially dried before being reprocessed, and there were three main ways of doing this. One was to pound the fish with wooden clubs or mallets and leave them to dry out completely, thereby forming a type of *stockfish* able to be cooked in a variety of ways. Another was to lay them out and allow slow drying, to form what were known as *haberdines* – a better-quality product, but with the same culinary purposes. The last was to resalt them and pack into casks as a means of storage and conveyance – and maybe for even further curative treatment later on. In addition to the fish caught on the voyage, a number of the vessels involved also acquired stockfish from the Icelanders themselves (often by the exchange of goods carried on the outward part of the journey, as noted on p. 129), this having been produced by drying alone, in the open air, without the use of salt. It was of better quality than the English version and highly marketable.

By the early modern period Lowestoft had specialist open-sided buildings on the lower terraces of the cliff in which fish caught by lining were laid out on racks to dry. They were known as *barf-houses* and were used also for the salting of herrings prior to their being hung in the fish-houses for smoking. Whether or not these were a feature of medieval times is not known, but it is possible – particularly as lining became more important as an enterprise and increased catches were taken. Initially, before this means of fishing became larger in scale, it is likely that the species caught locally, if not to be eaten fresh, were salted and dried down on *The Denes* close to where they were

[31] The term derives from a Dutch word, *traen*, meaning 'oil'.

landed. The mix of sand and gravel to be found here, with its thin top-layer of salt-tolerant vegetation, would have lent itself to such use, and nor would it have been difficult to have constructed racks or poles on which to lay or hang the fish, if that was what was desired.[32]

Whatever the treatment given to cod and ling once it had been landed, one factor remained constant: its preparation prior to cooking. First of all, it had to have as much as possible of the preservative salt drawn out of it by long soaking in fresh water (up to three days, according to John Collins in *Salt and Fishery*). Then it was either boiled or roasted and flavoured with various marinades and sauces before being presented at table, usually with a range of vegetables. Given the expense of the sweeteners and spices that went into producing the flavouring agents, this kind of culinary practice would have taken place only in the more affluent houses. In poorer households the fish would probably have been mainly employed in producing stews and pottages.[33] Fresh fish would have been altogether more palatable and versatile, but was far less easy to obtain by people who did not live within a relatively easy distance of the sea.

This is why stockfish and the like, and white and red herrings, became so important. They remained usable for long periods of time and could be conveyed over considerable distances without deterioration. Nothing has been said about the cooking of herrings up till now, but they too were prepared in a number of ways, with all kinds of sauces used to add flavour; one favourite recipe was to make pies of them baked with spices inside a pastry case. This may well have applied to white (or pickled) herrings, as well as fresh ones, and it is interesting to note that one of the conditions of Norwich being granted its charter in 1122 was that it should make an annual gift to the monarch of twenty-four fresh herring pies (the source of these probably being Great Yarmouth). Red herrings were so well cured that they did not need to be cooked and could be skinned and eaten off the bone, just as they were – a practice that continued well into the twentieth century.

[32] In Iceland, especially, it was customary to tie split cod (in pairs) by the tail to poles or posts and leave them to dry. The term *stockfish* reflects this practice, as the first element derives from the Dutch word *stok*, meaning 'a pole'.

[33] For a range of recipes (ancient and more recent) relating to cod, see Kurlansky, *Cod*, *passim*.

The role of women

There is a strong possibility (it may even be a fact) that girls and women in fishing families were involved in helping to service and support the work carried out by their menfolk. Even in the Britain of today, female participation in aspects of the industry has not died out entirely in certain long-established maritime communities, which have managed to keep working in the face of the manifold difficulties that afflict deep-sea fishing as a means of livelihood. Again, no documentation has survived (if it ever existed) for Lowestoft – or anywhere else, as far as the writer is aware – to confirm female activity during medieval times. However, given the contribution made by women, young and old, along the British littoral fringe during the eighteenth, nineteenth and twentieth centuries – to say nothing of North European coastal regions – it seems reasonable to assume that earlier antecedents for the practice had once existed.

Two main areas of activity would have made use of female labour: the manufacture and repair of nets and lines (together with the preliminary spinning of the hempen twine from which they were made) and the curing and processing of catches. Some of the hemp would have been grown in Lowestoft itself, but the bulk of it would have been brought in from the hinterland – especially the Waveney Valley area. Fishing families would have worked as small collectives, producing and maintaining gear, and the contribution of the womenfolk would have been significant – particularly during the autumn herring season, when their carrying out of maintenance tasks during the two months or so that it lasted would have enabled the men to maximise the effort devoted to fishing itself and keep the boats working. Equally, with the handling of catches (again, particularly during the autumn), their input in processing both red herrings and the pickled variety would have increased the effectiveness of the total operation.

Once the town's general maritime trade had become established and began to increase in scale during the fourteenth and fifteenth centuries, some of the Lowestoft women would have found themselves as periodic surrogate heads of household simply because their husbands were away at sea for considerable lengths of time, the larger fishing craft switching over to the carriage of goods when not otherwise employed. It would be unwise to describe this situation as one of proto-emancipation on their part, but it would have given them an important role to play and may have enhanced their standing within the community. By the early modern period, the importance of leading mariners' wives (as well as those of the merchants involved in maritime activity) in the social fabric is plain to see, with an impressive degree of literacy in evidence on their part – and this was a process which was likely to have begun 200 to 300 years earlier.

A clash, or a combination, of interests?

In the absence of suitable documentation, one matter which cannot be satisfactorily resolved (and which should not, perhaps, be allowed to impact too obtrusively upon the overall narrative) is that of the organisation of the Lowestoft male workforce in meeting the labour requirements of both farming and fishing. Did both occupations, each of them essential to the community's well-being and viability, mesh together as a collective operation, or did they compete for the available manpower? There is no ready answer and, again – as in other matters – the only clues to hand are those which manifest themselves during the early modern period. Historical back-projection has, of necessity, to be exercised with some degree of caution, but it is the only means of assessing possible previous practice when documentation is not available.

Using a range of appropriate sources (including parish registers, probate material, manorial records and tithe accounts), it can be clearly demonstrated that between 1560 and 1750 farming and fishing were discrete activities.[34] The only area of overlap is that to be found in the tithe accounts of the eighteenth century, where a handful of seafarers can be seen cultivating small plots and yards within the built-up area of the town (growing root crops such as carrots and parsnips, for the most part) or keeping small numbers of poultry (especially geese).[35] It is reasonable to suppose from this data that, once maritime activity had become a major feature of the town's economy (especially with overseas and coastal trade added to the equation), agriculture required its own full-time operatives for successful practice.

During an earlier period, things may well have been different. At the time of the Hundred Roll (1274–5) it is entirely likely that the male inhabitants of Lowestoft carried out farming and fishing activity concurrently – the autumn herring season fitting in neatly with the completion of harvest and most autumn ploughing activity. Once the township had relocated, however, and sea-based enterprise (both fishing and carriage) become increasingly important, the two basic industries must have diverged, with each of them requiring its own dedicated labour force in order to function effectively. The separation would have been reinforced by the introduction of the cod-lining voyages to Iceland during the first half of the fifteenth century, an enterprise which further broadened the town's maritime horizons and kept part of its workforce away from home for months at a time.

Another imponderable regarding the town's adult male workforce is that concerning the bottom echelon. So-called unskilled labourers feature notice-

[34] Butcher, *Lowestoft*, pp. 61, 64, 69 and 71 (Tables 17–20).

[35] Butcher, *Lowestoft*, pp. 209, 217 and 218.

ably during the early modern period in Lowestoft's occupational structure (especially in the first half of the eighteenth century, with regard to both agriculture and building trades). But again, in the absence of documentary evidence, their presence during the medieval period cannot be established or confirmed. The writer is not even prepared to assume that it existed, because it may have been possible for the tenants of the demesne and villeinage lands described in the Hundred Roll to have worked their holdings themselves, with the help of family members. It has been observed that, with the bulk of English farmland distributed in relatively small parcels among households using family labour (a pattern established, certainly, by the fifteenth century), relatively few villagers had lands sufficiently extensive to need hired workers.[36]

Once the divergence of agriculture and sea-based trades had taken place, with an increasing proportion of the workforce drawn into the latter, a need for labourers to assist in the former may have been created, especially on lands held by men involved in maritime pursuits also. The manor roll of 1618 and the eighteenth-century parish tithe accounts clearly show a number of merchants and leading tradespeople involved in agriculture to a greater or lesser degree,[37] and it was a combination of interests which probably developed progressively during the second half of the fourteenth century and the first half of the fifteenth. Just how much menial labour was employed to work the land (if, indeed, such a group of workers existed in Lowestoft) can only be speculated upon – and, in any case, it would never have been a significant number of people. Thus the figure of the landless labourer earning his 1d–2d a day for routine tasks (enjoying increased remuneration only at harvest-time), with any female equivalent being paid about half the going rate, is but a shadowy presence at best – one without the means of having his (or her) existence verified.[38]

Maritime trade

In contrast with the wealth of data presented in Nicholas Amor's comprehensive and detailed study of trade and industry in the county town of Ipswich during the late medieval period, Lowestoft has very little information avail-

[36] J. Hatcher, 'Unreal wages', in B. Dodds and C.D. Liddy (eds), *Commercial Activity, Markets and Entrepreneurs in the Middle Ages* (Woodbridge, 2011), pp. 8 and 9.
[37] Butcher, *Lowestoft*, p. 218.
[38] Hatcher, 'Unreal wages', p. 10, cites the 1d–2d a day payment – a sum broadly in line with that given by J. Langdon, 'Minimum wages and unemployment rates in medieval England', in B. Dodds and C.D. Liddy (eds), *Commercial Activity, Markets and Entrepreneurs in the Middle Ages* (Woodbridge, 2011), pp. 30–32. The data in the latter case is drawn from records relating to the royal manor of Old Woodstock, 1256–1357.

able to create any kind of picture regarding its seaborne commerce, other than that relating directly to fishing. Until the year 1679 it had no standing as a port in its own right, being of *creek* status only under the authority of the head-port, Great Yarmouth. This meant (in theory, at least) that all its overseas and coastal traffic had either to exit or enter via the Norfolk town or be accounted for by its duly appointed officers. The inconvenience of this probably meant that, from its beginnings as a coastal trading station, Lowestoft avoided Yarmouth's legal control of its activity as much as it was able to.

Given the lack of customs or borough records of its own, it is not possible to create a coherent statement of the town's medieval maritime trading activity, and such evidence as does exist is slender. Reference has already been made in this chapter to the carriage of red herrings to the port of Southampton during the first half of the fifteenth century (p. 127) and further information relating to specifically named vessels engaged in marine traffic will be given in the next. There are five instances of Lowestoft craft being named in either the Calendar of Patent Rolls or Calendar of Close Rolls, in 1403 (twice), 1412, 1437 and 1457. This would seem to suggest that the town's maritime trade had probably become a pronounced feature of its overall economic structure by the later years of the fourteenth century, with reinforcement in terms of the number of vessels involved resulting from the opening-up of the Icelandic cod fishery during the early years of the fifteenth.

Also to be revealed in the next chapter is the carriage to London of a locally produced linen cloth known as *loesti*, which was then trans-shipped to Venice for distribution among Middle Eastern countries (p. 156). Nearer to home, a trading connection of some kind seems to have been established with Ipswich during the later part of the fifteenth century, because Lowestoft is shown as featuring in that town's petty court proceedings between 1486 and 1500 – a very small number of its inhabitants being involved in legal cases there. No such connection, drawing upon records available for the years 1400–1415, is evident at an earlier period.[39] An overland association (given the fifty-mile distance between the two towns) is most unlikely, so the link was probably one established by coastal trade of some sort.

No details are available for the size and carrying capacity of Lowestoft's medieval dual-purpose trading and fishing craft, but a national list of vessels returning from the Iceland voyage in 1533 shows the seven ships involved to have been in the range of fifty to seventy tons burden (see Appendix 4). A more extensive military survey record of 1544 lists fifteen craft in all for the town, with capacities ranging from fifty to 120 tons (*tuns*). It is likely that the earlier ships, mentioned above, were in the lower range of thirty to fifty tons,

[39] Amor, *Ipswich*, pp. 195 and 91 (Maps 4 and 6).

but there may also have been ones of greater size. In all probability, however, there was nothing sailing out of the town during the late fourteenth century of dimensions to compare with the Hanseatic cog found in the bed of the River Weser, at Bremen, in 1962 (it sank in 1380): seventy-six feet in length, twenty-five feet beam and fourteen feet high amidships, with a hold capacity of over 5,500 cubic feet, capable of carrying ninety tons (*tuns*) of cargo and drawing four feet of water unladen and seven feet loaded.[40]

Crewing levels on medieval vessels were high, with thirty hands cited for a craft of 120 tons (*tuns*) burden and twenty-seven for one of eighty tons.[41] Even further down the scale, with the number of men serving on smaller ships proportionately higher than that employed on larger ones, the overall total of adult males and boys actively engaged at sea would have been considerable, although there is no means, in Lowestoft's case, of estimating how many it might have been. During the early–mid fifteenth century merchant shipping's need for greater carrying capacity and improved seaworthiness resulted in the adoption of Mediterranean-influenced carvel-build (flush planking on the hull), as opposed to the traditional North European clinker method of construction (overlapping planks).

Methods of shipbuilding have been widely covered in a number of other publications and it is not intended to become engaged in the discussion here. Suffice it to say, however, that one of the Lowestoft vessels mentioned above was a kervyll (*sic*) named *The Michael* (November 1457). This shows that the new style of building ocean-going craft, with its greater strength in hull and decking and its improved handling qualities at sea, had been adopted by the town. Together with the advent of larger vessels and the increased use of timber came greater costs of construction and fitting-out, and it has been noted how (in the port of Ipswich, at least) the extra expenditure resulted in shared, rather than single, ownership of vessels.[42]

The middle years of the fifteenth century, from the 1440s to the 1470s, have been characterised as the time of the so-called 'Great Slump', when the national agrarian economy was undergoing what has been described as 'savage retrenchment' in the face of falling commodity prices, rising wage-costs and the consequent reduction in the demand for labour.[43] Poor harvests during the late 1430s had acted as a preamble of misfortune, while the European bullion shortage created liquidity problems among people involved in com-

[40] Amor, *Ipswich*, p. 80. The vessel's full carrying capacity was 5,650 cubic feet, or 141 *net tons* in modern maritime terminology. See *Tunnage* (Glossary) for a full explanation of space below decks.

[41] Amor, *Ipswich*, p. 79.

[42] Amor, *Ipswich*, pp. 136–7.

[43] Hatcher, 'Unreal wages', in B. Dodds and C.D. Liddy (eds), *Commercial Activity, Markets and Entrepreneurs in the Middle Ages* (Woodbridge, 2011), p. 11.

merce.[44] Then there was the matter of the Wars of the Roses, providing a backdrop of political instability in the country as a whole and mayhem in those areas of it unfortunate enough to be the venues for the major battles which periodically took place. Among the overall negative effects discernible on everyday trade was the decline in numbers of local markets and of the business carried on there.[45] It was a time of difficulty for nearly everybody involved in agriculture, manufacture or commerce.

Changing fortunes for the people engaged in maritime trade must have been an accepted part of the business, not only in the matter of the ebb and flow of economic trends but also because of the many risks involved. Overseas trade was at the mercy not simply of the elements but also of piracy and acts of war, as the volatile European political situation went through different phases and changes. Even coastal traffic – which formed the majority activity for most East Anglian ports and havens[46] – was not without its attendant risks, with even smaller, handier vessels than their deep-sea counterparts liable to founder on the many treacherous shoals that lay offshore. Even so, a detectable increase in affluence on the part of a number of Suffolk communities has been detected during the later medieval period, based on the littoral fringe's trade in leather and dairy produce and on fishing activity (including in Iceland). Between 1334 and 1524 (both years of nationally imposed subsidies) Aldeburgh, Lowestoft, Southwold, Walberswick and Woodbridge all increased their share of local taxable wealth.[47] And, in Lowestoft's case, the advances made were probably the largest of all five townships.

Conflict with Great Yarmouth

An examination of Lothingland Half-hundred's commercial differences with Great Yarmouth has already been made (pp. 49 and 58–60), and it is now time to look specifically at the rivalry between Great Yarmouth and Lowestoft – something that was partly the result of the Suffolk town becoming, firstly, the emerging force in Lothingland and, ultimately, its leading community. A four-man royal commission of 1228, previously mentioned, was authorised to investigate the causes of disputes between the Yarmouth burgesses and 'the men of Lothingland' (to use the terminology of the time) and to make rulings

[44] Amor, *Ipswich*, pp. 141 and 139.
[45] J. Hatcher, 'The great slump of the mid-fifteenth century', in R. Britnell and J. Hatcher, *Progress and Problems in Medieval England: Essays in Honour of Edward Miller* (Cambridge, 1996), pp. 245–6.
[46] Bailey, *Suffolk*, p. 130.
[47] Bailey, *Suffolk*, p. 282.

concerning them. Basically, their decisions favoured the Norfolk town, giving it primacy in matters of local trade but allowing traffic in lesser goods and victuals (i.e., not grain, wool, woven cloth or wine) to take place on the Suffolk side of the river.

The question as to whether or not this waterway was under Yarmouth's jurisdiction on the northern side and Lothingland's on the southern bank was also settled in the former's favour. A ruling was given that 'the same Water or Haven is but one port and not divided; and so passeth unto Beccles and Bungay, and divideth the two counties of Norfolk and Suffolk, and doth belong to Great Yarmouth only'.[48] There was no argument as to the clarity of that pronouncement: Yarmouth controlled the water on both banks and thus had the means to stifle Gorleston and Southtown. There was less certainty as to the interpretation of 'lesser victuals', once grain (and perhaps malt) and wine had been ruled out. For instance, were herrings to be included in this category? Their widespread use at the time must have elicited the answer 'no' from most right-thinking people. But the inhabitants of Lowestoft wouldn't have seen it that way – and therein lay the problem.

From early on, Yarmouth's autumn herring fair had drawn in fishermen from around the eastern and southern coasts of England and from Flanders and north-western France. It was one of the largest concourses of maritime activity of its kind anywhere in Europe. At some point during the thirteenth century the Cinque Ports (originally Dover, Hastings, Hythe, New Romney and Sandwich, with Rye and Winchelsea added later) were allowed to have partial control of its activities. This arrangement was fraught with difficulty from the start, with understandable resentment felt by the Yarmouth bailiffs and other leading townsmen at what they saw as outside interference from the Kentish officials (known as *barons*), and there was much ill-feeling between the opposing parties. Relationships became so strained towards the end of the thirteenth century that open conflict between their vessels even occurred, and periodic dissension continued for another 200 years until formal resolution of the disputes was made in 1575.[49] With continuing trouble of this nature to occupy it, the last thing that Great Yarmouth needed was a problem in its own backyard.

However, that was just what Lowestoft provided, as it began to develop its own civic and economic autonomy during the first half of the fourteenth century, and Yarmouth was quick to see the emerging threat to its own interests, particularly in the matter of the herring trade. Thus it was that, in 1357, at a time of great difficulty in the aftermath of the Black Death, it was able to use

[48] Ecclestone, *Manship's Great Yarmouth*, p. 96.
[49] Ecclestone, *Manship's Great Yarmouth*, pp. 102–8.

its considerable importance to the Crown (as a supplier of ships in times of war) to have a government ordinance passed in its favour. This particular Act of Parliament became known as The Statute of Herrings and it did a number of things to regularise the conduct of the autumn herring fair. These included confirming the *long hundred* measure of 120 fish as the standard means of reckoning, fixing the sale-price of *the last* (12,000 fresh fish and 10,000 cured) at 40s, ruling that no fish should be sold out at sea but be brought ashore in Yarmouth itself, and giving the town exclusive rights of landing and sale within seven leagues (*leucae*) of the town quay.

It was the last-mentioned clause that was the crucial one as far as both Yarmouth and Lowestoft were concerned, because everything hinged on the interpretation of the size of the league – or *leuk*, as it was sometimes rendered. This was a variable measure at the time, with accepted distances other than that customary later on, of three miles. As far as Yarmouth was concerned, it was a length of two miles, which put Lowestoft (nine miles distant) comfortably within its sphere of influence; to Lowestoft, however, it meant a statutory mile, and no more. Each side took a stand on its own interpretation of the distance and there then followed three centuries of argument and dispute as to the length of the *leuk*. A judgement of 1597, in Lowestoft's favour, fixed this at one mile only and ordered that a post be set up on the shoreline to mark the limit of Yarmouth's jurisdiction – an action that was duly carried out. However, the Norfolk town continued to contest the decision, and it wasn't until February 1662 that the House of Lords gave what became the final pronouncement in the matter and confirmed the earlier ruling. Just under a year later a new oak marker was put in place – and its successors continued to be erected right into the twentieth century.[50] Seventeen years later, in May 1679, Lowestoft freed itself of Yarmouth's influence further when it was granted port status in its own right and enabled to handle a wide range of goods other than fish – merchandise which, in theory at least, was supposed to have passed through Great Yarmouth first.[51]

Yarmouth's constant concern about its rival is understandable, not only from a commercial angle but also because of the trouble it was having with its harbour entrance at the time, which affected both incoming and outgoing traffic. The illustrations of Lothingland Half-hundred in Maps 1, 3 and 4 all demonstrate the problem: the lengthy sand-spit stretching southwards, which produced a narrow approach channel that was usable with ease only at high tide. This particular difficulty would not have affected the landing of herrings caught during the autumn season, because they were brought directly onto the

[50] Butcher, *Lowestoft*, p. 187.
[51] W.A. Shaw (ed.), *Calendar of Treasury Books*, vol. 5, ii (London, 1911), p. 1219.

Yarmouth denes and conveyed from there to wherever curing took place. But outward-bound processed fish packed in casks would have followed the route of the river out to sea, and from thence to whatever destinations awaited. By the 1330s the harbour entrance was beginning to cause major problems to the larger vessels using the port.

The southward movement of sand and gravel along the shoreline, caused by longshore drift, had not only caused elongation of the spit over many, many years but also resulted in the sanding-up of the entrance, and, because the flushing action of the ebb tide was greatly diminished by the length of the channel it was not able to keep the channel sufficiently clear to allow boats easy passage. Periodic blockages caused the river to find other exits and, between 1347 and 1560, seven of these altogether were made into entry- and exit-points. The last one, completed by a Dutchman, Joas Jonsson, in 1566 is still in operation today – though with a solid concrete southern pier having replaced his original stilted oak version in the early 1960s. A good account of the so-called Seven Havens can be found elsewhere and will therefore not be pursued any further here.[52]

Late fourteenth-century documentation admirably illustrates the cut and thrust of the contentious issue between Yarmouth and Lowestoft regarding the conduct of not only the autumn fishery but general maritime trade also. Beginning with a restating of the privileges of Yarmouth's local control by royal charter in August 1372, there were at least three repeals of this decision (April 1376, September 1381 and December 1385) and three restatements of its validity (November 1378, February 1385 and November 1386), as each side attempted to influence government thinking to its own advantage, using influential people of knightly status (county sheriffs, MPs and the like) to achieve what it wanted. Such changes of mind on the part of the king and his council probably resulted from what today would be termed parliamentary lobbying – a process which, on the evidence of the Lowestoft–Yarmouth dispute, has very long-established precedents indeed.

The charter of 1372 deserves detailed discussion because it provides a great deal of insight into the root causes of the friction and the local topographical conditions underlying it.[53] It makes reference to the obstruction of the Yarmouth harbour channel by the action of the sea and periodic storms and also to the detrimental effect this had had upon the town. There is mention, too, of Yarmouth's trading supremacy regarding herrings and other merchandise within seven leuks of the town (the length of a leuk not being defined) – privileges which were further reinforced by authorising that *Kirkelerode* (*sic*)

[52] Ecclestone, *Manship's Great Yarmouth*, pp. 74–87.

[53] H.C. Maxwell Lyte and A.E. Stamp (eds), *CoCR*, vol. 5 (London, 1916), pp. 224–5.

be annexed to it and stating that it was 'a place in the sea near the entrance of the port'. *Kirkley Roads*, as they were known, were the inshore reaches of the sea off Lowestoft and the coastal parishes to the north and south of it (loosely, Corton to Kessingland); but here was a new definition, with a real sting in the tail where Lowestoft was concerned.[54]

The entrance to the port of Yarmouth at the time of this declaration was located at the northern end of Corton (the first of the seven artificially created harbour entrances), and it was already experiencing the problems of its predecessor, eventually being superseded in 1393 by one much further to the north. However, it was the annexation of Kirkley Roads to become part of Yarmouth's jurisdiction, together with the identification of its northern limit as being near the harbour entrance, that caused real problems for the Suffolk town. Even if the leuk was only a mile in length, it still put Lowestoft well within Yarmouth's area of control and made it subject to any regulations regarding the landing and loading of goods. Even more threatening was the specific warning given to 'the men of Lowestoft' not to contravene any of the rulings made in Yarmouth's favour – something that left the town with only one realistic option, as far as its inhabitants were concerned: to flout the rules and get away with what it was able to.[55] This is a matter which will be investigated in the next chapter, along with Lowestoft's increasing involvement in both national and international trade and in the legislation which accompanied it.

[54] The term *Kirkley Roads* (and *Kirkley Haven*) has, over the years, led to much misunderstanding. Kirkley itself was never a port, or even a fishing station. Its fleet was mythical and could never have anchored up on the southern shore of Lake Lothing, as has been claimed, as the shingle bar at the mouth of the mere prevented passage. Kirkley Roads were given that particular name because the township of Kirkley (small though it was) was once closer to the sea than Lowestoft – a fact still reflected in the respective sitings of the two parish churches. Until Lowestoft moved to its new cliff-top location, it was sited inland and with relatively little maritime activity to distinguish it, hence a neighbouring community being chosen to give its name to the local inshore reaches of the North Sea. Up until the late twelfth century, and beyond, Lowestoft's involvement with the marine environment was subsidiary to agriculture; its relocation to the cliff-top signalled an important change.

[55] This book is, of course, primarily about Lowestoft (and the emphasis has, of necessity, to be placed there), but Great Yarmouth's history was inextricably linked with that of its rival throughout the whole of the late medieval period. For focused and perceptive studies of Yarmouth see the work of A.R. Saul: 'Great Yarmouth in the fourteenth century: a study in trade, society and politics' (unpub. PhD thesis, Univ. Oxford, 1975); 'The herring industry at Great Yarmouth, c. 1280–1400', *Norfolk Archaeology*, 38 (1981); 'English towns in the late Middle Ages: the case of Great Yarmouth', *Journal of Medieval History*, 8 (1982).

– 5 –

Misdemeanour and mishap in Kirkley Roads

Great Yarmouth's attempted control of Lowestoft and its trade came to an end only during the second half of the seventeenth century, when its legally backed dominance was ended and the Suffolk town placed beyond its jurisdiction. For 300 years the head-port viewed its upstart rival as 'a town of great smuggling' – not in the popular, clichéd sense of casks of spirits, packs of tobacco and bales of silk being brought ashore at night (an eighteenth-century image), but simply in reference to the evasion of customs duties payable on a wide range of commodities being imported and exported, at all times of day and night and at any time of year.[1] This chapter is intended to give the reader some idea of the problems faced by Great Yarmouth in its attempts not only to maintain its legally granted authority but to collect customs duties owing to the Crown (a major source of revenue) and to maintain some degree of order and legality within its area of head-port jurisdiction. For Lowestoft's part, the material presented will serve to show its growing commercial activity, its bending of the rules as far as it was able (or dared) to, and its place (as a coastal community) in the trade and politics of the nation.

The town's development as a maritime community is attested by the number of references to be found in public records of the fourteenth and fifteenth century, and Map 7 gives some idea of why so much activity took place close by. A safe anchorage for vessels was available between the outlying sandbanks and the shoreline in times of bad weather, as long as the channels between could be safely negotiated (particularly *The Stamford/Stanford* and the *St*

[1] A.R. Michell, 'The port and town of Great Yarmouth and its social and economic relationship with its neighbours on both sides of the sea, 1550–1714' (unpub. PhD thesis, Univ. Cambridge, 1978), p. 325, cites the description used here of Lowestoft.

Nicholas Gat). If not, then the banks could easily be the means of causing craft to founder, especially in north-easterly gales, with loss of life and property. In calmer conditions, though, *Kirkley Roads* – later to become known as *Lowestoft North Roads* and *South Roads* – provided a haven for shipping either locally bound or in transit for other destinations, both in England and on the continent.

There is a good description of its capacity, written on a map possibly drawn as a precursor of some kind to the survey of coastal defences carried out by the duke of Norfolk in May 1545, referred to above (p. 110). Here is what was said: 'From the Stamparde [Stanford] to Saint Nicholas Gat there is harbour for five hundred ships and they may ride at low water at eight fathom and may come to land at all times and hours what wind so ever blows and lieth five miles in length.' There are a number of other annotations, two of which give the depth of water at high tide in both the Stanford Channel and the St Nicholas Gat: three fathoms and five fathoms, respectively (eighteen feet and thirty feet).[2] The inshore shelter available off Great Yarmouth was nowhere near as good or extensive as that at Lowestoft, which is why so many vessels (even those headed for Yarmouth) laid up off the Suffolk town. And, while riding at anchor there, they were sufficiently far removed from the head-port and its officers for their operators to think that illegal trading activity was worth taking a chance on.

Customs duties had been applied to a number of standard goods exported from England towards the end of the thirteenth century, during the early years of Edward I's reign (1272–1307). Payment on the export of wool (the country's main staple) was imposed, as well as on sheepskins, hides, leather, lead, tin, butter, cheese, lard and grease. During the fourteenth century cloth and wax (beeswax) were added. There were standard rates of payment for each commodity, with 6s 8d being levied on each sack of wool and every 300 sheepskins (later reduced to 240) and 13s 4d on every *last* of hides (200 in number).[3] All other goods paid 3d per pound's worth of value. The first ten items named were classified as *ancient custom* and, after 1303, foreign merchants were required to pay an extra 50 per cent surcharge on them.[4] Certain imported products were also liable for the payment of duty – notably, wine, which was rated at 2s per tun and which seems to have been customed

[2] BL, Cottonian MSS. 1i/58/7950160.

[3] A sack of washed wool, ready for export, was generally reckoned at twenty-six stones in weight (364 pounds).

[4] These would have been non-resident ones, commonly referred to as *aliens*; those who lived in England for at least part of the year were usually called *denizens*.

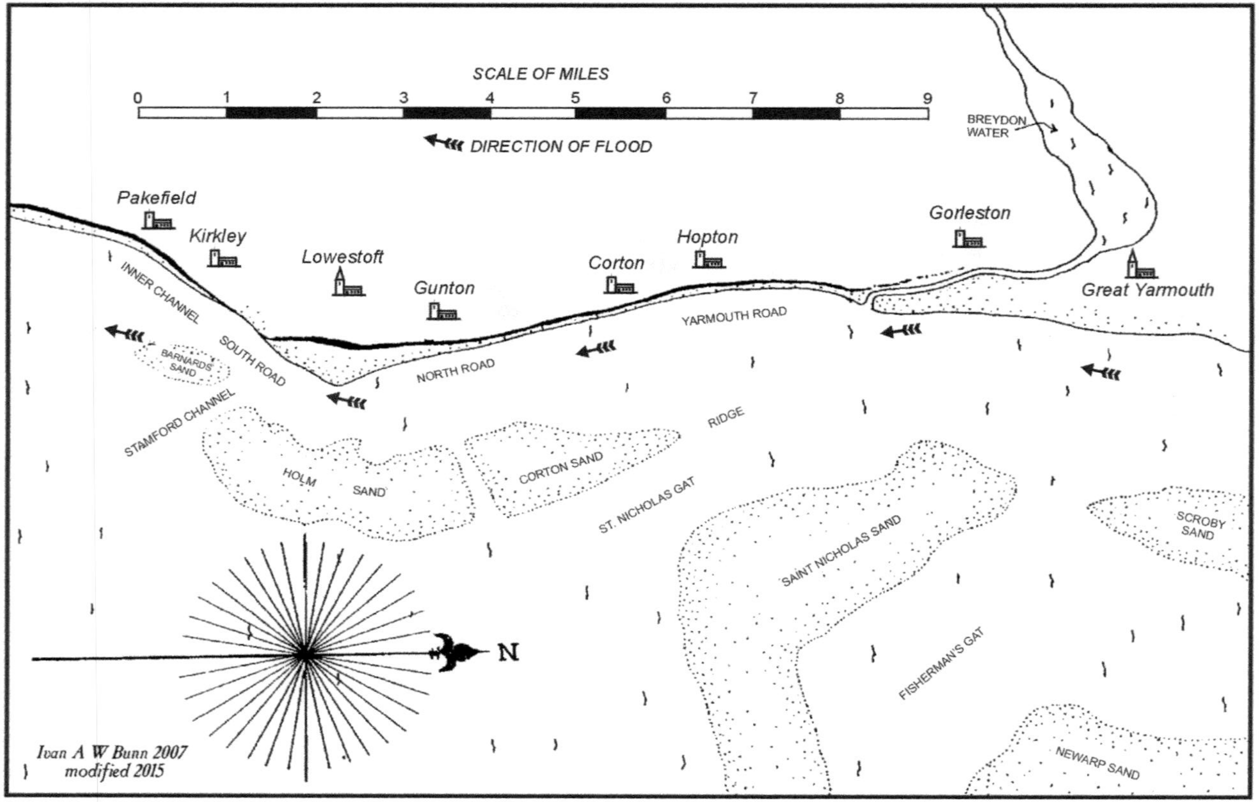

Map 7. The local coastline in the late eighteenth century.

Notes to Map 7:

- This shows how the Lothingland coastline looked by the late seventeenth century, with the sandspit forming the entrance to Yarmouth harbour now washed away by the rise in sea levels and by tidal action.
- Erosion had also destroyed the parish of Newton, leaving a narrow cliff-edge strip to become part of Corton.
- Although the offshore sandbanks changed from time to time in terms of size, this was not a major factor as far as navigation was concerned and their configuration remained basically the same.
- The Holm Sand, off Lowestoft, derived its name from OE *holm* (meaning 'small island'), which is probably indicative of the mass of marine sediment discernible at low tide.
- Breydon Water (with the rivers Yare, Bure and Waveney feeding into it) held a sufficient amount of tidal stream to provide a significant flushing action on the ebb, thereby enabling Yarmouth's harbour mouth to be kept largely clear of silt and sand.

early on in the fourteenth century (the levy had risen to 3s by the fifteenth century).

It has been noted how port towns occupied an important place in the urban hierarchy during medieval times, with eight of the twenty wealthiest English communities in 1334 (Lay Subsidy) being ports and seven of the most populous having the same status in 1377 (Poll Tax). By 1524 (Lay Subsidy), half of the country's wealthiest towns were seaports.[5] Great Yarmouth, with its area of jurisdiction covering most of the Norfolk and Suffolk coasts (from Blakeney to the Orwell estuary), would have been among them – its adjacent head-ports to either side being Lynn and Ipswich. It has been calculated that, in 1203–4, Yarmouth had 1.4 per cent of national overseas trade (Ipswich had 0.7 per cent); by 1478–82, it had declined to 1.0 per cent (Ipswich's share was 2.1 per cent).[6] In neither case was either port numbered among what might be termed as the 'big players'. That distinction went firstly to Boston, followed by Hull, Lynn, London and Southampton during the earlier phase cited, and to London, followed by Hull, Southampton and Bristol during the later one. What is not indicated in the figures is the importance of coastal trade, which went unrecorded in national customs records, but which would have played a vital role in the distribution of imported goods from the ports of entry to other coastal stations for sale and dispersal.[7] It would also have

[5] M. Kowaleski, 'Port towns: England and Wales, 1300–1540', in D.M. Palliser (ed.), *The Cambridge Urban History of Britain*, vol. 1 (Cambridge, 2000), p. 467.
[6] Kowaleski, 'Port towns', vol. 1, p. 477, Table 19.1.
[7] Kowaleski, 'Port towns', vol. 1, p. 480.

involved the use of smaller, handier craft than the ones employed in overseas carriage.

In the opinion of one leading maritime commentator, coastal trade might possibly have constituted 75 per cent of all English trading voyages and, in being carried out by smaller ships, was largely in the hands of owner–masters of vessels, such seafarers being the predominant presence in the command of craft up to around twenty tuns' carrying capacity.[8] In contrast to this pattern, ownership of the larger deep-sea trading ships tended to be vested in merchants of different kinds, who hired masters and crews for specific voyages and for the length of time these took. Rates of pay were agreed in advance and the mariners could choose to request right of *portage* on board the particular craft in which they served. This entailed their being allowed an allotted area of hold-space for the storage and conveyance of goods of their own, which could then be sold when their destination was reached – an arrangement which could stand in lieu of part, or even the whole of, their wages.[9] This privilege – which was collaborative one, not awarded on a purely individual basis – was most claimed on the wine run to France, where one *tun* (a measure of 252 gallons) free of freightage cost was allowed, but other victuals (notably, garlic, onions, herrings and grain) also had portage claims made.

Such flexibility regarding earnings may have been one factor in shipmasters of the medieval period developing a degree of entrepreneurial skill. Commanding a vessel which ventured overseas was a many-faceted responsibility, requiring navigational skills, commercial acumen, man-management ability, oversight of provisioning the ship, knowledge of foreign ports, awareness of danger(s) at sea, a certain grasp of maritime law, and knowledge also of the current European political situation.[10] Geoffrey Chaucer included a ship's commander among his assembly of pilgrims and the man of Dartmouth presented in *The Prologue to the Canterbury Tales* (begun c. 1387) may perhaps have been typical of a late fourteenth-century high-ranking mariner. The portrayal is not an entirely flattering one, with theft of cargo (wine from Bordeaux!) and acts of piracy attributed to him, but his navigational expertise is also referred to, as well as his extensive knowledge of the southern North Sea and the Mediterranean. Chaucer, as Comptroller of Customs in the port of London from 1374 to 1386, probably based his Shipman on people he had met in the everyday course of his official duties. For most of his period of

[8] Kowaleski, 'The shipmaster', in B. Dodds and C.D. Liddy (eds), *Commercial Activity, Markets and Entrepreneurs in the Middle Ages* (Woodbridge, 2011), pp. 168 and 170.
[9] Kowaleski, 'The shipmaster', pp. 174–5. See also J.P. Van Niekerk, *The Development of Insurance Law in the Netherlands, 1500–1800*, vol. 1 (Cape Town, 1998), p. 332.
[10] Kowaleski, 'The shipmaster', p. 165.

service he collected the levy due on wool, hides and skins, commodities to which wine was added in 1382. His salary was £10 per annum.

Imports

Wine

The earliest reference to any of the nationally taxable commodities in connection with Lowestoft concerns an order of December 1308, given to John Aleyn and Henry de Drayton (citizens of Great Yarmouth), to collect 2s per tun on imported wine in Yarmouth, Cromer, Blakeney and Kirkley.[11] Twenty-three years later, in October 1331, similar authorisation was given to Hamo de Borton, with Cromer being omitted – while, in September 1334, William de Wylimound was appointed to act in Kirkley and Yarmouth only, probably because to deal with north Norfolk as well would have been stretching his capabilities somewhat.[12] Some notion of the difficulties inherent in the duties of customs officers may be seen in an directive of December 1370 given to Hugh Fastolf of Great Yarmouth, sub-admiral of the king's fleet, ordering him to confiscate twenty tuns of uncustomed wine (5,040 gallons), plus the offending ship and its other cargo.[13] The vessel, of unnamed origins and identity, had anchored in Kirkley Roads and sold the wine to certain Norwich merchants, both parties hoping to gain by avoiding payment of the duty (amounting to the sum of £2 – a not inconsiderable amount, considering that a labourer of the time would probably have taken the best part of a year to earn this amount of money). There are other passing references to wine as part of vessels' cargoes in a number of recorded incidents other than those connected with smuggling, and these are sufficient to show that the importation of French wine was an important activity.

The chief port of dispatch for French wine was Bordeaux and its product to satisfy the English market consisted mainly of claret. There was a wide pattern of distribution for its reception and sale and the three East Anglian head-ports all played their part. During the late fourteenth century (1372–86) Lynn had 3.6 per cent of the ships involved in carriage, with 4.3 per cent of the overall carrying capacity; Yarmouth had 3.7 per cent and 3.9 per cent, respectively;

[11] H.C. Maxwell Lyte (gen. ed.), *CFR*, Edward II, vol. 2, p. 33. The wine in question was probably coming from Gascony.

[12] Maxwell Lyte, *CPR, Edward III*, vol. 2, p. 196, and vol. 3, p. 23. Further authorisations are to be found in October 1361 and February 1362: Maxwell Lyte, *CPR, Edward III*, pp. 92 and 75. *Kirkley* was a generic term used of the Lowestoft inshore area.

[13] H.C. Maxwell Lyte (gen. ed.), *CCR, Edward III*, vol. 13, p. 167.

and Ipswich, 3.2 per cent and 3.1 per cent. By the middle of the fifteenth century (1442–9) carriage had declined as follows: Lynn 1.9 per cent and 3.4 per cent; Yarmouth 0.7 per cent and 0.3 per cent; and Ipswich 1.5 per cent and 1.5 per cent. London, in comparison, had figures of 7.3 per cent and 9.9 per cent (1372–86) and 8.5 per cent and 12.7 per cent (1442–9). Altogether, the east coast ports (including London) had 32.7 per cent of the ships and 40.6 per cent of the carrying capacity during the earlier phase of the trade and 27.1 per cent and 34.9 per cent during the later one.[14] This shows that the greater share of traffic lay with ports along the south and south-west coasts of England, particularly in the later phase – which, given their proximity to the area of production of the wine, should come as no great surprise.

Exports

Wool and cloth

Of the main outgoing commodities, it may well be unsurprising that the most commonly referred to in terms of both general traffic and illegal conduct was wool, up to 35,000 *sacks* (364 lbs per unit) of which were exported annually during the early fourteenth century. English wool was highly rated on the European mainland for its length and durability of fibre and it always fetched a good price; hence the temptation to maximise profit by evading the high duty imposed upon it (half a mark per sack) – even though it could be a capital offence for any Englishmen caught offending. By the middle of the fourteenth century it seems to have become a problem for the authorities along much of the Suffolk coast, and in February 1343 a commission of five local men was authorised to arrest any craft smuggling wool and other goods at Ipswich, Orford, Dunwich and Kirkley. Less than three months later, in May, a Flemish vessel (the *Skynkewyn*, meaning 'wine-pourer') was arrested in Kirkley Roads for smuggling wool and, in November, continuing investigation in the area was ordered to be carried out by a man named John Sigor.[15]

A separate incident in June of the same year shows a government official named Saier Lorymer being authorised to deliver to Henry Speke and Haukyn Sunderman (a German?) forty quarters of wheat – or the money for this, if it had been sold – which had been taken from a ship arrested by him in

[14] Kowaleski, 'Port towns', p. 490, Table 19.6, in D.M. Palliser (ed.), *The Cambridge Urban History of Britain* (Cambridge, 2000).

[15] Maxwell Lyte, *CPR, Edward III*, vol. 6, pp. 27, 75 and 180. Amor, *Ipswich*, p. 60, refers to a craft named *Skenkewyn*, from Brouwershaven, carrying coloured cloth from the Suffolk port in 1368. It could well have been the same ship.

Kirkley Roads. The vessel had loaded in Newcastle-on-Tyne and was bound for Guelders (Gelderland, in central Holland). Certain uncustomed wool had been found on board, which did not belong to either of the men named and of which they had no knowledge.[16] Fifteen months later, in September 1344, Lorymer was ordered to sell, as quickly as he could and for the best possible price, 120 wool-fells (sheepskins, with the wool attached) and a sack and a *pocket* (half-sack) of wool, all of which had been found uncustomed in a Berwick-upon-Tweed ship called the *Godyer.*

Also to be sold at the same time was a mixed cargo belonging to a vessel called the *Nowell* from Picardy, in northern France, consisting of a pipe and rundlet of salmon, five *pers(e)* cloths (grey or blue-grey material) and thirty-one bird-bolts or arrows (*tribulos*).[17] But that wasn't the end of the matter, because in November 1344 it transpired that Lorymer had not acted upon his orders concerning both of the offending craft, but had committed their merchandise to the custody of Robert Rivsshale (Ryveshale), the Lowestoft constable, who was now withholding it from him on the orders of Thomas de Drayton (collector of customs in Great Yarmouth and citizen of the town). De Drayton, in his own turn, was now being required to return the goods to Saier Lorymer – presumably so that the latter could then sell the uncustomed cargoes as previously ordered to.[18] It is not possible to work out exactly what was going on between these three men, but some kind of corrupt practice may have been taking place, as the collection of customs duties was a notoriously dishonest activity. Another interesting aspect of this particular incident is the way in which two officials of bitterly opposed towns seemed to have sunk their civic differences in a matter of mutual advantage!

There seems to have been a lull in illegal activity during the 1350s and 1360s, which was probably at least partly the result of major disruption to all kinds of activity, economic and administrative, caused by the Black Death. However, general orders concerning the searching of ships in Kirkley Roads for uncustomed wool and wool-fells, as well as other merchandise, may be found during the 1370s, 1380s and 1390s, and specific examples of evasion of the tax due on the material continued well into the fifteenth century. In

[16] Maxwell Lyte, *CCR, Edward III*, vol. 7, p. 77. The two men named had either successfully argued their way out of a crime committed or had been used as unknowing 'mules' to convey illicit cargo. A *quarter* of wheat was eight *bushels* by volume and forty such units would have weighed about four tons.

[17] Maxwell Lyte, *CFR*, Edward III, vol. 5, p. 389. A *pipe* was a measure of 126 gallons, a *rundlet* one of eighteen. Fish was transported in casks and they were probably of the smaller capacity cited here, meaning seven containers in all (the salmon probably being salted). *Pipes* and *tuns* (the latter of double capacity at 252 gallons) were extremely large containers usually reserved for the bulk storage of wine where it was produced.

[18] Maxwell Lyte, *CCR, Edward III*, vol. 7, p. 427.

March 1408, for instance, John Drax, a serjeant-at-arms, was ordered to seize a Newcastle ship that had anchored up after being driven in by bad weather and fear of 'the King's enemies' and which was loaded with uncustomed wool, wool-fells, hides and other merchandise.[19] It was said that the cargo was intended for a continental port other than the official English point of reception at Calais, but there is no mention of where this was. A month later a request was recorded from a group of Berwick-on-Tweed merchants that the ship and its cargo be released.[20] It was claimed by them that the vessel, called the *George* of Camfer (Veere, in the province of Zeeland), had been legally loaded at Berwick, was bound for Middleburgh in Seland (Zeeland) and that false accusations of evasion of customs duty had been made. The plaintiffs were placed under the huge penalty of 1,000 marks (£666 13s 4d) if their claim proved to be incorrect, but the outcome is not known.

On occasion, it would seem that direct avoidance of the law concerning wool was carried out even by local people operating from their own coastline. In January 1444 one John Hampton was granted a *crayer* called the *Katerine* belonging to the port of Flysshyng (Flushing) in Seland, and also an accompanying boat.[21] Both craft belonged to, and were commanded by, Adrian Hughson, and they had been arrested early in December 1443 for smuggling wool. It was said that the boat had carried seven *fardels* (loads) of the commodity out to the crayer, leaving both vessels forfeit to the Crown after their arrest. No local people are named in connection with the offence, so presumably they had managed to avoid detection by some means or other.[22] A crayer was a small, single-masted trading craft and its boat (propelled by oars) would have been carried on board and used for a variety of tasks. Interestingly, the East Anglian herring boats, which worked directly off the beaches, were known as *fartill boats* – the first element deriving from *fardel*, meaning 'a pack' and thereby indicating limited carrying capacity.

Very occasionally, mistakenly confiscated wool was returned to the owners. One such example is to be found occurring in December 1398, when an order was given to customs officers in Great Yarmouth and Kirkley to make restitution of a cargo of wool and sheepskins.[23] The owners, John Grene and John Clyf of Grantham and John Belasisse and John Swaby of Lincoln, had petitioned that the ship carrying the merchandise – a vessel belonging to the town

[19] H.C. Maxwell Lyte (gen. ed.), *CPR, Henry IV*, vol. 3, p. 473.
[20] Maxwell Lyte, *CPR, Henry IV*, vol. 3 p. 475.
[21] H.C. Maxwell Lyte (gen. ed.), *CPR, Henry VI*, vol. 4, p. 229.
[22] Amor, *Ipswich*, pp. 122–3, notes an increase in local wool-smuggling activity after the duke of Burgundy had caused disruption to the normal pattern of trade by a declaration of war on England in 1436.
[23] H.C. Maxwell Lyte (gen. ed.), *CCR, Richard II*, vol. 6, p. 358.

of St Botolph (Boston) and owned by Robert Dey – be allowed to proceed to Calais, its cargo having been duly customed in its home-port. According to the official record, it had foundered and split in Kirkley Roads and (while no mention is made of this) it had also obviously undergone repair to its hull and become seaworthy once more, able to continue its journey to France.

In addition to export of the raw material itself, there is also evidence from the mid-fourteenth century onwards of a developing English cloth industry employing the skills of immigrant workers from Flanders. A general order of April 1347 to ports around the country laid down a scale of charges to be imposed on woollen cloth being sent abroad.[24] It gave two rates of payment: the first to be made by merchants living in England, the second (with the 50 per cent surcharge mentioned above) by those visiting from across the sea. Six types of material of varying size and type are referred to: assized, scarlet, mixed colour, worsted, single bed and double bed, with the appropriate charges to be levied.[25] Evidence of the government's interest in encouraging the native production of cloth may perhaps be seen in another general order, of February 1357, this time to bailiffs of ports along the whole of the east coast (including Kirkley Roads). It concerned a wide range of goods leaving the country that were not to be taken anywhere (on pain of forfeiture) except Bordeaux, Calais and Berwick-on-Tweed – ports under English control at the time – and the prohibited merchandise included woollen thread.[26]

Twenty-five years or so later, in May 1383, there was direct focus by the authorities on the Island of Lothingland and its inshore reaches, with an order being given to John Seynesbury and Henry Gryme of Suffolk to search all ships in Kirkley Road (the singular form was used), Lowestoft and Lothingland for uncustomed wool, wool-fells, hides, cloths and other merchandise.[27] Arrest(s) and confiscation(s) were to be carried out where appropriate. A decade on, and Lowestoft men were entrusted with the same task, only with a much wider area of scrutiny: from Blakeney to Ipswich.[28] William Spenser was the first one to be given the post of *searcher*, in February 1392, to be followed by Richard Reynkyn (Rankin) in August 1394 and William Denys and Robert Spexhale (Spexhall) in July 1395. It was possibly in recognition of Lowestoft's growing importance in the local area that such appointments were

[24] Maxwell Lyte, *CPR, Edward III*, vol. 7, p. 276.

[25] The *assized cloth* mentioned might well have been the standard English *broadcloth* of some twenty to thirty yards' length and two yards' width. The term *assized* itself suggests that the item had fulfilled an officially approved standard of size and quality.

[26] Maxwell Lyte, *CCR, Edward III*, vol. 10, p. 401.

[27] Maxwell Lyte, *CFR*, Richard II, vol. 9, p. 360. Note that the *Fine Roll* calendar series is numbered continuously across all the reigns covered and not *per* individual monarch.

[28] Maxwell Lyte, *CFR*, Richard II, vol. 11, pp. 30, 129 and 158.

made, with perhaps an element – in William Spenser's case, at least, given his limited geographical brief – of personal knowledge (experience, even!) of what was going on with regard to the evasion of customs.

One particular case from the early fourteenth century makes for interesting reading, as it shows something of the developing cloth-making industry in north-east Norfolk. Towards the end of May 1407 it was recorded that John Sudbury, the Yarmouth searcher, had seized a large quantity of *saye* and worsted from a boat making towards the *George* of Camfer – a craft mentioned above – which was lying in Kirkley Roads. The cloth was not *cocketed* (customed and approved) and had therefore been forfeited to the king. The owner of the goods, John Baxster of Honing, paid a £100 fine for his subterfuge, received a pardon and regained his merchandise.[29] Again, as in the case noted above, it would seem that the contraband material was being rowed out from the shoreline to a waiting vessel.

At other times, wool or cloth featured as items of salvage when vessels grounded on local sandbanks. One such occasion was recorded in May 1405, when the Lowestoft bailiff of Michael de la Pole (earl of Suffolk and lord of the manor of both Lowestoft and Lothingland) was ordered to surrender six and a half cloths salvaged from the *Godberade* of Camfer, owned and commanded by Arnold Johnsoun. The goods had been legally loaded at Kingston-upon-Hull and the vessel split in a storm off Lowestoft.[30] The bailiff, whoever he was, was (at least, on the face of things) acting in accordance with local manorial law, which gave right of foreshore to the lord of the half-hundred. The ordinance also stated that half the value of whatever was recovered from a wrecked vessel or was washed up on the beach went to the lord and the other half to the finder(s). The case here may have been one of genuine salvage of goods from a stricken ship which, after repair, was able to continue its journey (compare with the incident recorded above), or it could have been the result of an opportunity to take advantage of the craft's temporary misfortune.

Another overturning of action taken is to be found seven years later, in May 1412. The customs officials in Great Yarmouth were ordered to allow a Lowestoft ship called the *Katerine*, loaded with cloth and belonging to John Rothenhale and Stephen Wylof (Wyolf), to sail abroad. This directive countermanded a recent royal pronouncement that no vessel over thirty tons'

[29] Maxwell Lyte, *CPR, Henry IV*, vol. 3, p. 434. *Saye* and *worsted* were fine woollen cloths, the former sometimes containing silk thread. Honing was a village in the North Walsham area, close to the eponymous Worstead.

[30] H.C. Maxwell Lyte (gen. ed.), *CCR, Henry IV*, vol. 2, p. 443. The vessel was possibly the same one as that mentioned in Amor, *Ipswich*, p. 61, spelt there as *Godbered* and commanded by Andrew Jonessone. The name means 'God riding beside'.

(*tuns*) burden be allowed to do so without special licence from the Crown.[31] It was a measure meant to control the movements of larger craft capable of carrying sizeable cargoes overseas and sometimes containing merchandise the passage of which across the North Sea was not always considered (for economic or political reasons) to be in the national interest.

The web of international trade and diplomacy was a complex one and nowhere is this better illustrated than in a directive of May 1343, which sanctioned the loading of wool by merchants of the Society of the Bardi in certain English ports (London, Great Yarmouth and Boston) for sale on the Flanders staple (possibly, Antwerp). The duty payable was to be the standard 6s 8d per sack and the merchandise included thirty and a half sacks of Scottish wool confiscated, in June 1341, in Kirkley Roads.[32] This act had been carried out against 'the King's enemies' by Thomas de Drayton, the Yarmouth *customer*, the merchandise having been taken from the wreck of a Calais vessel and then passed on by him (for safekeeping) to John Toteler (Tuteler) and William, Robert and Thomas de Ryveshale of Lowestoft.[33] These four men were then to hold the goods on behalf of the king. The reference to the Society of the Bardi is a particularly interesting one, for the Bardi family (along with their associates, the Peruzzis and Frescobaldis) were Florentine bankers. All of them had been major lenders of funds to Edward I, Edward II and Edward III to help finance their wars, and it was the last-named of these monarchs, through his failure to repay loans taken out in the earliest phase of the Hundred Years War (beginning in 1337), who caused the Bardis and Peruzzis to go bankrupt.[34] The authorisation for the Bardis to purchase and ship wool abroad at a preferential rate of duty – to foreigners, at least – may therefore have been intended to be some small act of compensation to them for the money they had lost.

It will not have gone unnoticed that, throughout the whole of this section, nearly all of the references to wool and woollen cloth have related to areas of production other than local ones. This is because Suffolk sheep produced fleeces that were lighter in weight and quality than those deriving from other breeds and were therefore not as highly rated for export abroad.[35] The main use of the material, therefore, to produce lighter textiles within the home

[31] Maxwell Lyte, *CCR, Henry IV*, vol. 4, p. 273. The term *tuns burden* refers to a vessel's load-capacity in terms not of weight but of volume. Thirty tuns would have meant a cargo – or its equivalent – of 420 *rundlets* (eighteen-gallon casks used for wet or dry goods). By the end of the seventeenth century the word *ton-tun* had become differentiated, with the former referring to Imperial measure weight and the latter to liquid storage capacity.

[32] Maxwell Lyte, *CCR, Edward III*, vol. 7, p. 28.

[33] Maxwell Lyte, *CCR, Edward III*, vol. 6, p. 180.

[34] A.R. Myers, *England in the Late Middle Ages* (London, 1963), p. 66. Robert de Ryveshale is the man named as *constable* of Lowestoft on p. 151, but with a different spelling of the surname.

[35] Bailey, *Suffolk*, p. 171.

county was undoubtedly a major factor in establishing cloth-making as an industry (especially in south Suffolk) by as early as the end of the thirteenth century.

Linen cloth

Among the textiles shipped out of England during the fifteenth century was a fabric known in Venice (the main point of reception for it) as *loesti*. At least two specialist economic historians have noted its existence, one referring to it in the glossary of her book as a coarse cloth of the time and the other detecting it in commodity lists for Damascus (1413) and Alexandria (1424) and in judicial material relating to its importation into Beirut (1417).[36] It also features in the Venetian state papers on two or three occasions, most notably in November 1456, when *Lowesto cloth* is referred to among the commodities handled at the state's London factory. This centre of its English trading operations was heavily in debt as a result of bad administration (and probably corruption also) and the authorities were trying to raise money to clear what was owed by imposing surcharges on cargoes carried by its vessels returning from London. A levy of eight *grossi* (the *grosso* being a coin worth 3d) was therefore to be paid on every piece of the cloth landed.[37] The linen has been identified as a product of the Waveney Valley, in Lowestoft's hinterland, and as being exported from the town.[38] In light of the number of linen weavers living there during the early modern period, it is likely that some of the material was produced in Lowestoft before being taken to London for shipment to Venice.

Hides

Periodic orders made to local officials in all parts of the realm to search ships for various kinds of proscribed goods often included hides among the items to be either temporarily or permanently seized. Two examples are to be found above (pp. 151 and 153) in relation to the orders given to William Spenser and his successors (February 1392, August 1394 and July 1395) and John Drax (March 1408). Leather was a commodity of great importance and value in the pre-industrial world – not just for footwear, gloves and other items of cloth-

[36] K. Fleet, *European and Islamic Trade in the Early Ottoman State* (Cambridge, 2006), p. 177, and E. Ashtor, *Levant Trade in the Middle Ages* (Princeton, 1983), p. 326.
[37] R. Brown (ed.), *Calendar of State Papers Relating to English Affairs in the Archives of Venice*, vol. 1 (London, 1864), no. 334. This work (along with many others) is available at British History Online, a service provided by London University: www.british-history.ac.uk.
[38] E. Kerridge, *Textile Manufacture in Early Modern England* (Manchester, 1985) p. 23.

ing, but for all kinds of tools, equipment and utensils – and governments of the time were obviously concerned about the raw material being sent to destinations overseas. This would have been not only because of the loss of revenue caused by cargoes being uncustomed but also because the hides were needed at home for the manufacture of all kinds of necessary goods. Some idea of the scale of operation may perhaps be seen in just one example relating to the community of Lowestoft, where a sufficiency of hides, it might be felt, would have been available locally from surrounding agricultural communities. In November 1380 Geoffrey Richer, barker (tanner) of the town, was granted a licence to convey sixty *dickers* of hides (a dicker being a unit of ten) from Newcastle-on-Tyne to Kirkley Road.[39] A cargo of 600 cattle skins would have produced a lot of leather (as well as £2 in duty for the Crown)! It would also have required a considerable quantity of ash or oak bark to create the tanning agent.

Fish

Prominent among the foodstuffs sent abroad (not surprisingly, perhaps) were cured herrings. The case of a French ship loaded with red herrings wrecked in a storm off Lowestoft in January 1362 has already been mentioned (p. 126). The vessel (called the *Grace de Dieu*, commanded by Saundes Demay) was making for Bayonne, its home-port, and most of the cargo had been washed ashore, together with items of gear, and been removed by local men.[40] It was one of the many cases recorded where the distinction between legitimate salvaging and theft of property was somewhat blurred. Both sets of merchants involved in the transhipment (four men from Bayonne and the vendor from Great Yarmouth) had lodged an official complaint regarding the incident, and a royal mandate was issued to the sheriffs of Norfolk and Suffolk to investigate the matter and retrieve and return the goods to the rightful owners if they did not constitute legal wreck.

Two further connected references to cured herrings are to be found about three years later, in November and December 1364.[41] The fish could have been either red herrings or white (pickled) herrings, or both varieties – there is no way of telling – but the directive given to the Yarmouth bailiffs was clear. No quantity of fish sent out of the town was to exceed the amount permitted by royal licence and any failure to comply should result in forfeiture of the

[39] H.C. Maxwell Lyte (gen. ed.), *CPR, Richard II*, vol. 1, p. 553.
[40] Maxwell Lyte, *CPR, Edward III*, vol. 12, p. 75.
[41] Maxwell Lyte, *CCR, Edward III*, vol. 12, p. 36, and Maxwell Lyte, *CPR, Edward III*, vol. 13, p. 75.

cargo. The bailiffs were further advised that that the owners and masters of vessels were answerable for the movement of herrings within the realm so as to limit export abroad and prevent shortages at home. Within a fortnight authorisation was given to 'all sheriffs, mayors, bailiffs, masters and mariners' in Yarmouth and Kirkley Roads to search all ships loaded with cured herrings in order to ascertain whether the cargoes exceeded the amount allowed by royal mandate and whether such mandate was now being used by parties to whom no grant had been made.

The restriction on the export of herrings continued for quite some time without it ever becoming clear which cured form is referred to in the records. The only reference to red herrings is the one cited on the previous page, all others using the word *cured*. As a broad indication of type, it is probably true to say that reds were generally sent to France and Mediterranean countries, while the pickled variety were more favoured in northern Europe. Therefore, it was likely to have been red herrings which were the object of a grant made in March 1382 to three Flemish merchants from Sluys allowing them to sell anywhere in England a certain quantity of herrings destined for France and captured in Kirkley Road.[42] This revoked an earlier order authorising Thomas de Holland, earl of Kent (Richard II's brother), and his bailiffs to sell them in either London or Sandwich.[43]

Even as late as December 1403 attempted illegal shipping abroad was continuing, as shown in an order given to the Great Yarmouth bailiffs and customs officials to release seven vessels (five Yarmouth, one Lynn, one Lowestoft) arrested on suspicion of preparing to take herrings and wheat overseas). The Lowestoft vessel, called the *Katerine* (see p. 154), was commanded by Henry Shyngle, and its origins may have been one reason why a townsman, William Pye, was one of four people (two others were from Little Yarmouth, or Southtown, and one from Great Yarmouth itself) who undertook to guarantee passage of the craft to English ports after the cargoes had been customed.[44] They must have been serious in their undertaking, because they paid a 500 mark surety (£333 6s 8d) as a pledge of good intent – evidence, perhaps, of the wealth generated locally by maritime trade.

It is interesting to note the close co-operation between rivals in this matter, for, as in Lowestoft, the inhabitants of Southtown had no great liking for their large and (as they saw it) overbearing neighbour. However, in spite of the commercial rivalry between Great Yarmouth and its neighbours,

[42] Maxwell Lyte, *CPR, Richard II*, vol. 2, p. 99.

[43] Thomas de Holland had become lord of the manor in Lowestoft and Lothingland the previous year (June 1381).

[44] Maxwell Lyte, *CCR, Henry IV*, vol. 2, p. 199.

there were times when compromise proved possible – such as in the case of the agreement of February 1401 between the bailiffs and burgesses of the head-port and the townsmen of Lowestoft enabling the latter to buy and sell herrings and other foodstuffs and merchandise within the hours of daylight, and to engage with any merchants and fishermen except those from Holland and Zeeland *hosted* to Yarmouth itself. The sum of half a mark (6s 8d) was to be paid to the port authorities for each *last* of fresh herrings traded (12,000 fish).[45]

With the establishment of the east coast cod fishery trade during the early 1400s, and its continuation for the rest of the fifteenth century, occasional references to its products are encountered. In July 1437 a licence was granted to John Steyngate of Lowestoft, owner of two ships (the *George* and the *Peter*), to go fishing in the craft, which were not currently under royal requisition (for military purposes), and to buy and bring back to England 3,000 *stock-fish* (*fungarium*) for the household of William de la Pole, earl of Suffolk. An express command was given not to sail into any 'forbidden regions'.[46] The order clearly shows authorisation of a fishing expedition to Iceland, with the additional duty of purchasing (while there) locally produced stockfish – a highly rated commodity all over Europe. De la Pole was lord of the manor of Lowestoft and Lothingland (the family having risen from mercantile origins in Hull to aristocratic levels during the late fourteenth century) and he was obviously using his influence at court to secure food supplies for his domestic establishment.

'Northern fish', as it was sometimes termed, also featured in a directive to the Lowestoft constables in January 1454, when they were ordered to arrest and hold a ship from Cley, in north Norfolk, carrying a cargo of 2,872 salted ling and 940 salted cod which had been stolen from a man called Richard Arnold. The vessel's name is not given, but it was owned by John Auger and commanded by John atte Hoo, and the alleged intended place of sale for the merchandise was Queneburgh (Queenborough, Isle of Sheppey) in Kent.[47] Eighty or more years later, in August 1536, a letter from someone called Richard Tomyow to Thomas Cromwell, Lord Privy Seal, concerning supplies of fish for the latter's household, advised that 200 ling and 800 cod (salted)

[45] Maxwell Lyte, *CPR, Henry IV*, vol. 1, p. 428. *Hosting* was the term used in English fishing stations for the process of allowing vessels from other parts of the country (and from the European mainland) access to fish stocks for the duration of a season. It often included finding the visitors onshore accommodation, if needed, for the duration of their length of stay and attending to their needs.

[46] Maxwell Lyte, *CPR, Henry VI*, vol. 3, p. 72. *Forbidden regions* were Icelandic waters made out of bounds to foreign ships.

[47] Maxwell Lyte, *CPR, Henry VI*, vol. 6, p. 168.

would be sufficient, at a total cost of £30 – the merchandise usually being sent from Boston or Lowestoft.[48]

The key ingredient in preparing all of the merchandise referred to in this section was, of course, salt. It never appears in any of the documentation relating to export restriction, but it does feature occasionally as an incoming commodity. Two particularly interesting references are to be found from June and July 1387. Both were general orders, issued to officials in sundry ports on the east and south coasts and in Devon, to allow Dutch/Flemish ships to sell cargoes of salt (after payment of customs duty) and then return home. In the first one the mayor and bailiffs of Kirkley were so commanded with reference to specific vessels, all from the port of Campe (Kampen, a Hanseatic base on the River Ijssel): the *Godberode* (master, Gerarde Wilte), the *George* (master, Henry van Homme) and the *Godberode* (master, Walter Clut).[49] In the second directive, which followed five weeks later, the original instructions were modified to allow merchants from Seland (Zeeland) to sell cargoes of salt 'at retail and not in gross for the advantage and relief of the realm'. Allowing foreign traders to have the retail price for their product and not the usual wholesale value – and there was an additional perquisite for them in not having to pay the normal customs duty – suggests that there must have shortages of salt at the time.[50]

Wheat

Next in number in terms of references concerning the illegal (or restricted) shipment abroad of fish was wheat – and the East Anglian coastline generally would have been an ideal place from which to send outward cargoes of the grain, from one of the leading areas of production anywhere in the country. The first reference encountered is one from February 1311, when the order was given for a proclamation to be made in Kirkele Rode (*sic*) and adjoining towns, stating the king's prohibition of the export of victuals. Foreign merchants were said to have been congregating there, discharging their own cargoes and then buying victuals without paying customs duty on them.[51]

[48] Gairdner and Brodie, *LPFD, Henry VIII*, vol. 10, p. 133.
[49] Maxwell Lyte, *CCR, Richard II*, vol. 3, p. 246. The directive was obviously aimed at the mayor and bailiffs of Great Yarmouth, using the title of their area of maritime jurisdiction rather than that of the town itself. There would have been nothing unusual in any European port of the time having the same name used by different vessels (ref. *Godberode* – a name previously encountered on p. 154).
[50] Maxwell Lyte, *CCR, Richard II*, vol. 3, p. 332.
[51] H.C. Maxwell Lyte (gen. ed.), *CCR, Edward II (1307–13)*, p. 301. The four volumes covering the reign of this monarch are not numbered.

Thus, it would seem that the objection (in this case, at least) was to the evasion of customs, not necessarily to the shipping out of foodstuffs. The word victuals, of course, can cover a wide range of provisions, but there is no doubt that wheat would have been one of the main items as it is specifically referred to as a restricted commodity right into the middle of the sixteenth century. Barley, on the other hand (and the malt made from it), does not feature in the records relating to the Yarmouth–Lowestoft coastline, so presumably both commodities were mainly utilised for the baking of bread and the brewing of ale, leaving nothing significant in the way of surplus to be sold abroad.

Comment has been made, in the case of Suffolk, that some grain was drawn into international trade, especially when grown in coastal districts, such locations being conducive to the shipment of a product that was otherwise expensive to move overland because of its low value relative to its weight and bulk.[52] It has been further observed that most grain in the county c. 1300 was sold and consumed locally, with rye (a crop suited to the light soils of the coastal belt) comprising most of the grain shipped abroad and with its traffic largely taking place out of Ipswich.[53]

A salvage case of June 1323 gives some idea of the size of cargoes carried at the time on the larger trading vessels. Reference is made to a ship from Hythe, in Kent, which was wrecked in a storm near Kirkley (Roads) and from which ten and a half quarters of wheat and twelve pipes of wine were retrieved.[54] The full cargo was 195 quarters and fourteen pipes, so the bulk of the wine was saved but not the grain. The full complement of the foodstuff would have weighed something in the region of forty tons, while the beverage would have measured out at 1,764 gallons. If this volume of liquid had been racked off into eighteen-gallon *rundlets*, it would have meant ninety-eight such casks being on board. The corn, if bagged up in four-bushel sacks, would have resulted in 390 of them being stowed away in the hold.

There are occasions when the amount of corn leaving the country might appear to have been small, but as far as the government of the day was concerned there was obviously a perceived problem of some kind regarding its leaving English shores (probably, shortages in London).[55] In January 1356 an order was given to the bailiffs of Lynn (later, Bishop's Lynn and King's Lynn), and to all bailiffs of the east coast and Channel ports (including Kirkley

[52] Bailey, *Suffolk*, p. 169.
[53] Bailey, *Suffolk*, p. 169.
[54] Maxwell Lyte, *CCR, Edward II (1318–23)*, p. 660.
[55] It has been observed that prohibition of grain exports was the commonest form of government response in times of dearth. See J. Lee, 'Grain shortages in late medieval towns', in B. Dodds and C.D. Liddy (eds), *Commercial Activity, Markets and Entrepreneurs in the Middle Ages* (Woodbridge, 2011), p. 73.

Roads), that no pilgrims be permitted to leave the country before the coming Easter or take any corn with them, except that bound for Calais.[56] Given that the devastating effects of the Black Death (which had occurred less than ten years before) took decades to work through, in terms of the labour shortage resulting and the dearth of cereals caused, any 'leakage' of a key food resource would have been noted. It was mainly wealthy people who went on pilgrimage at the time, to the major European shrines and to the Holy Land, and it is entirely likely that members of the merchant class might well have taken the opportunity to carry stores of wheat with them on the ships they had hired for passage (or which they even owned) to sell in whatever port they landed at – either for profit or even to finance the pilgrimage itself.

Some idea of shortages of basic foodstuffs during the second half of the fourteenth century, especially in large urban centres (London particularly), may be had from a directive sent to the mayor and bailiffs of Dunwich and to the bailiffs of Lowestoft in March 1375. This required that William Neuport, citizen and fishmonger of London, be allowed to load 300 quarters of wheat, beans and peas and convey them to the city for the provisioning of the populace. A similar command was given regarding William Kelleshull, also citizen and fishmonger of London, regarding 200 quarters of the same items, with both these orders overriding any proclamations made as to the prohibition of grain and pulses being shipped out of areas of production.[57] Eight years later, in May 1383, an order was given to the bailiffs of Lowestoft (following the petition of John de Vautort of London) to release from arrest a crayer called the *George* (also of London) and allow it to sail to 'northern parts'. The destination is not revealed, but the vessel was carrying wheat and had been attacked by Frenchmen off Dunwich. The crew had left their craft, gone ashore to seek help and managed to regain control of it. They had then sailed to Lowestoft and put into Kirkley Roads, with the Dunwich men claiming salvage rights on the cargo for their part in the rescue.[58] The outcome of this questionable claim is not known.

Much earlier in the fourteenth century, during the famine of 1315–17, the shortage of grain became a national matter, not one relating just to the

[56] Maxwell Lyte, *CCR, Edward III*, vol. 10, p. 298.

[57] Maxwell Lyte, *CCR, Edward III*, vol. 14, p. 126. Lest it be thought strange that fishmongers were given the task of moving corn and pulses to the capital, their gild was one of the strongest and most influential in the city and, given the nature of their trade, its members would have had easy access to ships.

[58] Maxwell Lyte, *CCR, Richard II*, vol. 2, pp. 270–71. The use of the term 'bailiffs of Lowestoft' is probably a generic one, applying to the local authorities in the town, because there were no port officials bearing this title. There was only one *manorial bailiff* (or steward), but there would also have been officers responsible for maintaining law and order working under his supervision.

capital. Exports of corn and other victuals from English ports were forbidden and the customs duty on the import and export of corn, salt and fish was removed so as to facilitate traffic in these basic commodities and encourage their distribution. Finally, brewers in London were prohibited from making malt because of the more pressing need to use barley in the baking of bread.[59] The compulsion to fill empty stomachs was not simply a matter of fulfilling a basic human need; there was also a moral imperative imposed on the ruling authorities to ensure that food was made available equitably across all levels of society.

The case of seven East Anglian vessels (including one from Lowestoft) arrested in December 1403 on suspicion of exporting herrings and wheat was referred to on p. 158. There had been a similar incident noted two days earlier, as shown in an order given to the Colchester bailiffs and customs officials to release from arrest the *Margarete* of Lowestoft (master, John Clif) and the *Christofre* of Yarmouth (master, William Sweteman), after customs duties had been paid on the cargoes.[60] In neither matter is the destination of the ships given, but it was an English port (or ports) and thus perceived evasion of customs payment seems to have been the issue, not the prohibited export of foodstuffs abroad. The same three men who pledged themselves as guarantors in the case previously cited also acted in the same capacity here. Keeping track of the illegal shipment of wheat to foreign parts was an ongoing and widespread problem well into the sixteenth century. A record of 1536 stated that fines for the illegal export of grain were due to the Crown from Thomas Miller and Thomas Walter of Lynn, Ralph Seymonds of Cley, John Dey of Wiveton, Andrew Stubbes of Bungay and John Botswayne and Richard Willat of Lowestoft.[61] Four years later, in November 1540, John Lissle of Lowestoft reported that a fellow-townsman, Thomas Bocking (along with others), was engaged in the same illicit trade.[62]

[59] D. Keene, 'Crisis management in London's food supply, 1250–1500', in B. Dodds and C.D. Liddy (eds), *Commercial Activity, Markets and Entrepreneurs in the Middle Ages* (Woodbridge, 2011), pp. 58–9.

[60] Maxwell Lyte, *CCR, Henry IV*, vol. 2, p. 225. Use of French forms of both vessels' names is interesting and must have been the result either of some quasi-legal convention or of an individual clerk's whim.

[61] Gairdner and Brodie, *LPFD, Henry VIII*, vol. 10, p. 532.

[62] Gairdner and Brodie, *LPFD, Henry VIII*, vol. 16, p. 605.

Precious metals and currency

Perhaps the most interesting items being shipped out of the country (as well as being brought in) were not exports at all in the true sense of the word, appertaining to either raw materials or manufactured goods. They were gold and silver bullion and the coinage made from them. As early as January 1311 an order was given to John Aleyn and Henry de Dreyton (members of the Great Yarmouth ruling elite) to keep watch for the inward and outward movement of counterfeit money 'of less value than the King's sterling'. Anyone found involved in such traffic was to be arrested and the money confiscated, reminted and given to the king. At exactly the same time as this directive was made, Aleyn and a man named John Akle (Acle) were also appointed to be wardens and searchers of money in Yarmouth, Cromer, Blakeney and Kirkley,[63] which was as wide an area of scrutiny as that given to Aleyn and de Dreyton three years before, when they had been appointed to collect the 2s duty on imported wine.

More than fifty years later the only other recorded case of counterfeit currency entering the local area was considered at an inquisition held on the seashore in December 1362 before Hugh Fastolfe of Great Yarmouth, deputy to Sir Robert de Herle, the king's admiral. It was said that a man called William atte Wood, from Lukrus (Leuchars) by Saint Andrews, Scotland, had put into Kirkley Road in a ship called the *Palmedagh* from Scluse (Sluys) in Flanders (master, Giles the Beste). Atte Wood was accused of bringing with him 'false money called *Lucenburghes*' (Luxembourgs), to the value of 7s or more, which he had used in the town of Lowestoft to buy cloth and victuals.[64] The sum cited may not appear to have been very large to make purchases of the kind referred to, and nor are the types of cloth or foodstuffs specified, but the attempted deception is interesting in being yet another of the illegal practices carried out in a locality that was very much a frontier with the rest of Europe and the wider world beyond it.

One singular case which certainly seems to have transcended national boundaries was that of 1 August 1356, when grant of a commission to John Mayn, the king's serjeant-at-arms (a personal attendant of the monarch) was recorded. Mayn was given the task of investigating the arrest by Robert de Reveshale (the Lowestoft bailiff) of one 'Lumbard de Melan' (i.e. a Lombard, from Milan), who had been taken in possession of 390½ marks of gold (£260 6s 8d) stolen from his master. Reveshale (Ryveshale) and a man named John

[63] Maxwell Lyte, *CFR*, Edward II, vol. 2, pp. 80 and 82. Re-minting of any counterfeit money would have been possible at Bury St Edmunds.
[64] A.E. Stamp (ed.), *CIM*, vol. 3 (London, 1938), p. 186.

Bould, who had been present at the arrest, were summoned to appear at Westminster with the offender and the gold.[65] Upon the accused's arrival in London (recorded on 12 August), John Mayn was ordered to hand him over (as well as a man named John de Hanham) to Henry Pycard, king's butler, together with 389 marks of gold found in his possession (£259 6s 8d). The Lombard was named as Nicholas de Portu, of Milan, and on 21 October his release was authorised, together with that of de Hanham, no wrongdoing having been found. An order was also made for the gold to be restored to him.[66] The discrepancy in the two sums of money cited is a detail to be noted (it must reflect spending of some kind during settlement of the case), as is the introduction of John de Hanham, who was obviously a business associate of de Portu – perhaps even his employer.

Inward and outward movements of cash and bullion – especially the latter – were a matter of concern to governments during the late medieval period. The discovery of south and central America, and the rich deposits of gold and silver to be found there, had not yet occurred and there was a shortage of precious metals over much of Western Europe. Put simply (perhaps even simplistically), the continent could not produce enough from its own resources to meet spending requirements. The ever-increasing demand on the part of the wealthier levels of society for luxury items from the east (particularly India), such as silks, spices, dried fruits and sweetening agents, created a constant flow of cash abroad and the only way to deal with the resulting deflation was to periodically devalue the currency.[67] Hence the complaints in England, during the fourteenth and fifteenth centuries, about the shortage of 'good money' and the attempts by successive governments to exercise some kind of control on the movement of both cash and bullion in and out of the country.

In February 1333 an order was given to port bailiffs in England and Wales (including Kirkley Roads) to ensure that no silver (money, vessels and bullion) was taken out of the country without royal licence. Anyone found doing so was to be arrested and the silver confiscated.[68] Within six months of this directive Reginald Reynald, constable of Lowestoft, and Henry Tristram of Rokelound (Rockland), bailiff of Lothingland Half-hundred, were accused of allowing Scotsmen and others to take silver coins and silver and gold objects

[65] Maxwell Lyte, *CPR, Edward III*, vol. 10, p. 450.
[66] Maxwell Lyte, *CCR, Edward III*, vol. 10, pp. 298 and 281. Strict time-sequence in these records is not always observed and later dates can sometimes be found on preceding pages. *King's Butler* was the title accorded to the country's chief collector of customs.
[67] Myers, *Late Middle Ages*, p. 71.
[68] Maxwell Lyte, *CFR*, Edward III, vol. 4, p. 347.

out of the country in return for payments (i.e. bribes).[69] The outcome of this particular alleged contravention of national policy is not known.

Thirty years later, in December 1364, similar orders were being issued to the bailiffs of Hythe and to those of other east coast, south coast and West Country ports – including Kirkley Roads. No one was to go abroad without the king's special licence, and searches were to be made for money, gold, silver and jewels. Merchants were to be allowed passage, but only with as much money as was necessary for the conduct of business.[70] Less than a year later, in July 1365, a further order was issued to the Constable of Dover Castle, the Warden of the Cinque Ports and the bailiffs of other east coast, south coast and West Country ports (Kirkley Roads included) concerning the smuggling abroad of currency: all merchants and seamen would be required to swear an oath that no persons engaged in such activity were on board their vessels.[71]

The problem was an ongoing one. In October 1370 Reginald de Shouldham was authorised to search all vessels between Lynn and Kirkley for a range of contraband goods, including gold and silver (both coin and plate) and jewels. Any such items detected were to be seized and all sheriffs, mayors, bailiffs, lords (of manors), masters (of ships) and mariners were ordered to help him.[72] In late April 1383 John de Seynesbury and Henry Gryme were given a commission to investigate the export (without licence) not only of gold and jewels but also letters of exchange in Kirkley Road, Lowestoft and Lothingland (see p. 153 for other duties required of them).[73] The last-named items were what became known later as promissory notes, in which the drawer, or a designated surrogate, promised to hand over a certain sum of money on a certain date to a named payee. They were the forerunners of bank cheques and were also the means of currency leaving the country, even if such exchange was legitimate. This right of enquiry granted to Seynesbury and Gryme was reiterated a week later, in early May, with the addition of uncustomed wool, wool-fells, hides, cloths, papal bulls and letters prejudicial to the king. It also went into more detail concerning the valuables by specifically referring to coin, plate and bar in connection with the two precious metals.[74]

Similar commissions to the ones cited here are also to be found recorded in February 1392, August 1394 and July 1395. The first one was issued to William Spenser of Lowestoft (see p. 153), followed by others to Richard Reynkyn (Rankin) and to William Denys and Robert Spexhale (Spexhall),

[69] Maxwell Lyte, *CPR, Edward III*, vol. 2, p. 501.
[70] Maxwell Lyte, *CCR, Edward III*, vol. 12, pp. 90–91.
[71] Maxwell Lyte, *CCR, Edward III*, vol. 12, pp. 135–7.
[72] Maxwell Lyte, *CFR*, Edward III, vol. 8, p. 94.
[73] Maxwell Lyte, *CPR, Richard II*, vol. 2, p. 198.
[74] Maxwell Lyte, *CFR*, Richard II, vol. 9, p. 360.

all three of them men from the same town.[75] The length of coastline to be inspected, however, was much more extensive, stretching from Blakeney to Ipswich, and this might perhaps be taken as an indication of the size of the problem. The reason for such a course of action in the formal granting of the duty of coastal scrutiny and inspection lay in the shortage of silver to produce lower-value coinage particularly, and the men charged with implementing the royal command must have employed helpers in order to carry out the task effectively. The lack of readily available bullion in Western Europe generally was sufficiently serious to cause a trading depression during the mid-1390s that lasted for a period of about twenty years.[76]

Anti-government feeling

It is evident from the references to papal bulls and prejudicial letters found in government pronouncements of the time that there was sensitivity on the part of the Crown concerning possible disloyalty on the part of its subjects during the reigns of Edward III and his grandson and successor, Richard II. Lowestoft, in being a coastal station facing out to the continent of Europe (even though theoretically under the jurisdiction of Great Yarmouth), therefore became part of the wider world of politics, as well as that of trade. There were two main areas of concern for the monarchs: in generalised terms, problems caused by difficult relationships with the papacy and discontent of varying kinds (and degree) among their subjects.

Edward III had contested the papal right to appoint clergy to English benefices with the enactment (in 1351) of the first Statute of Provisors – a law reinforced two years later by the first Statute of Praemunire, which declared that jurisdiction over appointments belonged to the king's court and provided for the punishment of anyone who sought from the papal curia any legal advice or instruction contrary to the royal prerogative.[77] This put English clerics in a difficult position, with a possible conflict of interests between loyalty to their secular and spiritual leaders, and it was a dilemma which was perhaps felt more keenly by the regular clergy living in communities (monasteries and the like) than by those engaged in parish ministry. This was because the majority of English abbeys and priories were, ultimately, under the direction of a mother house located somewhere on the continent (particularly in France) which, in its own turn, was likely to incline to papal rule rather than

[75] Maxwell Lyte, *CFR*, Richard II, vol. 11, pp. 30, 129 and 158.
[76] Amor, *Ipswich*, pp. 49–50.
[77] Myers, *Late Middle Ages*, p. 83.

that of a foreign country. Between 1378 and 1417 the matter was made more complex because of division in the papacy known as The Great Schism, which resulted in an Italian pope making pronouncements from Rome and a French one doing the same from Avignon.

The first reference to papal documents coming into England (in a local context, at least) is found in December 1364, in the order recorded above, which also covered precious metals and currency. It is interesting to note that such items are listed with other potentially anti-government literature – a generalised classification which says a good deal about the attitude of government towards any kind of material emanating from Rome, no matter what its content. In April 1383 (again, in a reference previously cited twice), the commission granted to John de Seynesbury and Henry Gryme used the expression 'trafficking in papal bulls', which would seem to suggest that a significant quantity of documents was entering the country[78] – although there may well have been a degree of official exaggeration used in order to have the desired effect of creating some sense of the scale of the problem in the minds of the officials charged with controlling it.

Richard II was only sixteen years old at the time, so it is fair to presume that the opinions of his counsellors weighed as heavily as his own in shaping any policies regarding the papacy. The Rome–Avignon split, with the rival claims made by Urban VI and Clement VII and the resultant conflicting loyalties among clergy all over Europe, created a complex state of affairs. There was pronounced anti-papal feeling in England at the time, reinforced among the educated classes by growing adherence to the teachings of John Wyclif, which encouraged an individual approach to the interpretation of Scripture without reliance on received teaching and authority. There were many people in England not prepared to go as far as Wyclif in his opinions regarding the governance of the church and the validity of its sacraments, but there still remained remained a general dissatisfaction with papal leadership. The order of 1383 regarding the potentially subversive nature of papal literature was still being repeated a decade later, when the composite directives issued were continuing to show official concern at the entry into the country of such material.

The later years of Edward III's long reign (1327–77) were troubled ones, with growing dissatisfaction at the way the ageing king was exercising his authority, and much of his successor Richard II's time on the throne (1377–99) was also fraught with difficulty of one kind or another. References in

[78] A bull was an edict, mandate or grant of some kind, named after the official lead seal (*bulla*) attached to it. The classical Latin word *bulla* meant 'a bubble', giving some idea of the shape of papal seals.

both 1364 and 1365 – previously cited with regard to the carriage of money and precious metals out of the country – refer also to anti-government literature being taken abroad. The word sedition was not current at this time, but this seems very much to have been the Crown's perception regarding the proscribed material, whatever it was (there are no specific details given). There was conflict with the Papacy, as noted above, regarding its claimed rights in the matter of controlling the English Church; the tide had begun to turn against England in the Hundred Years War; and there were continuing economic and social problems resulting from the Black Death.[79] All of these factors combined, in one way or another, to create discontent among the population as a whole and encourage those who felt sufficiently strongly (and who were able to do so) to express their opinions to contacts overseas – both fellow countrymen and foreigners.

Richard II faced his first great challenge, at the age of fourteen, in 1381: The Peasants' Revolt. The courage he showed in confronting the rebels at Smithfield played a large part in the successful suppression of the uprising, but he then had the best part of a decade to learn the arts of kingship and the harsh realities of political manoeuvring before he was able to govern in the way he wanted. His excessive cultivation of the royal persona was one of the factors that ultimately led to his downfall and, in the shorter term, made him sensitive to criticism of his style of government. Again, as had been the case with his grandfather thirty years before, the searches of ships for literature deemed prejudicial to the monarch (which were authorised during the early 1390s) show a combination of resentment at papal interference (as it was perceived to be) in English affairs and concern for any show of disloyalty towards the Crown on the part of residents of the country and expatriates alike.

Perhaps the most interesting of all the incidents associated with Richard II's reign, which had a connection with Lowestoft, concerns his banishment in September 1398 of the duke of Hereford and duke of Norfolk. The former, Henry Bolingbroke (Richard's uncle), was exiled for ten years and the latter, Thomas Mowbray, for life. The two peers' rivalry and expulsion forms a key moment in the opening act of Shakespeare's play *Richard II* (Scene 3). It was Mowbray's departure from English shores which was both witnessed and confirmed by the townspeople of Lowestoft.[80] On 19 October, at two o'clock in the afternoon, the duke embarked on board a ship with a company of thirty people (servants, retainers and the like) to cross to Dordrecht. The taking leave of his native land was attested by Thomas Thornton (king's searcher),

[79] A further serious outbreak of plague in 1361 did not help in the cause of restoring stability.

[80] C. Given-Wilson et al. (eds), *PRME*, C65/59. The source used here was the digitised one, provided by British History Online: www.british-history.ac.uk.

men of Lowestoft Geoffrey Richer, John Boof, Geoffrey Palmer, Stephen Wyolf, John Lacy Snr, Richard Reynkyn (Rankin), William Wymer, William Spencer and Thomas Calke (Chalk), and others – William Menhyr, Edmund Billingford and Robert Spryg. It was said that more 1,000 people had assembled to watch. If the authorities had chosen Lowestoft as the embarkation point in preference to Yarmouth because it was smaller and less well known, their hopes of keeping the event low-key seem not to have worked.

Contrasting with this notable example of banishment under a royal order is the attempted restriction of people's movement abroad at various times. The embargo of January 1356 on pilgrims travelling for Easter devotion at continental shrines and taking grain with them has already been referred to (pp. 161–2). In April the following year an order was given to the sheriffs of London and the bailiffs of various ports (including Kirkley Roads) that no religious persons (or any others) be allowed to cross the seas without the king's special licence and that no Augustinian friars were to leave the land, even though granted licence to do so.[81] Pilgrims featured again in June 1362, along with men-at-arms and archers (plus their horses and weapons)[82] – this latter category being not without interest, as the Treaty of Bretigny had ended the first phase of the Hundred Years War in 1360. Two years later, in December 1364, restrictions on travel abroad were still being imposed, with movement out of the country possible only with royal approval.[83]

Foreign conflict

Many of the incidents and cases already cited took place against a backdrop of the country's wars, notably those with France and Scotland. Ongoing strife with the latter nation is revealed in orders issued to Thomas de Drayton, the Yarmouth collector of customs, in November and December 1340. The first of these required him to bring the bishop of Man under safe conduct to London, so that he might be examined in matters concerning the king – his ship having been driven ashore near Lowestoft while on a voyage to Rome. The other people on board, and the vessel's goods, were to be kept in safe custody until further notice, and a valuation of the ship and its contents was to be made. John Tuteler and Robert de Ryveshale, of Lowestoft, were the men entrusted with this supervision and, in due course, they were ordered to

[81] Maxwell Lyte, *CCR, Edward III*, vol. 10, p. 393. The term *religious persons* applied to anyone in holy orders.
[82] Maxwell Lyte, *CCR, Edward III*, vol. 11, pp. 405–6.
[83] Maxwell Lyte, *CCR, Edward III*, vol. 12, pp. 90–91.

release the bishop's goods and chattels (and, presumably, the crew), as it had been established that he and his men were loyal to the king.[84]

Six months later, in June 1341, another incident involving a Scottish ship was noted – one that has already been referred to in connection with thirty and a half sacks of confiscated wool taken in Kirkley Roads (see p. 155), though the *Close Rolls* source cited talks about a Calais vessel. The Patent Rolls contain a great deal more in the way of information and say that the wrecked craft was Scottish. In addition to the wool (worth £61), it was carrying sixty dickers of hides (£20), sixty wool-fells (15s), and sail and cable (10s).[85] These items of salvage had been taken by John Tuteler, William de Ryveshale, Robert de Ryveshale and Thomas de Ryveshale of Lowestoft, with lesser cargo and parts of the vessel in the hands of other men. Reginald de Brundale (Brundall) was in possession of twelve hides (worth 8s), twelve wool-fells (3s) and a yard (3s), while Edmund Ode, Geoffrey Grym, John Grym, William Deckne, James Hulot, Richard Reynald and Adam Hoddon had timber of no great value, and John de Dope 18d worth of wool. In resolution of the matter, Tuteler and the Ryveshales were allowed to keep the hides, but had to surrender the wool and sheepskins to the Crown.[86]

Further evidence of conflict with Scotland is to be seen in December 1342, in the authorisation given to James de Artefeld to release a Calais ship (master, John Petreman) loaded with wool, hides and other merchandise at Aberdeen and driven into Kirkley Roads by a storm. The vessel was sailing under the *cocket* (customs authority) of David de Bruys (Bruce), the king's enemy, and had therefore been arrested by John Totiller (Tuteler) and others of Lowestoft. The vessel was to be released in exchange for one belonging to John de Eccles, which had been arrested in Bruges at the request of John Petreman – the request for this to be done having been made by Margery de Reveshale (Ryveshale) and John de Eccles himself.[87] De Bruce was king of Scotland and the arrest of the Calais ship, with Scottish goods on board, was legal under the terms of warfare of the time (and those of any other time). The web of international trading connections is made clear in the retaliatory arrest of the local ship in Bruges and shows the way in which

[84] Maxwell Lyte, *CCR, Edward III*, vol. 5, pp. 573 and 594. The Diocese of Man consisted of the island of that name, plus the isles of Iona, Bute and Skye.

[85] Maxwell Lyte, *CPR, Edward III*, vol. 5, p. 220.

[86] Reginald de Brundale, Edmund Ode, Geoffrey Grym, John Grym, William Deckne, James Hulot and Richard Reynald were either listed in the 1327 Lay Subsidy (see p. 62) or of families having members referred to there. The Tuteler family had moved into Lowestoft from Kirkley. The *yard* referred to in connection with Reginald de Brundale was a spar from which a sail hung and which had become separated from the mast.

[87] Maxwell Lyte, *CCR, Edward III*, vol. 6, p. 693.

communication could be made with the European mainland using the seaways as the means.

Eventually, in 1369, a truce (lasting fourteen years) was established between England and Scotland and an order of 10 May that year shows the change in official attitude towards the country's traditional enemy. Robert de Aston (king's admiral), or his lieutenant in Great Yarmouth and neighbouring parts, was to enquire into the loss of goods suffered by William de Lyth (Leith), John Wode, John Foldmouth and other merchants of Aberdeen and to make full restitution to them or their attorneys. The merchants had loaded the *Seint Marie* of Westcapel (West-Kappell) in Seland (Zeeland) at the port of Lescluses (Sluys) with 100 tuns of wheat flour, ten lasts of herrings (pickled fish) and various other goods to the value of £1,000, and also with gold and silver coins and silver bullion worth £500. The vessel, commanded by William Mone, had been wrecked on the return journey to Aberdeen off the coast of Kyrkeleyrode (*sic*), though the master had survived the mishap and the stricken craft could not therefore be termed a wreck (a legal technicality of some kind). Men from Kirkley, Corton and Lowestoft had taken the goods washed ashore and asked the king to make provision for their recovery.[88]

A different perspective is given in other accounts of the incident. In June 1369 an assize session of *oyer and terminer* was granted to William de Wychyngham (Witchingham), Edmund Gourneye (Gurney), John de Bernye (Berney) and Reynold de Eccles concerning 'evildoers' who had broken a vessel called the *Seint Marie* and carried away cargo.[89] The inquisition was eventually held at South Yarmouth (Southtown) on 19 December and it was reported there that everyone on board had died, except William Mone, who was named as both master and owner of the vessel. It was carrying coin, linen cloth, tackle (possibly, ropes and blocks), wax, pepper, ginger, furs, madder, alum and other merchandise, which had been washed ashore in late January. William Lucy (Lacy) Snr and others had seized £102 worth of the goods.[90] The detail given regarding the cargo shows that it was of high value and gives some idea of mixed carriage of the time.

The matter seems not to have been resolved, because in March 1370 a similar right of trial was granted to William de Wychyngham, Nicholas de Tamworth, Hugh Fastolf and William de Tamworth on the complaint of the following Scottish merchants: William Lyth, James Henrison, Thomas Marcher, John Wode, Thomas Recyvet, John Scot, Adam de Dalgarnok, Walter Gopeld, Simon de Abbeye, Alan Hog and Thomas Clerk. Two vessels, the

[88] Maxwell Lyte, *CCR, Edward III*, vol. 13, p. 27.
[89] Maxwell Lyte, *CPR, Edward III*, vol. 14, p. 343.
[90] D.L. Evans (ed.), *CIM*, vol. 4 (London, 1957), p. 282.

Seint Marie of Zeeland (master, William Mone) and the *Seint Anne* of Cagent (*sic*) in Flanders (owner–master, Florence Johanneson) had loaded with cargo at Lescluses for passage to Scotland and been driven ashore in a tempest at Kirkley Road. Robert Clerk of Lyth (Leith) and Richard de Waldaston of the *Seint Marie* had laid claim to the cargoes on behalf of the rightful owners, but local men had stolen the goods, in contravention of the treaty between England and Scotland.[91] Three months later, in June 1370, a commission was given to Edmund de Thorpe, sheriff of Norfolk and Suffolk, and to John de Berneye, Reynold de Eccles and John de Lakynghethe (Lakenheath), keepers of the peace (JPs), to investigate the case, see that the goods were returned to the rightful owners and arrest anyone who refused to hand over stolen property.[92]

The long-term enmity between England and both Scotland and France (these latter two countries often being in alliance) is seen more in terms of Scottish vessels rather than French ones being apprehended, which may have had something to do with the traditional trading routes taken by the ships. Sometimes, as in the case cited in the previous paragraph, the demarcation between what was legitimate and what was not tended to become blurred, but there were also occasions where government directives left no doubt as to which course of action should be taken. In October 1415, for instance, Stephen Wyoll (Wyolf) and John Wryght of Lowestoft were among twenty-one Norfolk and Suffolk men appointed to 'keep the sea' for the protection of fishermen and other subjects. The other ports and havens represented were Dersingham, Wiveton, Cley, Salthouse, Cromer, Winterton, Yarmouth, Covehithe, Easton, Southwold and Aldeburgh, and specific orders were given that no goods were to be taken from any vessel, except French and Scottish ones.[93] A relative of John Wryght named William had been chosen in January the same year by Thomas Chaucer, the chief butler (head collector of customs), to serve as customer in Kirkley and Yarmouth, and this was followed in December by Stephen Wyolf being similarly authorised.[94] What the burgesses and bailiffs of Great Yarmouth thought of such appointments can only be guessed at.

The year 1415 was one which saw Henry V invade France (in a major renewal of engagement in the Hundred Years War) and win his great victory at Agincourt. Another thirty-eight years was to pass before the conflict finally ended, but even in the final, sporadic years aspects of its conduct

[91] Maxwell Lyte, *CPR, Edward III*, vol. 14, p. 424.
[92] Maxwell Lyte, *CPR, Edward III*, vol. 14, p. 471.
[93] H.C. Maxwell Lyte (gen. ed.), *CPR, Henry V*, vol. 1, p. 363.
[94] Maxwell Lyte, *CPR, Henry V*, pp. 272 and 400. Chaucer was son of Geoffrey Chaucer, the poet – a previous holder of the post.

manifested themselves in local maritime activity. In June 1442 Miles Stapleton (lord of a manor in Kessingland, which bore his family's name) was authorised to requisition local vessels in Kirkley Roads and take them to Caumbre (Cambrai) by 1 August.[95] This particular city was an independent bishopric at the time, and more part of The Netherlands than of France, but it was obviously seen to have some strategic significance from an English point of view. Even after the long drawn-out conflict had formally ceased, in 1453, England then found itself increasingly preoccupied with the onset of the Wars of the Roses and the increasing mental fragility of its monarch, Henry VI. As early as August 1457 the French saw an opportunity to cross the Channel and launch raids on both Sandwich and Fowey, burning much of the former town to the ground. This was probably the background to an order given in November the same year to Roger Treweman of Lowestoft, master of a *kervyll* (carvel) called the *Michael*, to arrest men for members of his crew in service against the king's enemies.[96] This authorisation shows that the pressing of men for naval service had antecedents going back long before the seventeenth and eighteenth centuries.

Sometimes, the requisitioning of craft in the national cause overstepped the mark. There was a case in November 1406 in which the Yarmouth bailiffs ordered the release of a ship called the *Laurence*, from Westcaple (West-Kappell) in Holland, under the command of Martin Maklore. This was at the request of Richard Frenssh (French), citizen of London, who had had the vessel loaded in Newcastle-upon-Tyne with a cargo of seventy chaldrons of coal and fifty-four grindstones (millstones). It had been driven ashore in Kirkley Roads while on its way to London, and arrested for the king's service.[97] It was probably a case of the ship being in the wrong place at the wrong time, but there was always the chance that foreign vessels were seen as fair game simply because they were from another country (even if it wasn't an enemy of England). Scottish craft were the most vulnerable, as has been noted, even during times of truce with England, and yet another wrongful detention occurred in July 1405 when William Spenser, John Boofe and John Palmere of Lowestoft, along with Nicholas Lomynour (Lumnor) and William Forthe of Norwich, were ordered to release six Scottish merchants and their goods. These men had been driven ashore in Norfolk, arrested by Sir William Calthorpe, released by him because

[95] Maxwell Lyte, *CPR, Henry VI*, vol. 4, p. 106.

[96] Maxwell Lyte, *CPR, Henry VI*, vol. 6, p. 404. A *carvel* was a vessel with a hull built of planks butted up flush to each other, not overlapping in *clinker* fashion.

[97] Maxwell Lyte, *CCR, Henry IV*, vol. 3, pp. 159–60. A *chaldron* was a measure of thirty-six bushels, reckoned at about one ton in weight at this point in history. As time passed, different-sized chaldrons developed for Newcastle and London (the main ports of export and reception), with the former being heavier than the latter.

of the truce between England and Scotland, then re-arrested by Spenser and the others and detained in Lowestoft.[98] Spenser, of course, has been previously encountered in an official capacity (p. 153), so he may have been exercising what he saw as a legal duty – even though it was a mistaken one.

Something of the internal procedures inherent in the arrest of vessels may be seen in the commission granted, in September 1377, to John Botild, William Lacy Jnr, Richard Perelees, John Lacy Jnr, Stephen Lacy and Robert Raveshale (Ryveshale). These Lowestoft men were charged with valuing the goods of Scottish merchants arrested on board a Flemish crayer in Kirkley Roads, with holding the merchandise and selling some for the payment of duty and the settling of the mariners' wages, and with retaining the residue of the property and the merchants themselves until further notice. Everything was to be done with due legality. The appraisal of the merchandise was to be carried out with the aid of 'good and lawful men of the district' and an indenture drawn up with the full knowledge of the merchants. The names of these men and the value of their goods were to be declared and money from authorised sale of the latter was also to be used for the expense involved in maintaining the arrest and distraint.[99]

Foreign conflict and dispute were not always limited to the political sphere; trading rivalries that lay outside of national aspirations and intentions sometimes caused problems. This was particularly true where the Hanseatic League was concerned – that federation of German Baltic ports which, because of its great commercial reach and efficiency, transcended Western European boundaries and formed a federation that achieved a supra-national status of its own during the later Middle Ages. Sometimes capable of high-handed behaviour in defence of its interests, it aroused resentment from those not included in its circle and this may have been what lay behind an incident recorded in February 1382.

It was in this month that an order was given to Thomas de Holland (second earl of Kent), or to his bailiffs or ministers of the town of Lowestoft and in the port of Kirkelerode (*sic*), that certain goods be returned to Conrad Fynk and John de Meudon, merchants of the Hanse, who had complained concerning their confiscation. The merchandise in question consisted of nine lasts, seven and a half barrels and one ferendell (farendell) of herring and 220 ells of linen cloth, which had been loaded at Scone (Skåne, southern Sweden) in a ship from Sluys (master, Baldwin van Seint Thomers) for conveyance to Flanders. Both the vessel and its cargo had been arrested on the pretext of belonging to

[98] Maxwell Lyte, *CCR, Henry IV*, vol. 2, p. 464.
[99] Maxwell Lyte, *CPR, Richard II*, vol. 1, p. 51 and Evans, *CIM*, vol. 4, p. 6.

France.[100] From the information given, and taking into consideration the time of year, it has to be presumed that the ship had been blown off course by a north-easterly gale on its return journey, eventually finishing up off Lowestoft.

A more straightforward example of commercial tit-for-tat manifested itself four years later, in February 1386. The steward of Lothingland and bailiff of Lowestoft were ordered to release a ship from Conyngesbergh (Königsberg) in Sprucia (Prussia), which had fetched up off the town and been arrested in retaliation for local goods seized in its home area of Germany. The vessel was called the *Bethleem* and it was the master, Henry Pousyne, who had made the request for its release. This was agreed, providing that he could find guarantors to stand surety for him.[101] The significance of this requirement lay in its being the means of securing the merchandise distrained somewhere along the Baltic coast and ensuring that it, or its monetary value, was returned to the legal owners. Relationships with the Hanse were often strained, in spite of the economic advantages attaching to contact with it and its trading partners, and open war with it (1468–74) eventually led to a serious dislocation of Baltic commerce.[102]

There has been more than a hint up until now of unlawful behaviour on the part of those involved in a number of the incidents previously cited. Such illegality was sometimes due to misunderstandings of the state of national relationships with traditional enemies (primarily, Scotland and France) – it not always being clear whether war or peace prevailed – and sometimes to what may be termed the 'grey area' between legal salvage claims and the theft of another's property. On other occasions it was simply a matter of breaking the law (in both moral and legal terms) in the cause of self-aggrandizement and taking a chance on whether or not apprehension followed the act. The government's action in its encouragement of mariners and fishermen to undertake privateering activity in the national cause during the Hundred Years War would have encouraged all kinds of illicit activity at sea and schooled English seafarers in the unsubtle arts of maritime plunder.[103]

Personal gain seems to have been very much the motivation in the earliest of the recorded unequivocal criminal cases, dating from July 1311 and noting

[100] Maxwell Lyte, *CCR, Richard II*, vol. 2, p. 35. Thomas de Holland was the half-brother of Richard II and lord of the manor of both Lowestoft and Lothingland. A *farendell* was a small quantity of cured herring and possibly a variant of *fardel*, meaning 'bundle' or 'pack'. The *ell* (or *cloth-yard*) was a measure of forty-five inches in England, but could vary in other countries.
[101] Maxwell Lyte, *CCR, Richard II*, vol. 3, pp. 54–5.
[102] Amor, *Ipswich*, pp. 5 and 138. The town was adversely affected by severance of its established links with Cologne.
[103] Kowaleski, 'Port towns', in D.M. Palliser (ed.), *The Cambridge Urban History of Britain*, vol. 1 (Cambridge, 2000), p. 492, and Kowaleski, 'The shipmaster', in B. Dodds and C.D. Liddy (eds), *Commercial Activity, Markets and Entrepreneurs in the Middle Ages* (Woodbridge, 2011), p. 181.

the detention in Ipswich gaol of local men involved in robbery both in Great Yarmouth and out at sea. Richard Tuteler of Kirkley and Peter de Beketon (Beckton), John de Wymdale (Wymundhale) and Robert le Ray of Lowestoft, in company with thirty-three accomplices, had stolen goods from two local merchants (Stephen de Drayton and John de Belton) and nine Flemish ones and were awaiting trial at an oyer and terminer sessions to be held before John de Mutford and Edmund de Hemgrave.[104] The outcome is not known, but the assemblage of persons engaged in the felonious activity was drawn from all over the local area (Covehithe and Dunwich are mentioned) and even included Roger le Man, the incumbent of Flixton church!

The scale of the theft, in terms of the number of people involved, was not untypical. In May 1343 an assize of oyer and terminer was granted to John de Shardelow, John de Berneye, Robert de Clere and Thomas de Drayton concerning a complaint received from Simon Chaudry, a merchant of Berwick-on-Tweed. It was the plaintiff's claim that the following people had forced entry to his ship: John Totelere (Tuteler), Robert de Rifshale (Ryveshale), John Gryme Snr, John Gryme Jnr, William Gryme, Richard Lacy, John Wartleyne (Watling?), Thomas de Yelverton, John Wyart (Wyatt) Jnr, John German, Richard Seneman, Henry Lacy, Henry de Eston, William de Rifshale (Ryveshale), Richard Vykerbrother, Robert Brid (Bird), John Fayrewedre (Fairweather) of Pakefield, Edmund Bone, William le Bowere, Richard Hed, Richard le Bailiff, Alice Sad, Henry Alman, Nicholas Dekne (Deacon), John de Rothenhale, Warin Benetesbrother, Adam Hodelow, Geoffrey Gryme, Adam de Blundeston, John Sewhat, William Clifhous, Henry de Blundale (Brundale?), Thomas of the Toune (Town), John Wyart Snr and others. The cargo had been removed, together with £20 in cash and 100 florins 'with the shield', and his servants assaulted and injured.[105]

The head-count of thirty-four named persons (including one woman), along with others not named, probably exceeds the total involved in the earlier incident. A number of the surnames are recognisable as those of Lowestoft people.[106] Four months later, in September, a much larger concourse of people

[104] H.C. Maxwell Lyte (gen. ed.), *CPR, Edward II*, vol. 1, p. 373. Peter de Beketon would have been from Pakefield, the Domesday vill of Beckton having been subsumed into that parish. Similarly, John de Wymdale would have had his roots in the Anglo-Saxon settlement of Wimundhall, which had been absorbed by Kirkley. John de Mutford was an eminent royal justice and Edmund de Hemgrave, his son-in-law, was lord of both Mutford parish and half-hundred.

[105] Maxwell Lyte, *CPR, Edward III*, vol. 6, p. 94. The *florins* referred to were probably not Italian gold coins from the city-state of Florence, but French *ecus* bearing the fleur-de-lis on the obverse. Both coins were widely used as trading currency in medieval Europe. John de Rothenhale was lord of the manor of that name (Rothenhall) in Pakefield.

[106] John Gryme Snr, John Gryme Jnr, William Gryme, John Wyart (Wyatt) Jnr, Henry de

– this time from Yarmouth and its surrounding area – came to Lowestoft, raided ships belonging to Sir Robert de Morle (Morley) and carried off the cargoes. No names are given, but the number engaged in the act of robbery was put at 137 or more. Not so much a felonious visit as an invasion! The task of investigating this act of rapine was given to John de Shardelowe, John de Berneye (both previously referred to), Peter de Ty and John de la Rokele.[107] The outcome is not known, but it would appear that the Yarmouth contingent had de Morley as its target rather than Lowestoft itself. He was a Norfolk knight whose family took its name from Morley St Botolph, near Wymondham, and he served as admiral of the king's fleet in the North Sea.[108] His commanding role at the great sea battle of Sluys in 1340 was a key factor in the crushing victory achieved over the French.

It is known that Great Yarmouth contributed perhaps as much as one-third of the ships in action at Sluys. De Morley would have requisitioned vessels to serve and it may well have been the case that some were still in service three years later. It is possible, therefore, that the incursion from Yarmouth was the result of people trying to reclaim their craft. During the Hundred Years War the owners of ships impressed into the king's battle fleet were paid 3s 4d per ton carrying capacity per three-month period of requisition, with the masters receiving 6d a day and crew members 3d – plus any bonuses which might accrue from prize money.[109] Even at these rates of remuneration, extended periods of use resulting in the disruption of normal trading operations must have been frustrating to both owners and crew.

Other than acts of robbery from vessels either moored up in harbour or lying at anchor inshore, there were also examples of piracy out at sea. In December 1404 a commission was granted to John Arnold, serjeant-at-law, to investigate the claims of two German ship-masters and two merchants from Dansk (Danzig, a Hanseatic port) that their vessels had been captured between England and Zeeland by a fleet of about twelve craft. Men from Cromer and Blakeney were mentioned as being involved, as was a crayer from Kirkley owned by William Pye and Thomas Chalk.[110] Three months later, in March 1405, a further reference to the incident named Pye as one of the persons involved, but mentioned only one German vessel as being victim of the outrage – a Prussian hulk called the *Holycrist*. Nine English boats, not

Eston, Nicholas Dekne (Deacon), Geoffrey Gryme and John Wyart Snr appeared in the 1327 Lay Subsidy.

107 Maxwell Lyte, *CPR, Edward III*, vol. 6, pp. 166–7.

108 T.C. Banks, *The Dormant and Extinct Baronage of England*, vol. 2 (London, 1808), p. 356.

109 Kowaleski, 'Port towns', in D.M. Palliser (ed.), *The Cambridge Urban History of Britain*, vol. 1, (Cambridge, 2000), p. 476.

110 Maxwell Lyte, *CPR, Henry IV*, vol. 2, p. 508.

twelve, were said to have been involved: six from London, one from Kirkley, one from Cley and one from Blakeney.[111]

The risks involved in maritime trade are also well illustrated in an incident in February 1441, when three Dutch craft (loaded with fish and other merchandise belonging to four London merchants) had brought up in Kirkley Roads through fear of 'enemies on the seas'. They were persuaded by a Plymouth *balinger*, with thirty-six armed men on board, that it would be safe for them to sail under its protection. Once under way, one of them (the *Buysse*) was attacked and its cargo stolen.[112] The vessel itself was taken to Beaulieu, near Southampton, and the mayor of that port was ordered to arrest John Cornyssh and his craft (the balinger) and restore the Dutch ship and its cargo to Clays Claysson, the master.[113] A similar act of aggression in April 1472 saw a Lowestoft vessel, the *Margaret*, captured and robbed in Kirkley Roads by the *Trynyte* of Hull. William Hardingham, a merchant, had reported the theft as it was his cargo on board, and a commission of enquiry was granted to Sir Thomas Walgrave (mayor and sheriff of Kingston-upon-Hull), Richard Doughty and Dominic Bukton. An order was made for the master (Robert Laverok) and crew of the offending vessel to be arrested and brought before the Court of Chancery.[114]

There were times, it would seem, when collusion between vessels belonging to different European countries took place in the committing of acts of piracy. Collaboration of this kind may have caused the granting of a commission in March 1476 to Sir John Howard (made duke of Norfolk in June 1483 by Richard III), Thomas Howard Esq. (his son), James Hobard (later to become Henry VII's attorney general), Thomas Sampson Esq., Thomas Appylton, William Smyth of Colchester and the sheriffs of Essex and Suffolk, whereby they were charged to investigate a complaint made by Henry Hoveman and Barnard Grefyngk, two merchants from Lübeck (a Hanseatic port). The men claimed that goods belonging to them (consisting of wheat, other merchandise and jewels to the value of £267) had been stolen from the *Marie* of Leith in Kirkley Road, while it was en route to Flanders. The offending vessels were named as the *Jenet Peryn* (master, Nicholas Schellem) and the

[111] Maxwell Lyte, *CCR, Henry IV*, vol. 2, p. 497. A *hulk* was a large vessel used for the transporting of goods.
[112] Kowaleski, 'Port towns', in D.M. Palliser (ed.), *The Cambridge Urban History of Britain*, vol. 1 (Cambridge, 2000), p. 492, notes how Devon and Cornish mariners became notorious for acts of rapine during late medieval times. *Buysse* was a variant of *buss(e)* – a craft used for general carriage.
[113] Maxwell Lyte, *CPR, Henry VI*, vol. 3, p. 506. A *balinger* was a stoutly built craft of the late medieval period, variously used for fishing, trading and military activity.
[114] H.C. Maxwell Lyte (gen. ed.), *CPR, Edward IV (1466–77)*, p. 353. The Lowestoft ship was probably named after the town's patron saint.

Marie of Sandwich (master, Richard Lokwode). It was said that the booty had been taken to Harwich and a plea was made for its safe return.[115]

This grant of enquiry is repeated almost word for word in another source, dated the same day (13 March), though with slight variation in the spelling of the names of those involved in the case and with additional information given.[116] The incident is said to have taken place on the Feast of the Assumption and specific instructions were given to ascertain who had carried out the robbery and to make restitution of the goods, if possible, and to make financial reparation if not. The religious holiday identified establishes that the robbery had taken place the previous year (1475), on either of two possible dates. If the festival named was that celebrating the Virgin Mary's ascension into Heaven, then 15 August was the one; if it referred to Christ's own ascension, then 4 May was the day for that particular year (Ascension Day being the Thursday following the fifth Sunday after Easter).

More detailed information is available, particularly with regard to the stolen cargo, from the enquiry eventually held at Ipswich (in October 1476) before the men charged with conducting it. There were 200 quarters of grain on board (worth £200), 100 yards of *musterdele* woollen cloth (worth 3s 4d a yard), eight pieces of *kersey* (worth £5 6s 8d), thirty-seven gold *ryals*, an old *noble*, two French *crowns*, a Scottish *crown*, half a *ryal*, a Flemish *rydere*, a gold signet (worth 25s), a diamond ring (worth 41s 8d), a coral rosary (worth 16s 9d), 300 ells of woollen cloth (worth £3 10s 0d) and a locked chest of goods (worth £9 10s 0d).[117] The blame for the theft was laid squarely at the door of Richard Lokwode, together with 'other evildoers and felons unknown', and the criminal act was said to have taken place on the Friday before the Feast of the Assumption (11 August 1375, if the Virgin Mary's festival; 28 April, if Ascension Day). And, far from Harwich being the point of reception for the stolen goods, Lowestoft was named. A man called John Hunton, lately of Mutford, had taken the grain, but the recipients of the other goods were not known – and neither were the whereabouts of the goods themselves. Further-

[115] Maxwell Lyte, *CPR, Edward IV (1466–77)*, p. 605. *Jenet Peryn* was probably the *Jenet* of Penrhyn (North Wales) referred to in naval lists of September 1513. See J. Brewer (ed.), *LPFD, Henry VIII*, vol. 1 (London, 1920), pp. 1023–42.

[116] C.S. Knighton (ed.), *CIM*, vol. 8 (London, 1969), p. 244.

[117] Knighton, *CIM*, vol. 8, pp. 244–5. *Musterdele* was produced at Muster-de-Villiers in Normandy; *kersey* was a woollen serge named after a village in the cloth-producing area of south-west Suffolk; the *ryal* was an English gold coin worth 6s 8d, minted during the 1460s to replace the earlier *noble*; the French *crown* or *coronne* was a gold coin named after the design on the obverse; the Scottish *crown* or *demy* was a gold coin worth 9–10s; and the Flemish *rydere*, or *chevalier*, was yet another European gold coin. The value given for the 300 ells of woollen cloth looks very low (even for a commodity of poor quality) and there may be an error in the length cited.

more, John Hunton and other suspected persons did not have possessions able to be distrained and sold to provide compensation.

A particular case

On 20 November 1352 a commission of enquiry was granted to Thomas de Drayton of Great Yarmouth, Lieutenant of the King's Fleet towards the North, in the counties of Norfolk and Suffolk, and to William de Ir(e)land, its purpose being to investigate a complaint made by men of Berwick-on-Tweed. This was to the effect that ships loaded with merchandise from Flanders had been broken near the coasts of Norfolk and Suffolk and the greater part of the cargoes washed ashore. The goods had then been salvaged by local men and illegally retained. Authority was given to de Drayton and de Irland to compulsorily reclaim this merchandise and restore it to the rightful owners – though any Scottish materials found were to be confiscated and kept safe for the use of the king. An identical plea from Newcastle men went hand in hand with that from the citizens of Berwick.[118]

What became of this enquiry is not known, but just over three months later, on 5 March 1353, similar authorisation was given by the Royal Council (meeting at Westminster) to Robert de Thorpe and Henry Grene concerning complaints made by certain merchants of Newcastle and Berwick-on-Tweed regarding ships loaded at Lescluses (Sluys) that had been driven ashore between 'Old Kirkley' and Lowestoft. The crews had been attacked by Sir Edmund Eingrave (Hemgrave – lord of Mutford parish and Half-hundred), Edmund de Thorpe and others under the pretence that they were Scottish craft. It was claimed that men had been killed in the water, as they swam ashore on pieces of wood, while others had been wounded and left for dead on the sand. The cargoes had been claimed as wreck and sold to Mary, the wife (widow) of Thomas de Brotherton, earl of Norfolk, to prevent recovery of the goods by the rightful owners. Redress was being sought by the injured parties.[119]

On 30 March 1353 reference is found to a further order being made in this matter, with power of enquiry now being granted to Richard de Kelleshull, William de Notton, Robert Clere and William de Lavenham, superseding that given previously but having to await execution until Robert de Thorpe and Henry Grene had reported back. It was said that three Flemish ships had been driven ashore on 1 November 1352 (a Friday) and their goods taken on

[118] Maxwell Lyte, *CPR, Edward III*, vol. 9, pp. 389–90.
[119] Maxwell Lyte, *CPR, Edward III*, vol. 9, p. 453–4.

the orders of Joan, wife of Edmund de Emgrave (*sic*), lord of the manor, and Edmund de Thorp(e) – this, in contravention of the king's peace. One person had been killed coming ashore, and the goods taken had a value of £1,300.[120]

Further information on the incident is to be found in a record of 3 May 1353, which notes the holding of an enquiry by Robert de Thorp(e) and Henry Grene at Beccles on 28 March concerning the wreck of two *hagbotes* from Seland (Zeeland) at 'Old Kirkley' on 2 November 1352. The vessels were carrying salt, onions, garlic and turves (peat) and there were no survivors. The cargo had been washed ashore and taken as wreck by Roger del Heth, bailiff of Edmund de Hemgrave. Soon after, on the same day, three ships foundered between Kessingland and *Old Kirkley mill*.[121] There had obviously been a storm of some magnitude locally on either 1 or 2 November 1352, with five vessels in all running aground on offshore sands and breaking up, and it is the wrecked trio which forms the main subject of the particular case under discussion here. Interestingly, neither the Patent Rolls nor the Close Rolls make reference to the loss of the two craft from Zeeland.

Grants of oyer and terminer sessions were made at the end of April to Richarde de Wilughby, Robert de Thorpe and Henry Grene to investigate two separate complaints. The first was from Gilbert de Duxfield, Robert de Duxfield and John de Bulkham (Newcastle merchants) concerning a ship called the *Godbernd* (*Godberade*), under the command of William Ladman, which had been loaded at Lecluses (Sluys) with wine and other cargo and which had been driven ashore at 'Oldkirkele' (*sic*). The crew and the merchants had survived, but cargo had been washed ashore at Kirkley, Pakefield, Lowestoft and Kessingland and been stolen by William de Parys, Roger Reymund, John Randolf, James Scot, Edmund Mellyng and others.[122] The second was from Richard of York, Richard de Stanhop, John de Ethale and John de Wymunderleye (Berwick merchants) that a ship called the *Nicholas* of Neuport (Nieuport), commanded by John Sevenskillynges, had been loaded at Lescluses with *avoirdupois* and other cargo and had undergone the same fate as the vessel previously mentioned.[123]

The third vessel, named the *Marie*, was also from Nieuport and belonged to a man named Clay Somer. Its crew had survived, as had other men on board: William Gretheved (the chief merchant), Christopher Coloyne, Robert

[120] Maxwell Lyte, *CCR, Edward III*, vol. 9, p. 590.

[121] Stamp, *CIM*, vol. 3, pp. 53–4. *Hagboats* were stoutly built, single-masted vessels used for general carriage and military purposes. The location given here was further to the south than that cited in Maxwell Lyte, *CPR, Edward III*, vol. 9.

[122] Maxwell Lyte, *CPR, Edward III*, vol. 9, p. 458. *Godberade* (or *Godberode*), used as a name for other continental ships, has been previously encountered on pp. 154 and 160.

[123] Ibid, p. 459. *Avoirdupois* was a general term used for bulk items of cargo, sold by weight.

Colle and John de Ederston. There is no indication given as to whether these traders were from Berwick or Newcastle (it was probably the former), but the vessel was carrying a cargo of drapery (fabrics), general goods, mercery (textiles), iron and steel worth £400.[124] The *Nicholas* belonged to John Sevenskele (*sic*) and Paul Reyner. The latter had survived, as had Richard de York (from Berwick) and Johan de Wollore – though the latter had been killed by Roger Dapesburgh and Richard Douwe on reaching the shore and his finger cut off for a ring he was wearing. The ship was carrying a cargo of wax (beeswax), groceries, iron, wine, cloth, wool, woolfells, mercery and general merchandise.[125]

The *Godberade* is said to have belonged to a William Ladman of La Scluse (Sluys) and was also commanded by him. Everyone on board had survived, including John de Bulkham of Newcastle (chief merchant) and his son Robert, John Gray, John de Whitewell and William de Muston (merchants). The cargo was one of drapery, mercery, general merchandise, wine, oil, wax and steel, worth £400, and the goods had been seized by Joan de Hemgrave and Edmund de Thorpe on behalf of Edmund de Hemgrave on the pretence that the merchants were Scottish. Reference was made to the enquiry held by Thomas de Drayton and William de Ir(e)land in November 1352, at which it had been established that certain *masers* (maple-wood cups), alum, pitch and other merchandise, worth £10, were in the hands of Richard Bonde of Pakefield and that other goods had been taken by other people. Edmund de Thorpe, Alexander Straunge (Strange) and others had demanded these goods, using bad language and threats in defiance of the law.[126]

It is difficult to arrive at the truth in this particular incident, which has the distinction of being the only one of its kind to feature in three types of record relating to national government: Patent Rolls, Close Rolls and Inquisitions Miscellaneous. This may have been due to the scale of the disaster, with five vessels in all being involved (though the focus was very much on the *Godberade*, *Nicholas* and *Marie*), or it might have been because eminent local people of legal standing and responsibility were involved. The merchants whose cargoes had been taken may well have exaggereated what had happened in order to further their cause, but the selling-on of their goods to a third party (the earl of Norfolk's widow) has the ring of truth about it. The introduction of Joan de Hemgrave into what had happened is interesting, as

[124] Stamp, *CIM*, vol. 3, pp. 53–4.
[125] Stamp, *CIM*, vol. 3, pp. 53–4. At this time *groceries* was a term which may have referred to unspecified bulk items of cargo rather than high-cost goods such as spices, dried fruits and sweetening agents.
[126] Stamp, *CIM*, vol. 3, pp. 53–4.

her husband was lord of the Half-hundred and (as such) entitled to wreck of the shore. This meant a legal claim to half the value of anything retrieved from the shoreline (either washed up or floating), so she may have been acting on his behalf. On the other hand, the merchants' testimony is unequivocal in at least one place as naming him as a prime mover in the incident.

Whatever happened on that particular day early in November 1352, there was obviously some degree of violence involved in the taking of salvaged cargo, with or without the owners' consent, and at least one person had died or been killed (the reference to the cutting-off of the dead man's finger in order to take his ring and the naming of the people who did this are very specific details). Another complication in the episode would appear to be the two references to Joan de Hemgrave and Edmund de Thorpe acting together – until some genealogical investigation is carried out. Edmund de Thorpe was the nephew of Edmund de Hemgrave, being the son of the latter's much older sister, Beatrice, who had married Sir Robert de Thorpe of Ashwellthorpe in Norfolk. It would therefore appear that some family collusion was at work in the episode or that it was simply a case of opportunism resulting from a localised natural disaster.

The final outcome of this fascinating piece of maritime disorder is not known, but Edmund de Hemgrave's position was not materially affected by it. It is interesting to note that one of the investigating justices, Robert de Thorpe, may have been a relative of one of the named main offenders. He was a leading legal servant of the Crown, acting as JP for Norfolk, Suffolk, Cambridgeshire, Huntingdonshire, Bedfordshire and Buckinghamshire. He rose later to become Chief Justice of the Court of Common Pleas and even served as Lord Chancellor for the last year of his life, in 1371. His colleague, Henry Grene, was also a high-ranking lawyer, eventually becoming Chief Justice of the Court of King's Bench in 1361. Edmund de Hemgrave himself was lord of the manors of Hengrave, Little Wratting and Westley, in west Suffolk (where the family had its roots), and of Fordham in Cambridgeshire – as well as being holder of the Mutford titles (parish and half-hundred). He had succeeded his father, Thomas, in 1349, at twenty-eight years of age and later served as MP for Norfolk and Suffolk in 1372–3 and as guardian of the latter county's coastline at the same time. He died in 1379.

Postscript

The final word in this chapter turns, once again, to Lowestoft's struggle with Great Yarmouth, which has manifested itself from time to time in the preceding material. Reference was made towards the end of the previous chapter (p. 142) to the sequence of repeals and regrants of Yarmouth's trading privileges during the final quarter of the fourteenth century, and there were periodic statements of the latter made in the rival town by duly commissioned officers of the Crown. Neither the proclamations nor the proclaimers were well received, and there were occasions when feelings ran high and breaches of the peace occurred. Some of these were sufficiently serious to draw the attention of the ruling authorities in London, with ensuing commissions of enquiry set up to investigate the unrest and bring the perpetrators to justice. Three such examples will be sufficient to illustrate the tension which existed between the two towns (at official level, especially) and serve to show that civil disorder is nothing new – whether planned in advance or simply the result of people reacting to what they saw as provocation.

There is no way of knowing for certain whether the people of Lowestoft had prior notice of when Yarmouth's mercantile supremacy was to be declared publicly within their civic bounds (though there must be at least the possibility that they did) or whether they simply responded to something they saw as unacceptable. On 1 May 1378 John de Foxley, under-sheriff of Norfolk and Suffolk, with the authorisation of his senior, Sir John Harsyk (himself under orders from the Crown), arrived in Lowestoft to proclaim Great Yarmouth's liberties and privileges in the matter of local trade and to show his audience the letters patent granting the same. He was met by a hostile crowd that prevented him from carrying out his task, threatened him with violence and chased him out of town in a shower of missiles and abuse.[127] Sir John Harsyk duly carried out an enquiry into the matter, which was held at Southtown on 12 September 1378. He was assisted by Roger de Hakenham, Walter Read, William Barker and other jurors, and the original wording of the proceedings is able to convey the atmosphere of what occurred on 1 May far more eloquently than any modern paraphrase:

> They [i.e. jurors/witnesses] say upon their oath, that whereas the aforesaid sheriff had sent certain liberties, granted by the aforesaid lord the king, to the bailiffs and commonalty of the town of Great Yarmouth, by John de Foxley, his under sheriff, by virtue of a certain order of the lord the king, to him directed on that account, to cause them to be proclaimed, viz. on the feast of the Apostles Philip and James, last past; on which day the aforesaid under sheriff, at Lowestoft, intended to proclaim the aforesaid liberties according to the form thereof, and there openly showed the letters patent of the lord the king; on that account came Martin Terry, Stephen Shelford, Andrew de Lound, Robert Shincale [Shingle], J. Coote, Roger Caley, Richard Gall, Thomas Smyth,

[127] Gillingwater, *Lowestoft*, p. 129.

> John Smyth, Thomas Murring, Thomas Soneman and William his brother, Henry Freberne and Emma his wife, J. Keene, Henry Boocher [Butcher], of Lowestoft; also John de Rookesburgh, John Spencer and Alice his wife, with a greater company of the men and women of the town aforesaid, of whose names they are ignorant, who, by the abetment and procurement of William Hammell, John Blower, Thomas de Wade, Richard Skinner, William Lacye, etc., they violently resisted and hindered him; some saying to the same sheriff, they would not suffer him to depart; others forcing his letters from him, and so with dangerous and reproachful words, etc., saying, that if he dared any more to come there for any execution of the lord the king, he should not escape. That for fear of death he durst not execute the writ aforesaid. And they drove him there and then with a multitude of rioters, with hue and cry, out of the town, casting stones at the heads of his men and servants, to the pernicious example and contempt of the lord the king, and against his peace.[128]

Edmund Gillingwater, Lowestoft's late eighteenth-century historian, does not reveal the source of this incident in his book and the writer has been unable to trace it. However, there are two similar episodes which are accessible, the first of which occurred six years after the one cited above and the second a further seven years on. The disorder may not have been entirely the result of Lowestoft's resentment of Great Yarmouth's commercial privileges. John Ridgard, the Suffolk medievalist, has noted that the Island of Lothingland was a centre of disturbance during the period of the Peasants' Revolt (1381), so it is possible that the Lowestoft–Yarmouth dispute(s) became enmeshed with the wider feeling of discontent present among the lower orders of society at the time.[129] This would have ensured that any visible sign of government authority provoked a reaction among people already far from happy with current social and economic trends and more than ready to vent their anger on anyone seen as representing the established order.

In September 1384 a commission was granted to Robert de Ufford, Richard Waldegrave, William Wyngefelde (Wingfield), Richard Hembrugge (Hamburg?) and the sheriff of Suffolk to enquire concerning 'divers rebellions and injuries to the king's ministers in the execution of his mandates at Lowestoft, co. Suffolk, so that they fled for their lives leaving the same unexecuted, and to seize and bring before the king in Chancery all persons indicted thereof'.[130] The outcome of this order is not known, but it has a familiar ring about

[128] Gillingwater, *Lowestoft*, p. 129.

[129] Bailey, *Suffolk*, p. 196, identifies Lowestoft as one of five Suffolk 'flashpoints', in company with Bury, Ipswich, Melton and Sudbury.

[130] Maxwell Lyte, *CPR, Richard II*, vol. 2, p. 503.

it and is mirrored in a record of October 1401, whereby the duke of Hereford (*sic*) gave the following report to the Royal Council. On 29 September the Yarmouth bailiffs were granted the right, by letters patent, to proclaim their privileges in Kirkley Road. One bailiff and three burgesses had gone to Lowestoft and presented the king's writ to William Spenser, Richard Langelee (Langley) and Geoffrey Palmer, the local constables. These three men had refused to receive the Yarmouth deputation and assembled 'a great crowd', which was armed and which threatened to kill the Yarmouth officials. The chancellor (Edmund Stafford, bishop of Exeter) was authorised to summon representatives from Yarmouth to Westminster and to send serjeants-at-arms to bring before him the three Lowestoft constables, plus John Boef (Boof) Snr, John Boef Jnr, Stephen Lacy, Thomas Somer, Simon Clerc (Clark), Thomas Calk (Chalk), John Pye, John Richer, Richard Stayngate and John Cof Baxter (baker), as well as others involved – all of whom were to be punished accordingly, if found guilty.[131]

Again, no outcome has been traced, but a clear picture is presented of civic volatility at the time and of people's willingness to use violence as a means of expressing their feelings and achieving what they wanted.

[131] J.L. Kirby (ed.), *Calendar of Signet Letters, Henry IV and Henry V* (London, 1978), p. 31. Duke of Hereford had been a title held by Henry IV prior to his accession to the throne. It merged with the Crown on his usurpation in 1399.

– 6 –

St Margaret's parish church

St Margaret's church was an integral part of Lowestoft in a manner which cannot be fully understood today. At the time that it was built, during the late medieval period, the Roman Catholic ecclesiastical structure throughout the whole of Western Europe was still largely intact and functional. A set of common beliefs was mainly adhered to by the various nations and their leaders, although dissatisfaction with papal authority manifested itself from time to time, as did matters of Biblical interpretation and sacramental practice. John Wyclif and the Lollard movement in late fourteenth- and early fifteenth-century England, for instance, can be seen as foreshadowing the storm that was eventually to break in 1517 when Martin Luther nailed his ninety-five theses to the door of All Saints Church, Wittenberg. But, for the most part, Catholic Europe was united (in a religious sense) by a set of common beliefs and values, which were not always adhered to on a personal or national level but which would have at least elicited lip-service on the part of most people.

Just how much a local parish church mattered to its congregation is hard to assess, but its presence was often sufficiently important for those who could afford it to pay for its construction. Once built, it was as much a statement of civic pride and personal affluence as God's house. But it was there for everyone, in the sense that people were baptised in its font, married at its door (within a porch, or not) and eventually laid to rest in its burial ground. The first two of these services provided were sacraments in their own right and, along with committal to mother earth, were the most fundamental acts for the majority of people. Of the other five recognised sacraments, one (the ordination of priests) did not concern them at all and another (mass) usually involved them directly only once a year – mainly, at Easter. Commitment to the other three – confirmation, penance and extreme unction – was probably desultory in nature and dependent in part on an individual's social and economic standing. The peasant, working the long and arduous hours that he (and she) did, would not have had a great deal of time for regular confession to the priest, or for the obligatory act of contrition which followed it, but someone of higher status might well have had. The last rites, as preparation for impending death, would have been irregular and spasmodic in administration and, again, more likely to have been given in the home to those of means and standing in the community. However, generalisation must not be carried too far and there were undoubtedly clergy of sufficient character (such as Chaucer's 'povre Person of a Toun') who would have visited the sick assiduously, regardless of rank. As for the confirmation of children (theoretically, at about the age of two or three) to follow up and reinforce their baptism, that really was a lottery, with many bishops not being able (or willing) to do it.[1]

The community had uses for the church building outside of the three key events of baptism, marriage and burial. Its nave was used for parish meetings and gatherings of different kinds as and when necessary (including those of gild fraternities, where these existed), and the yard outside was also available for the periodic holding of religious spectacles to celebrate major feast days and to stage church ales – again, events held on days of religious significance and approximating loosely to the fetes of today. Holidays were important in the medieval calendar and the church was the means of providing the entertainment and diversion so necessary to breaking the grinding routine of everyday toil. It was also the instrument of delivering a basic system of poor relief, the money being raised by the voluntary contributions of people who could afford it (collected as alms in church) and disbursed by the priest to those in need. There might even have been the opportunity for a handful of local boys (from families who could spare them) to attain a degree of literacy from their incumbent, if he was so inclined and competent to educate, and his own skills would certainly have been used from time to time to write documents of one kind or another and to read material for those not able to do it for themselves.

Such a broad and general view is limited by the very fact of its own simplification, but it may serve to give some sense of the ways in which the medieval church touched people's lives. Certainly, no one lived in isolation from its teachings and ceremonies and it was difficult in most communities, whether urban or rural, not to know who the local priest was and what he stood for. Even the largest towns and cities – some of them, like Norwich, containing a considerable number of separate parishes – would have had a sense of identity attaching to the individual churches which served those particular areas. And if the gifts made during the fourteenth and fifteenth centuries to both clergy and places of worship are anything to go by, there seems to have been genuine

[1] R.H. Moorman, *A History of the Church in England* (London, 1973), pp. 101 and 124.

affection on the part of many people for their local parish church. This would have resulted, at least in part, from regular acquaintance with the building and its custodian; from the wording of a number of late medieval wills it would seem that genuine friendships between priests and the members of congregations were sometimes formed.

Anglo-Saxon times

Reference to the origins of St Margaret's Church was made earlier, in Chapter 1. Edmund Gillingwater took the building's presence at face value and assumed that a church had existed in the town since soon after the introduction of Christianity into East Anglia by Felix the Burgundian in AD 631.[2] This assumption, in turn, was repeated by Hugh Lees in his monograph on the building, its clergy and its registers,[3] but it is very doubtful that St Margaret's had such an ancient pedigree. There is no way of telling when the church was founded, but it was probably during the late Anglo-Saxon period – and, of course, it was not directly connected with Lowestoft itself, but with the township's outlier, Akethorpe. The building occupied an elevated position in the local landscape about a half-mile in distance from the larger settlement, and eventually, by process of adoption, became its parish hub.

The Domesday Survey refers indirectly to the existence of the church by naming the holder of Akethorpe's eighty-acre manor: Aelmer, an Anglo-Saxon priest. His presence probably meant that of a church also, but without any endowment of land to make it taxable it would not have featured in the Domesday data. Significantly, perhaps, the three churches specifically recorded in Lothingland Half-hundred – Burgh Castle, Flixton and Somerleyton – all had lands attached to them (see p. 23), and so did the four noted in the Mutford jurisdiction: Barnby, Mutford, Pakefield and Rushmere. However, Mutford Half-hundred almost certainly had its own equivalent to Akethorpe in Kirkley township, as the place-name means 'church in an open space, or clearing'. No priest is mentioned, but the incumbent of Pakefield, a community immediately adjoining, could easily have officiated.

Priests in Anglo-Saxon times were sometimes known as *alter-thegns*, a term which recognises both their religious function and their social status. A number of them (such as Aelmer) held manorial titles, while others had extensive holdings which simply lacked the name of manor. In both cases they would have worked the land, usually with the help of men of lesser standing (Aelmer

[2] Gillingwater, *Lowestoft*, p. 255.
[3] H.D.W. Lees, *The Chronicles of a Suffolk Parish Church* (Lowestoft, 1948), p. 1.

had three bordars). Their priestly duties were clearly defined: they were to instil Sabbath observance in their flocks (Saturday afternoon until Monday morning), to encourage attendance at church on Saturday evenings (for evensong) and Sunday mornings (for high mass), to preach whenever possible, to teach recitation of the Lord's Prayer and the Creed and to educate children (male ones) if their parents were willing to have them undergo instruction.[4] Receiving communion was encouraged among the laity on a more regular basis than was the case after the Conquest and it was administered in both kinds, not just the bread alone. Ritual gradually assumed more and more importance as the medieval period wore on, until the people's part in the celebration of mass became mainly that of spectators, while the priest and his acolytes presented an act of holy theatre at the altar.

The dedication of Lowestoft's church to St Margaret of Antioch was, on the evidence of the patron chosen, a post-Conquest one. The Normans' knowledge of the wider world, through being a continental people, brought them into contact with a greater range of Christian thought and practice than was the case among the insular English, and it is noticeable during the twelfth and thirteenth centuries, as a pronounced expansion in the building of parish churches occurred, that a greater variety of Christian saints (both male and female) featured in the naming of them. Anglo-Saxon dedications tended to draw upon associations linked with the earliest phase of Christianity, not with its later spread throughout the Roman world and its ultimate adoption by Constantine as the official religion of that vast empire. Hence, in Lothingland, the three Domesday churches mentioned were dedicated to St Peter and St Paul (Burgh Castle), St Michael (Flixton) and St Mary (Somerleyton), while the patron of the one implied by the presence of a priest (Akethorpe) is not known. In Mutford Half-hundred the dedications of the Domesday churches – which, of course, were not usually recorded at the time – were St John the Baptist (Barnby), St Andrew (Mutford) and St Michael (Rushmere); that of Pakefield is not known.[5] Kirkley, whose church is not recorded, probably had the same patron as that of later times: St Peter.

From the late eleventh century onwards (and particularly during the twelfth and thirteenth centuries), as parishes firmed up in terms of their boundaries and as new ones formed from older settlements, Lothingland acquired

[4] Moorman, *Church in England*, p. 51.

[5] Mutford parish had two churches at Domesday, both of them connected with the same estate. One disappeared at some point during the post-Conquest period. The church at Pakefield was what later became the northern mediety of the 'two churches in one', having a post-Conquest dedication to St Margaret. The southern part, All Saints, had a connection with the manor of Rothenhall, this estate being the successor of a Domesday settlement of the same name absorbed by Pakefield and its neighbour, Kessingland.

fourteen new churches: Ashby, Belton, Bradwell, Corton, Flixton, Fritton, Gorleston, Gunton, Herringfleet, Hopton, Lound, Newton, Somerleyton and Southtown. Some of these were named after traditional patrons, while others adopted newer ones. Two of the foundations, Flixton and Somerleyton, were the result of topographical changes whereby new communities formed from older ones (see Map 3, p. 30). A large part of Domesday Flixton went to form the new parish of Oulton (including the church of St Michael) and a smaller building (St Andrew) was raised to serve a much reduced community. Much of the eastern and south-eastern sectors of Somerleyton helped to create another newcomer, Blundeston, and the church of St Mary was part of the area taken. A replacement building, also dedicated to St Mary, was then built further to the west to serve a diminished Somerleyton. Additionally, Ashby, Bradwell, Gunton and Southtown were also post-Domesday creations that required churches of their own.

Two of the new Lothingland foundations, Fritton (St Edmund) and Herringfleet (St Margaret), have architectural features that suggest construction soon after the Conquest, in that Anglo-Saxon techniques are combined with Norman ones. Both have round towers, as do Ashby (St Mary) – though with a later octagonal modification – Belton (All Saints), Bradwell (St Nicholas), Gunton (St Peter) and Lound (St John the Baptist). The rest of the towers, at Corton (St Bartholomew), Gorleston (St Andrew), Hopton (St Margaret) and Somerleyton (St Mary, as previously stated), are square, all of them being later rebuilds of earlier (probably) round ones. The ruined church of Flixton (St Andrew) has vestigial remains of the nave only; the parish of Newton and its church have disappeared completely (a late sixteenth-century vignette taken from a map of the coastline shows a building with a square tower); and Southtown church (St Nicholas) has also long gone. Oulton (St Michael) is a much modified version of a Norman tripartite building, with a square central tower at the meeting point of nave and chancel and with transepts long demolished. Lowestoft (St Margaret), lineal successor to Akethorpe, has a square-tower replacement of an earlier one (probably round, as was the fashion of the time).

Mutford Half-hundred is equally mixed in its church buildings and their dedications. The Domesday foundations recorded have already been referred to above, but the decades following the great survey saw additional churches built at Carlton (St Peter), Gisleham (Holy Trinity) and Kessingland (St Edmund). Of the eight churches seen today, three have round towers (Gisleham, Mutford and Rushmere) and five have later, square ones (Barnby, Carlton, Kessingland, Kirkley and Pakefield). A dedication in each half-hundred to Edmund of East Anglia, king and martyr, killed by the Danes in AD 869 and still England's true patron saint (though largely unrecognised), is extremely interesting.[6] Was it some way of asserting Anglo-Saxon identity in a changing world of Norman dominance? Or did it result from a conciliatory gesture made by a Norman lord in two communities that had a pronounced native freeman element in the local population? In both cases, patronage of the church was vested in a former Domesday manor, with control of each estate passing to the Crown (in the case of Fritton) and to the earl of Chester (in the case of Kessingland). There would have been no personal interest or input from either of these parties, their only concern being the rents due, but a lot would have depended on the surrogates charged with the day-to-day administration of both land and assets – a task that might well have included sanctioning the establishment of a parish church.

St Margaret's, Lowestoft, did not stand in isolation, then, as the centre of religious life in its own community. It was part of a wider structure, both in its own local area, in its diocese, in the realm of England and in Western Europe as a whole. The congregation would not necessarily have been aware of the wider geographical and theological context, nor perhaps some of the priests in the earlier stages of its existence – but, after the Conquest, the English church became much more a part of the European mainstream in terms of organisation and sacramental practice. All the Anglo-Saxon bishops (apart from Wulstan of Worcester) were replaced by Norman successors and the indigenous monasteries were increased in number from thirty-five or so to over fifty main establishments, with another seventy-five lesser houses and dependencies – all of them under the command of imported clergy.[7] And not only was the structure of the native church drastically reformed; a programme of construction in stone, in the Romanesque style, radically altered the layout and appearance of religious buildings.

The later medieval period

What may be termed the Anglo-Saxon phase of English medieval history loosely coincides with a half-millenium period of the development of Western Christianity after the collapse of the Roman Empire. During this time Christianity developed in a number of ways (not all of them good), spread into northern parts of Europe previously unevangelised and established

[6] There are seven churches in Suffolk dedicated to Edmund (including that of the ruined abbey where he was once buried) and thirteen in Norfolk. Four loose groupings manifest themselves: Fritton, Kessingland and Southwold in north-east Suffolk; Downham Market, Emneth and Walpole Highway in north-west Norfolk; Caistor, Costessey, Norwich and Taverham in mid-Norfolk; and Acle, South Burlingham and Thurne in south-east Norfolk.

[7] Moorman, *Church in England*, pp. 60 and 68.

uniformity of doctrine and practice centred on Catholic practice.[8] It was a lengthy phase of growth and influence, the cohesion of which was eventually and irrevocably torn apart in the second decade of the sixteenth century by the Reformation. During its formative phase the English church experienced three major developments of its own: the initial evangelisation of the country by Roman missionaries (beginning with Augustine in AD 597), the established primacy of Rome in matters of doctrine and procedures over that of the native Celtic church (decided upon at the Synod of Whitby in AD 664) and the introduction of updated ideas and institutions from the European mainland following the Battle of Hastings in 1066.

Initially, following its evangelisation by Felix the Burgundian in AD 631, East Anglia (consisting mainly of Norfolk and Suffolk) was formed into a single diocese centred on *Domnoc* (Dunwich). In the year 672, probably because of the size of the area, Theodore, archbishop of Canterbury, created the diocese of Elmham, with its mother church or cathedral located in the Norfolk community of North Elmham, five miles or so to the north of East Dereham. Thus, Dunwich became the diocese for Suffolk and Elmham that for Norfolk. By the 950s both jurisdictions had been combined into a single entity bearing the name of Elmham and this was the way things remained until transference of the diocese to Thetford in 1075 by Bishop Herfast, a Norman replacement of an Anglo-Saxon cleric. The new location was in use for only twenty years before it was moved to Norwich in 1094–5 by Herbert de Losinga upon his appointment to the post of bishop in 1091, following the death of William de Beaufeu, Herfast's successor. Norwich Diocese has remained in operation ever since, though the Diocese of St Edmundsbury and Ipswich was created in January 1914 (out of part of Norwich Diocese and part of the Diocese of Ely) to serve the county of Suffolk.[9] Thus do wheels come full circle in the onward flow of history.

It is not possible to establish when the church of Akethorpe was founded, nor at exactly what point it became the parish church of Lowestoft. But, even if it was an eleventh-century creation, it formed one small part of three different dioceses within quite a short span of time, with three different locations for the

[8] This interpretation does not take into account the so-called *Great Schism*, which took full effect in the year 1054 and made the Western and Orthodox churches into separate entities after a long period of difference between Rome and Constantinople.

[9] Both Norwich and St Edmundsbury retain something of their earlier, combined histories in having *suffragan bishops* named *Thetford* and *Dunwich*. The one part of Suffolk remaining in Norwich diocese is the extreme north-eastern sector: the old Hundred of Mutford and Lothingland, formed in 1763 from the two earlier half-hundreds for Poor Law administration and eventually becoming a rural district council in 1894. Its parishes (with the exception of those annexed to Norfolk in 1974, and of Barnby) now constitute *Lothingland Deanery*.

mother church, or cathedral. The nature of the building is not known, but it was probably of simple rectangular Anglo-Saxon form, consisting of nave and chancel with the division between the two obvious only from the inside. The structure would either have been of timber and daub or of flint masonry, and (if it was the latter, particularly) it might also have had a round tower attached. It is not possible to make any further observations concerning its build, except to say that it almost certainly had a thatched roof, probably of reed.

The church's adoption by Lowestoft – or, at least, when it became viewed as serving the larger community nearby rather than its parent, Akethorpe – probably occurred at some point between Domesday and the later years of Henry I's reign (1100–1135). In 1123 an Augustinian canon in London named Rahere established a priory in West Smithfield on land donated by the king. It was dedicated to St Bartholomew and it grew into one of the great religious houses and hospitals, not only in the capital but the country as well.[10] At some point between 1123 and 1135 Henry I made a gift to the priory of five churches located on lands belonging to the manor of Lothingland Half-hundred: those of Gorleston, Little Yarmouth (or Southtown), Northville, Belton and Lowestoft. The last named (as Akethorpe) was probably in existence at the time of Domesday, but the other four must have been founded afterwards, and just why the monarch should have chosen to make this particular endowment can never be known.

St Margaret, Lowestoft, and St Andrew, Gorleston, both remain in use today, their respective locations still retaining topographical prominence in built-up urban surroundings. St Nicholas, Southtown, which later became the church of an Augustinian priory founded during the late thirteenth century, has long gone, but the presence of the religious house itself (which actually accommodated friars) is perpetuated in the name Priory Lane at the northern end of Gorleston town. The chapel of St Mary, Northville, stood on the west side of the present-day Southtown Road, just to the south of where the former Southtown railway station once stood, and it was demolished in 1548. All Saints parish church, Belton, is still standing above ground and involved in Christian ministry – a medieval survivor in a village changed out of all recognition by the spread of extensive late twentieth-century housing development.

Part of the arrangement, in the gift of the five Lothingland churches to St Bartholomew's Priory, was that the convent appointed vicars to staff them in return for receiving their great tithes and other emoluments. Augustinian *canons secular* did not live in a closed community, like their brother *canons regular*, but were members of an order intended to go out and perform

[10] 'Bart's', as it is known, is still with us and the apse (rebuilt), chancel and transepts of the Norman church remain in use as London's oldest place of public worship.

ministry in the wider world – a task that made them ideal to serve as parish priests.[11] At some point, an arrangement was made between the London priory and the diocese of Norwich regarding the appointment of clergy to the Lothingland parishes, whereby the right of nomination was vested in the bishop when a vacancy occurred but the act of presentation (or appointment) of the nominee lay with the prior and convent, after the said nominee had met with him and senior clergy and been found acceptable.[12] Thus was some kind of balance maintained between local and outside interests.

After passing into the hands of St Bartholomew's Priory, St Margaret's Church had a connection with it for 400 years, before the dissolution of the monasteries severed the link in 1539. At some point after the Norman Conquest the Domesday building was probably replaced by a larger one, which then remained in use until superseded by the structure seen today. Neither of the earliest church's successors would have been built by the London priory. The myth of religious houses building parish churches up and down the length of the land has been long exploded; their main interest in acquiring or receiving appropriations was to appoint clergy and receive rents and tithes in return. In Lowestoft's case, the great tithes (the most valuable ones) would have consisted of the money due on grain only, the parish having very little productive managed woodland for the production of timber and not much grassland for making hay on any significant scale. When the Rev. John Tanner, vicar of Lowestoft (1708–59), was able to purchase the great (or *rectorial*) tithes in 1719 – mortgaging himself to the limit in order to do so for the benefit of the living, not for personal gain – he increased the incumbent's annual income by £70 from a fluctuating average of c. £40–£65.[13]

The medieval incumbents of St Margaret's (as was the case with their post-Reformation successors) lived on the parochial small tithes and on the crops grown on their portion of the glebe land. The tithes consisted of herbage (all field crops other than corn), lactage (milk and dairy products), pigs and poultry, and one half of an individual share of the profit made by each fishing vessel in operation (known as Christ's half-dole).[14] The 10 per cent of produce

[11] Both types of canon lived under a community discipline developed by St Augustine of Hippo (a North African diocese in what is now Algeria) during the early fifth century. It became a model widely adopted throughout much of medieval Europe. The split into *canons regular* and *secular* was a late eleventh-century development.

[12] E.A. Webb, *The Records of St. Bartholomew's Priory and St. Bartholomew the Great, West Smithfield*, vol. 1 (Oxford, 1921), pp. 321 ff.

[13] Butcher, *Lowestoft*, pp. 245–7.

[14] The boats had a certain number of shares attached to them, varying according to the number of people who had an interest (owners, crew members and any outside investors). In the early modern period cod-fishing vessels usually had thirty to thirty-five shares each, while herring-fishing vessels (often the same craft) worked out at seventy-five to eighty-five.

due to the priest was either paid in kind, to be stored in the parish tithe barn (Plate 23), or commuted to an agreed (and more convenient) cash payment. If late medieval wills are anything to go by, parishioners were often in arrears with their tithe payments and the settling of such debts feature prominently among the bequests made. Presumably, if things were to be right with the Almighty following death, being in debt to his earthly surrogate was no way to begin Eternity!

Plate 23. The tithe barn, an aisled structure of the late fifteenth century. The rearward section, as seen, is the barn itself, with a nineteenth-century cross-wing fronting it. The timber framing from wall-plate downwards remains intact, but the roof is a nineteenth-century one, probably contemporaneous with the front extension.

A rental of Easter 1306 incorporating all of St Bartholomew's Priory's possessions outside London provides interesting information on St Margaret's Church.[15] The annual value to the priory of the church and its tithes was £9 6s 8d (£4 13s 4d, church; £4 13s 4d, tithes) out of an overall value of £26 (£6, church; £20, tithes). The money deriving from the church itself would have been the result of various fees due for services provided and obligations met, and it is interesting to note that the lesser tithes at this time were worth

[15] Webb, *St. Bartholomew's Priory*, vol. 1, pp. 428 ff. The original document is in the Bodleian Library collection and is referred to as *Middlesex Roll 1.*

more than the great ones – unlike the situation referred to above. This would seem to suggest that less grain was produced in Lowestoft during the medieval period than was the case later on, when agricultural improvements (particularly the use of crop rotation to avoid resting land every third year) had improved yields considerably and led to more consistent levels of production and when more land had been put under the plough.

In addition to the income from fees and tithes, the priory also received the rental money due from the church's glebe land, which was largely leased to tenants. There is no mention of the priest's own share of the land, but he would have had an area that he would have either tended himself or paid someone to look after. Originally, the glebe would have been part of the manorial demesne, given to St Bartholomew's Priory as part of the church endowment. Henry I probably had little or no direct knowledge of his manor of Lothingland, so it was probably someone with local knowledge and influence who was instrumental in arranging the transfer of the five churches – the overseer of the royal lands, probably Hugh Bigod.[16] Gorleston was the hub of the manor at Domesday, with 600 acres of arable land; Lowestoft and Belton were outliers, with 450 and 120 acres respectively. Thus there was ample capacity to convey the churches gifted to their new patron with an endowment of land and accompanying rents.

The Lowestoft glebe land was probably dispersed throughout the three common fields rather than concentrated in one place. There were nine tenants altogether, whose annual combined rent came to 6s 10d (payable at Michaelmas), and six of them were also responsible for the payment of a specified number of hens and cockerels as part of their lease agreements. The birds were to be taken to Gorleston on 26 December (St Stephen's Day) and handed over to members of the Bacon family, who held title to Gorleston manor from the Crown, and to William de Leegh (Leigh), the incumbent of both St Andrew's Church, Gorleston, and St Margaret's Church, Lowestoft. A meal for the tenants was to be provided.[17] The year 1306 was the very point at which the manors of Lothingland and Lowestoft were transferred by Edward I to his nephew, John de Dreux, earl of Richmond, so the procedure of tenants taking their fowls over to Gorleston (a distance of some seven miles) is one of those interesting throwbacks so often encountered in manorial history. It was a procedure probably dating back to the mid-twelfth century, when the Lowestoft glebe land was first rented out to tenants by St Bartholomew's Priory (Table 11) and when Gorleston was still the focal point of the half-

[16] The son of Roger Bigod, sheriff of Norfolk and Suffolk – William I's 'enforcer' in East Anglia.
[17] Webb, *St. Bartholomew's Priory*, pp. 428 ff.

hundred manor. The matter of Gorleston and Lowestoft sharing a priest at this time is interesting also and, given his being based in the former town, he must have employed a curate to officiate in the latter.

Table 11. Glebe tenants and rents (1306).

Name	Status	Holding	Rent	Poultry
Thomas s. of Walter	Villein	1 messuage and 5½ acres	17½d	2 hens and 1 cock
Nicholas Brun	Villein	1 messuage and 5¼ acres	18d	2 hens
Nicholas le Niweman (Newman)	Villein	1 messuage and 3¾ acres	12½d	2 hens one year and 1 the next
Richard Thowre (Thrower)	Villein	1 messuage and 2 acres	5d	
Adam de Rothenhale	Villein	7½ acres	24d	3 hens and 1 cock
Edmund s. of the Deacon	Freeman	¼ acre	1d	
John de Goseford and Henry Basset	Freeman	1 acre	3½d	1 cock
William Rymshale (Ryveshale)	Freeman	½ acre	½d	
		4 houses and 25¾ acres	6s 10d	9(8) hens and 3 cocks = 1s 3d value

Notes:

- These holdings show varying levels of rent, which probably reflect particular conditions of some kind relating to location and soil quality.
- The villein houses were almost certainly in the township, with the strips of land (located in the common fields) attached to each one worked by the occupants at any given time.
- The three freeman holdings were probably individual strips of land.
- The half-acre held by William Rymshale had formerly been in the tenancy of William Regnald (Reynald), the largest identifiable landholder in the 1274 Hundred Roll.
- The reference to four freemen is the only direct one to persons of this status connected with Lowestoft found up until now by the writer. Edmund, son of the Deacon, might have been connected with any of the three tenants bearing that title who feature in the Hundred Roll data (Table 6, p. 33). The other three men do not seem to have had antecedents there, nor in Tables 7 and 8 (pp. 38 and 62), and may have moved into Lowestoft during the interim. Members of the Ryveshale family featured prominently in the previous chapter.
- Three of the four villeins referred to also have no apparent connection with people referred to in Chapter 2, but Thomas, son of Walter, may have been related to the Richard Walter(s) listed in Table 6.

Another vital aspect of Lowestoft's development during the early fourteenth century was the town's relocation to a cliff-top location from its original site at the bottom of the hill surmounted by the parish church. As it is seen today, St Margaret's is one of Suffolk's great Perpendicular glories and deserving of being much better known than it is. Externally, it is on a par with Southwold, Blythburgh, Lavenham, Long Melford and others. It is also (at 182 feet) the third longest church in the county, after St Mary (213 feet) and St James (195 feet), Bury St Edmunds – the latter being the cathedral of St Edmundsbury and Ipswich Diocese. However, it is the nave and integral chancel, the side aisles and the south porch which date from the period 1440–80; the extremities are over a century older, having their origins in the first half of the fourteenth century. It was pointed out in Chapter 3 (p. 113) that there appears to be a contradiction between the comparatively modest tax burden imposed on the town by the 1327 Lay Subsidy and the money being spent by Lowestoft residents on relocating the town and building a grand new parish church. However, the finance must have come largely from within the community, even if it is not possible to determine how.

St Margaret's imposing presence is a combination of its siting and its construction – just like the church of the Holy Trinity at Blythburgh, standing above the marshes of the river from which the parish takes its name. Both churches have large integral naves and chancels that are out of proportion with earlier, fourteenth-century towers – the latter never updated, in each case, to match the rest of the building, probably because of the inconvenience and cost. St Margaret's tower is, in any case, an impressive structure for its period (the early fourteenth century, on the evidence of the first stage's west-facing Y-tracery window and the second-stage lancet above), of good size and solid proportions. It would appear that three stages were completed before work came to a halt, probably as a result of the Black Death. At the other end of the church a similar interruption occurred. A crypt had been constructed beneath the intended site of the high altar (probably to function as a charnel house), and that was as far as things progressed.[18] It was to be about another century before construction resumed (Plate 24).

In common with other parts of the country during 1348–9, Lowestoft lost probably half or more of its population from plague.[19] Demographic and economic recovery would have been slow, but eventually progressed sufficiently

[18] A charnel was customarily used for the storage of human bones exhumed from recycled graves, which were reused at periodic intervals in churchyards of limited area (as most were, at the time).

[19] Benedictow, *Black Death*, Table 38, p. 383, puts overall mortality in England at 62.5 per cent.

Plate 24. St Margaret's Church from the east end, showing the building's imposing appearance. The crypt is located beneath the mighty east window, with two apertures to light it visible at ground level.

to allow the townspeople to complete the building of their grand new civic church. Once the chancel was constructed (allowing the priest to celebrate mass) and the adjoining section of the nave was standing, demolition of the earlier church could proceed and its replacement be brought to completion. The fourth stage of the tower (in which the bells were hung) was built and a battlemented parapet added, with flushwork decoration along its four faces. A wooden leaded spire was then set within the parapet to give the steeple a finished height of 120 feet. The main body of the building had north and south aisles added to the nave, giving it an overall external width of 62 feet, and the main entrance to the church (on the south side) was given a sumptuous two-storey porch. No expense seems to have been spared in making St Margaret's a statement of belief in God Almighty, of the community's pride in itself and of its increasing affluence (Plate 25).

Plate 25. St Margaret's Church from the south, showing the structure's overall mass and appearance. The original churchyard was comparatively small, relative to the size of the building, and had to be greatly expanded (especially on the southern side) during the mid-nineteenth century to take account of the town's rapidly growing population.

It is no part of this narrative to create a church guide, but the construction of St Margaret's church, inside and out, shows craftsmanship of the highest order. The southern elevation of the building – the side approached from the town – is eye-catching and ornate (the northern side being plainer and comparatively unadorned), with superb fenestration of the aisles and with the buttressing enhanced by flushwork panels set within delicately canopied limestone frames. This work is continued at the east end of the church, where the great five-light window takes up more than half the surface area of the wall and has skilfully contrived tracery in which the height of the transoms is varied to create a most striking alternating pattern. The porch, too, is impressive, with lavish use of arcaded flushwork on its exterior, and the ceiling of the lower section is supported by a tierceron rib-vault with three bosses at the intersections. Inside the main building the nave and aisle arcades (six bays in extent) have finely moulded piers and arches and are surmounted by an excellent timbered roof of castellated tiebeams supported by hammerbeams, restored in 1897–8 by G.F. Bodley, one of the leading Victorian church architects.[20] Most of the medieval fittings have been removed or replaced at different stages of the church's development, but a brass eagle lectern dated 1504 has survived and is still in use, as is the fine (but mutilated) font on its raised triple platform at the western end of the spacious and beautifully proportioned interior.

A lifetime's work carried out by the late Peter Northeast in transcribing and analysing Suffolk wills of the late medieval period, showed little information relating to the main constructional aspects of raising parish churches but a great deal of detail connected with exterior modification and interior embellishment.[21] This feature holds true for St Margaret's Church, and therefore the people who raised the money to pay for its construction must remain anonymous. It is doubly impressive that the town's inhabitants felt able to embark upon the raising of such a large edifice at the same time as they were relocating their township and that, having recovered from the most disastrous epidemic ever to hit this country, they were prepared to see the work through to its conclusion. The building stands as a tribute to their determination and dedication, reinforced in all likelihood by pride in membership of one or other of the five religious gilds which existed in the parish during the mid–late fifteenth century. More significantly, it demonstrates the economic power of the town, in terms of the wealth its leading citizens were able to lay out.

One small insight into the resumed building of St Margaret's during this period may perhaps be found in a will dating from the third decade of the sixteenth century. It was made on 15 April 1529 by Richard Jetur (Jettor) of Wyberton (East or West), near Boston in Lincolnshire, as he prepared to visit the shrine of St James the Great at Compostela in northern Spain. Among the early clauses in the document are recorded the gift of 10s to the high altar in Laystoft (*sic*), Suffolk, and the sum of £14 for 'the reparation of the glass windows in the said church of Laystofte, on the north side, to be made after the same work that my father caused to be made in the windows of the

[20] George Frederick Bodley was a student of George Gilbert Scott, becoming in his own turn one of the leading exponents of the Neo-Gothic style. St Margaret's was fortunate in its choice of restorer.

[21] This foremost Suffolk medievalist was never quite sure how many wills had come under his scrutiny, but it was in the region of 18,000 (out of a possible maximum number of c. 25,000). His working time-scale was from c. 1350 to c. 1550.

south side of the same church'.[22] Richard Jetur was a younger son of John Jettor (or Jetour), a leading Lowestoft merchant and member of one of the town's wealthiest families (if not the wealthiest of all). He had six children, all of whom were below the age of twenty (at which point they were to receive their respective legacies), so he may have been forty years of age or more when he made his last will and testament. Two of the children were from his first marriage, the other four from a later union, and the elder pair (Robert and Margery) were obviously living in Lowestoft with their father's older brother, John.[23]

The reference to Jetur's father having work 'caused to be made in the windows of the south side' of St Margaret's Church is interesting, as it could refer to the windows of the south aisle or of the nave clerestory above, or to both. Interpreting the wording of medieval (and later) documents and establishing an accurate meaning is sometimes difficult, but there seems to be the implication, at least, that the statement made here was referring to the glass of the windows, not the stone frames and tracery. Glazing was a very expensive process, but it may not necessarily have been considered as part of the structure of a church, which leaves the question of who provided the money for building still unanswered. In all probability John Jettor made notable contributions towards this cost, but it was the glazing of the south-facing windows which his son, Richard, had in mind when he made his will. Exactly when the work was carried out cannot be established, but it could have been as late as 1500. And if it was, and there had been similar activity on the north side of the church, what had caused this to require reparation within three decades of its having been done?

There are three possibilities. The first is that the work had not been done particularly well in the first place, either in the manufacture of the glass or in the fitting of it; the second is that severe weather, in the form of a northerly winter gale, might have inflicted hailstone damage (there are examples of this having happened in both medieval and modern times); and the third is that glass was replaced in order to keep up with the latest fashion in religious decoration. Medieval churches were constantly being modernised and re-embellished by private donation, and the seriousness of the loss of Christian artwork caused by the Reformation cannot be emphasised enough, doing irreparable damage to this country's creative legacy.

[22] TNA, Prob 11/24/35 (PCC wills). Jetur seems to have returned from his pilgrimage, as probate was granted to his wife, Matilda, on 15 October 1532.

[23] Robert Jettor was eventually to become the most heavily fined of all Suffolk recusants during Elizabeth I's reign, when a penalty of £1,500 was imposed for his non-attendance at church. See Butcher, *Lowestoft*, p. 301.

According to the 1524 Lay Subsidy, Richard Jetur's older brother John was the wealthiest of all the inhabitants of Lowestoft, paying £6 on movable goods worth £101.[24] The family had come into Lowestoft at some point during the fifteenth century and quickly established themselves among the town's mercantile elite. Their impact in the community and their commitment to its parish church may perhaps be seen in the number of graves they occupied within the walls of the building. Some very interesting remarks are appended at the end of the first surviving parish register book by the vicar of the time, James Rous.[25] In recording the arrival of the Puritan visitor (Francis Jessop of Beccles) on 12 June 1644, he writes about the removal of the memorial brasses from the floor of the church carried out by this man and his assistants. Jessop's commission authorised him to remove all inscriptions in the church with *orate pro anima* (often shortened to *ora paia*) written or engraved upon them, but he went far beyond this and removed practically every brass there was. Rous described him as 'a wretched commissioner not able to read or find out that wch his commission injoined him to remove', and claimed that 'there were taken up in the middle ally [*sic*] twelve pieces belonging to twelve severall generations of the Jettors'.

There are ninety-five grave slabs of one kind or another marking burials inside the church, thirty-eight of them medieval and fifty-seven dating from the seventeenth and eighteenth centuries.[26] James Rous's claim concerning the generations of Jettor brasses removed from the middle aisle (the nave's) should not be taken literally in the modern sense: what he meant was that twelve brasses commemorating different members of the family were taken up, and this may be accepted as fact. There are eleven medieval slabs in the floor of the middle aisle out of a total of sixteen, eight of them having indents only and three retaining remains of brasses (one of which is early sixteenth century and commemorates Margaret Parker, ob. 1507; Jessup and his helpers overlooked her somehow). Two of those now marked by indents only have eighteenth-century inscriptions added to Francis Kettebrow (Kettleborough) (ob. 1721) and to a former incumbent, John Arrow, and his wife Rebecca (ob. 1789 and 1784). Four of the later slabs date from the seventeenth century and commemorate members of the Wilde, Canham and Daynes families, while a fifth is of early nineteenth-century origin and marks the resting place of John Brown (ob. 1803), a Lowestoft man who had moved to Great Yarmouth but

[24] S.H.A. Hervey, *Suffolk in 1524*, SGB 10 (Woodbridge, 1910), p. 243. The father, John Snr, paid the sum of 5s on £10 worth of goods. He had presumably scaled down his trading operations and had probably given much of his wealth to the church already.
[25] NRO, PD 589/1.
[26] They were meticulously recorded by Hugh Lees. See Lees, *Chronicles*, pp. 18 and 291–2.

wished to be buried in his native town. Any of these later stones could easily have replaced medieval ones and therefore a total of twelve Jettor brasses, as described by Rous, is entirely believable. He would not have been mistaken, in any case.

The interior of St Margaret's is a cemetery for the town's 'great and good' (of all ages) of the medieval and early modern periods, with elegant memorials of the latter time adorning the walls as well. Practically the whole of the north aisle floor is covered with medieval slabs, with only a single grave (containing the remains of mother and daughter, Mary Mighells and Elizabeth Rivet), out of the total of sixteen, dating from the reigns of William and Mary and the early years of George II. Ten of the medieval gravestones have indents of effigies and inscriptions, or of inscriptions only; two have illegible inscriptions; and one is blank. There is also a truncated slab bearing an inscription indent at the extreme southern end of the north aisle's benched area and a fine matrix (without the brass) of a late fifteenth-century incumbent in its War Memorial Chapel, at the opposite end.[27] The latter was moved at some time during the nineteenth century from its original position in the middle of the chancel's floor.

Two medieval slabs remain in the chancel, one on each side of the aisle. That on the south carries the indent of a coat of arms or merchant's mark, the other an inscription indent. Returning down the south aisle, towards the west end of the church, there are four medieval slabs out of a total of ten set in the floor. The first of them has the remains of a brass showing shrouded skeletons. After an interposing mid-eighteenth-century slab to a member of the Arnold family, there comes one with an indent of effigies, inscription and shields, followed by a damaged brass depicting a man and his wife (the latter headless) and with two groups of children missing from the matrix.[28] This latter memorial also has a merchant's mark in evidence, as well as the badge of the Salt-fishmongers' Company, a London-based livery organisation. Next to it is the slab of William Colby (ob. 1534), commemorated by his name and year of death on a small brass plate.[29] Finally, there are four inscription-indent stones immediately west of the font, which is largely surrounded by much later memorials.

[27] It commemorates Thomas Scrope, a Carmelite friar, one-time bishop of Dromore, in Ireland (1434–40), and *suffragan* in Norwich diocese (1450–77). He served as parish priest at Lowestoft 1478–90, dying at the advanced age of about 100 years.

[28] Lees, *Chronicles*, p. 115. The writer of the work cited was drawing upon E. Farrer, *A List of Suffolk Monumental Brasses* (Norwich, 1903) for his information.

[29] This man was the wealthiest inhabitant of Pakefield, shown in the 1524 Lay Subsidy as paying £1 10s on movable goods worth £30 (Hervey, *Suffolk in 1524*, p. 261). He had obviously moved into Lowestoft at some point afterwards.

One fortunate survival that illustrates the practice of burying people inside the church, rather than out in the yard, is to be found towards the end of England's long period as a Roman Catholic country. In his will of 16 April 1535 John Goddard, merchant, another of the town's wealthiest citizens, made the following request: 'to be buried within the church of St. Margaret, within the chancel door, whereas I do sit, upon the north side'.[30] If his wish was carried out (and there is no reason to believe that it was not), then his place of inhumation probably lies somewhere beneath grave-slabs of the late seventeenth and early eighteenth century. As one of the town's trading elite and a likely contributor of money to the church, Goddard's will shows that he had both a privileged position from which to observe the celebration of mass and the conduct of other services and, ultimately, one where he could be laid to rest. The chancel of a medieval church was separated from the nave by a wooden screen to differentiate between the priest's domain and that of the laity, and to be allowed beyond this division was a privilege not given to everyone. In fact, it was extremely unusual to find a layman allowed into the chancel and Goddard must have been of some special standing, perhaps as a major donor towards the construction of the church.

The fee paid to the vicar for burial inside the church during late medieval times is not known, but by the fourth decade of the seventeenth century it was 11s. This is revealed in the accounts of the administration of Thomas Mighells, merchant, who made his last will and testament on 26 July 1636 (probate granted 3 November 1636) and wished to be buried within the walls of St Margaret's.[31] The document itemising the sale of Mighells' worldly goods, the collecting of money owing to him, the settling of his debts and the apprenticing of his eight-year-old son, James, survives only by accident, and makes for fascinating reading. It is inserted into the pages of the Lowestoft tithe accounts,[32] put there at some stage by John Tanner (incumbent from 1708–59) to prove his entitlement to such payment. He had married into a branch of the Mighells family and had found the accounts among his in-laws' effects.

The interior of the church today, benched throughout during the 1870s with solid oak, is very different from what would have been present c. 1500. The restored roof gives some idea of the use of colour in a late medieval church, as does the font cover, which was the creation of church architect and restorer

[30] TNA, Prob 11/25/419 (PCC wills). Probate was granted to his wife, Anne, on 20 November 1535.
[31] TNA, Prob 11/172/179 (PCC wills).
[32] NRO, 589/80.

J.N. Comper – one of the last great exponents of the neo-Gothic tradition.[33] There is also an ornate wooden screen separating the War Memorial Chapel from the rest of the north aisle that is similar in style to a medieval one but lacks its bright colours and the painted figures of saints or angels on the dado (the chapel was dedicated in April 1923, as a memorial to the townsmen killed during the First World War). At one time such a screen, richly embellished and coloured, would have run across the whole width of the interior, with the rood (cross) crowning it beneath the chancel arch.

The rood group itself, consisting of Jesus on the cross flanked by his Mother and St John the Evangelist (sometimes St John the Baptist, his cousin), was an object of veneration in medieval times and much care and attention was given to it. The great double beam on which it was set was, in fact, a narrow walkway along which an attendant could move in order to keep wax lights perpetually burning before the crucifixion scene. The approach to it was by a stairway constructed within the width of the wall (aisle or nave, depending on the design of the church), one of which may be seen next to the War Memorial Chapel's screen. Of all the symbols of Roman Catholic practice within a church, it was probably the rood that caused many Protestant reformers most offence and the majority of crucifixion groups were among the first things to be taken down during the reign of Edward VI (1547–53). His sister Mary restored them during her brief reign (1553–8), then down they came again when Elizabeth I acceded to the throne (1558).

Apart from the illumination of the rood beam, lights of different significance were a major feature of a late medieval church interior – and St Margaret's was no exception. Symbolically, they represented the triumph of good over evil; in practical terms, they served to focus the attention on specific features and to create the sense of a living building during the hours of darkness. Wills of the period make reference to four different lights, with the testators leaving money to fund the purchase of beeswax candles in order to maintain a constant illuminating presence. The *common light* found referred to was the hanging sanctuary lamp in front of the high altar, which burned night and day without fail, representing Christ as the Light of the World and proclaiming that his body and blood were ever-present in the holy elements held within their tabernacle. The *light to the Blessed Virgin Mary* would have stood before a statue of her and the infant Christ, mounted either on a bracket or set within a niche and probably located in the chapel dedicated to her. Another image of her, holding the body of her crucified son, would

[33] Comper is best known locally for his restoration of the church of St John the Baptist, Lound, where the organ case and rood screen particularly (executed in 1914) demonstrate the high quality of his work.

have been the *Our Lady of Pity* mentioned from time to time – again, with a light burning perpetually in front of it. Finally, the *Sepulchre light* would have been located in an arched recess (with decorative surrounding tracery) in the north wall of the sanctuary, this particular space representing Christ's tomb. On Good Friday the holy wafer (or *host*) was put in a box and placed in the sepulchre, which was then veiled over, to be brought out on Easter Day for celebration of the high mass – a cyclical ritual representing the death and resurrection of Our Lord.

There was one other light known to have been located inside the church. It was dedicated to St Rock (or *Roch*), a high-born fourteenth-century native of Montpellier, in France. At one point in his life he performed relieving work in northern Italy (he is known there as St Rocco) during an epidemic, from which actions he achieved cult status and, following the Black Death, became invoked as a protection against plague. His feast day was held on 16 August and he may have been celebrated in Lowestoft because of a residual memory of how the initial stages of building the new St Margaret's had been disrupted in the first place. A one-acre piece of land next to the south-western corner of the churchyard (see Map 2, p. 25) had been given at some point to endow a light in his memory, the income deriving from the rent generated by hire of the ground.[34] It had been taken from the glebe, so one of the Lowestoft vicars (with the approval of St Bartholomew's Priory) must have originally been responsible for its donation.

The ritual practice of the time is further revealed in references to *tabernacles*. These were ornate boxes for preservation of the bread and wine used to celebrate mass and there would have been two of them, kept for use on the high altar itself. Two others are specifically referred to, dedicated to St Margaret and St Mary Magdalene, but these would have been portable cases made of wood or stone, embellished with tracery and intended to house an image or statue of a saint. The former would have been located in the chapel commemorating the church's patroness, the latter perhaps in a space used for hearing confessions. Mary Magdalene (or Mary of Magdala) was the great Christian symbol of penitence during medieval times, the model of a reformed life. She was also one of the most trusted members of Christ's inner circle and the person who first discovered that he had risen from the dead.

There were no fewer than seven altars within St Margaret's Church towards the end of the fifteenth century, five of them connected with religious fraternities or gilds. The two exceptions were the high (main) altar itself and that

[34] It was referred to as St Rook's in later times. See Butcher, *Manor Roll*, pp. 54 and 55. There was also a light to St Rock in the parish church of St Bartholomew, Corton, two miles to the north.

of the sepulchre, which would have stood close to it. The others would have been located within chapels formed by partitioning off spaces within the two side-aisles and their dedications were to the Blessed Virgin Mary, St Margaret, The Holy Trinity, St Gregory and St George. Together they form a typical selection of medieval patrons and patronesses and the gilds represented by them would have been socio-religious groups of people whose spiritual lives found focus through association with their chosen objects of devotion. The different patronal feast-days would have been celebrated with processions and feasts; vigils would have been kept on the evenings preceding; prayers would have been offered within the various chapels for the souls of departed members; and masses would have been said or sung in the same cause. Major festivals would have been celebrated also, with all due ceremony – a notable one being *Corpus Christi*, on the Thursday following Trinity Sunday, when the creation of the eucharist itself was commemorated.

In the absence of any surviving gild records or churchwardens' books of the period (in which their business might have been recorded), a good overview of typical activity is to be had elsewhere. The three main distinguishing features of gilds have been outlined in the previous paragraph: a religious patron, a base in the local parish church and an annual patronal mass and feast.[35] Reference was also made to the saying of prayers for departed members, but there was more to gild function than religious observance alone. Social and economic matters came within the remit too. Care was taken of sick members, financial support given to those of the respective fraternities in need and fund-raising undertaken for what would currently be termed 'community projects' aimed at improving the town. Local politics featured in the members' protection of what they saw as important areas of commercial interest and means of social control were exercised through the ethos of the fraternities and their sense of moral purpose. Note has been taken of the positive effect on local economies resulting from the (sometimes) lavish spending on the annual processions and feasts – and comment has been made, too, on the effect of gilds as instruments of community cohesion and divisiveness (both features having been examined by different observers).[36] Rivalries no doubt existed, and tensions sometimes came to the fore, but, with their duly elected officers (wardens, stewards and councils) and their religious and civic function, gilds made an important contribution to the life of any late medieval community and reflected its economic strength.

[35] K. Farnhill, *Guilds and the Parish Community in Late Medieval East Anglia* (York, 2001), p. 10.

[36] Farnhill, *Guilds and Parish Community*, pp. 11–19.

In the Addenda appended to his history of the town, Edmund Gillingwater says that he had been 'credibly informed' that there had once been two or three gilds in the town. He goes on to identify them as 'trading companies' and speaks of the difficulty of determining which houses (i.e. gild halls) belonged to them.[37] As far as is known, there were no trade gilds in Lowestoft during medieval times and, while Gillingwater makes reference to religious gilds and their function, he obviously did not know of their existence in the town. The nearest he got was speculating whether or not the light kept burning to St Rock belonged to a gild. It has been observed that the growth of religious gilds became numerous in towns after the middle of the fourteenth century,[38] which may suggest that they were part of the recovery process from the psychological trauma caused by the Black Death – a refounding of religious faith and practice in a changed and chastened world.

It is not known when the Lowestoft gilds were formed, but they were certainly active by the mid–late fifteenth century. They were probably directly involved in building the new nave and chancel and it is likely that the vicar himself was connected with them. Chaplains are also referred to in documentation relating to the town and it is likely that they, too, were associated with the fraternities and were probably paid by members for the services they provided. The most tangible evidence today of gild activity is the presence of a banner-stave locker in the north-west corner of the nave of St Margaret's. This tall, narrow recess within the fabric of the wall, with its canopied stone hood and its pierced traceried door (not an original one), was used to store the rods on which ceremonial banners were set for processional use. Its survival is probably mainly down to chance, but it is interesting nevertheless and gives another of those tantalising glances into a lost world.[39]

The location of the gild altars is not known and there is little or no visible evidence to suggest where they stood. It is reasonable to suppose that the one dedicated to the Virgin was situated at the east end of the south aisle, where the organ now stands, as this would have been a prime setting (being on the favoured lighter side of the building) for a lady chapel. Equally, with St Margaret of Antioch being patroness of the church, it is conceivable that her dedicated space might have been situated on the north side in an

[37] Gillingwater, *Lowestoft*, p. 483.

[38] Bailey, *Suffolk*, p. 149. Lowestoft's number of five gilds compares favourably with other Suffolk towns of the time. For a county-wide distribution of gilds see P. Northeast, 'Parish gilds', in D. Dymond and E. Martin (eds), *An Historical Atlas of Suffolk* (Ipswich, 1988), pp. 58–9.

[39] There are thirteen surviving banner-stave lockers in Suffolk, all of them in churches located in the north-eastern part of the county. Norfolk has eleven examples, spread across the southern half of the county from Yaxham to the Broads. See H.M. Cautley, *Suffolk Churches and Their Treasures* (Ipswich, 1954), p. 192, and *Norfolk Churches* (Ipswich, 1949), p. 43.

identical position, occupying the area now taken up by the War Memorial Chapel[40] – though any altar in the chapel would not have been dedicated to her, as that honour would have been accorded to the high altar itself. The space devoted to the Holy Trinity was possibly located in the upper room of the south porch. The central boss of the vaulted stone ceiling below depicts the Trinity in the form of God the Father, shown as an old man (how else would mere mortals be able to depict the Creator?), supporting his crucified Son between his knees and with the Holy Spirit, in the form of a dove, carved upon his breast.

It is likely that members of the gild gave the money to build the porch and commissioned the boss to represent their organisation, and the use of the parvis(e) above as their chapel is a far more likely explanation of its purpose than a later story that grew up concerning it. At some point the room became known as The Maids' Chamber, in which two sisters (Elizabeth and Katherine) are said to have lived as recluses. These ladies, having withdrawn from the world, performed a charitable act on behalf of their fellow townspeople and paid for public wells to be dug a quarter of a mile or so from their cell, on the eastern edge of *Church Green*.[41] These then became known as *Basket Wells*, a name coined from the pet forms of their names, Bess and Kate: a far more fanciful origin than simply sinking shafts into the ground and lining them with wicker (p. 94). Interestingly enough, in her will of 6 January 1496, Katherine Wylton left an undisclosed sum of money for the repair and maintenance of the wells for a period of ten years – but she was no anchorite.[42]

Other bequests make reference to the three chapels either directly or indirectly, some of them showing the connection of townswomen with the gilds. On 17 February 1497 Margaret Wullysby left half an acre of land in the *North Field* to be sold and the money used to provide 'a common curtain in the chapel of Our Lady' – a hanging, perhaps, to act as a screen for the doorway.[43] Alice Hatter, whose husband John (a wealthy citizen of the town) had predeceased her, may (along with him) have had an affiliation to the gild of St Margaret, because in her will of 14 November 1508 she left her sister, Mary Wrenne, 'a token of silver enclosing a lock of St. Margaret's hair', with a little pax attached to it. This object of personal devotion was obviously a treasured personal possession – one of a large number of such items to be

[40] It is likely that John Goddard's request for burial inside the church, in this particular area (p. 207), indicates that he was a leading member of the St Margaret gild.
[41] Gillingwater, *Lowestoft*, pp. 270 and 271.
[42] NRO, NCC 38–39 Multon. She also left quantities of wood and coal as fuel for the poor of the parish and bequests of bedlinen to pregnant poor women. Surplus clothing and bedding in her shop (after legacies had been made) was also to be given to the poor.
[43] NRO, NCC 96 Multon.

found in the late medieval period associated with holy relics of very dubious provenance.[44] Finally, on 1 December 1506, Robert Jetor left an acre of land butting onto *Folde Lane* (location unknown) to be rented out for twenty years and the money used to provide a lamp to burn for twenty years 'on holy days' in the Holy Trinity gild chapel, at the end of which time the plot was to be sold and the money used to fund the saying of prayers for his soul.[45] The holy days are not specified, but one of them would almost certainly have been Trinity Sunday.

The chapels to St George and St Gregory may well have been set up at the western extremities of the two side-aisles, flanking the tower archway. There would have been sufficient room on either side to incorporate the parcloses required, even on the south side of the church, where the doorway to the south porch's staircase was located. George, of course, was a soldier-saint and well on the way to becoming the country's national figurehead after having begun life (in England, at least) as patron of the Order of the Garter, inaugurated by Edward III in 1348 as the country's highest order of chivalry. St Gregory was Pope Gregory I (known also as Gregory the Great), one of the foremost scholars of the Western church and often referred to as one of the four Latin Doctors (the other three being Ambrose, Augustine and Jerome).[46] One interpretation of the possible symbolism lying behind the choice of these two men as gild patrons is that one represents action (as well as being symbolic of the triumph of good over evil) and the other learning.

Further symbolism within the church's interior would have been found in the wall paintings which would almost certainly have once been there. Popular, instructive bible stories (the selection varied) were represented to draw the eye and exercise the mind, and cautionary legends were sometimes present also. Probably the best known example of the latter during late medieval times was the story of The Three Quick and the Three Dead, shown as three kings on horseback confronted by three skeletons, surmounted (or underwritten) by the caption: 'As you are now, so once were we; as we are now, so you shall be.' It was a powerful reminder of the fragility of human life, delivered (it has to be said) in an era when people probably had sufficient evidence of the statement's truth in their everyday lives.[47]

[44] SRO(I), ASu., R5/53. A *pax* was an object of personal devotion. See Glossary.
[45] NRO, NCC 435–436 Ryxe. He also made provision for coal and wood to be given annually to poor people.
[46] The Orthodox church had its equivalents in Athanasius, Basil, Gregory of Nazianzus and John Chrysostom.
[47] All Saints Church, Belton, has a much faded example of the painting superimposed on earlier representations of St James the Great and St Christopher.

Two specific references to paintings within the church are to be found in late fifteenth-century wills. On 10 December 1524 Margery Lowis left the sum of £10 to her husband Geoffrey to pay for a picture of St Christopher (and also to provide a tabernacle) – this, in fulfilling the wishes of her father, William Jetour.[48] St Christopher, of course, was a popular apocryphal figure, the patron of travellers, who had carried the Christ child across the flooding river near his cell one stormy night (the Greek *Christophoros* means 'one who carries Christ'). It was believed that whoever looked upon an image of him would come to no harm that day, which is why depictions of this particular saint were among the most common of all paintings to be found within medieval churches – usually on the wall opposite the main entrance. In St Margaret's case, this would have meant the north wall – a location where two fine examples in local churches may still be seen. The church of St Edmund, Fritton, has a good fifteenth-century representation of the saint in which it may be seen, on close scrutiny, that his staff is in fact an eel-pick – a delightful example of something in everyday use in a marshland environment being worked into the picture. The other image is to be found in St John the Baptist, Lound, where a modern version by J.N. Comper (part of his restoration of the interior in 1914) takes the eye, even down to a detail of the creator's Rolls Royce car driving up a hillside!

The other painting referred to in connection with St Margaret's Church is to be found in the will of Katherine Wylton, already mentioned. She wished for a picture of St Sebastian to be executed somewhere within the building. Again, this late third-century martyr was a very popular figure during medieval times, though most surviving images of him are Renaissance paintings showing him tied to either a tree or a post and stuck with arrows. He was a Roman soldier of Gaulish origins killed during the time of the emperor Diocletian (c. AD 288) for his adoption of Christian beliefs. His execution was attempted with bows and arrows, but he is said to have survived this and, later, to have been clubbed to death. Because of his military background he became a patron of soldiers and his initial ordeal also associated him with archers. It would be interesting to know why a Lowestoft woman should have chosen to commemorate this particular early Christian hero.[49]

[48] NRO, NCC 171 Briggs. William Jetour's own will is TNA, Prob 11/16/292 (dated 15 February 1510).

[49] A medieval book known as *The Golden Legends* describes Sebastian as 'being as full of arrows as an *urchin*' – i.e. a hedgehog (the word deriving from the Latin *ericius*). The image challenges the imagination!

Vicars of the parish

Much has been written so far of the church's origins and of the building, but what of its clergy? Both Gillingwater and Hugh Lees have lists of priests in their respective works (the latter drawing upon the former and continuing up until 1938), but each contains errors that require correction.[50] Gillingwater made use of bishops' registers to identify the Lowestoft incumbents, beginning with the appointment of John Ayshe (Ashe) in February 1308. This man's predecessor, of course, was William de Leegh (Leigh), referred to above (p. 198), so he must be given the distinction of being the first recorded priest of St Margaret's, though (as has been noted) he held the benefice in plurality with that of St Andrew, Gorleston. He wasn't the only medieval priest in Lowestoft to have held two livings, as will be seen.

Ayshe's successor was Richard of Walcote (Walcot), in November 1330, and he was followed soon afterwards in September 1331 by John of Garboldesham (Garboldisham), who was rector also of the north Suffolk parish of Ringsfield.[51] He, in turn, was succeeded by Matthew of Rollesby in June 1339, who held Burgh Castle as rector, and yet another pluralist came along in February 1347 in the person of John Everard, who was rural dean of Brooke in south Norfolk. He seems to have survived the ravages of the Black Death and was replaced in February 1360 by John of Welberham (Wilbraham), who served also as rector at Lound.[52] Wilbraham was the last recorded of the fourteenth-century pluralists and was succeeded five years after his appointment (in February 1365) by William Homfrey (Humphrey), who remained in post until his death in September 1383.

There is no way of knowing whether the four men who were appointed to St Margaret's but had other responsibilities spent time in the parish. Lound was about four miles from Lowestoft, which was relatively close, but thereafter the distance (and the time spent travelling) increased. Burgh Castle was eight miles away, Ringsfield ten miles and Brooke fifteen – and these are distances given as the crow flies, not the length of the journey by road. The priests named would not have had the capacity to exercise a full-time ministry and, if they did, then curates must have functioned in the other parishes held. Conversely, if the other parishes were the centres of their activities then curates must have had cure of souls in Lowestoft. John Everard, as rural dean

[50] Gillingwater, *Lowestoft*, p. 340, and Lees, *Chronicles*, p. 38.

[51] Gillingwater shows de Garboldesham as being appointed in September 1330; Hugh Lees corrected the error.

[52] Benedictow, *Black Death*, p. 356, states that the death rate of beneficed parish clergy in Norwich diocese was 48.8 per cent, compared with a figure of 45 per cent nationally (p. 343).

of Brooke, certainly wouldn't have had the time to devote to the parishioners of Lowestoft.

After William Homfrey's incumbency had come to an end there seems to have been an hiatus of some kind in recording the sequence of Lowestoft vicars. Gillingwater draws a line against the year 1383 and appends the word *Apostolicus* beside it. On the line beneath is the name William Smoggett, with the year 1385 placed beside it. *Apostolicus* must refer to the pope rather than the bishop of Norwich, for whom the abbreviation *Epi* is used throughout the source of information (from *episcopus*), but this was the time of the Great Schism (1378–1417), when two rival popes were trying to exercise control over the church from Rome and Avignon. William Smoggett was never appointed as priest at St Margaret's. Revocation of his presentation is recorded on 1 July 1387 (he is described as a chaplain) on the plea of Robert Aylesham (Aylsham) that the living was not vacant and that incorrect information had been given to the king, who was controlling the temporalities of the bishop of Norwich at the time.[53] Eight months later, on 25 February 1388, Aylesham was confirmed as vicar of Lowestoft.[54]

He must have been in post from at least 1385 (possibly 1384), because Richard II had assumed punitive financial control of Norwich Diocese in October 1383. The bishop, Henry Despenser (a notable soldier–cleric), had led a five-month campaign into Flanders (May–September 1383) ostensibly in support of the city of Ghent in its opposition to the French-backed Anti-pope, Clement VII, who presided over the breakaway papacy in Avignon. The expedition was termed a crusade, but its motivation was as much commercial and economic as religious, and it was in some ways a continuation of the Hundred Years War by the back door. It ended with the failed attempt to take the city of Ypres and Despenser had to face impeachment by parliament on his return, at which point the king took control of his temporalities. Eventually, he managed to re-establish himself as a leading figure in public life and restitution of diocesan resources was made during 1385.

John Aylesham seems to have remained at St Margaret's until 1410. He was succeeded by Simon Baret (Barrett) who, like his predecessor, does not appear in the published list(s) of incumbents. The first reference to him is to be found in a record of 4 April 1413, when a papal *indult* (licence) was granted allowing him the use of a portable altar.[55] He is described as Simon, son of Simon Baret of Heacham and perpetual vicar of Lowestoft (perpetual vicar being the term used

[53] Maxwell Lyte, *CPR, Richard II*, vol. 3 (London, 1900), p. 329.
[54] Maxwell Lyte, *CPR, Richard II*, vol. 3, p. 363.
[55] W.H. Bliss and J.A. Twemlow (eds), *Calendar of Papal Registers Relating to Great Britain and Ireland*, vol. 6 (London, 1904), p. 346.

for a clergyman who lived off the small tithes of his parish), and six months later he was petitioning the Antipope, Benedict XIII, for ratification of his appointment by Pope Gregory XII (following the death of Robert Aylesham) for fear of 'molestation' in his post.[56] No further details are given, but this particular record, of 2 October 1413, shows that Baret was a bachelor of canon and civil law and that he had been in post for three and a half years.

Permission to have a portable altar for personal use is referred to a number of times in papal registers of the fifteenth century, and not exclusively for clergy. Such altars would have been kept in the home and could have been taken with other possessions on journeys at home and abroad, for the celebration of mass as and when required. Among the grants recorded is one of 6 April 1468 to Simon Dolfin, nobleman, 'lord of a place in Lowystoft', and another of 10 May 1438 was to John Fastolf, lord of one of the two manors belonging to the parish of Oulton.[57] Another privilege awarded regularly to members of both clergy and laity was the personal choice of a confessor to grant full remission of sins at the hour of death. One such concession is to be found on 7 March 1411, when William and Mabel Pye of Lowystoft (*sic*) were accorded the honour.[58] The husband, it may be remembered, had been involved in act of piracy carried out against German shipping seven years earlier (p. 178). Perhaps this was one of the things that he remembered in his final confession.

That the incumbency of William Baret was not without complications is suggested, aside from his own fears concerning 'molestation', in the nomination of Adam Gele (chaplain) for the post in April 1407.[59] This was done by Henry IV, the Norwich Diocese temporalities once more being in royal hands, this time as the result of an interregnum between the death of Henry Despenser (23 August 1406) and the consecration of his successor, Alexander Tottington (23 October 1407). Gele was the man who had been granted a pardon in September 1398 for raping Margaret, wife of Richard Olderyng (Oldrin) of Rushmere, at her house in Lowestoft – breaking through her fence and forcing his way into the dwelling on two separate occasions (27 October 1395 and 5 February 1397) to reach the object of his desire.[60] There is no further information on either Gele or Baret, but the presence of the former

[56] Bliss and Twemlow, *Papal Registers*, vol. 6, p. 417.
[57] J.A. Twemlow (ed.), *Calendar of Papal Registers Relating to Great Britain and Ireland*, vol. 12, p. 619, and vol. 8, p. 393 (London, 1933 and 1909). Dolfin's Lowestoft property at the time may have been the High Street messuage, located on freehold land to the north of *Swan Lane*, which later became *The Dolphin* inn.
[58] Bliss and Twemlow, *Papal Registers*, vol. 6, p. 330.
[59] Maxwell Lyte, *CPR, Henry IV*, vol. 3 (London, 1907), p. 318.
[60] Maxwell Lyte, *CPR, Richard II*, vol. 6 (London, 1909), p. 410.

(especially if he was a gild chaplain at St Margaret's) may have been what caused the latter to express concern regarding his tenure as vicar.

If Baret managed to stay in post until the next officially listed incumbent, then his period of service was a comparatively long one. William Sekynton (Seckington) was appointed in January 1432 and was vicar for ten years, being succeeded by John Mildewell in June 1442. Mildewell was followed in December 1456 by Thomas Shirecroft, who seems to have been the shortest-serving priest of all, being replaced three months later, in March 1457, by John Manyngham (Manningham). Manyngham performed his parish duties for over twenty years and three years into his incumbency, in June 1460, he was given a dispensation to hold one other benefice for life.[61] This was a privilege allowed to many clergy during the medieval period, but by no means all of the grantees exercised their right (they had to be offered preferment, in any case), and there is no evidence that John Manyngham did. In fact, the dispensation was repeated fourteen years later, in October 1474, with no evidence, once again, that the right was ever implemented.[62] Personal circumstances regarding the man are revealed in a record of August 1472, in which he is shown to have held an MA degree and to have had a deformed left shoulder, arm and hand (what would once have been commonly described as a withered arm). A dispensation was granted to him to retain his position and continue his ministry, even though his disability had not been made known when he was appointed.[63]

His physical condition obviously concerned him during his later years in Lowestoft. He worried that he would lose strength in the arm (which was shorter than the right one), reaching a point where he would find it difficult to exercise his priestly function. Reassurance, however, was given to him from the highest level and Pius II authorised his continuation in office as long as his handicap did not become too much to bear. This directive also made reference to the fact that he was the brother of a knight called Sir Oliver Manyngham.[64] The most distinctive feature of his time in Lowestoft was perhaps his endowment of almshouses in the town, which were located on the north side of *Fair Lane* (now Dove Street) near its junction with *West Lane* (now Jubilee Way) and which, with various changes made, remained in operation

[61] Twemlow, *Papal Registers*, vol. 11 (London, 1921), p. 575.

[62] Twemlow, *Papal Registers*, vol. 13 (London, 1955), p. 37.

[63] Twemlow, *Papal Registers*, vol. 13, p. 20. Priests with an MA degree were referred to as *Master*; non-graduates held the honorary title of *Sir*.

[64] Twemlow, *Papal Registers*, vol. 13, p. 409. Oliver Manyngham had married into the aristocratic Moleyns family (Barons of Hungerford) in 1468, though his own antecedents were in Yorkshire. His PCC will (TNA, Prob 11/11/642) was made on 16 May 1499 and proved on 8 June immediately following. He was buried at Stoke Poges, Buckinghamshire.

well into the early modern period. The buildings are referred to in a manorial rental of June 1545 as 'the allmes howssis late master manyngom' and they carried an annual payment to the lord of the manor of 10d.[65] There was one other set of charitable houses, which stood on the west side of the *High Street* at its southern end (currently shop units, Nos 113–115), but which do not seem to have had a clerical connection in their founding. The 1545 rental describes them as 'the allmes howssis sumtym [some time] John Reynolds' and they were assessed at 6d annual rent.

The priest who eventually succeeded John Manyngham was Thomas Scrope (a member of the noble family of that name), who was appointed in May 1478. He has been previously referred to in this chapter (fn. 27, p. 206) and was already well into his eighties when he took up his post. According to Gillingwater, he had been a notable itinerant preacher in his day[66] – even when suffragan bishop in Norwich Diocese under Walter Lyhert and James Goldwell – and it may be that the gift stayed with him in his later years and was able to edify his Lowestoft congregation. He died on 15 January 1491 and was succeeded by Robert Tomson (Thompson) in March of the same year. Tomson was followed in March 1507 by John Wheteacre (Wheatacre) and he, in turn, by Edward Lee in October 1508. Lee's incumbency lasted only about eighteen months, for John Bayley (Bailey) replaced him in May 1510 and served a similarly short period of time, making way for John Brown in October 1511.

Brown was the longest-serving of the recorded medieval priests at St Margaret's, his ministry there coming to an end in 1540. The last decade of his incumbency was arguably the most turbulent time of all in the history of the English church: Henry VIII's divorce from Catherine of Aragon, his marriage to Anne Boleyn and the subsequent break with Rome, his assumption of titular head of the national church and the dissolution of the monasteries, all of which was set against the background of growing Protestant influence emanating from Germany and Switzerland. What effect such profound change would have had upon the parish of Lowestoft cannot be known and even the suppression of St Bartholomew's Priory in 1539 would probably not have mattered to any significant degree, the great tithes simply passing from its control into private hands (Sir Richard Rich, the perjured solicitor-general, initially, and then a London family named Burnell).

What the people of Lowestoft would have witnessed during the time of its next two incumbents, John Blomevyle (Bloomfield) and Thomas Downing, was the sequence of change in the liturgy and practice of the English church.

[65] SRO(L), 194/A10/71. See Butcher, *Lowestoft*, pp. 237–8.
[66] Gillingwater, *Lowestoft*, p. 341.

Blomevyle was instituted in September 1540 and served as priest until 1555. He would have taken up his post at a time when the first officially sanctioned English translation of the Bible had been produced and was just finding its way into parish churches (1539) – not so much for use during services as to act as a work of reference for anyone wishing to access its text.[67] He would then have have experienced the Protestant reformation implemented under Edward VI, during whose reign (1547–53) he would have seen the abolition of the mass, the abandonment of the use of Latin during church services (in favour of English), the adoption of the Forty-two Articles of Faith,[68] the removal of images and paintings inside churches such as might lead to 'superstition', the destruction of rood lofts, the introduction of an English prayer book and the suppression of chantry chapels. Thus, St Margaret's would have lost much of its artwork inside the building and its five gild chapels would have ceased to function. No more ceremonies and processions on high days, no more prayers being made for departed members, and no more masses offered for the repose of their souls.

The will of John Goddard (April 1535) has already been referred to in connection with his privileged burial place on the north side of the chancel, near the entry door from the outside (see p. 207). Another of his expressed wishes was to have 'an honest priest, being a *singing-man*, that shall sing for me and my friends in the church of St. Margaret of Lowestofte for the space of two years, and he to have every (each) year for his wages £6'. It is likely that Goddard was an officer of the St Margaret Gild and that his request for burial was therefore within its chapel, at the northern end of the north aisle of the church. He was well within the 'safety period' for obits to be uttered on his behalf following his death, probably within the gild chapel itself, but in historical terms the time for such practice was drawing to a close.

Blomevyle would have lived through all of the Edwardian upheaval and shaped his conscience and practice as best he could. Then, having made all of the radical adjustments necessary, he would have been faced with the restitution of Roman Catholic practice under Edward VI's much older half-sister, Mary (1553–8). Henry VIII, though separating the national church from Rome, had remained Catholic in belief throughout his reign, simply making himself head of ecclesiastical organisation. His daughter, however, returned the apostate country to the authority of the pope and did her best to reverse the Protestant measures adopted by her half-brother. Thus the traditional

[67] Moorman, *Church in England*, p. 172.

[68] These were the guiding principles of Protestant practice in the Church of England. They were reduced to thirty-nine in number during Elizabeth I's reign and remain the foundations of Anglican belief and observance.

Latin mass was restored, stone altars were rebuilt in place of wooden communion tables, images, ornaments and vestments were reintroduced, married clergy were removed from their posts, and trial and punishment for Protestant heresy were carried out – culminating in the notorious burnings at Smithfield and in various provincial towns throughout the realm (including nearby Beccles).

Halfway through the Marian reaction Blomevyle resigned from St Margaret's, presumably because he did not agree with the changes in religious policy. He was replaced in June 1555 by Thomas Downing, who had also served as vicar of Besthorpe (in south Norfolk) from March 1528. The two parishes were combined into one living for the term of his life, because the income from each of them was modest.[69] The likelihood is that he did not spend a great deal of time in Lowestoft, given his long-standing Norfolk connections, and his incumbency was a short one in any case as he died in 1559, not long after the accession of Elizabeth I and the country's return to Protestantism. There must then have been an interregnum, before he was succeeded in 1561 by William Nashe, who was to serve the town for thirteen years, marrying into the Witchingham family (mariners and blacksmiths) and producing children – among whom was the future Elizabethan wit and satirical writer Thomas Nashe. The year of his arrival in Lowestoft is, coincidentally, the earliest year of survival for the parish registers and a fitting point at which to end this sequential account of the town's clergy.

There remains the opportunity to say something of the Lowestoft medieval clergy's function and practice within the parish. Cure of souls was the priest's main responsibility, together with observance of the daily round of set services and the celebration of major feasts in the Christian calendar (Christmas, Epiphany, Passiontide, Easter, Pentecost, Ascension, Trinity and Corpus Christi). The patronal festival of St Margaret (20 July) would also have been a notable high day during the year, with the festivities shared by the whole congregation and members of the patron's gild. The daily office was probably not as strictly observed as the routine within monastic communities and it would probably have been a matter of personal discipline on the part of individual priests as to whether (or not) the first two services of the day, matins (post-midnight) and lauds (dawn), were said. The pair were often conflated, in any case, and carried out at some point during the 'small hours'. It is likely that the first main service of the day at St Margaret's would have been prime (6 a.m.), followed by terce (9 a.m.), sext (noon),

[69] Gillingwater, *Lowestoft*, p. 344, quotes Francis Blomefield (the notable eighteenth-century Norfolk clerical antiquarian) as saying that the unification was one of the first examples he had encountered where the reason for implementing it was stated.

none (3 p.m.) and vespers (early evening). Compline was the final service of the day, said after supper – and, again, this was one which may not have been regularly observed.[70]

The daily mass (simplified in form rather than the full, high variety) would probably have been celebrated at terce, though sext was also a possibility (some priests may have observed both). It was also possible in Lowestoft to hold services in the *Town Chapel* (see p. 97), which had been built on a *High Street* site next to the *Corn Cross* and which was intended for public devotion during the winter when the roadways to the parish church were difficult to traverse. It is doubtful whether mass would have been celebrated there and nor is it known whether baptisms or marriages were conducted. The only clue as to possible uses and procedures is to be found in a post-Reformation record of 11 November 1570, when John Parkhurst, bishop of Norwich, issued a licence for public prayers to be said in the building but prohibited the celebration of communion (as it had become) or the carrying out of baptisms.[71] The sacrament of marriage is not referred to and burial services would obviously have had to be carried out at St Margaret's. It is likely that the bishop was following earlier practice concerning the chapel, but there is no conclusive proof of this.

With regard to the priest's domestic accommodation, it would seem from the available evidence that the vicarage house had two sites at different phases of its existence. The 1274 Hundred Roll implies that it was within the earlier of the two townships (see pp. 38 and 41), but at a later period it was situated at the south-west corner of the churchyard. The first location would have meant a half-mile walk up and down the hill for the incumbent – not a great distance, it has to be said (especially in the minds of people living in an age without modern means of transport), but not as convenient as a dwelling abutting onto the churchyard wall. According to Gillingwater, this house was destroyed by fire in 1546 and it is not known whether or not it was rebuilt.[72] It was definitely not on site when the 1618 manor roll was compiled, because the triangular quarter-acre plot on which it had stood (see Map 2, p. 25) is simply described as 'a piece of arable land' held by the vicar, John Gleason.[73] Whoever wrote up the document was obviously using an earlier, less complete

[70] The names of the eight services all derive from Latin, with the four main daily ones called *first*, *third*, *sixth* and *ninth* after the hour at which each was held – six o'clock in the morning being reckoned as the starting point.

[71] A copy of the document is to be found inserted in the pages of the parish tithe book, put there by the Revd John Tanner (NRO, PD 589/80).

[72] Gillingwater, *Lowestoft*, p. 251.

[73] Butcher, *Manor Roll*, pp. 54 and 55. Original document: SRO(L), 194/A10/73.

record of 1610, because John Gleason had died that year and been succeeded by Robert Hawes.[74]

Altogether, Gleason had three pieces of glebe land next to the churchyard, the other two (one acre and a half-acre in size, respectively) lying to the south of the wall, abutting onto *St Rook's acre* on the western side (see p. 209). This gave him one and three-quarter acres altogether and he seems to have farmed it. His burial is recorded in the parish registers on 26 June 1610 and, though his will has not survived, the probate inventory of his worldly goods (dated 2 July 1610) is still able to be studied.[75] It shows that he had a crop of barley worth 13s standing on the half-acre field and that he owned 'a little old horse', two pigs, six hens and a cockerel, and three geese. He lived in a house just off the *High Street*, in *Webb's Lane*, and the dwelling contained some hemp fibre and a spinning wheel. According to a note in the first surviving register book made by Thomas Warde (yeoman), the parish clerk of the time, John Gleason's house had suffered a fire on 6 March 1606 in which the previous register had been destroyed.[76] Luckily Gleason had made a paper copy (its predecessor would have been vellum), which then became the official register.

During the incumbency of Robert Hawes, Gleason's successor, it would seem that a new vicarage house was built close to the church again – unless it had been there since its predecessor was destroyed in 1546 and Gleason used his residence in town in preference to it (or even in tandem with it). The 1618 manor roll shows that Gleason's former residence was held by Thomas Smiter (yeoman) in addition to an inn close by (*The Pye*), but it also makes reference to Robert Hawes holding 'one house called *The Vicarage* and a piece of arable land' situated next to *Park Close* and *Church Green* (see Map 2, p. 25).[77] This places the house on the larger of the two arable pieces (one acre in size) immediately south of the churchyard wall. Again, like his predecessor, Hawes was involved in farming. No probate inventory is available for him, but his will of 26 August 1639 shows that he owned horses and beef cattle, while stocks of corn, wool and hemp are also referred to.[78] His burial took place on 3 September 1639, which shows that he was in a very fragile state of health when he made his will (as was John Gleason) – a situation which was fairly typical of the time.

The evidence of these two seventeenth-century clergymen working their glebe land for field crops and grazing livestock elsewhere is as near as it is

[74] The reference for the manor roll of 1610 is SRO(L), 194/A10/72.
[75] NRO, NCC INV 23/114.
[76] NRO, PD 589/1.
[77] Butcher, *Manor Roll*, pp. 24 and 25 and 42 and 43.
[78] NRO, NCC 92 Green.

possible to get regarding the Lowestoft incumbents' involvement with farming, and it may not have been typical of the practice of their medieval predecessors. The time that clergymen spent on church services after the Reformation was far less than had been the case in medieval times; there was no longer the daily round of at least five or six offices to perform (including one celebration of mass), the days of obligation during the year were greatly reduced in number, and use of the church by religious gilds had ceased. A conscientious vicar of the seventeenth or eighteenth century probably held matins (morning prayer) every day and possibly evensong as well, preached morning and afternoon on a Sunday, and celebrated communion either once a month or quarterly (Christmas, Easter, Whitsun and Michaelmas) – again, on a Sunday. Even with a pastoral duty of visiting of the sick and the distressed and conducting services of baptism, marriage and burial, he probably had more time at his disposal than his earlier counterpart.

One responsibility remained with Church of England clergy after the Reformation: keeping the chancel in good repair (the nave being the responsibility of the churchwardens and congregation). If the incumbent was a rector, enjoying the benefit of the whole of the parish's tithe value, then the burden was his alone. If, however, as at Lowestoft, he was a vicar and in receipt of the small tithes only, then he acted as agent on behalf of the organisation or individual who held the great tithes: St Bartholomew's Priory before the dissolution of the monasteries and a series of private individuals afterwards, beginning with Sir Richard Rich. A further duty laid upon the medieval incumbents of St Margaret's was responsibility for keeping the various service books and ornaments in good order – the latter almost certainly referring to chalice, paten, vestments, altar cloths and the like, as well as to candlesticks and other artefacts used in the visual embellishment and beautification of ritual and practice.[79] They were also responsible for the upkeep of the vicarage house and its surrounds, and an archdeacon's visitation of 1533 noted that the churchyard fencing was defective – 'the fault of the vicar in the part of it of which the repairs relate to him' (i.e. the section which abutted onto his house).[80]

According to an inquisition held at the beginning of the reign of Elizabeth I (accession 17 November 1558), the valuation of the Lowestoft vicarage was put at £25 17s 10½d (cf. £26 in 1306).[81] This was exclusive of the great tithes, which were now in private hands, and the calculation was reckoned by the churchwardens to be too high. A second enquiry duly took place on 31 January 1566 and its proceedings were noted by the Revd John Tanner and added

[79] Webb, *St. Bartholomew's Priory*, vol. 1, pp. 321 ff.
[80] NRO, ATC/46.
[81] Gillingwater, *Lowestoft*, p. 266.

to the pages of the Town Book.[82] The commissioners took evidence from five leading residents of the town – Richard Mighells (around fifty-five years old), Anthony Jettour (around forty-three years), John Grudgefield (around eighty-four years), Thomas Webb (around forty-eight years and recently moved to Norwich) and Richard Gooch (around fifty years) – and, as a result of their testimony regarding the church's income, the figure was lowered to £9 4s 5d. However, there was a sting in the tail and, in order to see that the church was liable for the payment of *first fruits and tenths*, it was raised to £10 1s 0d.

First fruits (or *annates*) and tenths were taxes paid by every church and chapel during medieval times and sent to Rome. The former were an agreed proportion (it varied) of the church's income paid by an incumbent during his first year of office, with a 10 per cent proportion paid annually thereafter. In 1540, with Henry VIII in charge of the English church and the monasteries dissolved, The Court of First Fruits and Tenths was set up to collect money sent previously to Rome and divert it to the Crown. Churches with an annual income of £10 or less were exempt, which is why the Lowestoft valuation was adjusted upwards by one shilling to make it liable for payment. Eventually, in 1703, the money collected was converted to Queen Anne's Bounty – a scheme devised by the monarch and sympathetic bishops to assist clergy in parishes with low incomes. Thereafter, any church with an income of less than £50 per annum was exempt from payment of the tax and the poorest ministers had their stipends augmented by the money collected from wealthier parishes.

The Good Cross Chapel

The final part of this chapter is given over to a lesser known part of Lowestoft's religious past. The foundation known as *The Good Cross Chapel* stood in the extreme south-eastern corner of the parish near the junction of the present-day Suffolk Road with Battery Green Road, close to the building which once served as the town's library and which is now incorporated into a local retail premises. It was a wayside place of devotion not far from the crossing point (a sand and shingle bank, or bar) over the eastern extremity of Lake Lothing, and it purported to have a piece of Christ's cross as an object of veneration (it has been said that there were enough of these wooden fragments in medieval Europe to have built a small fleet of ships!). It is not known when it was built, nor who endowed it, but it was an important part of the town's religious

[82] NRO, PD 589/112. This book is a collection of hand-written material relating to the town, contributed by leading citizens during the seventeenth and eighteenth centuries. A microfilm copy of it is available in SRO(L).

culture and it raised an income of £8–£9 annually from the offerings made by people resorting to it. One of the witnesses referred to above (John Grudgefield) was the person who provided this information to the commissioners enquiring into the value of the vicarage in January 1566. He gave the chapel's demise (caused by the suppression of the chantries) as one of the major factors in the fall in parish income.

As a creator of income for the vicar the chapel would undoubtedly have come under his jurisdiction, but parish duties and the observance of daily services would have kept him fully occupied. A chaplain would therefore have been employed to administer the chapel, holding services there as and when required and seeing to the needs of visitors. There is at least one reference to it as a place of pilgrimage from the mid-fifteenth century, in the nuncupative will of Thomas Pekerell of Rickinghall Superior, in West Suffolk.[83] In declaring his final wishes, on 25 January 1458, the testator requested (among other things) that his wife do pilgrimage either in person or by surrogate to the following places: Norwich (shrine of the boy-saint, William, at the Cathedral), Ely (St Etheldreda's Shrine, at the Cathedral), Walsingham (the Shrine of Our Lady, in the Priory), Bury (the Shrine of St Edmund in the Abbey church) and Lowestoft. At each place prayers for Thomas Pekerell's soul would have been offered, and it can be seen that *The Good Cross Chapel* was in elevated company.

After its demise,the building would have been stripped of its fittings and the holy relic probably destroyed. It seems to have been converted to domestic use at some point, and it is referred to in the 1618 manor roll as 'a house called the *Good Cross Chapel*'. It was held under copyhold tenure by a man called Thomas Wilson at an annual rent of 4d.[84] Just over a century later, in c. 1725, the Revd John Tanner drew up a list of copyhold properties in the town, together with an accompanying series of court baron transfers relating to each property.[85] He does not mention the Chapel in his listing, but the transfer material contains the following information, translated here by the writer from the original Latin: 'a piece of land from the waste of the lord, with a house built thereon called *The Good Cross Chapel*, sixty feet in length by fifty in breadth'. Thus is the size of the chapel's plot established. Two details of transfer are given: Laurence Robson, on the surrender of Richard Watson, at the leet court of 1550; Thomas Webb, on the surrender of Laurence Robson, June–July 1563.[86]

[83] SRO(I), SA R2/9/240. A nuncupative will was one made verbally by a testator, who was usually close to the point of death.
[84] Butcher, *Manor Roll*, pp. 20 and 21.
[85] SRO(L), 454/1 and 454/2.
[86] Thomas Webb was one of the five witnesses who gave evidence as to the value of the Lowestoft vicarage in January 1566.

The route of today (moving from east to west) formed by Suffolk Road, Bevan Street East, Bevan Street West and Norwich Road was once known as *Chapel Lane*. It had an earlier pedigree as an ancient track skirting the southern perimeter of *The South Field* and linking with the route southwards to Kirkley and Pakefield over the shingle bank separating Lake Lothing, or *The Fresh Water*, from the sea (see Map 2, p. 25). The name continued in use well into the nineteenth century and it is possible that the building itself stood above ground until the second half of the eighteenth – though its fate thereafter is not known. A decorative transfer-print design used on blue-and-white porcelain produced at the Lowestoft factory during that period is known as the Good Cross Chapel pattern (Plate 26).[87] Its provenance or assignation has never been established, but it could possibly date from the 1770s or thereabouts. The scene presented seems to be a composite one of five local buildings of the time. Working from left to right, there is a bridge built of masonry (possibly the one crossing the meeting point of the broad at Oulton and Lake Lothing), a tall house of some kind with an end-stack, a much smaller building fronting it (which may represent a fish-house), a tower surmounted by a lantern (representing the cliff-top lighthouse) and a four-bay building with cross-wing and doorway and three large, ecclesiastical-looking windows (the Good Cross Chapel itself).

There can, of course, be no absolute proof that this architectural conflation contains a significant vestige of Lowestoft's medieval past, but there is more than an even chance that it does.

Plate 26. The Good Cross Chapel pattern. This late eighteenth-century blue-and-white teapot shows the scene described, with the five local features combined into a single decorative motif.

[87] G.A. Godden, *The Illustrated Guide to Lowestoft Porcelain* (London, 1969), plate 98.

– 7 –

The early to mid-sixteenth-century community

Although much of the documentation used throughout this book up until now has given insights (sometimes substantial ones) into Lowestoft's developing status as the dominant town in its local area, the first real sense of an established urban community (albeit of middling proportions) is to be found in a national tax record. The 1524–5 Lay Subsidy lists residents liable for payment of a levy made nationally by Henry VIII and his government for the conduct of war with France.[1] It gives a comprehensive view of the names of the contributors and the levels of wealth present in the Lowestoft society of the time. The particular source used to explore the data presented is a transcription of the original documentation carried out by the great Suffolk antiquarian and historian the Revd Sydenham Henry Augustus Hervey, vicar of Wedmore in Somerset but a member of the notable aristocratic family of Ickworth.[2] Because of defects present in the 1524 collection list, he supplemented a shortfall detected there (in the amount of money collected) with additional material from the following year in order to create balance in the overall picture.

The structure of the levy made upon the population of England was created in such a way as to ensure that all its citizens made a contribution, regardless of how they earned their money. Land was assessed at 12d (1s) in the pound

[1] The parliament of 1523 granted an annual subsidy for four years (1524–7), aimed at raising a sum of £800,000. Land, movable goods and wages were taxed, thereby allowing the authorities to reach all levels of society in their attempt to collect the money required. The collection day for each year was 9 February.

[2] Hervey, *Suffolk in 1524*, pp. 243–7. Hervey used Exchequer documentation in the Public Record Office, now classified as TNA, E179/180/141 and 184 (the former relating to 1525 and the latter to 1524).

(£) value, regardless of how much was held; goods (i.e. trading stock and trade equipment) were assessed at 12d in the pound for those people having £20 worth or more and 6d in the pound for those having £1–£20 worth; and wages of £1 or more per annum were assessed at 4d and of £2 or more at 6d. Any alien (foreign) wage-earners paid double that amount. Thus, in broad and generalised terms, the landowning classes (aristocracy and gentry) were taxed on their main source of income, the merchants, master craftsmen, seafarers and farming community on theirs, and the artisans and labourers on theirs.

As long ago as the early 1960s the economic historian Julian Cornwall produced a social structure relating to English country towns, using the 1524 Subsidy as the means of establishing it.[3] Taking the assessment on goods as his indicator, he devised the following financial bands to identify the different social groupings paying the different fixed levels of tax: 1. £2, small craftsmen and husbandmen (often partly independent and partly earners of day wages); 2. £3–£5 and £6–£9, a kind of 'lower middle class'; 3. £10–£19, richer tradesmen and husbandmen, and lesser yeomen – 'a substantial middle class'; 4. above £20, prosperous master craftsmen, merchants, yeomen and gentlemen. The work was later cited by Margaret Spufford in her classic book on Cambridgeshire rural parishes, *Contrasting Communities*, and it can be taken as relating to Lowestoft in a generalised sense – but with one important exception: the lack of any references to maritime activity. This is entirely understandable, as the work was dealing with inland communities, but coastal ones differed from their rural counterparts and their socio-economic structure was partly determined by fishing and seaborne trade. It will also be noticed that the bottom-most band of £1 per annum (largely, servants, labourers and men in a very small way of business) does not feature at all.

Society, economy and taxation

The wealthiest merchants in Lowestoft would all have been involved in the ownership of sea-going vessels employed in fishing and trading, and would have had a direct interest in the processing of the catches landed. The men serving on board would have varied a good deal in status and earnings, with the masters possibly placed as high as the third category referred to in the previous paragraph – though with a different means of assessment applied to their tax liability. At the other end of spectrum, the lesser crew members would have earned much lower wages and been taxed accordingly. The level of expense involved in the building, fitting-out and maintenance of vessels

[3] J. Cornwall, 'English country towns in the 1520s', *EHR*, 2nd series 15 (1962), p. 63.

would also have created a number of specialist craftsmen and artisans (shipwrights, carpenters, smiths and the like) whose skills would have been in high demand and whose stocks of materials and equipment probably carried quite a high capital value.

The information relating to the economic status of Lowestoft's inhabitants in 1524–5, and to their consequent tax assessment, is quite lengthy – which, in itself, shows that the town's population had grown to the point where it had attained a definite urban character (Table 12). This had probably begun at the point when the township relocated to the cliff (c. 1300–1350), but exactly when it was that Lowestoft could truly be considered to have become a town is not possible to declare. Certainly, by the later years of the fifteenth century it had a large enough number of inhabitants and a sufficiently complex occupational structure to merit the title. Mark Bailey places it in tenth position among the top ten Suffolk towns, based on the number of taxpayers recorded (144), though it does not enter the list based on the amount of tax it paid – its £35 18s 7d being below the £40 raised by Dunwich (the sums of money cited relate to the year 1524; the number of taxpayers to 1525). It also features in a map of Suffolk showing the location of towns 1200–1500.[4]

Bailey based his hierarchy of 'top ten' towns on the work of the historical geographer John Sheail, which gives a detailed breakdown of the tax details relating to the whole of the country.[5] The total amount of money collected in Lothingland Half-hundred in 1524 was £63 11s 8d, with Lowestoft paying the £35 18s 7d cited above – 57 per cent of the whole. The number of taxpayers was 311, but Lowestoft's figure is not given because of defects in the list. However, using Sydenham Hervey's information it would seem to have been about 133, which would make the Lothingland total 444 – giving Lowestoft 30 per cent of the overall number of contributors. The following year, 1525, cites a total sum of £54 0s 3d for the half-hundred, with Lowestoft paying £29 11s 8d, or 55 per cent. The overall number of taxpayers is given as 408, with Lowestoft having 144, or 35 per cent. It leaves one in no doubt as to which Lothingland community was the dominant one in terms of size of population and levels of wealth. Interestingly, however, it may be that the town should not have been included in Suffolk's top ten urban communities based on the number of taxpayers, as Nayland is shown to have had 147 of them in 1525 – three more than Lowestoft's 144.[6]

[4] Bailey, *Suffolk*, pp. 282 and 122 (Map 1.4).

[5] J. Sheail, 'The regional distribution of wealth in England as indicated by the 1524–5 Lay Subsidy' (unpub. PhD thesis, Univ. London, 1968), part 2, p. 487. This thesis was eventually put into print by the List and Index Society in 1997.

[6] Ibid, p. 473. See Appendix 2 for a detailed examination of Suffolk's 1524–5 Subsidy return.

Reference was made in the first paragraph of this chapter to Sydenham Hervey's making good a shortfall in the stated amount collected for 1524 (£35 18s 7d). The individual entries listed produce a sum of c. £5 15s 0d less than this, so he extracted a list of contributors from the 1525 return whose payments added up to this particular amount. Forty-one individuals were selected and only four of them featured in the 1524 collection, which looks very much as if the town's tax was collected in stages, rather than from the whole population at once. The collector for Lothingland and Mutford half-hundreds was none other than John Goddard, who featured in the previous chapter with regard to his wishes regarding his burial arrangements (pp. 207 and 220). His task, as outlined by the Commissioners for Suffolk (John Jernegan, John Harvy and John Debden), was to take possession of a parchment document issued by them on which were listed all the taxable people in both jurisdictions (arranged by parish) and the individual sums of money they had been assessed at. The constable(s) of each parish was/were to be responsible for collecting the money, before handing it to Goddard, who would then pass it on to the commissioners.[7]

Given the level of detail concerning the individual inhabitants of each parish, it is just possible to make approximate population estimates for the contributing communities. But they are no more than that and must therefore be approached with caution. The taxpayers in any given community would have varied widely in age and marital status, and the factor of gender has also to be taken into account, with a small minority of women featuring in the statistics.[8] Therefore, it is practically impossible to arrive at an accurate number of family heads in order to use the commonly accepted multiplier of 4.75 and produce a notional population figure. If Lowestoft's combined number of taxpayers was 277 (133 for 1524 and 144 for 1525) and a quarter of them (male and female) were ineligible for inclusion in the process of calculation for one reason or another, that would leave 207 as possible family heads to produce a population of around 1,000 people, using an accepted multiplier of 4.75. Demographic analysis of the town's parish registers for the period 1561–1600 (using an approved crude-death-rate formula based on the number of burials which took place) gives a population of c. 1,500 people.[9] Expansion of the

[7] Hervey, *Suffolk in 1524*, pp. 242–3.

[8] Lowestoft also has the added complication of a noticeable number of foreigners in its population, who may have been married with families but who could also well have been young male servants without dependants.

[9] This total is arrived at by using an annual death rate of 30 per 1000. This chosen number of 30 is divided by an average number of burials over a given period (at least a decade) and the resulting figure then used as the divisor with a dividend of 1000. In Lowestoft, such a calculation produces a population of c. 1470 for 1561–75 and c. 1540 for 1576–1600.

town during the second half of the seventeenth century and the first half of the eighteenth added about 200 people every twenty-five years, so an increase of 500 or so between the 1520s and the 1580s is entirely possible.

Table 12. The 1524–5 Lay Subsidy.

Name(s)	Category	Value	Tax paid
John Jettor Jnr*	Goods	£101 (*sic*)	£6
Thomas Kidwell and Richard Thompson	Wages	£1 each	8d
Robert Hodds Snr	Goods	£100	£5
Richard Stevens, Robert Scarlet* and Thomas Curtis	Wages	£1 each	1s
Thomas Wood	Goods	£40	£2
William French*	Goods	£40	£2
Robert Bache*	Goods	£50	£2 10s 0d
Thomas Spink and Walter Cooper	Wages	£1 each	8d
John, servant of Robert Bache	Wages	£2	1s
John Goddard*	Goods	£40	£2
Alice Drawer*	Bequest	£2	1s
John, servant of John Goddard	Wages	£1	4d
Bernard (French man), servant of John Goddard	Wages	£1	8d
John Jettor Snr*	Goods	£10	5s
Geoffrey Lobbes	Goods	£18	9s
John Harman*	Wages	£2	1s

Notes:

- All names are given in modern spelling format.
- There is a break in the sequence of taxpayers at this point, punctuated by the editor's following comment: 'Here a part of the membrane is torn off. The valuations and payments of ten persons can be read, but not their names. Their valuations are £1; £8; £4; £8; £2; **£30**; £12; £2; £16; £10. The one pounder pays 4d in the £, the thirty pounder pays a shilling, and the rest 6d. Their payments amount to £3: 1: 4. The payers of about £5: 15: 0 appear to be lost altogether.' The person paying the sum of 4d in the pound on £1 wealth was a wage-earner; the two people paying 6d in the pound on £2 were either upper-level wage-earners or lower-level craftsmen/traders; everyone else paying 6d was a merchant or tradesman of varying status; and the shilling in the pound contributor was a substantial merchant.

Name	Category	Value	Tax paid
Robert Willett	Goods	£6	3s
? Stevenson	Goods	£2	1s
John Fairweather	Goods	£5	2s 6d
Ralph Dean	Goods	£8	4s
Nicholas Swain*	Wages	£1	4d

Table 12 *cont.*

Name	Category	Value	Tax paid
John Smith*	Goods	£2	1s
John Arnold*	Goods	£5	2s 6d
Thomas Baron	Goods	£6	3s
Alice Coe (widow)*	Goods	£2	1s
Thomas Pine	Goods	£13 13s 4d	6s 10d
William Randall	Wages	£1	4d
Agnes Davey (widow)*	Goods	£2	1s
Agnes Fuston (widow)	Goods	£4	2s
Richard Allcock	Goods	£1	6d
Richard Clarke*	Goods	£2	1s
John Holmes	Goods	£14	7s
John Dixon and Andrew Norman	Wages	£1 each	8d
James ? (Dutch man)	Wages	£1	8d
Richard Landeville and William Neslyn	Goods	£3 each	3s
John Leman and William Hooker	Goods	£1 each	1s
Thomas Barker*	Goods	£12	6s
Harry Gronge and John Freeman	Goods	£2 each	2s
John Botson and Thomas Ager	Goods	£4 each	4s
Nicholas Fellow	Wages	£1	4d
William Wynne and John Winston	Goods	£3 each	3s
John Neville, Thomas Holland*, William Cooper and Robert James*	Goods	£1 each	2s
William Pond*	Goods	£8	4s
Thomas Hanks*	Goods	£5	2s 6d
John Youngs	Wages	£1	4d
Thomas Oldring	Lands	£2	2s
Andrew Benton, Thomas Rutherford, William Levery and Martin Brend	Goods	£1 each	2s
Richard Heron, John Hooker, John Ireland and Austin Dent	Goods	£1 each	2s
Robert Blackman and John True	Wages	£1	8d
William Wilde*	Goods	£2	1s
William Hatch*, John Carr, Roland Hall and Nicholas Dikeman	Goods	£1 each	2s
Thomas Dixon and Robert Barnard*	Goods	£2 each	2s
William Savage and John Dean	Goods	£4 each	4s
John Fowler, John Gedge, Anthony White* and William Benns	Wages	£1 each	1s 4d
John Butcher	Goods	£3	1s 6d
Roger Wright	Wages	£1	4d

Table 12 *cont.*

Name	Category	Value	Tax paid
William Cooper, Roland Seward, Harry Mason, Robert Melton, Robert Wilson, John Knightley and ? Johnson	Goods	£1 each	3s 6d
John King and Richard Moore	Wages	£1 each	8d
William Stone	Goods	£14	7s
Alexander Love	Goods	£2	1s
John Decker, Richard Steyngate and John Carter	Goods	£1 each	1s 6d
Richard Selling and John Currier	Goods	£5 each	5s
William Harman*	Goods	£4	2s
John Barker*	Goods	£4	2s
John Hadley and Richard Sinston	Wages	£1 each	8d
Edmond Hill*	Goods	£1	6d
Sir John Brown (vicar)	Goods	£7	3s 6d
Lawrence Dodson	Wages	£2	1s
Alice Jettor*	Bequest	£4 2s 8d	2s 2d
John Rabue (French man)	Wages	£1	8d
William Marshall (Scottish man)	Wages	£1	8d
William Youngs (French man)	Wages	£1	8d
Thomas Youngs (Scottish man)	Wages	£1	8d
Philip Groat (Guernsey man)	Wages	£1	4d
John the Breton	Wages	£1	8d
Matthew ? (French man)	Wages	£1	8d
Nicholas ? (Guernsey man)	Wages	£1	4d
Thomas Parnell	Goods	£10	5s
Roger Gage (gentleman)	Lands	£5	5s
John Booty	Wages	£1	4d
Christopher ? (servant with Richard James*)	Wages	£1	4d
Peter ? (Dutch man)	Wages	£1	8d
James Coppe	Goods	£1	6d

Notes:

- This is where the 1524 list ends, with the total sum collected of £35 18s 7d stated at the bottom of the column indicating the individual sums paid. Small supplementary sums (referred to as *oblites* and *increments*) totalling £1 7s 10d are included without explanation of the terms' meanings. The original document is set out as two columns: the first one consisting of the information presented in the first three columns of the table, the second showing the sums of money paid. In the published version of the text there then follows an editorial note from Sydenham Hervey: 'The printed items fall short of this total by about £5: 15: 0, the roll being imperfect. I here give an extract from the roll 180/141, being for the second year's return of this subsidy, which will more or less supply the deficiency in the first year's return.'

Table 12 *cont.*

Name	**Category**	**Value**	**Tax paid**
Geoffrey Lobbes	Goods	£18	9s
John Harman	Wages	£2	1s
Robert Murdock and Robert Woodshed*	Goods	£8 each	8s
John Palmer (gentleman) and Robert Gare	Goods	£4 each	4s
Robert Brown and Theodore Ovey	Goods	£2 each	2s
John Robson (the consideration of his decay is that he lost a ship upon the sea, the which was taken with the Scots to the value of £28)	Goods	£2	1s
Thomas Annot*	Goods	£12	6s
Roger Chancellor*	Goods	£16	8s
Robert Fly and Gilbert Humbleton	Goods	£1	6d
Thomas Ovey and Avis Andrews	Goods	£5 each	5s
John Everard	Goods	£10	5s
Robert Chever	Goods	£20	£1
Robert Hodds Jnr	Goods	£19	9s 6d
Walter Stubbard	Goods	£3	1s 6d
Audrey Stanbridge (widow)	Goods	£2	1s
Thomas Allen*, Richard Scarlet* and Cornelius Rogerson	Goods	£6 each	9s
Richard James*, John Mutton and John Sale	Goods	£4 each	6s
John Tubbing	Goods	£4 13s 4d	2s 4d
Robert Fowler*, Robert Gilbank* and Ralph Dean	Goods	£8 each	12s
John Rutter	Wages	£1	4d
Mangle (a Scottish man)	Wages	£1	8d
John Beveridge, Thomas Shotsham* and John Fairweather	Goods	£5 each	7s 6d
Martin Cornelius (Dutch man)*	Goods	£7	14s (*sic*)
Cornelius ? (Dutch man) and Peter ? (Dutch man)	Wages	£1 each	1s 4d
William Collis and Robert Willett	Goods	£6 each	6s
Lucas Martinson (Dutch man)	Goods	£12	6s (*sic*)

Notes:

- The end of the Lowestoft data has an editor's note to the effect that the sums of money paid in his 1525 supplement add up to £7 11s 8d, which is larger than the £5 15s 0d he remarked upon at the end of the 1524 list.
- The six names in bold font in the first part of the table, together with the anonymous sum of £30, show that these seven persons paid 58 per cent of the town's 1524 total tax liablility. They represent 14 per cent of the people featuring in the goods category in the 1524 list and just over 5 per cent of all the names recorded (including the ten missing).

- John Jettor Jnr has the editor's appendage (*sic*) against his valuation, implying that £101 is perhaps an error. It may be that he had entered another tax band and that the extra £1 worth of goods cost him £1 more in tax.
- Though not stated as such, it is likely that the wage-earners following the names of John Jettor Jnr and Robert Hodds Snr may well have been these men's servants. Both taxpayers are in a category of assessment described as 'remarkable' in Amor, *Ipswich*, p. 37 – the example cited here being a foreign merchant named John Vancleve, who also paid tax on £100 worth of movable goods.
- Ralph Dean, John Fairweather, John Harman and Geoffrey Lobbes are names given in both the 1524 and 1525 data, with identical assessments and payments recorded. This may mean that payment had not been made first time round and was being collected the following year.
- At the end of the 1525 supplement it would appear that Martin Cornelius (as an alien) paid double his double-amount of tax due. It should have been 7s on £7 worth of goods. Similarly, Lucas Martinson seems to have paid the same rate as native-born taxpayers, as his alien's contribution should have been 12s. Sydenham Hervey makes no comment on either person's payment.
- Use of an asterisk indicates surnames to be found in the 1568 Lay subsidy.
- Only seven women are recorded as taxpayers (4 per cent of the total number of 174 people listed in the table). Four of them were widows taxed on movable goods, while two more were probably widows also, having assessments based on legacies. The remaining one (taxed on movable goods) could have been either married or single and possibly running her own business enterprise. Female servants and menials do not feature in the assessment.

While the tax liability of 1524–5 shown in Table 12 is interesting, it is the additional data incorporated that is of value in presenting a more detailed picture of Lowestoft in the third decade of the sixteenth century. It will not go unnoticed that the surnames listed in two previous taxation rolls, of 1274 and 1327 respectively (see Tables 6, 7 and 8, pp. 33, 38 and 62), have scarcely any replication in the list above (Allen and Steyngate being the two exceptions, with the possibility of Dean having derived from Deacon). Nor is there any notable presence of surnames belonging to the men recorded in connection with the town's maritime activity during the fourteenth and fifteenth centuries (the subject of Chapter 5). The Boofs, the Boulds, the Grymes, the Lacys, the Palmers, the Pyes, the Reynalds, the Ryveshales, the Tutelers and the Wymers – community leaders, many of them – are not to be found. Only the Bochers (Butchers) and the Steyngates are visible – the latter family running all the way through from the 1274 Hundred Roll. The Black Death would have taken its toll of all families at the time of its first appearance (1349), but a number of the names are to be found after the ravages of this most destructive epidemic, as well as before. So what had occurred to create the turnover in population by 1524?

The answer probably lies in spatial mobility, which is evident in Suffolk from the thirteenth century onwards and was caused by a number of factors.[10] Firstly, the high rate of free tenancy recorded at Domesday (estimated to be as high as 45 per cent of all landholding, against a national average of 14 per cent) created individual freedom of choice and the ability to move from place to place. Then there was the relatively low degree of villein tenancy (c. 20 per cent of the county total), which resulted in fewer people being tied to their manors and unable to move as they might wish to. And, finally, a substantial (but unquantifiable) proportion of the lower orders was landless and therefore rented small holdings as best they could on a short-term basis, before moving on somewhere else. Following the ravages of the Black Death, and its great demographic, economic and social dislocation, the opportunity (or compulsion) to change one's surroundings probably increased further. Lowestoft's fortunes had burgeoned from c. 1300 onwards through fishing and seaborne trade, and this upturn in economic enterprise would have acted like a magnet, drawing in people endowed with practical skills from both near at hand and further afield.

A scrutiny of the 1524–5 Subsidy record relating to the half-hundreds of Lothingland and Mutford suggests that a number of the Lowestoft taxpayers may have had antecedents in the surrounding parishes. For instance, the name Allen is to be found in Pakefield, Annot in Southtown, Arnold in Blundeston and Carlton, Bache in Gorleston, Barker in Bradwell, Kirkley and Pakefield, Booty in Gunton and Oulton, Chancellor in Herringfleet, Coe in Somerleyton, Fairweather in Corton, Gorleston, Fritton, Hopton and Oulton, Fowler in Kirkley, Hill in Kessingland and Pakefield, Holland in Mutford, Nestlyn in Corton and Rushmere, Thompson in Carlton and Kirkley, White in Gorleston, and Wilde in Carlton, Corton, Kessingland and Rushmere. Moving further southwards, down the coast, the Dunwich bailiffs' accounts of the early fifteenth century have not only Arnold and Chancellor but Cooper, James and Wright also.[11] A wider search would no doubt yield even more recognisable surnames.

There is little or no way of accurately assessing the turnover of population during the medieval period, and it is not until the introduction of parish registers during the sixteenth century and the listings of residents sometimes made in communities during the seventeenth and eighteenth that such movement can be calculated. In Lowestoft's case, it is possible to estimate from register material (using marriage and baptism data, and burial entries to a lesser

[10] Bailey, *Suffolk*, pp. 36, 41 and 54. The facts presented here cogently summarise the overall effect on population movement of the varying types of land tenure present in the county.
[11] Bailey, *Bailiffs' Minute Book*, passim.

degree) that, between 1561 and 1730, 25 per cent of the town's population had a residency period of three years or less and 33 per cent one of twelve years or less.[12] The mobile element of the population, on the evidence of occupational references given in the registers, consisted largely of servants, labourers, lesser tradespeople and artisans, with a small number of gentry thrown in. Very little information is given as to the places of origin of these people, but a book of settlement orders (beginning in 1698 and ending in 1769) provides crucial insight.[13] It reveals that, for the first three decades of the eighteenth century, most of the inward migration came from places within a fifteen-mile radius of Lowestoft, with the strongest 'pull' exerted by the town on local parishes lying within a five-mile distance. And that may also have been largely the case in medieval times.

Having noted that there is very little tie-up between the surnames of the thirteenth, fourteenth and fifteenth centuries and those of the 1524–5 Subsidy, there is not a great deal, either, between Henry VIII's taxation and that of his daughter Elizabeth in 1568. The latter records 112 names (seven of them women), with a total sum of £34 19s 8d collected.[14] On the evidence of parish register entries the people taxed do not constitute a full head of population by any means and the way they were selected is not known. Given that there is a gap of only forty-four years between the two subsidies, there is relatively little overlap in the surnames recorded, which again suggests continuing turnover of population as people moved from place to place for whatever reasons. In the case of the lower orders (especially servants and labourers), it was probably a matter of moving on to find improved conditions of employment, while craftsmen and tradespeople (including merchants) would either have gone to where more money could be made or to where they might elevate their social standing on the strength of the wealth they had accrued in their previous place of residence.

In terms of surname replication, the following ones are to be found in both lists: Allen, Annot, Arnold, Barnard, Chancellor, Cornelius, Drawer, Gilbank, Hatch, Hill, Holland, James, Jettor, Scarlet, Shotsham, White, Wilde and Woodshed. The total of eighteen represents about 12 per cent of the overall number of surnames listed in the 1524–5 data and one of the people taxed at that time, a merchant named Thomas Annot, was still alive, living in the town and paying tax, in 1568. Robert Barnard (shipwright) is another possibility, but his presence cannot be proved as that of Annot can

[12] Butcher, *Lowestoft*, p. 40. The surviving Lowestoft parish registers begin in the year 1561.
[13] SRO(L), 01/13/1/3.
[14] S.H.A. Hervey, *Suffolk in 1568*, SGB 12 (Bury St Edmunds, 1909), pp. 186–9. The original document is TNA, E179/182/359.

be. Annot had increased his wealth and status since his earlier days, paying £2 13s 4d on lands worth £40 a year – the most heavily taxed by far of all Lowestoft citizens. He was into the final decade of his long life and his burial is recorded on 15 November 1577. Another link may be seen with William Wilde, son of the man who had paid 1s on £2 goods in 1524 – the year that he was born. Wilde paid 6s 8d on goods worth £8 in 1568 and did not die until 23 March 1611 at the age of eighty-seven years, being buried two days later. Thomas Annot's grave slab is located behind the organ at the end of the north aisle in St Margaret's church; that of William Wilde, which recorded the date of death and his age and said that he 'lived harmless as a child', is no longer present in the middle aisle as it once was.[15]

Both men represent the best in the civic responsibility shown by people of their time. Annot, who was the end of his male line (having no living sons), is best known for endowing a free grammar school for forty local boys in June 1570,[16] while Wilde was the founding father of a family which remained in Lowestoft for over 200 years and gave dedicated service to the town in all kinds of ways – including, eventually, a free grammar school of their own. The latter was established in principle by the will of John Wilde in July 1735, but the testator's intention was not carried out until 1781 owing to the longevity of a particular legatee.[17] The building in which the school was once housed is still in existence (located on Wilde's Score, off the High Street), currently serving as the headquarters of the Lowestoft Heritage Workshop Centre. It is fitting in some respects that both of these schools (which had changed radically from their original intention and form) were eventually amalgamated, thereby merging two notable charitable acts, and the work of education continued in enlarged premises until bomb damage sustained during the Second World War effectively brought it to an end.

Authorisation for the Elizabethan taxation was granted on 18 December 1566 and the official date of collection was 24 February 1568. Lowestoft's contribution, as cited above (£34 19s 8d), was 47 per cent of the Lothingland total of £74 8s 6d and its 112 taxpayers constituted 42 per cent of the half-hundred's contributors (265 in number). These figures confirm the town's dominant position in its local area, just as those of the 1524–5 collection did (see p. 230 above). The 1568 Subsidy was structured differently from its predecessor in the way that the assessment was made. It had the same basic

[15] Gillingwater, *Lowestoft*, p. 293, and Lees, *Chronicles*, p. 155.
[16] Butcher, *Lowestoft*, pp. 291–5. He also left a legacy for the grammar school in Woodbridge, which probably indicates a family connection with that town suggestive of its perhaps being his place of origin.
[17] Lees, *Chronicles*, p. 147.

framework of payment on lands and goods, but wages (and the people who earned them) do not feature at all and aliens made a poll-tax contribution of 2d instead of a payment based on their earnings. What is noticeable in the Lowestoft data is how many more of its citizens paid tax on land than had been the case in 1524–5: thirty-four of them (30 per cent) as opposed to two (1 per cent). Goods remained the dominant category, at sixty-two people (55 per cent), as it had been previously with 123 (71 per cent), but both it and land had a different calculation applied as the basis of collection. The term land is misleading to a certain degree, as it included buildings of various kinds, and it is perhaps best referred to as real estate. It was assessed at 1s 4d per £1 annual rental value of the property. Goods referred to trading-stock and equipment of various kinds, as it had done previously, and had the sum of 10d per £1 capital value applied.

The calculations of the subsidy's best potential yield must have been worked out prior to collection and local knowledge must have been used to work out whether a payment on land or goods would be most productive of funds. What the Lowestoft assessment shows is that a substantial proportion of its inhabitants had invested in property both as a base for their homes and businesses and also as a means of creating income from the rents charged on the houses in which other people lived and (perhaps) worked. Using parish register and probate data, it has been possible to establish occupations for seventy-six of the 112 contributors (with an additional five possibilities) and both main categories of assessment show a mix of merchants, tradespeople, seafarers and craftsmen as contributors. From the authorities' point of view, it was all a question of whether it was the value of the real estate held by each individual or the value of his stock-in-trade that was able to yield the most tax.[18]

What the increase in property-holding shows to the modern observer is a rise in the amount of disposable income in the echelons of society above the servant and labouring levels, which allowed people the opportunity to purchase real estate for the reasons referred to above. It is a feature observable in most of the other communities in Lothingland Half-hundred as well.[19] Only Ashby (a sparsely populated parish) and Bradwell show no one taxed on land in either subsidy, while Blundeston and Gunton (the latter, again, with a

[18] The most interesting contribution made was that of James Cutting, who paid the sum of 12s on £9 *annuity* (a 1s 4d per £1 value, as with *land*). He was a master-gunner at the town's shore battery, sent originally from the tower of London armouries and paid 6d per day for his services – a yearly salary of £9 2s.

[19] Flixton, the most populous settlement in the half-hundred at Domesday, and the one with by far the biggest area of cultivated land, is not referred to in either subsidy. The loss of most of its former area to Oulton, as the latter developed, meant that it was considered to be part of its larger neighbour for assessment purposes.

small population) showed a state of no change. All the other places showed an increase in the number of people taxed on land, with Gorleston providing the best comparison with Lowestoft because it, too, was urban in nature. Its 36 per cent of people listed paying tax on land compares quite closely with the 30 per cent established for Lowestoft.

Reference has already been made to the assessment of aliens (or foreigners) living in the community for the purposes of collecting tax. Twelve of them are listed in the 1524–5 data (7 per cent of the whole) and fifteen in 1568 (13 per cent). The first set consisted of five Dutch, four French (one a Breton) and three Scots – all of them men (two Channel Islanders, from Guernsey, were rightly classified as English), but the second has far less detail concerning countries of origin. Once again, all of them are male and seven of them are named individually – but that is all.[20] Another one is simply referred to as the brother-in-law of one of the named men, but given neither name nor origin, while yet another is identified merely as being a particular merchant's servant. Two further anonymous ones are described as strangers (both living with the same local mariner), while another couple are referred to as 'Iceland boys' (each of them living and working at an inn). Finally, there were two surnameless Johns, one Dutch and the other French, both employed as servants by two of the town's merchants.

Incomers from abroad

Chapters 4 and 5 (particularly the latter) demonstrated the widespread European links created by fishing and maritime trade, and the countries of origin referred to in the previous paragraph confirm these immediately, the common factor of herring and cod fishing being strikingly obvious. There was considerable immigration from the Continent during the fifteenth century and the first half of the sixteenth along the whole of the Suffolk coast, details of which are now available online.[21] With the omission of men referred to in Table 12 (who are also present in the published lists), there are fifty-five foreign nationals referred to altogether in connection with Lowestoft, six of whom were women. The reason for their entry into the town's population, be it long term or of shorter duration, can probably be termed economic migration, but

[20] One of them, James Philip, is found referred to in parish register entries as both *mariner* and *rope-maker* – the latter occupation probably being one that he adopted after having given up going to sea.

[21] Arts and Humanities Research Council (University of York), *England's Immigrants, 1350–1550*: www.englandsimmigrants.com.

personal factors other than mere financial ones cannot be ruled out. Table 13 presents the data in as cogent a way as it is possible to devise.

Table 13. European immigrants, 1346–1544.

Name	Year	Origin	Occupation	Status	Source of information
John Gerard	1436	Germany	Webster	Fealty oath	*CPR, Henry VI*, vol. 2. p. 572
Henry Johnson		Holland	Skinner	ditto	p. 573
Richard Raulenson		ditto	Cordwainer	ditto	p. 572
John Treke		ditto	Tailor	ditto	p. 573
Henry Wolbranderson		ditto	Cooper	ditto	p. 572
Simon Wolbrandeson		ditto	Cordwainer	ditto	p. 572
Tymon Brewer (dec'd)	1440		(Brewer)	Householder	E179/180/92 (tax assessment)
Hugh Brewer			(Brewer)	ditto	
John Brundyssh (moved)				ditto	
John Bysshoop				Non-householder	
Henry Coppe				ditto	
Deryk Cowpere			(Cooper)	Householder	
Gerard Ducheman		(Holland)		ditto	
Hans Ducheman (moved)		ditto		ditto	
Jacobus (James) Ducheman		ditto		Non-householder	
John Duchemen		ditto		ditto	
Helewyse Duchewoman		ditto		ditto	
Meyse Duchewoman		ditto		ditto	
Jacobus Dunkyll (moved)				Householder	
Janyn Frensheman (moved)		(France)		Non-householder	
Joan Frenshewoman		ditto		ditto	
William Gybbeson				Householder	
John Hymmys (moved)				Non-householder	
John Jacobson (moved)				ditto	
Hugh Man (moved)				Householder	

Table 13 *cont.*

Name	Year	Origin	Occupation	Status	Source of information
Evenot Matyse				Non-householder	
John Noven				Householder	
John Parys		(France?)		ditto	
Elys Reynold				Non-householder	
Isabella Shomakere (widow)				Householder	
Walter Skotman (moved)		Scotland		Non-householder	
Henry Skynnere			(Skinner)	Householder	
Peter Skynnere (moved)			(Skinner)	ditto	
Peter Sowee (moved)				Non-householder	
Simon Sowtere			(Souter)	Householder	
Thomas Taylowr (moved)			(Tailor)	ditto	
Gertrude Veyma				Non-householder	
Katherine ?			Servant	ditto	
William Berbrewer	1456	Flanders	(Beer brewer)	Householder	E179/235/67 (tax assessment)
Joceus Couper			(Cooper)	Non-householder	
John Fley			Tailor	ditto	
Henry Shomaker			Shoemaker	ditto	
John Bolton (al. Whightetopp)	1483			Householder	E179/180/111 (tax assessment)
Heyn Cowper			Beer brewer	ditto	
John Cowper			Cooper	ditto	
William Cowper			Ditto	ditto	
John Denys			Tailor	Non-householder	
Keysar Ducheman		(Holland)	Souter	Householder	
Everard Wresteler			Smith	ditto	
Deryk ?			Beer brewer	ditto	
Gilbert ?		Scotland	Tailor	ditto	
? ?			Servant	Non-householder	
? ?			Hatmaker	ditto	
William Cowdere (al. Hasill)	1544	Normandy			WAM 12261 (denization)
James Phelip		ditto	Mariner		

Notes:

- Spaces in the Origin and Occupation columns indicate lack of information. The use of brackets in those columns gives information which is implied by the person's name.
- The first six people recorded took oaths of fealty to the Crown before being granted citizenship; the last two of all were given *denizen* status, by letters patent, after lengthy periods of residence in England (thirteen years in the former case, eleven in the latter).
- All the other men (and women) referred to are recorded in three Alien Subsidies, granted to Henry VI (1440 and 1453) and Edward IV (1483).
- James Phelip (last named of all) was the same man as the one referred to in fn. 20 on p. 241.

A perusal of the names above shows the Low Countries or Netherlands as the most frequently named place of origin for the incomers (thirteen in all), where such information is recorded, and it is likely that many of the other people listed also originated from the same area of Europe. Five immigrants of French nationality (two of them from Normandy) are noted and one of them, James Phelip, is detectable in both the 1568 Lay Subsidy and the Lowestoft parish registers, his burial being recorded on 18 December 1588. One man from some part of Germany is the first one of all to be listed and his trade of *webster* (weaver) was almost certainly connected with the textile trade of the time (either woollen or linen cloth). Finally, there are two men from Scotland included in the information relating to place of origin and, just to correct any foregone conclusion that a maritime connection must be the reason for entry to Lowestoft (especially one connected with herring fishing), one of them was a tailor.

Skilled workers required

If the column showing the occupations of the incomers is scrutinised, it will be seen that (apart from James Phelip's calling) nearly all of them relate to trades or crafts of one kind or another – a similar pattern of occupation to that observed in Ipswich.[22] Phelip was a seafarer and there are two servants mentioned, a female by Christian name only and an unnamed male.[23] Of the other twenty-six, five were brewers, five were coopers, five were shoe-makers

[22] Amor, *Ipswich*, pp. 32–3.
[23] The woman worked for John Noven and the man for Everard Wresteler.

(the category includes the cordwainers and souters),[24] five were tailors, three were skinners, one was a weaver (previously referred to), one was a hatmaker and one was a smith. It is a selection of activities that probably reflects the town's development and growth during the fifteenth century in terms of both its everyday economic activity and its becoming more affluent and socially complex. It is also interesting to note that thirty-eight of the fifty-five people listed (69 per cent) had come into the town on the eve of the so-called 'Great Slump' (c. 1440–79), just before it began to exercise its depressive influence on the national economy, that only four (7 per cent) were recorded while its effects were being felt, and that the eleven (20 per cent) recorded in the tax assessment of 1483 may be indicative of recovery taking place.

Coopering was clearly a necessary trade to provide the many barrels used in the preparation and transhipment of cured fish, but casks were also used for the conveyance of many other goods and products, wet and dry – and, as Chapter 5 showed, Lowestoft was a focal point for all kinds of cross-North Sea activity. There may also have been a connection with the number of brewers recorded, too, because any increase in that particular enterprise would have required extra containers for the storage of the product. Pertinent comment has been made by Mark Bailey regarding the commercialisation of brewing in Suffolk during the fifteenth century and the consequent increase in the scale of production, with particular emphasis placed on the role of Dutch immigrants in changing the English taste for ale to the newer, more flavoursome beer.[25] Dunwich, Ipswich and Walberswick were the examples chosen to demonstrate this change and it would probably be safe to add Lowestoft to the list.

Bailey also cites butchery as a rising activity in many Suffolk towns of the time, as the consumption of meat grew, and while this cannot be proved as part of Lowestoft's development it was likely to have been. Occupational data for the second half of the sixteenth century shows the presence of twenty-seven individual butchers in the town between 1561 and 1600, by far the biggest trade relating to the production of food and drink for the community and also for the coastal trading vessels which stopped offshore to take on victuals[26] – and this must have been the result of a cumulative process, rather than something which had occurred during the particular period of data-collection. The killing of animals for meat (especially cattle) would have led to

[24] Originally, *cordwainers* had produced high-quality footwear from Spanish leather produced in Cordoba (hence their title) – a distinction which had largely disappeared by this time. *Sutors* were sometimes regarded as lesser operatives, mending shoes rather than making them, thereby placing them in the *cobbler* category.

[25] Bailey, *Suffolk*, p. 267.

[26] Butcher, *Lowestoft*, p. 61.

the production of large numbers of hides and skins, and it is noticeable that three skinners feature among the overall number of immigrants recorded in Table 13 – men whose skills were needed in the slaughter trade and in the use of the animals' pelts once the carcasses had been processed.

Trades associated with leather were among the most important manufacturing activities of the medieval and early modern periods, and it has already been shown above (p. 157) that there was a demand in the town for cowhides over and above what local resources were able to supply. Data of the early modern period shows the importance of leather production in Lowestoft and in uses of the product after it had been manufactured,[27] a feature of the local economy that was already well established by the middle of the sixteenth century. There were three tanneries in town, all located at the northern end on land at the base of the cliff off *Whaplond Way* (now Whapload Road), which took advantage of the supplies of water issuing from a natural spring-line that is still detectable. Two of them stood at the bottom of what is now Lighthouse Score; the other was situated in the present-day Sparrow's Nest gardens. In addition to large quantities of water, the other main ingredient used in producing leather was the tanning agent itself, made from the long steeping of oak and ash bark and also used in the preservation of fishing nets and lines.

Such was the importance of the product in the town's economy that two manorial officials were elected each year at the annual leet court (first Saturday in Lent) to serve as searchers and sealers of leather and ensure that a satisfactory standard of manufacture was maintained. The use of the material went far beyond the mere making of boots and shoes. It was also employed in producing harness, tack, buckets, domestic containers, hinges, aprons, leggings, detachable sleeves, gloves, hats and a host of other items, with different types in use according to particular requirements. Pigskins were used for finer grades of the material, as were horse-hides and even dog-pelts, and such were the intricacies of the trade that investigating it in depth would require a chapter all of its own.

The presence of five shoe-makers (see Table 13) ties in immediately with the skinning of slaughtered animals and the manufacture of leather from their hides. Again, the early modern evidence shows the importance of this trade in Lowestoft's occupational structure,[28] which operated at three levels of production: heavy-duty working boots, everyday shoes and luxury footwear. The hatmaker would almost certainly have used leather to make a good proportion of his wares and he would probably also have operated at different levels, producing both standard and fine headgear. The occupation may even

[27] Butcher, *Lowestoft*, pp. 224–6.
[28] Butcher, *Lowestoft*, pp. 61, 64, 69 and 71.

be suggestive of a developing consumerism in local society, whereby disposable income was available among the wealthier members of the community to spend on personal luxury items. The same could be said of the tailors mentioned because they, too, would have made items of clothing for different purposes and different levels of cost. In a sense, the weaver referred to precedes them, in that he made the material used in their workshops, though it is not revealed whether he was a worker with wool or linen. Textiles were definitely a part of Lowestoft's occupational structure during the second half of the sixteenth century and the first half of the seventeenth, though their importance diminished thereafter – partly the result, perhaps, of the town becoming much more focused on maritime activity and trades.

There is no evidence in the data relating to incomers from the European mainland (nor in other sources known to the writer) suggestive of what may be termed 'high-end' consumer goods, such as precious metals, silks and spices. Small town luxuries, such as they were, tended to be recognisable in trades or occupations such as goldsmith, spicer, grocer, glazier, mercer, mason and skinner (the last-named in connection with furs).[29] Non-luxury categories included the food and drink trades, textile production, leather-working, building, woodworking and metal crafts – though the possibility of the people involved satisfying wealthier customers than their normal clientele is acknowledged.[30] Certainly, with clothing, footwear, house construction and fitting-out, as well as the making of everyday implements and utensils, different levels of manufacture and finish to suit the individual customer's financial means would have been carried out. The previous paragraph referred to finer-quality headgear, footwear and clothing; there would have been a range of other products available too, to satisfy the aspirations of people with disposable income who, unlike their less affluent, wage-earning fellow-citizens, did not have to spend a majority of their household budget on food alone.[31] And if Katherine Wylton's will of 1496 is to be believed (see p. 212, fn. 42), the existence of shops serving as retail outlets is further evidence of Lowestoft's urban nature.

The one trade remaining for discussion is blacksmith – an occupation of great importance in the medieval period, and in the one which succeeded it. Metalworkers were called upon to make a wide range of artefacts (domestic, agricultural, industrial and, in Lowestoft's case, maritime) and it is difficult to appreciate, in today's society, just how vital a part they played in the

[29] C. Dyer, 'Luxury goods in medieval England', in B. Dodds and C.D. Liddy (eds), *Commercial Activity, Markets and Entrepreneurs in the Middle Ages* (Woodbridge, 2011), pp. 230–31.
[30] Dyer, 'Luxury goods', p. 231.
[31] Dyer, 'Luxury goods', p. 223.

communities they served. Everard Wresteler (Table 13) makes an interesting case study, because information regarding him has survived and his inclusion in an Alien Subsidy list of 1483 shows that the government was on what might be described as a 'catch-up exercise', because he had been in the country for a number of years already. The will of his wife Agnes was made on 3 May 1479, as she was about to set off on a pilgrimage to Compostela in northern Spain.[32] Wresteler was her second husband (William Whyte being the previous one) and, in the event of her death, he was to have her house for the term of his life. Provision was also made for his falling upon hard times, in the event of which he was to be allowed to sell the dwelling and its messuage and take forty marks (£26 13s 4d) from the sum raised. The household was obviously a substantial one and it would appear that Wresteler had made a good choice in deciding to settle in Lowestoft.

It is possible that the anonymous male servant referred to in connection with him was a journeyman blacksmith rather than a domestic factotum. Whatever the case, though, Everard Wresteler eventually became a man of substance in his adopted community and he, too, made a will.[33] It was written on 14 March 1486 (proved 15 July 1487) and in it he left 10s to Father John Teward of the Order of Preachers in Great Yarmouth to pray for his soul and that of his wife. Although all friars were trained in preaching, the term 'Order of Preachers' applied specifically to the Dominicans, or Black Friars, whose house in Yarmouth was located at the southern end, near the town wall, and whose existence is perpetuated in the name Blackfriars Road. Wresteler's will also reveals that he had two sons, named Everard and William (the latter of whom had a son named Everard), and that the house he lived in was his own. He directed that half of the messuage was to be sold (with his wife, Agnes, receiving the sum of £5 from the proceeds) and that she be allowed to live in the other half for the term of her life, keeping it in good repair at her own expense. Agnes Wresteler's will was proved four months later by Everard Wresteler Jnr, on 10 November 1487, which would seem to suggest that both husband and wife were in failing health concurrently. Wresteler Snr had obviously come into Lowestoft from abroad and married a comfortably-off local widow, eventually being granted title to her house and holding it in his own right. He had prospered in the town through a combination of a fortunate marriage and his own practical skills.

There would have been other incomers, perhaps, whom fortune smiled upon, but their stories are not known. In Table 13, in the section relating to the Alien Subsidy of 1440 (the most substantial of all, with thirty-two of

[32] NRO, NCC, 113 Aubry.
[33] NRO, NCC, 72 Aubry.

the fifty-five overall references), it is shown that a third of the people named (all of them men) had moved on to other places. Only two references to a subject's occupation are made (those of skinner and tailor), so the trades of the others are a matter of speculation. It may well have been the case that a number of them were at the lower end of the working spectrum, being journeymen, labourers and servants – people who tended to move from place to place, as opportunity offered, in the cause of bettering themselves. This was very much the pattern of the sixteenth, seventeenth and eighteenth centuries and there is no compelling reason to think that the mid-fifteenth differed to any great extent regarding this particular level of society.

The use of *Dutchman* or *Frenchman* as a surname substitute helps a good deal in the identification of European immigrants (though the term 'Dutch' was sometimes used of Scandinavians) – particularly when an attempt is made to establish long-stay connections with a community. Of the names listed in Table 13, only two might have some possible link with those found in the 1524–5 Subsidy (Couper and Johnson) and they are, in any case, ones in fairly general use whose origins would be difficult to establish. It is likely, given the forty-year gap between the Alien Subsidy of 1483 and Henry VIII's national levy (and even longer periods of time relating to earlier data) that most of the incomers arriving in Lowestoft from abroad had moved on to somewhere else. As previously noted (p. 238), there are not even a great deal of connections to be made in a comparison of the 1524–5 subsidy with that of 1568, though it is possible to connect some of the wealthier citizens of both taxations to houses located in the town. These were mainly situated in the *High Street* area, as might be expected, and the information leading to their identification is to be found mainly in the 1618 manor roll, backed up by the Revd John Tanner's court baron extracts concerning the transfer of individual properties.[34] Table 14 presents the information in a conveniently summarised form.

Table 14. Properties held by 1524–5 and 1568 taxpayers.

Name	Description	Location today
Thomas Annot (merchant)	Dwelling house	49A–50B High Street
Robert Bache (merchant)	Houses and land below the cliff House and garden	Below 3–4 High Street North of St. Margaret's Plain
Robert Barnard (shipwright)	Land below the cliff Dwelling house below the cliff	Below 87 High Street Old Nelson Street (Police HQ site)
Roger Chancellor (merchant)	Dwelling house	33 High Street

[34] SRO(L), 194/A10/73 and 454/2.

Table 14 *cont.*

Name	Description	Location today
William French (merchant)	Land and fish-house below the cliff	To the rear of 55 High Street
Richard Fulwood (merchant)	Dwelling house	49 High Street
Thomas Gilbank (merchant)	Dwelling house	160–161 High Street
Robert Hodds (merchant) – Snr or Jnr	Dwelling house	63 High Street
	Dwelling house and croft	159–160 High Street
John Jettor (merchant) – Snr or Jnr	Dwelling house	4 High Street
Richard Scarlet (merchant)	Dwelling house	Between 4 and 26 High Street
	Dwelling house	102–104 High Street
	Dwelling house and chief tenement	North of St Margaret's Plain
Thomas Shotsham (merchant)	Fish-house and land below the cliff	Lighthouse Score area
	Dwelling house	70–71 High Street

Notes:

- The information here results from chance alone, deriving from references made in the manor roll to previous owners of the properties listed (which just happen to go back far enough in time to reveal the people named).
- The properties held by these men do not indicate relative levels of affluence. Robert Hodds and John Jettor (whether father or son) were wealthier than Richard Scarlet and would have held a good deal more real estate than that shown here.
- It is not known whether the houses listed were lived in by the property-holders or rented out.
- It is not possible to determine which Robert Hodds or John Jettor is being referred to.
- The locations given are generally accurate. The houses between Nos 4 and 26 High Street were destroyed by enemy bombing during the Second World War and not replaced, the surface area being grassed over and left as open space. The house belonging to Richard Scarlet was the next unit but one to No. 4.
- Some of today's High Street buildings (largely shops) observe original plot frontages; others stand on subdivided plots. The only one possibly mentioned in the table is Nos 102–104 High Street (Richard Scarlet), a fine timber-framed house of c. 1520–30 with a jettied first floor, long converted into three shop units.

Urban characteristics

Reference has been previously made to the quality of build in the Lowestoft houses, as noted by the third duke of Norfolk in his survey of coastal defences in May 1545 (p. 110). The High Street property held by Richard Scarlet, referred to in the last note immediately above, certainly fits the description of 'right well builded', as do Nos 27, 30, 31, 36, 43–44 and 148 – all of which would have either been standing at the time the comment was made or were raised within a decade or two afterwards. The late Alan Carter, an authority on the buildings of Norwich, once remarked to the writer that, on the evidence of the buildings he had seen during a day's inspection of the High Street area (Nos 27, 36, 43–44, 102–104 and the cellars beneath Nos 41–42 and 160), the standard of both materials and craftsmanship was as good as anything he knew of in Norwich and, in some cases, was better. His visit was made during the 1980s, more than 400 years after Thomas Howard had made his own assessment of the town, and its domestic architecture of the time was still able to create a favourable impression.

The following have been noted as among the distinguishing features of the medieval small town: commercial activity in industrial and craft-based enterprise, a densely concentrated population, closely built housing, problems caused by the build-up of waste products and the pollution issuing therefrom, a certain degree of civil disorder, and the presence of taverns and ale-houses.[35] Lowestoft would have had all of these by the early 1500s, and they are plain to see in documentation from the late sixteenth century onwards. Diversity of trades and occupations is another noted characteristic, with fifteen to twenty callings able to be identified and with specialisation apparent in three primary activities: fishing, leather-working and textile manufacture.[36] Again, Lowestoft fulfills the criteria in all three areas, though with an emphasis on linen cloth rather than woollen materials. It has been identified as a lesser centre of woollen production during the second half of the fifteenth century, producing fewer than 200 cloths a year,[37] but this may have been as much the result of manufacture in the hinterland as in the town itself. Having said that, a residual woollen industry may still have existed as late as c. 1600, if the presence of a dyer in the table below is indicative and if some of the weavers listed worked in wool – to say nothing of a shearman (Wyllyam Beckett), who occurs in a parish register burial entry of December 1603.

[35] Bailey, *Suffolk*, pp. 145–8.

[36] Bailey, *Suffolk*, pp. 154 and 155.

[37] Bailey, *Suffolk*, p. 273, Map 16. The data shown derives from N. Amor, 'Merchant adventurer or jack of all trades? The Suffolk clothier in the 1460s', *PSIA*, 40 (2004).

A further definition of urban status, as applied to small towns, may be summarised thus: a population of 300–2,000 inhabitants, a weekly market, a distinctive occupational structure and a specific topography.[38] Yet again, Lowestoft fits the requirements. It had an estimated population of 1,000 people in 1524 (p. 231), a market (pp. 94–102), an occupational structure with some degree of complexity (discussed above and below), and a distinctive local topography in terms of its geological and coastal features (Chapter 3). The community as a whole was a balanced one, with an economy based on maritime and agricultural activity and on the numerous associated service trades. Additionally, it had a sound system of manorial self-governance and a sense of civic identity and pride stemming from its ability to order its own affairs.

Mark Bailey has argued that the institutional and legal standing of a town was an important determinant in its governing process and that royal boroughs (c. 30 per cent of all chartered foundations) had far greater autonomy than seigneurial (manorial) ones – the latter being subject to the control of their lords.[39] Lowestoft had no charter of any kind and was a manorial unit, but its lord's control was weak because of his (or her) absence. Local control was in the hands of a steward, or bailiff, and as long as the rents were paid over to the lord his (or her) interference in the running of the community would have been minimal, perhaps even non-existent. This point has been previously made, and the status of successive Lowestoft lords during the medieval period ensured a remoteness that was as distant as it could possibly be, in social terms particularly but also in geographical ones.[40] This placed a great deal of autonomy in the hands of the manor's chief tenants, the lineal (not familial) descendants of the people named as holding the villeinage tenements in the Hundred Roll of 1274–5.

The *chievers* (or *chevers*), as they later became known, were the men who mattered in Lowestoft and who ran its everyday affairs in co-operation (even collusion, when it came to malpractice) with the steward. On the slender evidence available, it would seem that the medieval stewards were men of comparatively humble social background (such as John Bonde, who featured

[38] C. Dyer, 'Small towns 1270–1540' in D.M. Palliser (ed.), *The Cambridge Urban History of Britain*, vol. 1 (Cambridge, 2000), pp. 505–6.
[39] M. Bailey, 'Self-government in small towns in late medieval England', in B. Dodds and C.D. Liddy (eds), *Commercial Activity, Markets and Entrepreneurs in the Middle Ages* (Woodbridge, 2011), pp. 108, 109 and 110.
[40] From the Norman Conquest onwards it was in the hands of the Crown (until 1228), the de Balliol lords of Barnard Castle (until 1294), the Crown (until 1306), the earls of Richmond (until 1376), Sir John de Surrey (until 1380), the earl of Kent (until 1385), the earl of Suffolk (until 1386), then, following his death, the queen (until 1390), the earl of Kent (until c. 1400) and the earl, then duke, of Suffolk (until 1509).

so prominently in Chapter 2), who may well have relied upon the services of a clerk to keep the necessary records and accounts, none of which have survived. During the early modern period the post was filled by members of the local gentry from outside the town, who usually acted as their own secretaries and who kept the proceedings of both court baron and court leet in an exemplary manner.[41] The former session was held every four to six weeks and dealt largely with property transactions (though it would originally have handled a wide range of business). The latter met annually, with those chief tenants attending (there were fines imposed for those who did not) first swearing the homage to the lord, then taking the traditional view of frankpledge, reporting the deaths of any of their fellows who had died during the year, electing the person charged with collecting lord's rents that year, considering the various cases of nuisance and misdemeanour brought before it, and electing the officers annually responsible for maintaining good order in the community.

A surviving minute-book dating from the 1580s shows that six men were elected each year to perform three specific functions connected with social cohesion and fair trading practice both within the town's inns, ale-houses and retail premises and at its weekly market: two constables, two ale-founders (or tasters) and two sealers and searchers of leather.[42] Thirty years later, the number of constables had doubled to four and two swine-reeves were being appointed annually to make sure that any pigs' movements were limited mainly to people's backyards and that their snouts were duly ringed. No leet records have survived from late medieval times, but the six officers referred to above were probably appointments of that period also and there seems also to have been a pinder at one point, whose duty it was to impound stray animals and levy a charge upon the owners for their release. There was also a court bailiff, whose task it was to inform wrongdoers of their particular misdemeanours and summon them before the leet, and two afferators (al. afferers), who fixed the level of the fines paid for the various offences committed.

Thus, by way of summary, it is true to say that the day-to-day government of Lowestoft was conducted by locally elected manorial officials and the chief tenants, under the supervision (in theory, at least) of a steward acting as surrogate for an absentee landlord. The town may have been 'simply subsumed' within the many estates of its lord,[43] but this was to its advantage, not its detriment. It may not have had a separate legal identity (it wasn't made a

[41] The following men have been identified: John Randall (1616–53), Thomas Plumstead (1668–79), Thomas Godfrey (1680–1704), Robert Lulman (1704–9), Robert Lowde (1709–25) and Richard Allin (1726 onwards). Lulman lived in Great Yarmouth; the places of residence of the others are not known.

[42] SRO(L), 194/A10/4.

[43] Bailey, 'Self-government', p. 108.

borough, in fact, until 1885), but it was able to conduct its own affairs – largely free from outside interference – as long as the income generated by the holding and transfer of property, and by the fines imposed at the annual leet court, were duly collected and handed over to the steward. There is no surviving evidence in the town's extensive early modern documentation as to the collection and disposal of income generated by the weekly market (other than the fines imposed annually at the leet court for malpractice, carried out by residents and out-of-towners alike), but the running of the facility would have been related to manorial practice in one way or another. What has been termed '*de facto* self-government' was definitely the Lowestoft model[44] – the result, very largely, of a centuries-old lordly absence.

Nicholas Amor has shown that, in Ipswich, with its fully developed borough bureaucracy and system of courts (including four geographically zoned leets), more than 100 men were involved annually in the running of the town: burgesses, bailiffs, portmen and the like.[45] Lowestoft was much smaller, both in physical extent and in population (the latter totalling about one-third of Ipswich's near-3,000 in the early 1500s), and its late medieval civic governance – including the manorial officers referred to the previous paragraph – probably added up to no more than twenty to twenty-five people directly involved each year. There were twenty-eight chief tenements surviving from the old villeinage lands, with fourteen of them reduced in size and status to form half-chieves, thereby making a total of thirty-five holdings altogether (see Appendix 3). These pieces of land entitled the different occupants to be community leaders, but they were not all held singly.

For some considerable time (it is not possible to say how long) it had been the practice of certain influential local men to acquire chief tenements in order to boost their standing in the community and become part of its governing structure. By about the year 1540 the plots were in the tenure of twelve individuals and the Lowestoft town trust, a charitable body functioning under the auspices of the parish vestry to assist indigenous poor people, and headed up by the two annually elected churchwardens.[46] This organisation held three chieves and two halves (five properties in all, therefore), with the rest of the tenements disposed as follows: lord of the manor (Sir Henry Jernegan of Huntingfield), two and a half; Edward Blomvil (esquire), two halves; George Harvey (gentleman), one half; John Jettor (merchant), nine and a half; Robert

[44] Bailey, 'Self-government', p. 124.
[45] Amor, *Ipswich*, p. 18.
[46] It had its origins in the will of William French, merchant (4 April 1529), who left the sum of £60 for the purchase of lands (twenty-eight and a half acres were acquired) to fund the gift of 1d each per week to thirteen poor people. A panel of trustees was enfeoffed to administer the land and the churchwardens made the weekly disbursements.

Hodds (merchant), three and two halves; Thomas Annot (merchant), one half; Richard Scarlet (merchant), one and a half; William Coult (merchant), one half; Robert Scarlet (merchant), one; Anthony Jettor (merchant), one; John Murton (merchant), one; John Lobbes (merchant), one.[47] This all adds up to thirty-four individual properties, with a late addition to the collection (known as Hunts or Moneys) not featuring. It will not go unnoticed that the two richest contributors to the subsidy, Jettor and Hodds, held nearly half of the chief tenements between them, with the former having double the number of his fellow townsman.

The affluence of men such as these, as well as that of those people taxed on smaller quantities of movable goods, is evidence of increasing wealth among the merchants and craftsmen of the town, which , in turn, probably reflects the improved living standards noted in Suffolk as a whole during the late medieval period.[48] Between c. 1340 and 1440 it is reckoned that skilled workers' wages nearly doubled and that even unskilled operatives saw a 50 per cent increase in pay. Improved living conditions were to be seen in a better diet, in higher-quality clothing, in the increasing number of personal possessions and, finally, in the standard of house-building that manifested itself across the whole of the county. The third duke of Norfolk was suitably impressed by what he saw of Lowestoft's housing stock in 1545, and his favourable comments upon the town generally are suggestive of a vigorous and buoyant community at the time of his visit.

The economic base for the high standard of the houses belonging to the wealthier members of Lowestoft society was founded on a combination of commercial factors which Table 15 broadly reflects, in terms of the range of occupations and the numbers of people involved. Maritime activity, both fishing and seaborne trade, was of considerable importance and the presence of only one fishermen recorded need not cause surprise. The larger vessels comprising the main element of the town's fleet were dual purpose, as has been previously noted (p. 130), and the terms 'mariner' and 'sailor' were largely synonymous for crew involved in deep-sea enterprise of all kinds.[49] Local merchants owned the vessels operating and carried out the curing and sale of the catches, and they were also among the larger holders of agricultural land in the parish. They sometimes worked it on their own behalf, using paid

[47] R. Reeve, 'A history of Lowestoft and Lothingland', vol. 4 ((unpub. ms c. 1810), pp. 154–5. Robert Reeve was a local solicitor of the late eighteenth and early nineteenth century and steward of the manor for a number of years. His unpublished four-volume work is of considerable interest.

[48] Bailey, *Suffolk*, pp. 242–5.

[49] It may well have been the case that the sole fisherman listed was a longshore operator, spending most of the year working close in to land.

labour, and they also rented it out to men of lesser standing in the community who managed it for themselves. It may appear at first glance that agriculture and animal husbandry was of no great importance in the Lowestoft economy, but merchant tenure of much of the land serves to conceal a lot of the activity taking place.

Table 15. Occupations, 1561–1600.

Category	Occupations and the number of people involved	Total	% of the whole
Maritime (at sea)	Fisherman (1), mariner (43), sailor (52)	96	18.6
Maritime (on land)	Cooper (14), hook-maker (1), hoop-maker (1), roper (3), shipwright (12)	31	6.0
Agriculture	Husbandman (6), neatherd (3), shepherd (1), yeoman (1)	11	2.1
Retail and distribution	Draper (5), fishmonger (1), goldsmith (1), merchant (22), merchant tailor (1)	30	5.8
Food and drink	Baker (8), brewer (5), butcher (27), miller (10)	50	9.7
Leather trades	Cobbler (1), cordwainer (5), currier (2), glover (3), knacker (2), shoemaker (5), tanner (3), tawer (1)	22	4.3
Clothing	Hatter (1), tailor (36)	37	7.2
Textiles	Dyer (1), weaver (9)	10	1.9
Building	Carpenter (9), glazier (1), joiner (4), mason (11), sawyer (2), thatcher (2)	29	5.6
Metalwork	Blacksmith (3), pewterer (1), smith (10), tinker (2)	16	3.1
Professional and services	Barber (4), innkeeper (3), minister (7), nurse (1), proctor (2), schoolmaster (1), scrivener (1), surgeon (1), victualler (1)	21	4.1
Miscellaneous	Carter (4), chimneysweep (1), fletcher (1), gunner (1), ostler (1), singing man (1)	9	1.7
		362	
Gentry	Gentleman (12)	12	2.3
Menial	Labourer (36), maidservant (6), servant (99–79 male, 20 female)	141	27.4
14 categories	62 occupations	515	

Notes:

- The information derives mainly from parish register entries, with probate material, manor court records and a muster list of 1584 as supplementary sources.
- The register material provides 372 of the 515 references (72 per cent) and therefore gives the broadest view of the society of the time, recording people's names and occupations regardless of their social status. Wills and inventories constitute a source skewed towards wealthier people.

- Most of the occupations listed probably describe what was regarded as the subject's main source of income.

The wide range of manufacturing processes and trades recorded reveals that most of the town's day-to-day needs were able to be met, with the suggestion in places that the number of operatives recorded seems to be in excess of what was required to satisfy demand. This seems to be particularly the case with butchers and tailors, and also perhaps with bakers, shoemakers and metalworkers. However, it has to be remembered that Lowestoft not only had its own population to sustain; it was both a provisioning place for coastal shipping (especially where meat and beer were concerned) and the market centre for most of the area making up the half-hundreds of Lothingland and Mutford.[50] This meant an area of c. 22,000 acres or more (around thirty-five square miles), consisting of about eighteen or nineteen smaller communities, whose inhabitants would have used the Wednesday market as the means of acquiring goods not always available in the parishes where they lived, as well as bringing stock and produce of their own for sale.

Perhaps the most noticeable feature of Table 15, in terms of plain statistics, is that the menial level of the social and economic order has the highest number of people recorded. If labourers and servants are separated, the former category accounts for 7 per cent of the total number of occupations and the latter for 20.4 per cent. The loading could be partly the result of the vagaries of the sources available, but the writer is also inclined to think that it shows the vital role of the lower orders (servants especially) in providing a bedrock of contributed labour on which much of the town's social and economic fabric depended.

It is likely that many (if not most) of the servants were young people, as it has been estimated that, from the late sixteenth to the early nineteenth century, servants constituted about 60 per cent of the national population in the fifteen to twenty-four age group.[51] Nothing much is known about the Lowestoft servants, other than their names, but their considerable presence in town shows that they were an important part of the workforce. Their almost total absence from a family reconstitution exercise carried out on the parish registers by the writer during the 1980s (under the auspices of the Cambridge Group) would appear to suggest that they were members of the age group

[50] Butcher, *Lowestoft*, p. 10. Lothingland's five or six northernmost parishes (including Gorleston) probably looked to Great Yarmouth as their market provider, while Beccles may well have exercised a 'pull' on some of the Mutford communities.

[51] A. Kussmaul, *Servants in Husbandry in Early Modern England* (Cambridge, 1981), pp. 51 and 59–63.

referred to above, meaning that most of them had not reached the typical age of marriage (mid-twenties) and set up households of their own. Their surnames suggest that a majority (about 65 per cent) were either from the town itself or from neighbouring parishes, but there is no information as to the ways in which they were hired or how long they stayed with an employer.

Another factor which has to be taken into account when considering the structure of pre-industrial societies is the matter of what has been loosely described as dual occupation, whereby a man had a primary trade or interest but was also involved in other areas of economic activity. The term may not be the best one to fit the situation, however. A detailed study of Lowestoft's occupational structure between 1561 and 1750 shows that only eight men (out of a total of 2,005 people recorded and 125 occupations identified) can be said to have carried on two different trades at the same time:[52] Hugh Bond, baker and brewer (ob. 1592); William Sewter, husbandman and tanner (ob. 1629); Christopher Swift, fisherman and linen weaver (ob. 1670); Thomas Pacy, yeoman and brewer (ob. 1680); John Colby, apothecary and merchant (ob. 1719); William Bull, innkeeper and carter (ob. 1739); John Day, innkeeper and barber (ob. 1748); and John Peach, yeoman and brewer (ob. 1749). It is possible, of course, that there was more of the practice than the available information suggests, but in the absence of firm evidence the figures have to be accepted for what they are.

There is also the matter of interpretation to be considered when reaching conclusions concerning dual (or multiple) occupation. Taking some typical Lowestoft employment situations of the early modern period, it is pertinent to ask a number of questions. Was the labourer who was involved in both agriculture and building work a farmhand or a construction worker? Or was he simply someone who could turn his hand to different operations as time and necessity dictated? Was the fisherman who hired and cultivated a quarter-acre plot in some part of town a seafarer or a smallholder? Or did his agricultural activities simply act as a supplement to a living made on the waves? Was the husbandman who used his horse and cart to provide conveyance for hire a farmer or a carter? Or was he merely using constituents of his primary calling to earn extra money as opportunity offered? And, finally, was the grocer or merchant who had an involvement in fishing, fish-curing and brewing skilled in all of these trades, or just a man who had diverse business interests?

In the end it all comes down to an understanding of what dual occupation or multiple occupation really means – definitions which may differ from person to person. What Lowestoft shows, particularly in extant probate material, is evidence of a mixed economy at various levels of society, not just

[52] Butcher, *Lowestoft*, pp. 74 and 77.

among the merchants and trading classes. It may be best, therefore, to view urban communities of the time as having a diversity of economic activity as one of their distinguishing features. This, then, directs the investigator to ascertain what a man's primary interest was (if the available documentation makes this possible) and to look for what he might also have been involved in by way of subsidiary activity. In the absence of the working structure familiar today, with its (largely) set hours, holiday allowance, maternity leave, sick-pay entitlements and other legal protections, and with eventual retirement from whatever job is done not part of the overall experience, people laboured in whatever way was best suited to them in the cause of maintaining themselves and their families.

No apology is offered for what may be seen as a digression into the economy and employment pattern of Lowestoft during the early modern period, because the situation prevailing then had begun during an earlier phase of the town's existence. A complex occupational structure did not suddenly manifest itself in the middle of the sixteenth century; it had been developing for some considerable period of time before then, as is suggested by the data in Table 13. The immigrants from across the North Sea, who have trades attached to them in the data, can be seen as bringing in skills required in traditional areas of work, such as brewing, barrel-making, butchery, metal crafts, the production of leather goods and the manufacture of clothes and hats, as well as working in domestic service. Their arrival suggests that there was work to be done in their chosen fields, which may well reflect growth in the size and economic activity of the town and increasing variety in the number of handcrafts required to sustain it. And the contribution the aliens had to make probably transcended the merely utilitarian aspects of manufacture; some of them (particularly where clothes and footwear were concerned) might well have been assisting the development of a trade in luxury items for those who had the money to spend on such things. Even the apparent growth in meat production and the consumption of beer may also suggest more disposable income to lavish on a greater intake of basic dietary items than had previously been possible for many people.

It is not possible to produce a detailed assessment of the structure of Lowestoft society in the early sixteenth century, as there is not sufficient documentation of the type required. However, the 1524–5 Subsidy data is more than sufficient to suggest that it consisted of a small number of leading merchants, a much greater number of lesser men involved in maritime and land-based trades, a large wage-earning element working for either of the two previous groups, and a number of men employed as servants. Crude and simplistic though this breakdown is, it is effectively the Lowestoft of 200 years later. The range of activities had undoubtedly increased over the years, but the basic structure remained the same, with the bulk of the wealth and civic influence concentrated in the top level of society. The control exercised was considerable, but not absolute, and tradesmen of all levels were elected each year to manorial office, serving as parish constables, searchers and sealers of leather, ale-tasters and fen reeves.[53] Some of them also, as part of the duties exercised by the parish vestry (as represented by the two churchwardens), served as overseers of the poor – four of whom were chosen annually, with each one serving a period of three months during which time relief-money was collected and disbursed.[54]

It is tempting (and it may be an accurate assessment) to see Lowestoft as being at a key moment in its overall development at the time of the 1524 Subsidy. The religious and social upheavals of the next thirty or more years would have had a significant effect on the local population in the matter of change and counter-change in established belief and practice, though there is no way of assessing the town's response to the abandonment of traditional Roman Catholic practice and the adoption of newer Protestant principles. The Jettor family certainly remained faithful to the old ways and paid dearly for it, eventually being forced to leave the town because of punitive recusancy fines during the early years of Elizabeth's reign and live in reduced circumstances in nearby Flixton (where adherence to their faith continued to be punished by heavy fines). Yet, at much the same time, new religious practices that were equally unacceptable to the authorities were developing. A bishop's visitation of 1597 noted what seems to have been a proto-Nonconformist group beginning to form, in the excommunication two years earlier of a local woman, Joan Rivet, for non-attendance at church – she having become a member of the Brownist sect.[55]

Another change in the town's nature was the structural, social one already noted (pp. 236–8), whereby many of the people named had moved on elsewhere (or perhaps, in the case of the less transient members of society, died out in the male line), leaving others to fill the spaces left. This is particularly noticeable at the upper end of the social spectrum, where nearly all of the wealthier merchants had gone, leaving lesser men to rise to a position of

[53] Butcher, *Lowestoft*, pp. 273–7, gives a summary of local government in the town during the early modern period. The only level of society not represented in holding office was the *menial* one (labourers and servants).

[54] Mariners were not usually chosen for annual manorial office because of their absences at sea, but they did sometimes function as overseers – presumably, slotting their three-month stint in around their work.

[55] J.F. Williams (ed.), *Bishop Redman's Visitation, 1597*, NRS 18 (Norwich, 1946), p. 125. The Brownists derived their name from Robert Browne of Norwich (a leading Puritan thinker) and later became known as *Congregationalists*.

influence and make their mark on the community. Thus, the names of Allen, Annot, Arnold, Barnard, Drawer, Hill, Shotsham and Wilde had become ones to be reckoned with, along with those of Burgis, Damerell, Forman, King, Mighells, Rook and Wells. This exercise of cross-matching surnames is not a precise one, and other men could be found to supplement the second list, but it does serve to illustrate a point: the constant turnover in the different levels of society in response to the economic ebb and flow of pre-industrial times.

If Lowestoft's early modern social structure as a whole is considered, taking the 200 years between 1550 and 1750 as the time-span, it can be seen that certain families became foundation blocks of the community. So-called 'ruling families' have been identified in a number of towns and Lowestoft is no exception. The Arnolds, Ashbys, Barkers, Durrents, Jexes, Mighells, Pacys, Risings, Utbers, Wards and Wildes all exercised considerable authority because of their wealth and their long periods of residency. Of lesser standing, but also of some importance, were the Canhams, Coes, Daynes(es), Feltons, Ferneys, Fishers, Fowlers, Frarys, Hawes(es), Kitredges, Landifields, Mewses, Munds(es), Neales, Spicers and Uttings. Patterns of marriage are observable among these families, which must have helped to consolidate their wealth and standing as community leaders, and their presence is both observable and measurable because of the registration of births, marriages and deaths. No such means of monitoring a community's life was available during the medieval period.

Economic prosperity or decline?

For the best part of three decades or more there has been continuing debate among historians as to the experience of late medieval towns, the discussion hinging upon whether they flourished or suffered a setback in their fortunes. This writer considers that it is possible to argue a valid case for either situation, depending on the community under scrutiny and the type of source material used. One particular means of judging the state of a town's economy, in terms of apparent poverty, has been the data contained in the 1524 Lay Subsidy, where the number of residents assessed on the £1 minimum level could be as high as half the total of taxpayers.[56] Lowestoft had thirty-five wage-earners and forty owners of movable goods taxed in this category, which was 56 per cent of its taxable population, but it must not be presumed from such figures that the town was poverty-stricken.

[56] Amor, *Ipswich*, p. 4, citing S.H. Rigby, *Medieval Grimsby: Growth and Decline* (Hull, 1993), p. 132.

The seventy-five people concerned consisted of the male servant population, the unskilled and semi-skilled workers (male, also), and the lower-level craftsmen in a small way of business. In many ways, this stratum of society underpinned the viability of a local community by performing many of the basic menial tasks, and the labourers at least were being taxed on 20 per cent of an annual income of around £5 (4d a day).[57] The presence of large numbers of such people in an urban environment should come as no surprise; the point has been already made that servants alone constituted about 60 per cent of the national population in the fifteen to twenty-four age group and comprised as much as 56 per cent of the hired labour in some communities.[58] These statistics relate to the early modern period, but the situation may not have been significantly different in late medieval times. Table 15 (p. 256) shows that Lowestoft had 115 male menial workers in its workforce during the second half of the sixteenth century, which was 22 per cent of the total number of occupations recorded. Male wage-earners in the £1 category (labourers and servants) in the 1524 Subsidy numbered thirty-five, which was 26 per cent of the total number of taxpayers.

Another point to have been made regarding the adversity versus prosperity discussion is that urban decline, as a historical feature, is 'a problematic concept that often lacks a precise definition or chronology'.[59] Two of the formative works on the subject were written by Charles Phythian-Adams in the late 1970s; in the first, harvest failure was identified as one of the causes of general urban malaise during the period 1520–70 (the others being the general expense of living in towns, problems facing industry and retailing, and crises in overseas trade).[60] This was followed by a study of Coventry during the earlier part of the sixteenth century, focusing particularly on the crisis years of 1518–25.[61] Again, there was scrutiny of the shortage of grain as a central factor in the problems faced by the town, with analysis of a listing taken of townspeople, of stocks of grain and of the main users of corn (bakers and brewers).[62] The idea behind this assembling of data, presumably, was to enable the ruling authorities to prevent the stock-piling of grain and to persuade the populace that fair distribution of an essential food resource was being implemented.

[57] It might well be argued that a large echelon of low-wage, unskilled workers is still necessary to enable developed, modern, capitalist-style economies to function effectively.
[58] Kussmaul, *Servants*, p. 51 and pp. 59–63.
[59] Lee, 'Grain shortages', in B. Dodds and C.R. Liddy (eds), *Commercial Activity, Markets and Entrepreneurs* (Woodbridge, 2011), p. 79.
[60] C. Phythian-Adams, 'Urban decay in late medieval England', in P. Abrams and E.A. Wrigley (eds), *Towns in Societies* (Cambridge, 1978), pp. 159–85.
[61] C. Phythian-Adams, *Desolation of a City: Coventry in the Urban Crisis of the Late Middle Ages* (Cambridge, 1979).
[62] Phythian-Adams, *Desolation*, pp. 51–67.

There seems little doubt that grain shortages had the ability to cause considerable disruption to the running of medieval towns (with food riots ensuing and anger directed at civic authorities for their inability to maintain adequate supplies) and that the surrounding countryside was a vital component in the supply of food for urban communities.[63] Periods of bad harvest have been cited for the years 1481–3, 1500–1503, 1519–21 and 1527–9, with specific dearths recorded in 1482, 1520 and 1527,[64] but there is no local data available to make any comment on the experience of Lowestoft at this time. Records of a relevant nature do not seem to exist. There was, in any case, no physical separation of town and country during medieval and early modern times. Most urban areas had evolved organically in their respective rural surrounds for a variety of reasons and there was no hard demarcation between one and the other. Nicholas Amor has described how Ipswich merged into the adjacent countryside,[65] and Lowestoft did just the same (except on a much smaller scale). Yes, the town was a transplant, rather than the result of a long evolutionary process in one location, but its soft western edge merged gently into the parish's smallest common green, beyond which lay pastures and arable fields.

Further on, a half-mile or so away, stood St Margaret's parish church – a building that perhaps makes the most compelling statement concerning the state of Lowestoft's economy during the second half of the fifteenth century. Its history was explored in detail in the previous chapter and its sheer size and quality of construction suggest that considerable wealth was available among the more affluent townspeople in raising such an impressive house of God. Loosely, a date of c. 1440–80 can be attached to St Margaret's, but work could well have continued until about 1500. The town's five gilds would no doubt have played an important part in seeing the structure through to completion and there is no evidence in any of the community's surviving wills of parts of the building being left unfinished. At neighbouring Corton, for instance, two wills of the year 1486 – those of Roger Pye and Walter Speer, the vicar – both carried respective sums of five marks for the completion of the tower, if the parishioners wished to see the work carried out.[66]

In a lesser number of cases concerning the construction of medieval churches, surviving documentation is able to reveal the building instructions given to masons by those commissioning the work and donors' identities are sometimes revealed by the incorporation of their names or initials in decorative

[63] Lee, 'Grain shortages', in B. Dodds and C.R. Liddy (eds), *Commercial Activity, Markets and Entrepreneurs* (Woodbridge, 2011), pp. 79 and 65.
[64] Lee, 'Grain shortages', in B. Dodds and C.R. Liddy (eds), *Commercial Activity, Markets and Entrepreneurs* (Woodbridge, 2011), p. 64.
[65] Amor, *Ipswich*, p. 12.
[66] NRO, NCC, 64–65 Aubry and 294A. Caston.

stonework as part of the design. Wealthy (even aristocratic) patrons are occasionally named as the driving force behind construction.[67] Lowestoft has no surviving documentary material of any kind; nor does its fabric contain clues as to any persons financing construction. William and John de la Pole, first and second dukes of Suffolk, were lords of the manor at the time, but there is no visible evidence of any input from them in the manner of the family's leopard-head badge, found as a decorative motif on the base-course of the tower of St Mary Redenhall, further up the Waveney Valley on the Norfolk side of the river. Thus, the funders of St Margaret's remain anonymous, with informed guesswork as the only means of identifying them. The names Jettor, Goddard, Hatter and Hodds spring to mind, among others, but there is no positive proof of the families' involvement in raising the building, other than the single reference to John Jettor paying for the windows on the south side of the church (p. 203).

Returning to the specific matter of urban fortunes, the evidence usually produced in arguing a case for economic and social decline may be summarised as consisting of declining rent-roll values, reduced population numbers, decaying buildings and a retreat from holding civic office.[68] On the credit side, the following features may be adduced: rising levels of personal wealth, the construction of impressive (if fewer) buildings, increasing urban culture and greater social mobility.[69] Lowestoft has little or no direct documentary evidence to support either view and there is the further complication of a lack of precision attaching to the terminology used.[70] What, for instance, do the words *decay* and *decline* actually mean? Or even the term *town* itself, for that matter? It is a reasonable supposition to make – given the way specialist historical research can lead the investigator down very narrow pathways – that the conclusions sometimes arrived at are but partial in extent and may not represent the broader reality.

It is also probably accurate to say that current majority opinion leans towards the fact of the fifteenth century having been a period of difficulty for many urban communities. The so-called 'Great Slump' of the 1440s–1470s would not have been so termed if its effect across much of the country was neither detectable nor measurable. The maritime activity and irregularity forming the subject of Chapter 5 certainly shows a far greater number of incidents for the fourteenth century than for the fifteenth, which may mean that less overseas

[67] D. Dymond and P. Northeast, *A History of Suffolk* (Chichester, 1985), pp. 50–51. On this topic see, for example, the work of Gabriel Byng, in particular his PhD thesis, 'Parish church building and the later medieval economy' (2014).

[68] Amor, *Ipswich*, pp. 2–3.

[69] Amor, *Ipswich*, p. 3.

[70] Amor, *Ipswich*, p. 8.

commercial enterprise was taking place both locally and nationally than had been the case earlier (it is unlikely to have been less illegal activity *per se*). However, the necessary carriage of local goods and products would probably have continued along the coast, especially those related to agriculture and the keeping of livestock, and fishing would also have remained an important primary occupation, with cured herrings and dried cod as its staples.

Subsequent to the explanation given above for Lowestoft's high proportion of taxpayers rated at £1 wages or £1 goods, it is worth also considering the more affluent members of society as part of the local economic structure. Two men (both merchants) were of a genuinely high level of provincial wealth at a £100 rating on movable goods, and below them were another four (also merchants) in the £40–£50 category – a substantial level of prosperity. Below them were seven individuals (merchants, once again) in the £10–£18 grouping – again, a relatively comfortable level of commercial activity and domestic lifestyle – followed by eleven in the £5–£8 bracket (including the parish's vicar and a gentleman who was assessed on property held). There were then twenty-eight people taxed on a £2–£4 rating, including one highly paid servant and a man who owned property, as well as five widows. Two of the women were taxed on the bequests of their husbands (goods or property, or a combination of both), the other three on goods alone – this perhaps indicating that they were carrying on their husbands' business activities. The two lower taxable categories would have covered a range of people engaged in trade of lesser scale and worth than that of the merchants, as well as various craftsmen and skilled workers. The whole assemblage from top to bottom (including the extensive bottom-most level of all) represents the town's means of making a living and sustaining its socio-economic structure.

If the data available for the second half of the sixteenth century is to be believed (especially when set against the 1524 Subsidy material), Lowestoft does not seem to have undergone a period of crisis of the kind described by Phythian-Adams between 1520 and 1570. In demographic terms it was exactly the reverse, with an increase in its population from c. 1,000 to c. 1,500 – this being due in some measure to economic success and also to the effect of urban recruitment exercised by a town on its surrounding rural area. Nicholas Amor, in his exhaustive and fascinating study of late medieval Ipswich, found that the town did not fit neatly into the urban fortunes debate regarding its having undergone either crisis or advancement, because both experiences were evident at different times. What was also detectable was the way that the local economy showed resilience in adapting to changing conditions and seizing new opportunities.[71]

[71] Amor, *Ipswich*, p. 230.

Lowestoft does not have an extensive fourteenth- and fifteenth-century documentary resource on which to base a major study of trade and society, but the impression given by peripheral material contained in such sources as the Patent Rolls and Close Rolls, as well as in its inhabitants' surviving probate material, is one of urban growth and development. A good quality of building construction was evident in both its housing stock and its majestic parish church. It refused to be over-awed by a large and influential near-neighbour, Great Yarmouth, in shaping its own economic autonomy (even though some of its maritime activity, locally, was undoubtedly illegal). It governed itself largely by means of manorial procedures, in the absence of its lord, and was sufficiently flexible to absorb newcomers (including those from the European mainland) into its social and economic structure. And, while it must have undergone times of difficulty, these were not sufficiently serious (as far as can be discerned) to cause major disruption to its continuing progress.

Maritime considerations

In conclusion, if a single choice has to be made from the key influences in Lowestoft's overall development, there is one overriding factor which bridges the late medieval and early modern eras and serves as the means of linking them together: the sea and its associated activities. It is hard, in the second decade of the twenty-first century, to see the town as a frontier community – but, in a maritime sense, that is what it was. It looked out to the wider world of the European Continent and, through fishing and seaborne trade, had had a long acquaintance with it. Though seemingly not on the scale of fourteenth- and fifteenth-century activity (especially the former), illegal practices and irregularities of one kind or another continued well into the seventeenth century, with evasion of customs duties (largely through bypassing Great Yarmouth's function as head-port) remaining the most significant problem right up until Lowestoft was granted port status in 1679. This privilege was, of course, hotly contested by Yarmouth, but there is no doubt that it resulted in greater control of maritime activity locally and less loss of revenue to the Crown.

It is interesting to note the concern expressed by people connected with Lowestoft, during the middle years of Henry VIII's reign, regarding the evasion of customs by both English and foreign ships. On 5 March 1528 it is recorded that Sir John Jernegan (of Somerleyton), John Harvey (of Oulton), Robert Hodds and John Botolf (both of Lowestoft) had advised the monarch's council that ships carrying illegal grain in local waters (some English and some foreign) had been arrested, some of which were carrying cockets from

Lynn (King's Lynn) that appeared to have been forged. The Great Yarmouth bailiffs and customs officers had been informed because there was no space available in Lowestoft to store the quantity of grain and malt confiscated, but the vessels were so deep in the water that passage into Yarmouth was not possible. Furthermore, if they remained at anchor in The Roads they were likely to suffer damage. All of this concern was probably genuine and well founded, but there may also have been an ulterior motive on the part of the petitioners: that of seeking the means of bolstering coastal defences. Significantly, perhaps, the communication finishes, 'if Wolsey will send orders for the building up of the Blockhouse at Lowestoft, it will go better forward'.[72]

Nothing seems to have happened in this matter because, eleven years later (19 February 1539), three of the same men (Jernegan, Harvey and Botolf) – with the addition of John Jettor and Gregory Payne (both of Lowestoft) – were drawing the attention of Thomas Cromwell (Wolsey's successor as Henry's chief minister) not only to customs evasion by English and foreign vessels carrying wheat, barley and malt but also to illegal export of the same and claiming that, if nothing were done, shortages at home might result.[73] This time action was taken and, within a month, the town is found named (among a number of other places in England) as a place to be fortified.[74] A year later, in February 1540, it is described as having had its ordnance cast in the Tower of London (location of the Royal Armouries), but not trimmed – this referring, of course, to the smoothing and finishing of the guns, inside and out, after they had been removed from the moulds.[75] The formal selection of trained personnel to man and service the guns followed, with each of the three men being paid 6d a day for their services. Nicholas Sendall is recorded as being appointed on 14 November 1541 and James Hayms (also found named in later documentation as Hines, or Cutting) two days later.[76] Three months or so later, on 6 March 1542, Simon Legge is noted as having been appointed gunner in the Lowestoft bulwark.[77]

It would appear from this information that three gun batteries had been established to protect the town and to give greater control of maritime activity offshore. Thomas Howard, third duke of Norfolk, carried out an inspection of coastal defences between Great Yarmouth and Orford in May 1545 in expectation of a possible attack by France. His comment regarding the quality of the town, both in terms of its construction and the honesty of its inhabitants,

[72] Brewer, *LPFD, Henry VIII*, vol. 4 (London, 1904), p. 1783.

[73] Gairdner and Brodie, *LPFD, Henry VIII*, vol. 14(i) (London, 1894), p. 124.

[74] Gairdner and Brodie, *LPFD, Henry VIII*, vol. 14(i), p. 330.

[75] Gairdner and Brodie, *LPFD, Henry VIII*, vol. 15 (London, 1896), p. 71.

[76] Gairdner and Brodie, *LPFD, Henry VIII*, vol. 16 (London, 1898), pp. 641 and 696.

[77] Gairdner and Brodie, *LPFD, Henry VIII*, vol. 17 (London, 1900), p. 102.

has been previously cited (pp. 110 and 251), and it is pertinent now to repeat the whole of his statement:

At Laystofte (sic), for small ships of 10 or 12 foot draught, are two very good roads called the North Road and the South Road, in either of which a good number of mean ships may ride against all winds. Between the landing place and the town is at least 40 score tailor's yards, and the landing place is more than half a mile in length. The town have [*sic*] made bulwarks of earth at each end of the road and in the middle, with three or four small pieces in each. The town is as pretty a town as I know any few on the sea coasts, and as thrifty and honest people in the same, and right well builded; but surely if an army royal should come come thither, considering the bulwarks, which should beat the road, be but of earth, as banks made of turves, and so far distant from the town, I think it should be no great adventure for a good puissance to land there and burn the said town.[78]

This appraisal of Lowestoft's defensive capability is of considerable interest topographically. It shows that three small batteries had been set up: at the northern and southern ends of *The Denes* (loosely, in today's terms, opposite the Sparrow's Nest gardens and the end of Hamilton Road) and also in the middle at *Ness Point* itself, England's easternmost extremity.[79] However, the duke's description of the distance between the town (on its cliff-top site) and the shoreline as being 800 *tailor's yards* (a tailor's yard, or ell, was forty-five inches in length) shows that The Denes were a great deal more extensive in those days than they are now. Whether the stated width (1,000 yards) was the result of a measured survey or a paced-out exercise of some kind is not known, but it tells today's reader that coastal erosion has carried away much of the former barrier between the sea and the base of the cliff, leaving it less than half its former size. Regarding the armaments referred to, the small iron cannons placed in each earthern redoubt (constructed on a timber framework of some sort) were probably *slings*, which fired a two-and-a-half inch shot a distance of about 1,100 yards. During the archaeological excavation work carried out to the rear of No. 80 High Street, during the year 2000 (p. 93), a spherical limestone missile about the size of a tennis ball was dug up. It could well have been a surviving piece of shot from one or other of the Lowestoft batteries (the southernmost one being the likeliest) – stone shot being as common as iron at that time and not nearly as expensive to produce.

[78] Gairdner and Brodie, *LPFD, Henry VIII*, vol. 20(i) (London, 1905), p. 370.

[79] Ness Point has tended to move both northwards and southwards over the centuries, according to the effect of tides and offshore currents at any one time. Since the early years of the twentieth century its position has become fixed by concrete sea defences and is probably further to the south than it was when Thomas Howard made his inspection.

Earlier in this book (p. 145) reference was made to a map possibly connected with the duke of Norfolk's coastal survey. There is, however, one crucial difference: the only defensive position shown at Lowestoft is the blockhouse at Ness Point, drawn as a rounded, castellated tower with three guns protruding from its ports (the promontory itself is referred to as *Mage Neshe* – i.e. Major Ness). An identical fortification is shown on a cliff-top location between Corton and Gorleston, with the following words written above it: 'Mind that notwithstanding the Blockhouse made by Leystoft [*sic*] Road, yet the enemies may come in at the North end of the said Road by Saint Nicholas Gat without danger of the said blockhouse at their pleasure and may land three miles in length unless they be stopped by a blockhouse to be made so against Corton as here is made in the plat [map]'. The latter strong-point was never built, but two supplementary positions were placed either side of the Ness Point battery, so the map described must have been drawn some time during 1539 or 1540 (between the times at which Ness Point was approved by Thomas Cromwell and subsequently built, and the three gunners being appointed during a four-month period from November 1541 to March 1542).

Leaving aside any preliminaries regarding Lowestoft's defences, the duke of Norfolk was obviously concerned about the town's vulnerability if subjected to a large-scale ('royal') assault because of the insufficiency of the weaponry and its detachment from the built-up area. In the event, the guns were never tested by an invading French force, and their deterrent effect on illegal maritime activity cannot be assessed. Admittedly, there is less recorded customs evasion and theft than was manifested in fourteenth- and fifteenth-century records, but illicit activity still went on. One notable example involved two local men of merchant status, one of whom was a leading late sixteenth-century benefactor to the town: none other than Thomas Annot, founder of Lowestoft's free grammar school in June 1570 – he who looked around him and saw local youth as being 'very uncivil and ignorant for want of good Instruction and Education And the more for that they have within the said Town small or no trade to bring up their youth of the younger sort until they shall be trained and used to the Sea or other Service to preserve them from Idleness and other Misdemeanour'. Thus runs the preamble to the original deed of gift, luckily preserved in the memorandum book of the Revd John Arrow, vicar of Lowestoft from 1760 to 1789.[80]

The incident in which Annot and his associate had been involved nine years earlier reached diplomatic level, involving Elizabeth I's government in remedial action. On 28 May 1561 (in response to complaints made by the Spanish ambassador) Thomas Burman, the servant of Thomas Annot, was examined

[80] NRO, PD 589/92, pp. 13–14.

as to the landing of certain quantities of canvas and poldavies robbed from a Spanish ship and landed in the town.[81] More detailed information was revealed two months later, when it was recorded (on 19 July) that merchants from Spanish-occupied Flanders had complained of acts of piracy carried out by mariners named Marichurch, Johnson and Handsam of Faversham.[82] The phraseology may suggest that the three offenders were all from the Kentish port, but (given the wording of the time) it may refer to Handsam alone. All three men were said to have had caches of weapons and munitions in sundry places and Marichurch's base is stated to have been at Penryn, in Cornwall (next door to Falmouth). One of the felonies commonly practised by these pirates was to take catches of fish and nets from Flemish vessels operating in the North Sea and sell the former as if they were their own.

It was further reported that Marichurch had been seen in Lowestoft during July (1561) and that a serjeant of the Admiralty (the Court of Admiralty) called Thackwell was acting in collusion with him and the other offenders. Also involved in their activities (or, at least, having some knowledge of what was going on) were Thomas Arnott (Annot), Jaggs (Jex – Thomas) and Thomas Barman (Burman), all of Lowestoft. Their involvement had become clear in an examination carried out by Sir Thomas Woodhouse and two of them (Annot and Jaggs) were said to be well able to answer, while the third one, a servant, had already admitted that his master had a 'good understanding' with the pirates. The writer has been unable to find any further information regarding this matter and is unable to say whether or not punitive action was taken against Annot or Jagges. What is undeniable is that both of them feature in the Lay Subsidy of 1568: Annot with his property producing £40 a year in rents and Jagges with his £8 worth of trade goods.[83] However, nothing further is known of Thomas Burman, who perhaps had to leave his master's service after turning 'queen's evidence' against him.

It has often been argued that, to be successful in business, a certain flexibility of conscience and practice is sometimes necessary. Applying moral judgements to things that happened over 450 years ago is not part of any agenda connected with this book, which is largely concerned with showing things as they were during different phases of Lowestoft's development. The maritime economy was potentially profitable, but a great deal of attendant risk attached to it – largely caused by variable and unpredictable weather, periodic restrictions

[81] R. Lemon (ed.), *CSPD, Elizabeth I*, vol. 17 (London, 1865), p. 176. *Poldavy* or *poldavis* was a coarse canvas, originally made at the town of Poldavide, in Britanny, and much used as sailcloth.

[82] J. Stevenson (ed.), *CSPF, Elizabeth I*, vol. 4 (London, 1866), p. 193.

[83] Hervey, *Suffolk in 1568*, pp. 186 and 187.

imposed on both goods and their intended destinations by the government of the day, disruption caused by frequent European conflicts, acts of piracy both on the high seas and closer in to shore, and the difficulty of establishing networks of trust which enabled goods to be traded when necessary on long-term credit. A useful indicator demonstrating the ups and downs of fishing and seaborne trade is to be had from sixteenth-century vessel data, largely deriving from official lists which were periodically put together by national government when ships were needed for warfare or some other purpose.

The earliest Lowestoft information dates from the year 1526, when it is stated that the town had twenty vessels and 200 men engaged in the fishing industry – totals which would appear to be accurate, as the larger craft were crewed by about ten men.[84] This was probably about the sum total of *big boats*, as they became known much later, with most (if not all) of them involved also in trading voyages with increased numbers of men on board. Seven years later, in 1533, seven vessels are reported as having returned from the Iceland cod voyage.[85] This was probably not the whole of the main fleet, but it does suggest a reduction in the number of craft working. The first detailed official list to give information concerning the size of the Lowestoft merchant fleet in the sixteenth century was the result of a military survey.[86] In 1544 the Royal Council was thinking of sending an expedition to Scotland and was investigating the number of serviceable ships available to carry men and materials. Lowestoft's fleet was put at fifteen vessels (third in size in East Anglia, after Great Yarmouth and Dunwich), a number which ties in closely with information revealed below.

The next piece of evidence regarding numbers of deep-sea craft working from the town is to be found in a survey of 1565, cited by the maritime historian Neville Williams, in which five ships are attributed to Lowestoft and another three to Pakefield.[87] The following year, at the end of January, in an enquiry held into the value of the Lowestoft vicarage (see p. 224), testimony was given by three of the five witnesses (Richard Mighells, Anthony Jetour and John Grudgefield) as to the adverse effect on parish income caused by the decline in the Iceland cod fishery and the consequent loss of tithe payments.

[84] E.M. Hewitt, 'Fisheries', in W. Page (ed.), *VCH Suffolk*, vol. 2 (London, 1907), p. 293. No citation for the source of this information is given.

[85] TNA, SP 1/80 f.65v. The document records the levy imposed by the Crown on the profits made by the sale of cod and ling. See Butcher, *Lowestoft*, p. 172, fn. 30. Other Suffolk communities involved that year were Dunwich (twenty-two craft), Orwell Haven (Ipswich) (seven craft) and Orford (1 craft).

[86] Gairdner and Brodie, *LPFD, Henry VIII*, vol. 19(i) (London, 1903), p. 76.

[87] N. Williams, *The Maritime Trade of the East Anglian Ports, 1550–1590* (Oxford, 1988), p. 218.

It was said that, twenty years previously, there had been thirteen or fourteen *doggers* involved in the activity (these would have constituted practically the whole of the fifteen craft recorded in the 1544 survey), but the number was now reduced to one.[88] This sole survivor may have been among the five craft listed by Williams, with the other four not involved at the time in the northern voyage.

Seven years later, in 1572, a recovery in numbers seems to have taken place. A survey of merchant shipping (exclusive of fishing vessels) made by Thomas Colshill, chief surveyor of customs in London, records Lowestoft as having sixteen craft – though (significantly perhaps) nothing is recorded for Pakefield.[89] This number put the town in fifth place out of nine Suffolk coastal communities, behind Ipswich, Aldeburgh, Walberswick and Southwold, but ahead of Woodbridge, Dunwich, Orford and Gorleston. The fluctuations in fleet numbers noted for the whole of the county during the sixteenth century may well have meant the movement of vessels from place to place as fortunes rose and fell, because (in Lowestoft's case, at least) there was nowhere to lay craft up when they were not in use. Therefore, selling them on to towns where there was greater maritime activity taking place would have made sense. In some cases, the owners of vessels almost certainly accompanied them to their new homes and relocated themselves to where more business on the high seas was to be done (a summary of the information to be had from the data relating to 1533, 1544 and 1572 is to be found in Appendix 4).

Fluctuations in fishing and seaborne trade continued to be Lowestoft's experience for another century or more, with one particularly severe period of depression occurring during the first half of the seventeenth century.[90] It was during times of difficulty that the town was able to continue functioning on its other activities: agriculture, the manufacture of goods and the provision of services for its local area, and its victualling role in supplying shipping which anchored offshore. During the eighteenth and nineteenth centuries the fishing industry and cross-North Sea trade saw a long period of expansion, greatly accelerated by the coming of the railway in 1847 and the introduction of steam propulsion to the fishing fleet during the late 1890s. Fishing, particularly, reached its peak during the first decade of the twentieth century, before encountering difficulty caused by fluctuating catches and uncertain markets during the 1920s and 1930s. After the Second World War there was a partial

[88] NRO, PD 589/112. Gillingwater, *Lowestoft*, pp. 266 and 267, repeats the information.
[89] M. Oppenheim, 'Maritime history', in W. Page (ed.), *VCH Suffolk*, vol. 2 (London, 1907), p. 216 – drawing upon information contained in M.A.E. Green (ed.), *CSPD, Elizabeth I, Addenda*, vol. 22 (London, 1871).
[90] See Butcher, *Lowestoft*, pp. 64 and 191.

recovery, followed by the collapse of the North Sea herring fishery during the mid-1960s and the gradual decline of mid-water trawling throughout the 1980s and 1990s, eventually reaching extinction during the early 2000s.

With but a handful of inshore craft left working now, and with the fish market a shadow of its former self, it would be a brave person indeed who felt able to predict the return of large-scale fishing to the port of Lowestoft.

Postscript

Close to a thousand years of Lowestoft's past are contained within the preceding pages and, given that length of time, any statement regarding the community's origins and subsequent development has of necessity to be an incomplete one. At the same time, it is hoped that the reader has gained some notion of the human activity which laid the foundations of the town of today. The process would not have been sensed by the people responsible for it in the earliest phase of development; their only concern was to take the physical environment in which they found themselves and shape it to their own requirements. Day-to-day living was the priority, with the provision of food, shelter and clothing being the main considerations. Once the settlement had become established and viable, it would have been possible for its inhabitants to take a broader view of their situation and see themselves as part of a social fabric transcending their own immediate surroundings – one that was founded, no doubt, on the model left behind on the North European mainland.

There is no means of accurately assessing at what point Lowestoft gained a sense of what may termed civic identity, whereby its people saw themselves as being an integral part of a social unit based in a specific location and with its own distinguishing features. The Anglo-Saxon period probably did not generate this, for the township was an outlier to the hub-manor located in Gorleston, without any freemen of its own and with a workforce dedicated to supplying the lord and his household with agricultural produce – perhaps even before their own immediate needs had been met. By the time of Domesday, the manor of Lothingland was one of the many held by Gyrth Godwinson, younger brother of Harold, whose only interest would have been in receiving the rents due to him, so the thegn Wulfsi (acting as surrogate for Gyrth) would have been the dominant presence in the jurisdiction. Lowestoft probably played little part in the monthly hundred court (both criminal and civil cases being handled there), because it was freemen who formed the juries and made the decisions, and its people would have appeared there only if they had offended in some way.

Such a limitation on a community, which prevented it from sharing in the process of local government, must have impeded the development of a sense of corporate being. What focus would there have been, if the settlement's only purpose (even beyond sustaining the physical needs of its inhabitants) was to service the manorial hub? It was probably at some point during the twelfth century that things started to change. The Lothingland communities began to assume a firm parish identity, with five of the Domesday settlements (Akethorpe, Browston, Caldecot, Dunston and Gapton) ceasing to exist in their own right and with six new ones (Ashby, Blundeston, Bradwell, Gunton, Oulton and Southtown) being formed from the redrawing of boundaries. The building of churches took place in settlements where there had previously been none (fourteen out of eighteen), and there obviously came the time when the need was felt for the half-hundred to have two centres of control – probably because of population increase and the consequent physical expansion of local communities.

The Hundred Roll of 1274–5 shows that Lowestoft had been chosen to assist Gorleston in the process of government (see pp. 29 and 55–7), and this must have raised both its status among the other Lothingland communities and its own inhabitants' sense of importance. Such a feeling had probably begun earlier, when the township became a manor in its own right at some point before the year 1212, and being granted the right to hold both a weekly market and annual fair in 1308 would have further boosted local pride. Relocation to a cliff-top site during the first half of the fourteenth century undoubtedly created great community cohesion in the planning and execution of the work, while a further sense of purpose and civic pride would have been felt (and expressed) in the construction of a large new parish church to replace the existing building. This project came to a halt as a result of the Black Death, but it was eventually completed 100 years or more afterwards, as the long period of recovery and readjustment reached its conclusion.

The best evidence of Lowestoft's emerging status as an economic force to be reckoned with is probably to be found in the attitude towards it of Great Yarmouth, as the latter sought to exercise control over its smaller neighbour – a process that began in earnest in the period immediately following the Black Death. Some of the Norfolk town's concern was well founded, because there was certainly a great deal of maritime irregularity taking place in home waters not far to the south – much of it causing loss of both revenue and prestige to the head-port. Some of the illegal practice was unarguably deliberate on Lowestoft's part, being aimed at breaking what was seen as unfair restrictions on its trade imposed by an authority that was at best grudgingly acknowledged and at worst openly contested. The commercial rivalry between the two communities was to last for the best part of three centuries or more, and was probably another factor in the creation of a corporate identity in the Suffolk town, whereby its civic sense was shaped (at least, in part) by its response to a larger and directly opposed neighbour seeking to check its maritime ambitions at every turn.

By the time of the 1524 Lay Subsidy a recognisably urban community was in existence at Lowestoft, with a population of c. 1,000 inhabitants and a range of different trades and occupations. The basis of its wealth derived from the sea, in the form of fishing and maritime trade, but agriculture also served it, with the cultivation of food crops and a certain amount of animal husbandry. A degree of economic and social complexity was evident in the range of business activities carried out by the townspeople and in the differing levels of their personal wealth and status. All of them lived in close proximity to each other in a planned late medieval environment, but social geography was discernible whereby the substantial members of the community lived largely along the High Street (with the merchants mainly located on the eastern side) and the lesser artisans in the side-street area to the west of it. In addition to its own in-house commercial activities, the town also functioned as the local weekly market centre for its surrounding group of parishes. Remarkably, and in contrast to the experience of many other English towns, both large and small, it had undergone two centuries or more of cumulative growth, with the Black Death arguably the only significant hiatus in the process.

In presenting a summary of the town's essential nature, seven predominant aspects are discernible. First was the presence of a suitable site for early settlement, accessible from the sea and able to provide the materials required to support a community. Next was the coastal location itself, which offered opportunity for involvement in marine fishing and seaborne trade. Accompanying this topographical factor was the distinctive configuration of offshore sandbanks which produced a safe haven, when needed, for large numbers of vessels engaged in commercial activity – a feature eventually reinforced in importance by proximity to Great Yarmouth, the head-port, which had ongoing problems throughout the fourteenth and fifteenth centuries with silting of its harbour mouth and considerable difficulty in controlling illegal trading activity on its doorstep. Fifth was Lowestoft's being granted manorial status at some point during the late twelfth or early thirteenth century, and sixth was the presence of an available cliff-top area on which to construct a relocated town, using land that had little agricultural value but which was able to yield productive annual rents once built upon. Finally, there was the vital matter of the manorial lord being a distant absentee – thereby creating opportunities for the more important members of the community to conduct their own civic affairs in the way they wanted.

All of this prompts the writer to say that, in studying the function of medieval towns, historians probably need to give greater attention to the geological and topographical aspects of a neighbourhood and not concentrate mainly (even solely) on surviving documentation to create a sense of its being. Good written records are an invaluable source of information, where they exist, but they don't tell the whole story. Towns and villages grow up and develop only where the local environment is conducive to settlement in the first place or where it can be shaped to suit human requirements. Lowestoft shows both characteristics in its evolution. It started off in an area favourable to the founding of a settlement, then moved to a location seemingly unsuitable for habitation: a bleak and exposed cliff-edge, with a steep, soft slope dropping to the beach below. It required a considerable investment of human belief and physical effort to create the new planned town.

During the early modern period the community was to continue its urban development in a modest but positive way. In spite of periodic demographic setbacks, particularly two serious plague epidemics in 1603 and 1635, its population continued to grow and its range of trades and occupations to increase in number. Maritime activity (both fishing and seaborne trade) increased in importance to the local economy, though with periodic declines in fortune caused by a variety of factors beyond the control of the people involved, and the town also continued to develop its role as a provider of goods and services to its immediate neighbourhood. In 1679 it was awarded port status in its own right (much against the wishes of Great Yarmouth), with specified rights of import and export and with the appointment of resident customs officers to supervise traffic – a privilege which validated the community's long-held maritime aspirations and raised its status both legally and socially.

The town had long been a self-governing unit, functioning under a manorial structure in which the crucial absence of a resident lord throughout the whole of its history allowed its leading citizens (especially if they were chief tenants of the manor) considerable autonomy in the way that they regulated the community. This was done with good sense on the part of the ruling families, whose members were sensible and far-sighted enough to involve people of lesser status in the responsibilities of holding office and performing civic duties. Thus was the burden of responsibility spread, and quite a wide cross section of local society (above the bottom-most stratum) was involved in maintaining order. A study of the available records shows that, for the most part, the task was effectively carried out and that, in the case of poor relief administration, a degree of warmth and understanding is detectable where less fortunate townspeople were concerned.

It may be the case that a maritime community, in the face of dangers inherent in going out upon the waves to make a living and in having contact with people from other parts of the country and from abroad, is less introspective in outlook and more disposed to tolerance of views not necessarily held at home. Certainly, the parish priests of the late seventeenth century, and of the whole of the eighteenth, seem to have enjoyed a cordial understanding with the ministers of the dissenting congregation. This was by no means the case, at the time, throughout the whole of England and Lowestoft can almost stand as an example of proto-ecumenical relations between the established church and nonconformity. With something like 10–15 per cent of its population being of Independent (Congregationalist) persuasion, there was the potential for a rift to develop between the two sets of believers. The fact that it never occurred is a tribute to both the lay people themselves and to their religious leaders.

In many ways, the middle of the eighteenth century marked a high point in Lowestoft's urban fortunes. Within a short period of time during the 1750s and 1760s, it began to hold assemblies in a purpose-built extension to a local inn, provide sea-bathing facilities on its beach and manufacture soft-paste porcelain for local people and visitors alike, while the stagecoach run between Great Yarmouth and London was re-routed to pass through the middle of town. Its growing importance locally was also acknowledged in its being granted the legal privilege of holding quarter sessions hearings for north Suffolk (alternately with Beccles) and of having the right to stage petty sessions of its own. These responsibilities were accompanied by the building of a small gaol or lock-up, in which malefactors could be either held for trial or punished for misdemeanours. Finally, in the last decade of the century, an expatriate townsman published a history of the town for the edification of interested local people, whose names (as subscribers to the work) preface the text which follows.

Edmund Gillingwater's account informs us that, in 1790, Lowestoft had 445 houses and 2,230 inhabitants. By 1831 the population had increased to 4,238 – still largely contained within its medieval and early modern boundaries. New harbour works to the south of the old town (constructed 1827–30) had just opened, but their potential to increase the town's economic fortunes was realised only after Samuel Morton Peto improved the existing facilities and provided railway links first with Norwich (1847) and later with the Ipswich–London line (1859). This innovation in transport, together with the reinvigoration of the harbour works and the establishment of a cross-North Sea cattle trade with Denmark, created an expansion of maritime enterprise that, in turn, was aided further by the introduction of trawling to the port by vessels from Kent and Sussex (during the 1840s and 1850s) and by increasing numbers of Scottish craft coming south during the autumn months to fish for herring. The town expanded rapidly and, by 1891, had a population of 19,150.

This growth continued as fishing, particularly, increased in profitability on the strength of a buoyant market at home and abroad and with the introduction of steam propulsion to the herring fleet (the trawlers tended to stay largely under sail). And hand in hand with the upsurge in fishing and the landing of catches went an increase in associated industries: fish-processing, shipbuilding and heavy engineering, transport and carriage, net-making and the production of cordage, chandlery and other activities too numerous to list. By 1911 the population stood at 37,886, and it has gone on increasing ever since. During both world wars Lowestoft was a major naval base for the conduct of minesweeping and patrolling duties (its fishing craft being ideally suited to conversion for the work involved) and the second conflict saw it become one of the most heavily bombed communities in the whole of Britain (if not *the* most heavily hit).

The inter-war years saw fishing remain Lowestoft's staple industry, but never at the same level of importance as had been the case during the years leading up to the First World War. This was partly due to the loss of traditional markets abroad for the shipment of cured herrings (especially the pickled variety), but a decline in the level of catches of the species – a factor compounded by a degree of seasonal unpredictability – also played a role. Trawling remained relatively strong, with more emphasis on the use of steam-powered vessels than had been the case earlier, but even there fluctuations in market price caused problems from time to time. The period following the Second World War saw the extinction of the large-scale North Sea autumn herring fishery during the 1960s – a staple activity that had sustained communities along the east coast of England for the best part of a thousand years. There were a number of contributory causes, and over-fishing was certainly a factor – perhaps even the primary one. Within twenty years trawling had begun to decline as well, as costs mounted (especially the price of diesel fuel) and the length of travel to find viable catches increased. Unfortunately for Lowestoft, this dip in fortunes coincided with the shut-down in much traditional industry that was taking place all over the United Kingdom at the time. Thus, the town lost its two shipyards (along with much associated back-up business), two of its three food-processing factories and its bus and coach-building works, while a takeover of its television factory reduced the labour force by more than a half.

Some sort of partial adjustment – it can't really be termed a recovery – was enabled by the development of a service and supply industry connected with the North Sea oil and gas rigs, which cancelled out some of the unemployment caused among fishing crews and kept at least some vessels in the port (this activity had begun during the 1970s, before fishing entered its terminal stage). The continuation of a reduced summer holiday trade has also played its part, as has the development of new (largely) service industries located on outlying industrial estates. But the structure of the old maritime-based economy has been destroyed and it is difficult to see it ever returning. The town is at another of its periodic crossroads and it seems impossible to make any predictions concerning the direction it will take. Engineering and service function for an offshore renewable energy industry offers the possibility of increasing employment, both onshore and at sea, but it is difficult to comment on the ultimate scale of the operation.

The one constant feature in Lowestoft's history during the period covered in this book, in the era investigated by its predecessor, and in the two centuries or more which followed, is population increase. The current count is one of c. 70,000 people (including those living in the adjacent satellite communities now absorbed into the town) – a process of outward growth which has resulted in the almost total building-over of the old ecclesiastical parish. Even so, it is still possible to find substantial traces of the medieval community within the outward urban spread. The most obvious one is the relocated settlement of 1300–1350, seen today as the High Street area or 'the top of town'. It retains its original street plan and the terracing of the cliff-face is still largely intact, though much neglected and decayed in places. The building plots along the roadway's length conform either to their original size or to later subdivisions, which occurred mainly during the sixteenth and seventeenth centuries. Nothing of the earliest phase of house-building remains above ground, but there is sufficient survival of later replacement dwellings to substantiate the duke of Norfolk's comments in 1545 about the town being 'right well builded' and also to give an idea of its growing importance in the 200 years which followed.

Below the cliff-top itself, The Denes remain a notable topographical feature at less than half their width in the mid-Tudor period. The southern sector has been turned into an industrial area, with the large Birds Eye food-processing factory providing the dominant presence, while much of the northern half is covered with holiday caravans. An open part remains between these two developed areas to give some visual sense of a former stretch of waste which was once so important in the town's economy, serving as both a source of rough grazing for its livestock and (more importantly, perhaps) as a natural wharf for the holding of goods both inward and outward bound. One small area still recalls something of the maritime past in the survival of wooden posts and cross-bars (known as *spars*) on which fishing gear was hung to dry after being treated with preservative agents against the deteriorating effect of constant exposure to salt water – a precious survival and one worthy of being noted by anyone who passes.

As for agriculture, Lowestoft's other sustaining mechanism of its earlier period of existence, very little remains to give any direct sense of it – the only crops grown these days being the vegetables produced in back gardens or on the remaining allotments (three of which are located on former areas of waste or heath). However, *The North Field* is still detectable beneath the masonry and tarmac (with St Margaret's Road running along the line of the central baulk and the adjoining streets following the north–south alignment of the strips), while a substantial part of the *South-West Field* has been preserved as the Normanston Park recreation ground. Half a mile to the east of it, with a housing development and former railway cutting interposing, is the site of the original township, long incorporated within a large municipal cemetery but with its two cardinal high-points still plainly visible. Hill Road makes its own topographical statement close by, though it is over 400 years since a windmill stood there, but the upward slope northwards is still crowned by the Church of St Margaret – impressive in its late Gothic splendour.

The South Field, third and last of the former common agricultural spaces, lies partly beneath the main present-day shopping area of town and also under the complex of terraced streets immediately to the west – a part of Lowestoft originally known as *The Harbour Village*, since it lay immediately to the north of the main quay. Construction of this part of town (beginning in the 1840s and 1850s) was the direct result of the improvements made to the port's facilities by Samuel Morton Peto and his creation of rail links to other parts of the country. In any overall appraisal of Lowestoft and its development, Peto's influence is probably on a par with the relocation of the town during the first half of the fourteenth century. In fact, it may have been even more influential in the light of the expansion which followed. He was not responsible for the creation of the harbour (which was in severe financial difficulty within a decade of its being built), but he saw the potential in it and thereby brought the town well and truly into the modern industrial age.

A millennium and a half ago Hluda and his followers accessed Lake Lothing from the sea by dragging their craft over a shingle bank; the vessels of today enter it on much the same alignment, via a bridge channel.

Appendix 1

Name analysis of the Lowestoft Hundred Roll tenants (1274–5)

Surname analysis

A. Patronymic/matronymic: 23 (5 equivocal) – including 5 of religious origin (0 equivocal).

B. Place-name: 7 (1 equivocal) – 1 in Lothingland; 1 in Mutford Half-hundred; 1 further removed in Suffolk; 2 in Norfolk (1 north, 1 south), 2 foreign (both Norman French, 1 equivocal).

C. Personal Features/circumstances: 10 (6 equivocal).

D. Topographical/locational: 11 (5 equivocal).

E. Occupational: 14 (5 equivocal).

F. Ecclesiastical: 4 (2 equivocal).

G. Nationality/ethnicity: 0.

H. Equivocal: 11.

Patronymic/matronymic (secular)

1 Aleyn (Breton, from Gaelic *ailin* = 'little rock').

2 Bonde (ON *bóndi* = 'bound tenant', 'serf').

3 Dean, of the (OFr *dien* and ME *deen*, both from L *decanus*; name indicates the head of a tithing-group).

4 Eywald (possible variant of Aylward, from OE *Aethelweard*: *æthel* = 'noble' and *weard* = 'watch').

5 Fellawe (OE *fēolaga*/ON *félagi* = 'financial partner' – later becoming 'companion', 'acquaintance').

6 Gele (OE *gal* = 'merry', 'jovial').

7 Gode (OE *gōd* = 'good'; a possible derivation also, by back-formation, from the female forename *Gode*).

8 Haenyld (a possible variant of the Anglo-Saxon name *Humbald*).

9 Jerald (variant of Norman-French Gerald: OHG *ger* = 'spear' and *wald* = 'rule').

10 Joyce, son of (possibly deriving from Breton name, *Juidcaelh* or *Iodoc*).

11 Man (OE *man(n)* = 'man'; the original sense may have been that of someone's servant or vassal).
12 Odo, son of (Norman French variant of OHG personal name, *Otto* = 'wealth').
13 Ray, le (possible derivations: OE *ēa* = 'river; OFr *rai* = 'beam of light'; OFr *raie* = 'ray' – a flatfish).
14 Reynald (OE *ragin* = 'prince' and *wald* = 'counsel').
15 Sewall (OE *Saewald or Sigewald*, from *sæ* = sea, or *sige* = victory, and *weald* = rule).
16 Thurkild (ON *Thor* and *ketill* = 'cooking vessel', 'cauldron').
17 Walters (OFr variant of OHG *Waldhar* – *wald* = 'rule' and *hari* = 'army').
18 Wyard (OHG *witu* = 'wood' or *wit* = 'wide').

- 8 Old English, 2 Scandinavian, 1 Old English/Scandinavian, 1 Old High German, 3 Old French/Old High German, 2 Breton, 1 Latin.

Patronymic/matronymic (religious)

1 Adam(s) (Heb *adama* = 'earth' – Adam, the first man, being made from the dust of the ground: Genesis 2.7).
2 Austin (variant of Augustine, famous fourth-/fifth-century bishop of Hippo – the name itself deriving from L. *augustus* = 'venerable', 'majestic').
3 Catherine (deriving from St Katherine of Alexandria, legendary fourth-century martyr; the name is an 'importation' from returning Crusaders, deriving from Gr *katharos* = 'pure').
4 Mariot (a diminutive form of Mary, from Heb *maryam*, and therefore relating to the Blessed Virgin Mary).
5 Thomas (Hebrew/Aramaic; the Apostle *Didymus*, 'the twin' – also a possible reference to Thomas Becket).

- 1 Latin, 1 Greek, 2 Hebrew, 1 Hebrew/Aramaic.
- A mixture here of the predictable linguistic sources and of Biblical figures and people connected with the early church.

Place-name (Lothingland Half-hundred)

1 Oulton [Altona].

Place-name (Mutford Half-hundred)

2 Wimundhall [Wymendhale].

Place-name (elsewhere, Suffolk)

3 Weston.

Place-name (Norfolk)

4 Bromholm, abbot of (Bacton).
5 Langley, abbot of.

Place-name (foreign)

6 Coleville, de [Colevilla] (Colleville, Normandy; the man in question here had served as sheriff of Suffolk and his family gave its surname as the second element of Carlton Colville, in Mutford Half-hundred).

7 Joyce, son of (possible derivative of Josse sur Mer, Normandy).
• Use of square brackets indicates spelling of the name in the original Latin text, where it differs from the usual form.

Personal features/circumstances

1 Bele (OFr *bel* = 'handsome').
2 Burt (OE *beorht* = 'bright', 'famous').
3 Cherrent, le (possibly from OE *scir* = 'bright', 'fair', with the suffix *-ent* appended).
4 Dun (OE *dun(n)* = 'dull, greyish brown'; hair-colour, complexion).
5 Gele (OE *gal* = 'merry', 'jovial').
6 Gode (OE *gōd* = 'good'; a possible derivation also, by back-formation, from the female forename *Gode*).
7 Monk (OE *munuc* and ON *munkr* = 'monk').
8 Pipewell, of (OE *pīpe* = 'tube' and *wel* = 'well'; the first element refers to a musical instrument).
9 Rustert (OE *rūst* = 'rust', perhaps relating to hair or facial complexion).
10 Storck (OE *storc* = 'stork'; also, a possible variant of OE *stoc* = 'tree-trunk').
• 9 Old English, 1 Old French.

Topographical/locational

1 Bele (OE *belle* = 'bell').
2 Cliff, of the (OE *clif* = 'cliff' or 'rock-face'; there may be a connection with one of the manorial chief tenements – Clifton's – and with the man, Thomas, referred to here).
3 Eyl(e)sted (possibly, OE *æl* = 'eel' and *stede* = 'place').
4 Lone House, of the (suggestive of an isolated dwelling, from OE *all āna* and *hūs* – the first element becoming ME *all ane* or *one*).
5 Moor, of the (OE *mōr* = 'waste land' or 'marsh'; the manorial chief tenement known as 'Jordan Atmeres' – perpetuating the name of the man here – was located on the edge of an area of heath).
6 Piledhil (OE *pil* = 'shaft' and *hyll* = 'hill).
7 Pipewell, of (OE *pīpe* = 'tube' and *wella* = 'well'; a possible connection here with water supply).
8 Rustert (possible derivation from OE *hrist* = 'brushwood').
9 Stonegate, of the (OE *stān* = 'stone' and ON *gata* = 'road', 'street' – possible reference to a Roman road).
10 Weyn (OE *weġ* = 'track').
11 Woodhouse, of the (OE *wudu* = 'wood' and *hūs* = 'house').
• 9 Old English, 1 Old English/Scandinavian, 1 Old English/Middle English.

Occupational

1 Bacon (OFr *bacon* = 'ham').
2 Bele (OE *belle* = 'bell').
3 Bonde (OE *bonda*/ON *bóndi* = 'tiller of the soil', 'serf').
4 Carpenter (OFr *carpentier* – 'carpenter').
5 Eyl(e)sted (possibly, OE *æl* = 'eel' and *stede* = 'place').
6 Justice (OFr *justice*, deriving from L *iustitia* = 'equity', 'righteousness').

7 Kadiman (ME *cade* = 'cask', deriving from L *cadus* = 'wine-jar' – therefore, perhaps, a cooper by trade).
8 Miller (OE *mylen* = 'to mill'; also ME *mulnere* and *mylnere* from L. *molinarius*).
9 Ringebell (OE *hring* and *belle*).
10 Rustert (OE *hrist* = 'brushwood').
11 Sefrey (possibly, OE *sife* = 'sieve' and *ryġe* = 'rye').
12 Shirreve, le (OE *scīrgerēfa* = 'sheriff').
13 Smith, the (OE *smiþ* = 'metalworker').
14 Weyn (OE *wæġen* = 'wagon').

- 8 Old English, 1 Old English/Scandinavian, 1 Old English/Middle English/Latin, 3 Old French, 1 Old French/Latin.

Ecclesiastical

1 Deacon (OE *deacon* or L *diaconus* = 'priest's assistant' – someone not fully ordained – originating from L *diaconus*/Gr *diakonos* = 'servant').
2 Dean, of the (L *decanus* = 'one of ten'; the name is more likely to have referred to a headborough than to a cathedral officer).
3 Monk (OE *munuc* and ON *munkr* = 'monk').
4 Vicar of Lowestoft (name not known).

- 1 Old English/Scandinavian, 1 Old English/Latin, 1 Latin.

Nationality/ethnicity

None identified.

Equivocal

1 Bele (personal features, topographical, occupational).
2 Bonde (patronymic-secular, occupational).
3 Dean (patronymic-secular, ecclesiastical).
4 Eyl(e)sted (topographical, occupational).
5 Gele (patronymic-secular, personal features).
6 Gode (patronymic-secular, personal features).
7 Joyce (patronymic-secular, place-name).
8 Monk (personal features, ecclesiastical).
9 Pipewell (personal features, topographical).
10 Rustert (personal features, topographical, occupational).
11 Weyn (topographical, occupational).

- These eleven names are the ones underlined in the individual categories.

The patronymic/matronymic category is the most generalised one, with surnames of widely varying origins also to be found in other, more specific categories.

Forename analysis (all tenants – number of times recorded)

Male	**Female**
Adam (1)	Alice (2)
Alan (2)	Christina (1)
AS Edmund (1)	Elina (1) – variant of Eleanor

Henry (8)
John (10)
Jordan (1)
Nicholas (2)
Richard (9)
Robert (6)
Roger (1)
Seman (3)
Symon (1)
Thomas (8)
William (5)
(14)

Lena (2) – variant of Helena
Margaret (2)
(5)

• AS = Anglo-Saxon.

Forename analysis (linguistic origins)

Male: 13 Norman-French/other.
1 Anglo-Saxon.

Female: 5 Norman-French/other.

Both: 18 Norman-French/other.
1 Anglo-Saxon.

As a closing comment, it is worth noting that whereas Old English is the predominant linguistic source where surnames are concerned, the opposite is true of forenames. Here, Norman-French is, with one exception, the sole influence – a fact that may be taken as representing the suppression of Anglo-Saxon culture following the invasion of 1066. Many of the old surnames continued in use because they had been established over generations, and there was no need to change them, but the members of the lower orders who carried them as their birthright were no longer baptised with Christian names of like origin. The language of the conquerors had created a new currency, which is most noticeable in the names of three of the monarchs: Henry, Richard and John.

Various sources were used in the compilation of this appendix, prominent among them being the online *Surname Database*: www.surnamedb.com.

Appendix 2

Suffolk's top 25 townships (1524–5 Lay Subsidy)

Order by wealth

Name	1524	1525	Hundred	Total	Comments
1. Ipswich	£255 8s 3d	£233 17s 2d	(*extra-*Carlford)	£489 5s 5d	
2. Lavenham	£179 13s 10d	£175 17s 6d	Babergh	£355 11s 4d	
3. Hadleigh	£106 6s 10d	£108 10s 4d	Cosford	£214 17 2d	
4. Bury		£169 8s 8d	(Thingoe)	£169 8s 8d	No data for 1524 – all collected 1525
5. Beccles	£73 13s 4d	£71 7s 9d	Wangford	£145 1s 1d	
6. Long Melford	£65 7s 0d	£65 4s 4d	Babergh	£130 11s 4d	
7. Sudbury	£60 14s 4d	£61 13s 2d	Babergh	£122 7s 6d	
8. Nayland	£58 13s 4d	£56 3s 2d	Babergh	£114 16s 6d	
9. Stratford St Mary	£55 0s 3d	£53 9s 10d	Samford	£108 10s 1d	
10. East Bergholt	£50 9s 0d	£50 6s 0d	Samford	£100 15s 0d	
11. Woodbridge	£45 3s 6d	£42 2s 6d	Loes	£87 6s 0d	
12. Bures	£37 17s 4d	£39 11s 9d	Babergh	£77 9s 1d	
13. Framlingham	£56 9s 8d	£16 13s 2d	Loes	£73 2s 10d	
14. Dunwich	£39 19s 1d	£32 0s 6d	Blything	£71 19s 7d	
15. Bungay	£34 4s 10d	£35 0s 2d	Wangford	£69 5s 0d	
16. Lowestoft	**£35 18s 7d**	**£29 11s 8d**	**Lothingland**	**£65 10s 3d**	
17. Stoke-by-Nayland	£31 1s 1d	£27 11s 8d	Babergh	£58 12s 9d	
18. Blythburgh	£25 6s 0d	£25 12s 4d	Blything	£50 18s 4d	
19. Southwold	?	£25 11s 2d	Blything	c. £50?	No data for 1524
20. Glemsford	£26 6s 4d	£23 12s 4d	Babergh	£49 18s 8d	

Name	1524	1525	Hundred	Total	Comments
21. Boxford	£23 15s 0d	£23 18s 6d	Babergh	£47 13s 6d	
22. Stowmarket	£22 16s 10d	?	Stow	c. £45?	No data for 1525
23. Aldeburgh	?	£22 14s 8d	Plomesgate	c. £45?	No data for 1524
24. Mildenhall	?	£19 8s 0d	Lackford	c. £39?	No data for 1524
25. Bildeston	£12 12s 0d	£11 10s 8d	Cosford	£24 2s 8d	

- The information contained in both tables in this appendix derives from J. Sheail, 'The regional distribution of wealth in England as indicated by the 1524–5 Lay Subsidy' (unpub. PhD thesis, Univ. London, 1968), vol. 2, pp. 473–98, and S.H.A. Hervey, *Suffolk in 1524*, SGB 9 (Woodbridge, 1906) – both sources previously cited.
- Ipswich, as an ancient Anglo-Saxon borough, stood outside the hundredal structure of Suffolk, but was located within the geographical area of Carlford.
- Bury (St Edmunds) was sometimes treated as part of Thingoe Hundred; at other times, it was considered an entity in its own right.
- Not all of the communities listed necessarily fulfilled all of the criteria required to be considered as genuinely urban in nature, particularly where a sufficiently complex occupational structure and self-governing mechanisms were concerned. Some of them may well have been large villages rather than small towns.
- The hierarchy of communities presented above shows a pronounced loading in favour of townships located in the southern part of Suffolk, particularly in the cloth-making area of the south-west. Babergh Hundred has 30 per cent of the places named.
- The county's coastal strip generally shows less affluence than inland areas, with Dunwich, Lowestoft, Blythburgh, Southwold and Aldeburgh all being in the lower half of the table. Ipswich and Woodbridge (the latter benefiting from proximity to the former), while not truly coastal, were accessible from the sea and able to take part in maritime trade. Ipswich was, in fact, head-port from Orwell Haven to the Thames Estuary, which effectively gave it control of the whole of the Essex shoreline.
- The disparity in the levels of wealth between coastal communities and certain inland ones does not necessarily show that the former were in a state of decline so much as reflect the buoyancy of the Suffolk cloth-making industry at the time.
- The four cases of missing data (Southwold, Stowmarket, Aldeburgh and Mildenhall) have had identical sums to the one recorded added on, in order to produce a notional total for both years. Scrutiny of the table will show the reader a close correlation, in many cases (not all), between the sums of money collected in 1524 and 1525.
- Framlingham shows a degree of complexity in the 1524 data, in that separate numbers of 50 and c. 110 taxpayers are shown has having handed over sums of £18 14s 2d and £37 15s 6d respectively, thus totalling £56 9s 8d. Thus, its number of contributors in 1524 was nearly double that of 1525. Walberswick shows a similar

disparity (though not quite as large, proportionally), while most of the other communities seem to suggest that the subsidy was collected on what may be described as a 'fifty–fifty' basis over the two years.

Order by number of taxpayers

Town	1524	1525	Total	Hundred	Comments
1. Ipswich	360	412	772	(*extra-* Carlford)	Incomplete data for both years
2. Bury		645	645	Thingoe	No data for 1524; all collected 1525
3. Hadleigh	311	303	614	Cosford	
4. Beccles	242	307	549	Wangford	
5. Dunwich	230	235	465	Blything	
6. Sudbury	218	231	449	Babergh	
7. Lavenham	199	195	394	Babergh	
8. Woodbridge	c. 192	169	c. 361	Loes	Approximate number given in 1524
9. Long Melford	154	186	340	Babergh	
10. Bungay	145	142	287	Wangford	
11. Lowestoft	**133**	**144**	**277**	**Lothingland**	
12. Mildenhall	136	?	c. 272	Lackford	No data for 1525
13. Aldeburgh	?	125	c. 250	Plomesgate	No data for 1524
14. Nayland	102	147	249	Babergh	
15.= East Bergholt	123	123	246	Samford	
15.= Framlingham	c. 160	86	c. 246	Loes	Approximate number given in 1524
17. Stoke-by-Nayland	117	128	245	Babergh	
18. Hoxne	126	c. 118	c. 244	Hoxne	Approximate number given in 1525
19. Boxford	112	122	234	Babergh	
20. Southwold	?	117	c. 234	Blything	No data for 1524
21. Stowmarket	99	134	233	Stow	
22. Glemsford	122	100	222	Babergh	
23. Stoke-by-Clare	102	?	c. 204	Risbridge	No data for 1525
24. Walberswick	126	77	203	Blything	
25. Bildeston	90	105	195	Cosford	

- Three communities featuring in the previous table – Stratford St Mary (159), Bures (165) and Blythburgh (137) – are not present in this one, their replacements being Hoxne, Stoke-by-Clare and Walberswick.
- Ipswich has incomplete data for both 1524 and 1525, with two of its four civic wards having the number of taxpayers recorded for the former year and three for the latter.

- Mildenhall, Aldeburgh, Southwold and Stoke-by-Clare have had the missing year recording the number of taxpayers given the same number as the one recorded – this, in order to give a notional number of contributors.
- The total number of taxpayers, being largely (but not exclusively) adult males, may be taken as a very loose indicator of the size of the different communities' populations relative to each other. However, it would not be safe to apply a standard multiplier (such as 4.75) in order to work out a specific number of people living in each place. Such a calculation would lead to considerable over-estimation of the individual populations.
- The top ten communities can be seen, in some ways, as a summary of Suffolk's history. Ipswich was the ancient county town, with its status as borough and port going well back into Anglo-Saxon times, while Bury St Edmunds had an equally lengthy pedigree as the major force in the west of the county based on the presence of its abbey and associated extensive liberty. Hadleigh, Sudbury, Lavenham and Long Melford were prosperous market towns and centres of the woollen cloth trade, while Woodbridge benefited from a close association with Ipswich, from serving a rich surrounding agricultural area and from being able to participate in both fishing and maritime trade (it was also next door to Melton, the administrative centre of the Liberty of St Etheldreda). Dunwich had once been the centre of the first East Anglian diocese and the major port of the whole east coast, though it was in a state of long and gradual decline from its twelfth century heyday – and Beccles and Bungay (up in the northern sector of the county) had histories as local centres of trade going back into the Anglo-Saxon period.

Addendum

It is stated in Hervey, *Suffolk in 1524*, p. 402, that a preamble to the Subsidy, known as *The Anticipation*, was published in advance of the main collection process beginning. This was a directive from Thomas Wolsey that every man with assets worth £40 or more was to pay his dues before the collection officially began – presumably to ensure that the richest people in the land provided a basic sum of money to serve as a type of 'bottom line'. It is further revealed, on p. 418, that John Jettor (Jnr) of Lowestoft had his wealth assessed at £120, with a £6 payment due thereon. Table 12 in the main text shows him liable for the same sum, payable on £101 worth of goods, and the third note following on p. 236 speculates as to the reason behind this. It is clear that he was indeed in a higher tax bracket – at the top of the one following the £100 category.

Appendix 3

The Lowestoft manorial chief tenements

Name	Hundred Roll ref.	1327 Subsidy ref.	Location
1. Wymers			North Field
2. Geralds	John Jerald	John Gerald	Park Field
3. Deacons	Seaman the Deacon	Henry, William & Thomas Dekne	South Field (south-east of market)
4. Katherine Fellows	John Fellawe		South-West Field
5. Thirkells	Richard Thurkild		North Field
6. Ringbell & Shelton	Henry Ringebell		South-West Field (to the west of Church Green)
7. Garneys			South Field
8. Herrimans	Henry Man		North Field
9. Jervis (half)			South End
Herrimans (half)	Henry Man		North Field
10. Burtis	Richard Burt		East of Skamacre Heath
11. Fishmans (half)			East of Skamacre Heath
Holetts (half)		John & Warin Howlot	West of Skamacre Heath
12. Holetts		John & Warin Howlot	South-West Field
13. Seaman Carpenters	Seman Carpenter		North Field
14. Cliftons (half)	Thomas of the Cliff		Flyes Close (part of the North Field)
Piswells (half)	Richard Pipewell		North Field (north of Goose Green)
15. Kirkley (half)			South Field
Herritofts (half)			North Field
16. Odes		Thomas & Richard Ode	North Field
17. Eastons		Thomas of Easton	South Field (south-west of market)
18 Phillippottis			South-West Field
19. Woodhouse (half)	Richard of the Woodhouse		North Field
Akethorpe (half)		Edmund of Akethorpe	South Field

Name	Hundred Roll ref.	1327 Subsidy ref.	Location
20. Hanolds	Thomas Haenyld		South Field (south-west of market)
21. Reynolds	William Reynald	Reginald Reynald	East of Skamacre Heath
22. Reynolds	William Reynald	Reginald Reynald	East of Skamacre Heath
23. Jordan Atmeres	Jordan of the Moor		South-West Field
24. Justice	Henry Justice		South-West Field
25. Jovelflete			South-West Field
26. Wellflete/Wylplete			South-West Field
27. Bacons (half) Walters (half)	 Richard Walter		South End North Field
28. Whitlocks (half) Hunts, or Moneys (half)			South-West Field Between Flyes Close & High Street

- The information is taken from the manor roll of 1618 and R. Reeve, 'A history of Lowestoft and Lothingland', vol. 4 (unpub. manuscript of c. 1810) – SRO(L), 194/A10/73 & 193/3/4, pp. 156–81 – with adjustments made in the interests of clarity.
- It can be seen that the half-chieves were paired off to form full tenements for the purposes of record-keeping. They were not necessarily located near each other and they were treated as independent units for the collection of lord's rents, a duty which fell periodically on the holders of the various properties.
- Note that nos 18, 23, 24, 25, 26 and 28 (Whitlocks) were all located next to each other, in a cluster, at the top of what is now Normanston Park – in the area currently occupied by a skate-park.

Appendix 4

Sixteenth-century merchant fleet details

1. Vessels returning from the 1533 Iceland cod fishery voyage: 22 Dunwich, 7 Lowestoft, 7 Orwell Haven (Ipswich) and 1 Orford – total 37 in all. Source: TNA, SP 1/80 f.65v.

Lowestoft details

Name of vessel	Capacity	Owner	Master	Merchant	Tax paid
Margaret	60 tonne	John Jetter	Robt Deyghton	[As owner]	£6
James	54 tonne	John Jetter	Andrew Ailam	[As owner]	£4
Xpofer [Christopher]	72 tonne	John Jetter & Rogir Cannsell	Thomas Dobs	[As owners]	£6
Mary Grace	60 tonne	Thomas Annot	Johannes Springolde	[As owner]	£6
John	60 tonne	Robt Hodds Snr	Robt Wollovir	[As owner]	£6
Mary	72 tonne	Robt Hodds Jnr	William Ryaldin	[As owner]	£6
Johanne [John]	52 tonne	John Robsonne	[?] Gardyn	[As owner]	£4
					Total: £38

- All names have been left in the original spelling because of the difficulty of converting some of them to modern forms. *Rogir Cannsell* is Roger Chancellor.
- The vessel names all have religious associations. *Margaret* was St Margaret of Antioch, patron of the parish church and town; *James* was the disciple brother of John, executed in Jerusalem in AD 44 by Herod Agrippa; *Christopher* was the saint and protector of travellers; *Mary* was, of course, the mother of Christ, and the *Mary Grace* form of the name given here reflects both her votive prayer ('Hail, Mary') and 'The Magnificat'; *John* (*Johanne* is a Latinised form) was the disciple, gospel writer and creator of the Book of Revelation.
- The carrying capacity per vessel was reckoned as the number of *tuns* (barrels of 252 gallons volume) able to be conveyed, the term *tonne* (or *ton*) – as used here – therefore having nothing to do with weight of cargo. The craft listed here were of medium size.

- The merchant column represents the possibility of the vessels being hired by operators other than the owners. It did not apply in the case of Lowestoft.
- The final column records the levy known as *composition fish* or *prise fish*, which was paid by people financing the Iceland fishery during the sixteenth century. It was introduced during the reign of Henry VIII and remained in place until the 1590s. Each vessel returning from northern waters was taxed at the rate of the sale price of *120 ling* or *240 cod* – this differential reflecting the relative commercial value of the two species. The amounts of money paid here in tax suggest a profitable voyage. In c. 1600, good-quality, reprocessed Iceland cod (hydrated and resalted), of good size, retailed at about 1s 6d a pair.

2. The 1544 Vessel Survey: the number of vessels suitable for military use in Norfolk and Suffolk townships, with carrying capacity rated in tons (*tuns*) per vessel (columns 2–12). Source: *LPFD, Henry VIII*, vol 19(i), p. 76.

Township	**160**	**140**	**120**	**100**	**90**	**80**	**70**	**60**	**50**	**40**	**30**	**Total**	**Position**
Yarmouth		1		6		4		6	4	4	7	32	1st
Dunwich								7	2	4	3	16	2nd
Lowestoft			3	1		3		5	3			15	3rd
King's Lynn				1		1		3	4		3	12	4th
Walberswick						2		4	3	1 (35)	1	11	5th
Southwold				1		2		3	2		2	10	6th=
Ipswich/Orwell	1		1			1				4	3	10	6th=
Aldeburgh				1		2			1	2	3	9	8th
Cley			1	1		1				3	2	8	9th=
Wiveton					1	1			4	2		8	9th=
Burnham							1		1	1	1	4	11th
Blakeney									1	1(38)	1	3	12th=
Wells							1			1	1	3	12th=
Sheringham							1				1	2	14th
	1	1	5	11	1	17	3	28	25	23	28	143	

- The sequence of townships in the table is presented in league-table order, according to the overall number of vessels listed. The original order was as follows: King's Lynn, Wells, Burnham, Blakeney, Wiveton, Cley, Sheringham, Yarmouth, Lowestoft, Aldeburgh, Dunwich, Walberswick, Southwold, Ipswich/Orwell. Thus, although there was movement eastwards (at first) and then southwards through the two counties, strict geographical progression from place to place was not observed.
- Two vessels in the 40-ton (*tun*) category (Walberswick and Blakeney) have a slightly lesser carrying capacity recorded.
- It is noticeable that 104 of the overall total of 143 vessels are found in the medium range of 30–60 tons (73 per cent).

- If taken at another time, this survey would have shown considerable differences in the ranking of the various townships, as maritime fortunes rose and fell.

3. Survey of merchant ships made by Thomas Colshill (1572). Source: *VCH Suffolk*, vol. 2, p. 216, drawing on information in *CSPD, Elizabeth I, Addenda*, vol. 22.

Suffolk details

Township	100 tons +	50–100 tons	20–50 tons	20 tons and under	Total
Ipswich	5	12	10	11	38
Aldeburgh	1	8	13	12	34
Walberswick		2	3	13	18
Southwold	1	2	4	10	17
Lowestoft		1	7	8	16
Woodbridge	2		4	8	14
Dunwich		1	3	2	6
Orford		1	1	1	3
Gorleston				1	1
	9	27	45	66	147

- Again, the sequence of townships is presented in league-table order, the original one being as follows: Ipswich, Woodbridge, Aldeburgh, Orford, Dunwich, Southwold, Walberswick, Gorleston, Lowestoft. The geographical progression was therefore from south to north, but not in strict order.
- A total of sixty-six vessels in the 20 tons (*tuns*) and under category represents 45 per cent of the whole. This reflects either a process of including smaller craft than was the brief in the preceding table or a reduction in construction-size.
- It is noticeable that Lowestoft had lost twelve craft in the 60–120 ton (*tun*) range between 1544 and 1572. Half of its fleet in 1572 consisted of vessels of 20 tons and under carrying capacity. Southwold and Walberswick show even larger proportions of smaller craft (59 per cent and 72 per cent, respectively).
- According to *VCH Suffolk*, vol. 2, fishing craft were not included in this survey.

Names of Lowestoft vessels in the table above

Name	Master	Tonnage
Charitie	John Sameys [Samweys]*	50
Grace of God (r)	Reynold Robynson	40
Jhesus (r)	Thomas Bosyld	40
John (r)	Thomas Belman*	40
Charitie	Thomas Wynson	30

Name	Master	Tonnage
James (r)	James Towne*	30
Clement (r)	John Dowsing*	25
Mary Fortune (r)	Matthew Bedowe*	25
Danyell (r)	John Dale*	25
John (r)	John Grudgfyld*	20
Peter (r)	Xtofer Michells [Christopher Mighells]	20
Jhesus (r)	Thomas Grudgfilde*	18
William	John Beswick [Beseck]*	18
Clement (r)	Robert Hutton	15
Thomasyn	John Watson*	15
Gabriell (r)	Robert Yates	15
Henne	William Dalton	10
Phenix	Nicholas Bedyram [Bedam]*	10

- The list above shows eighteen vessels, not sixteen as shown in the previous table: with one extra craft in the 20–50 tons (*tuns*) category and another in that recording 20 tons and under. Thus, it is possible that there are other concealed errors in the data.
- The names with asterisks are those of known Lowestoft residents (eleven of the eighteen listed), traceable through the parish registers or other documentation. Of the remaining seven, some could have been living in the town at the time the list was compiled, while others may have been based in either Kirkley or Pakefield.
- The names of the vessels are largely (but not completely) religious, the symbol (r) indicating ones which definitely are. *Grace of God* and *Jhesus* (*sic*) speak for themselves; *John* and *James* were explained in the notes following the first table above; *Clement* was an early bishop of Rome, venerated as a saint and martyr and a patron of mariners (his emblem, an anchor); *Mary Fortune* was a name used to invoke the influence of the mother of Christ; *Danyell* (Daniel) was the great Old Testament prophet of the Babylonian Captivity period; *Peter* was the leading disciple and first bishop of Rome; and *Gabriel* was the archangel of The Annunciation.
- Of the remaining names, *Charitie* may well have had a religious motivation (its most famous use being in 1 Corinthians 13, where the Apostle Paul uses the word to mean Christian love in its widest and most embracing way). *William* and *Thomasyn* (Thomasine) are male and female Christian names, while *Henne* (Hen) and *Phenix* (Phoenix) represent the most common type of domestic poultry and the mythical, self-combusting bird of Arabia – extremes of a feathered kind, one is tempted to say!
- The appearance of non-religious names may reflect changes in thought and attitude caused by the disappearance of the old Roman Catholic order and the establishment of Protestantism as the official religion of England, though the Elizabethan settlement was only four years old at the time the survey was carried out.

Appendix 5

Fairs and markets in Lothingland and Lowestoft

Lothingland

As explained in Chapter 2, the original grant of a market in Lothingland Half-hundred was made by King John in the year 1211 – three years after Great Yarmouth had received its charter of incorporation (March 1208) with specifically stated trading rights. With only Crown income in mind, the monarch either had no idea of the contention and strife these opposing privileges would cause or was unconcerned about them. No positive first-hand identification of the person, or body, to whom the grant was made has been found by the writer, but in at least one printed secondary source it is said to have been to the 'men of Lothingland', in return for a gift to the king of one palfrey (a small riding horse generally for women).[1] Specific reference to the source of this information cites the Patent Rolls of 13 King John (May 1211 to May 1212), but the published reproduction of these royal grants and authorisations has the years 1209–12 missing.[2] If the manor itself (together with its revenues) was wholly in the hands of the king at the time of the granting of market privileges, it is conceivable that he might have conferred this right in exchange for the lesser gift of a horse – be it a one-off payment or an annual one.

The term 'men of Lothingland' (if this was the term used of the grantees) probably referred to leading landholders in the half-hundred. The manor of Lothingland was a royal one which, in typical fashion, was leased to private individuals as a means of generating revenue for the Crown. It is recorded that from Easter 1199 onwards the estate was held by the brothers Geoffrey and Reginald du Bois (al. *de Bosco*) for an annual rent of £61

[1] S. Letters (ed.), *Gazetteer of Markets and Fairs in England Wales to 1516*, vol. 2, List and Index Society, Special Series 33 (London, 2003) (online resource), p. 332. This work is also available in digitised form on the internet.

[2] T.D. Hardy (ed.), *Rotuli Litterarum Patentium*, vol. 1 (London , 1716). Reprinted on the order of William IV in 1835. Again, this particular source may be found in digitised form.

4s 0d, but there is no indication of their length of tenancy.[3] It had presumably terminated before 1211, with full title returning to the monarch, in order for the grant of a market to be made to residents of Lothingland. The following year it was leased once again – to William de Longspée, earl of Salisbury (half-brother of John), who seems to have remained in occupation until his death on 7 March 1226.[4]

The location of the market place must have been at the northern end of Gorleston parish, on low-lying, open ground adjoining the River Yare, opposite what was in those days the undeveloped beach area well to the south of Great Yarmouth town. It would have been located somewhere in the area where the present Malthouse Lane joins Beccles Road and Southtown Road, and it was troubled by tidal inundation from time to time because of its proximity to the water. William de Longspée had it moved during his time as Lothingland lord and also changed the day it was held from Sunday to Thursday.[5] The area providing the new market place was probably on slightly higher land to the north of its original siting, thereby making it closer to Southtown than to Gorleston – which is no doubt why the residents of the former community felt able to encroach upon it and build houses, as recorded in the Hundred Roll enquiry of 1274–5 (p. 58).[6]

The description given in the Hundred Roll of this encroachment being 'thirty feet on all sides' suggests a square trading area, and the fact of its being built upon would seem to imply limited use of the facility at best. Following the death of William de Longspée lease of the Half-hundred manor was taken on by Roger Fitzosbert, lord of Somerleyton, for a period of three years at an annual rent of £80, the grant itself being made on 8 May 1226 and backdated to Easter (19 April).[7] During his tenancy Fitzosbert contested Great Yarmouth's trading privileges, even going so far as to claim the right of taking certain customs duties in the Norfolk port – a move which simply prompted the burgesses there to make counter-claims of their own and assert their authority over the Suffolk side of the river (see pp. 59–60). He seems to have been unsuccessful in making his investment in the Half-hundred pay and, on 17 July 1230, title was transferred to the 'men of Lothingland'. The length of lease was stated as being for one year as from 24 June, but no rental cost was mentioned.[8] The grant was renewed or confirmed on 17 April 1231, at an annual payment of £70,[9] and further reiterated on 27 April, in the same sum, when it was also declared to be 'in perpetuo'.[10]

This particular term is probably to be taken as meaning 'for as long as it lasts', rather than 'for evermore'. And, indeed, the manor of Lothingland was conveyed in due course by Henry III to Dervorgille de Balliol in December 1237 in exchange for lands held by her in Cheshire. The annual rental remained at £70 and the men giving evidence in the Hundred Roll enquiry were in no doubt that the £10 differential between the £80 paid

[3] Arts and Humanities Research Council (University of Sheffield), *The Lands of the Normans in England, 1204–1244* (online resource, 2007): www.hrionline.ac.uk.

[4] Maxwell Lyte, *Liber Feodorum*, vol. 1, p. 139. His holding of title is further confirmed, on 13 March 1225, in Arts and Humanities Research Council, *CFR, Henry III*, C60/22, no. 130.

[5] Letters, *Gazetteer of Markets and Fairs*, p. 332.

[6] Hervey, *Hundred Rolls*, pp. 72 and 73.

[7] Arts and Humanities Research Council, *CFR, Henry III*, C60/24, no. 162.

[8] Arts and Humanities Research Council, *CFR, Henry III*, C60/29, no. 410.

[9] Arts and Humanities Research Council, *CFR, Henry III*, C60/30, no. 156.

[10] Arts and Humanities Research Council, *CFR, Henry III*, C60/30, no. 164.

by Roger Fitzosbert and the lesser sum charged thereafter (still current in 1274–5) was the result of Great Yarmouth's interference in Lothingland's commercial activity and the detriment resulting therefrom. As far as the market itself is concerned, those testifying in the Hundred Roll process maintained that the residents of Southtown (or 'Little Yarmouth', as it was referred to at the time) had made their encroachments onto the trading area after Dervorgille de Balliol had become lord of Lothingland,[11] which suggests both a lack of use and the remoteness of an absentee landlord. There is no record of any order being given for the encroachments to be cleared, but there is slender evidence of the market place being moved once again in recognition that the houses were a permanent feature. The southern end of Gorleston High Street, near the junction with Baker Street and Church Lane, broadens out into what looks very much like a former trading space, and it is possible that this is where the failing Lothingland market ended its days.

It is possible (perhaps even likely) that the Half-hundred of Lothingland, although some forty square miles in area, was not sufficiently well populated at the time to support a viable market, especially one that had its centre of trade located in the far north-eastern corner. This made access difficult for a substantial number of local people, and added to this was the market place's proximity to Great Yarmouth, the major town on the East Anglian coast between Dunwich and Lynn. Not only did this highly developed urban area dominate trading activity to the north of the river Yare, it was also able to exercise a restrictive influence to the south and west by virtue of a judgement of 1228 which gave it control of the area occupied by Southtown and Gorleston.[12] Thus, although the grant of a market to the lord(s) of Lothingland may have had a degree of prestige about it, local factors militated against the privilege in terms of it ever being of a profitable nature for its holder.

Lowestoft

The town has been noted as 'probably the successor to Lothingland as a commercial centre',[13] but this shows some degree of topographical misunderstanding. Lothingland, in being a half-hundred, was not a trading centre in itself, but an administrative area consisting of eighteen individual parishes and as many hamlets and outliers (see Maps 4 and 5). Its market place was situated in Gorleston, which was the hub of the manor during the eleventh and twelfth centuries but then diminished in importance as Lowestoft was granted manorial status in its own right (a fact first referred to in the year 1212) and grew steadily in importance thereafter.[14] It is important to note that when John de Dreux was awarded the right of a market and fair on 15 November 1308, the conferring of these privileges refers specifically to his manor of Lowestoft, not that of Lothingland – of which

[11] Hervey, *Hundred Rolls*, pp. 72 and 73.

[12] The order to set up the commission of enquiry into the disputes between the citizens of Great Yarmouth and Lothingland was given on 15 February 1228. See H.C. Maxwell Lyte (gen. ed.), *CPR, Henry III*, vol. 2 (London, 1903), p. 210.

[13] Letters, *Gazetteer of Markets and Fairs*, p. 332.

[14] Maxwell Lyte, *Liber Feodorum*, vol. 1, p. 134.

entity he was also lord. Therefore, the grant had nothing to do with Lothingland *per se*, but was conferred upon one of its single-parish manors, held by the same lord.[15]

The market day was Wednesday and the fair an extended one, beginning on the vigil of St Margaret (19 July) and lasting for a total of eight days. With many fairs being granted only a three- or four-day duration, it would seem that high expectations were held of the one awarded to Lowestoft (which may reflect the town's growing economic strength), but no records exist to show whether or not they were fulfilled. Nearly a century and a half later, on 14 December 1445, the lord of the manor of the time, William de la Pole, marquis of Suffolk, was awarded a regrant of the weekly market and of two fairs per annum: the first on the feast day of St Philip and St James (1 May) and the second on St Michael's Day (29 September), each with a three-day period on either side of the festival.[16] With two seven-day fairs replacing the original eight-day one, it would seem that Lowestoft was enjoying a period of economic prosperity – but, again, no records exist to confirm this.

Both the market and the fairs were discussed in detail in Chapter 3, and it would be unnecessary to cover the same ground here. The surviving leet court records for the seventeenth century, and for much of the eighteenth, show that the market was a buoyant enterprise, though its annual proceedings were dealing with the trading misdemeanours that took place with almost predictable regularity. Surprisingly perhaps, Edmund Gillingwater, Lowestoft's late eighteenth-century historian, has very little to say about the market and gives little insight, either, into the conduct of the fairs. All he has to reveal is that, according to a document lodged in the diocesan registry at Norwich, the regrant of privileges awarded to William de la Pole in 1445 entitled him (via his steward) to hold courts of market and fair. He also reveals that, in 1768, the lord of the manor (Sir Ashurst Allen) allowed the townspeople, upon their request, to move the fairs from the green where they had been traditionally held onto the market place – suggesting, perhaps, that they had declined in size and importance and no longer required such a large venue.[17]

[15] Crump and Trimmer, *CoCR*, vol. 3, p. 123, gives the details concerning Lowestoft being granted a market and fair.

[16] Cunningham, *CoCR*, vol. 6, p. 59.

[17] Gillingwater, *Lowestoft*, p. 55. The writer seems to be referring to the smaller overspill market area on the southern corner of *Tyler's Lane* (now Compass Street), where it met the High Street. This had been created in 1703 because of the encroachment of houses onto the main market, reducing the space available; it was situated close to Fair Green.

Appendix 6

Local place-name derivation

Lothingland Half-hundred

*1 **Akethorp**: OE āc = 'oak'; OD Þor*p* = 'farm' or 'outlier'.
*2 Ashby: ON *Aski*, personal name, or ON *ask* = 'ash tree'; ON *býr* = 'village', 'homestead'.
*3 **Belton**: ON/ODan *bil* = 'interspace'; OE *tūn* = 'enclosure', 'homestead', 'village'.
*4 Blundeston: OE *Blunt*, personal name; OE *tūn*, as above.
5 Boyton: OE *Boia*, personal name; OE *tūn*, as above.
*6 Bradwell: OE *brād* = 'broad'; OE *well* = 'stream'.
7 Brotherton: ODan *Brother*, personal name; OE *tūn*, as above.
*8 **Browston**: OE *brocc* = 'badger', poss. used as a personal name; OE *tūn*, as above.
*9 **Burgh [Castle]**: OE *burg* = 'fort'.
*10 **Caldecott**: OE *calde* = 'cold'; OE *cot* = 'hut', 'cottage'.
11 Carlton: OScand *Karla*, personal name, or a Scandinavian form of OE *ceorl* = 'free-man'; OE *tūn*, as above.
12 *Claydon*: OE *claeg* = 'clay'; OE *dūn* = 'hill'.
*13 **Corton**: ON/ODan *Kari*, personal name; OE *tūn*, as above.
14 Dale, The: OE *dael* = 'valley'.
*15 **Dunston**: OE *dūn* = 'hill', or OE *Dunn*, personal name; OE *tūn*, as above.
16 Enges: unresolved derivation. Possibly, a variant of OE *–ingas* = 'descendants', though without a patronym indicating a particular family group. Another possibility is OSw *ang* = 'water-meadow'.
*17 **Flixton**: ODan *Flic*, personal name; OE *tūn*, as above.
*18 **Fritton**: OE *friÞ* = 'enclosure'; OE *tūn*, as above.
*19 **Gapton**: OE *Gabba*, personal name; OE *tūn*, as above.
*20 **Gorleston**: OE *gyrele*, meaning 'child' or 'young person'; OE *tūn*, as above.
*21 Gunton: ODan *Gunni*, personal name; OE *tūn*, as above.
*22 **Herringfleet**: ODan *Herela* + OE *-ing*, personal name; OE *flēot* = 'tidal stream'.
23 Hobland: OE *hop* = 'dry land in/near a fen'; ON *land* = 'estate', or *lundr* = 'grove'. It is also possible that the first element, as 'Hob', could be a personal name.
*24 **Hopton**: OE *hop* = 'small enclosed valley' or 'enclosed land in the midst of fens'; OE *tūn*, as above.

25 Houton: OE *hoh* = 'spur', 'hill-ridge'; OE *tūn*, as above.
26 *Lanthorp*: OE *lang* = 'long'; ODan Þorp = 'farm' or 'outlier'.
*27 Little Yarmouth: a settlement to the north of Northtown and perhaps encompassing it. Yarmouth derives from OE *Gariannos*, the name of a specific river, later called the Yare, and OE *mūÞa* = 'mouth' – which fits the local topographical situation of an estuarine location. The first element is from the OE *lytel* = 'small'. The settlement is first recorded in the *Book of Fees*, 1219, as *Parva Gernemuta.*
*28 **Lound**: ON *lundr* = 'grove'.
*29 **Lowestoft**: ON *Hloðvér*, personal name; ON *topt* or OE *toft* = 'house-site', 'homestead'.
30 *Manthorp*: ODan *Manni*, personal name; ODan Þorp = 'farm' or 'outlier'.
31 Nes(s), The: ON *nes* or OE *ness* = 'headland'.
*32 **Newton**: OE *nēowe* = 'new'; OE *tūn*, as above.
33 Northtown (al. Northville): OE *norÞ* = 'north'; OE *tūn*, as above.
*34 Oulton: ODan *Ali*, personal name; OE *tūn*, as above.
35 Peneston: Brit *pen* (?) = 'hill', 'promontory', or OE *pen(n)* = 'enclosure'; OE *tūn*, as above.
36 Reston: OE *hris* = 'brushwood'; OE *tūn*, as above.
37 Smallmoor: OE *smael* = 'narrow'; OE *mōr* = 'moor' or 'fen'.
*38 **Somerleyton**: ON *Sumarliði*, generic personal name ('summer raider'); OE *tūn*, as above.
*39 Southtown: OE sūÞ = 'south' and *tūn*, as above (a later, alternative name for *Little Yarmouth*). The community does not feature in the *Hundred Roll* under this name.
40 *Thorpe*: ODan Þorp = 'farm' or 'outlier'.
41 Wheatcroft: OE *hwæt* = 'wheat'; OE *croft* = 'enclosed arable land'.

- The seventeen communities in bold font are the ones referred to in the Domesday Survey as constituting the settlements of Lothingland Half-hundred.
- The thirty-five places underlined are all referred to in the Hundred Roll of 1274–5.
- The four italicised hamlets, or farmsteads, are not mentioned directly in either document. Claydon, Lanthorp and Manthorp feature in the Hundred Roll as part of tenants' names, while Thorpe is known to have existed from other medieval sources.
- Asterisks indicate the larger and and/or longer-established settlements.
- Eighteen settlements/communities show definite or possible Scandinavian influence in their names (including eleven of the twenty-three major ones).
- Maps 4 & 5 give the locations of all places referred to above.
- Brit = British; OE = Old English; ODan = Old Danish; ON = Old Norse; OScand = Old Scandinavian; OSw = Old Swedish.

Mutford Half-hundred

1 **Barnby**: OScand *Biarni*, a personal name; and ON *býr*, meaning 'village', 'homestead'.
2 ***Beckton***: OE *bæce/bece* – cf. ODan *bæk* & ON *bekkr* – meaning 'stream'; and *tūn*, meaning 'enclosure', 'homestead', 'village'.
3 **Carlton**: OScand *Karla*, a personal name; or a Scandinavian form of OE *ceorl*, meaning 'freeman'; and OE *tūn*, as above.
4 **Gisleham**: OE *Gysela*, a personal name; and OE hām, meaning 'homestead', 'village'.

5 ***Hornes***: OE *horn*, meaning 'spit, or tongue of land'.
6 **Kessingland**: OE *Cussa/Cyssi*, a personal name, and *-ing*, meaning 'descendants of'; and OE (or ON) *land*, meaning 'estate'; or ON *lundr*, meaning 'grove'.
7 **Kirkley**: OE *cirice* or OScand *kirkia*, meaning 'church'; and OE *lēah*, meaning 'glade' or 'clearing'.
8 **Mutford**: OE *mōt*, meaning 'meeting'; and OE *ford*, meaning 'shallow place in water'.
9 **Pakefield**: OE *Pacca*, or ON *Pacci*, a personal name, and OE *feld*, meaning 'open country'.
10 ***Rothenhall***: poss. OE *rod* or *roþ(u)*, meaning 'clearing', or OE *Hroþ*, a personal name (+ *-ing*); and OE *halh*, meaning 'secluded place' or 'nook'.
11 **Rushmere**: OE *risc*, meaning 'rush' (the aquatic plant); and OE *mere*, meaning 'lake' or 'stretch of water'.
12 ***Wimundhall***: poss. OE *Wigmund*, a personal name; and OE *halh*, as above.

- All twelve Domesday communities are shown in bold font, but those which were later incorporated into other communities are also italicised.
- Scandinavian influence is less marked in Mutford Half-Hundred than in Lothingland, but is present nevertheless.
- Six of the names above are unequivocally English in origin (Gisleham, *Hornes*, Mutford, *Rothenhall*, Rushmere and *Wimundhall*), one is Scandinavian (Barnby) and four show, or may show, Scandinavian influence (Carlton, Kessingland, Kirkley and Pakefield).
- Of the latter four, Carlton may be a ***Grimston hybrid***, showing a combination of Scandinavian personal name and the Anglo-Saxon *tun*; Kirkley is either Scandinavian in the first element of the name or an example of a 'Scandinavianised' English form, using the 'harder' letter k in place of c (probably the latter); Kessingland seems to be a combination of an Old English personal name and an Old English or Old Norse tenure term; and Pakefield has a personal name first-element that may be either Old English or Old Norse. The possibility of the *land* element in Kessingland being a variant of Old Norse *lundr* (meaning 'a grove') has been considered, but Domesday records no woodland in the parish.
- *Beckton* is slightly problematical in the two forms of the name given in the Latin text of Domesday: *Bechetuna* and *Beketuna*. The former spelling would seem to suggest OE *bæce/bece* as the first element's origin, the latter either ODan *bæk* or ON *bekkr*. It is possible that the name may show the effect of Scandinavian influence on an existing Anglo-Saxon word, or the variance might be the result of clerical foible in representing it.

Sources: E. Ekwall, *The Oxford Dictionary of English Place-Names*, 4th edn (Oxford, 1960); P.H. Reaney, *The Origin of English Place Names*, 8th imp. (London, 1985).

Glossary of medieval terms

Absentee: a manorial lord who did not live on the estate, but dwelt elsewhere and drew the revenues.

Account roll: a yearly statement of the receipts (such as rents) and expenditure of money on a manor, and usually the receipts and use of agricultural produce and stock from the manorial ***demesne***.

Ad terminum (qui preteriit): words used in a writ of ***entry***, to recover possession of property from a tenant whose occupancy had exceeded the term agreed. The phrase may be translated as 'for the term which has passed'.

Advowson: the right to present/appoint a clergyman to a ***benefice***.

Agist: 1. common land which was let out (often in summer) for the controlled grazing of cattle at a certain monetary rate per beast. 2. The verb used to define such practice.

Agistment: 1. The right to graze cattle under controlled conditions. 2. The payment made for this.

Alienate: to transfer/convey land or real estate to another person or agency.

Alms: charitable gifts of money or materials for the poor and needy, often made through the agency of the church.

Ancient demesne: manors and other lands once in the ownership and direct control of the monarch in the time of Edward the Confessor and William I. Its tenants were free of a number of duties (including jury service at hundred and shire level) and also not liable to certain taxes – particularly market tolls and levies for road maintenance.

Appropriation: the acquisition or annexation, by an ecclesiastical organisation, of a ***benefice*** and also of the ***great tithes*** attaching to it. See also ***Impropriation***.

Appurtenance: a right or obligation attached to a landholding or piece of real estate, and passing with it upon transfer to another tenant.

Array: the raising of troops (usually infantry and archers), at a local level, for military activity in the service of the king.

Assize: 1. The sitting of a legal body, at either a petty or more elevated level. 2. A legal case.

Assize of bread and ale (or beer): a royal statute (created in the late twelfth century) designed to fix the sale price of these two staple commodities in local markets across England and Wales, according to the current value of grain and malt, and also intended to ensure a satisfactory standard of production. By the early modern period the process had become one of quality control and fair trading, with fines imposed for short weight and measure and for adulteration of the product(s).

Assumption of the Blessed Virgin Mary: a feast held on 15 August to commemorate Mary's ascension into Heaven.

Attach: 1. To arrest a person or seize goods under a writ authorising such action. 2. To place someone or something under the control of a court.

Attainder: 1. The process, or result, of attainting. 2. The legal outcome of the passing of the sentence of death, or outlawry, in the matter of treason (mainly) or major felony.

Attaint: 1. To convict a jury of having given a false verdict. 2. To bring an action to reverse an unjust verdict. 3. To subject to the process of attainder.

Attorney: a duly appointed legal representative.

Austin canons: known as *Black Canons*, because of the colour of the habit worn, these clergy either lived in closed communities as *canons regular* or in the wider world as *canons secular*. Both types could (and did) serve as parish priests. St Augustine of Hippo was their founding father.

Austin friars: a religious order founded in 1244, which adopted the principles of Christian life expounded by St Augustine of Hippo and whose members bore an abbreviated form of his name.

Bailiff: 1. A manorial lord's steward or estate manager. 2. A man appointed by the monarch to collect the rents due from Crown tenants in a hundred or half-hundred.

Balinger: a stoutly built craft, used variously for fishing, trading and military activity.

Bark: a vessel of sturdy build used for fishing and trading. It became particularly associated with the northern lining voyages for cod.

Benefice: an ecclesiastical office and the income deriving from it (usually with reference to a parish and the priestly duties attaching to its care).

Benefit of clergy: the privilege for those in holy orders either of exemption from trial by a secular court or of being given immunity from due legal process.

Black friars: a religious order founded by St Dominic in 1216, which was also known as the *Friars Preachers*. Its members wore a black habit, hence the name.

Blanched money: silver coin, often paid as rent.

Boat (small): 1. An undecked rowing craft worked directly off the beach for fishing and ferrying work. 2. A similar craft (possibly of shorter length) carried on board ship for various uses.

Bond tenant: a manorial tenant holding land by bond tenure which was also known as unfree, customary or ***villein*** tenure. The wealth of such people varied widely.

Bond tenure: the holding of manorial land by unfree tenants in return for specific obligations and services. See ***villein tenure***.

Bondsman/bondswoman: see ***serf***.

Boon-work: labour service performed on the manorial ***demesne*** of a lord by some tenants, which obliged him to provide food for the workers (ploughing and harvesting were common forms). The use of the word *boon* (meaning 'a gift') suggests that the work was possibly extra labour, over and above what manorial custom demanded – hence, the personnel involved being provided with meals.

Bordar: a 'middling' peasant landholder at Domesday, tied to the manor and ranking between ***villan*** and ***slave***. He had a modest amount of land allotted to him for the support of a family. The term is sometimes found translated as 'cottager'.

Bovate: an area of arable land one-eighth the size of a ***carucate*** (and, therefore, fifteen acres). In deriving from the Latin *bos-bovis* ('an ox'), it was notionally the area of land which represented one animal of the eight making up a plough-team. The word *oxgang* was sometimes used as an alternative term.

Breach of contract: the breaking of a legally enforceable agreement.

Bruery: managed heathland, which was sometimes divided into sections used by individual people.

Canon: 1. A law or decree of the church (ecclesiastical law is still referred to as *canon law*). 2. A clergyman living within the precinct of a cathedral. 3. An ordained member of an enclosed religious order (especially Augustinian) living within a community and according to its rules of conduct.

Canons regular: male clergy living in communities under the rule of St Augustine. They were allowed to leave their house and serve as parish priests under the orders of their ***prior*** or through a sense of personal vocation. On doing do they became ***canons secular***.

Cartulary: 1. The place where records or documents were kept. 2. A register of (usually) monastic lands and privileges.

Carucage: a tax paid to the Crown by individual ***hundreds*** on the amount of arable land present. 2s per *carucate* is one rate noted in *The Book of Fees* (al. *Liber Feodorum*), vol. 1, which covers the period 1198–1242. Richard I introduced the levy in 1198, but it was discontinued thirty years later.

Carucate: a term for 120 acres of arable land, introduced by the Normans to replace the Anglo-Saxon word for the same unit (***hide***). The word derived from the medieval Latin *caruca* ('a plough') and was reckoned to be the amount of land able to be tilled in a year by a team of oxen.

Chancery: the court of the Chancellor of England, located at Westminster – and the most important agency in the handling of civil administration.

Chantry: an endowment for the maintenance of priests to sing masses (usually for the donor's soul).

Chantry chapel: a partitioned space within a church in which masses were offered for the soul of the donor.

Chapel-of-ease: a place of worship within a parish that was subsidiary to the parish church itself. They were often built in the remoter parts of very large parishes for the convenience of people living there.

Chaplain: a priest without a ***benefice***, who may have ministered to the spiritual needs of a private family or been responsible for the supervision of a ***chapel***.

Chapter: the collective body of clergy making up the governing establishment of a cathedral.

Charter rolls: Chancery records of royal grants of land, borough privileges, markets, fairs etc.

Chattels: movable/portable possessions. Under the common law, ***serfs*** were their lords' chattels.

Choir: the part of a church in which divine service was sung. In a cathedral (or in any other large church with a central tower and supporting transepts) it was situated to the east of the tower and to the west of the high altar.

Christ's half-dole: the incumbent's entitlement, in coastal parishes, to a half of one individual share in the profits (if any) of a fishing voyage. Fishing craft had a set number of shares allotted to them (it varied from place to place and according to the type of fishing practised), which were held by the interested parties – vessel owners and crew – according to their rank and status. After expenses had been met, the money remaining was shared out *pro rata*.

Churl: in Anglo-Saxon times, the lowest grade of ***freeman*** (deriving from OE *ceorl*), but in later times sometimes mistakenly applied to unfree tenants.

Clerk: 1. A man in training for Christian ministry who had not reached the status of deacon or priest, but who assisted with church services in various ways. 2. A man in ***minor orders***, who was not fully ordained. 3. An ordained ***secular clergyman*** of diaconal or priestly status. The legal term for a Church of England clergyman today is 'clerk in holy orders'.

Close: an enclosed, fenced space – sometimes applied specifically to the surrounds of a dwelling.

Close rolls: records of the court of Chancery concerning grants made to individuals by the Crown. These documents were originally folded (hence 'closed') and impressed with the Great Seal, and they date from the year 1204.

Cog: a strongly built, broad-beamed trading or fishing vessel with rounded bow and stern and often a single mast stepped amidships. The Hanseatic cogs had a raised stern-castle and a bow angled at about sixty degrees to the water.

Collation: the term used of the appointment of a priest to a ***benefice***, carried out by a bishop in the diocese over which he presided.

Commonage: 1. The practice of using common land. 2. Rights attached to the use of common land.

Commendation: a system of feudal obligation, whereby a ***freeman*** pledged himself and his military support to a chosen lord or superior. It was a major feature of late Anglo-Saxon society.

Commission: legal authority granted (usually by the Crown) to a person to carry out a particular stated act.

Commissioner: a person charged with carrying out a specified duty on behalf of the Crown.

Commission of array: authorisation to the ***sheriff*** of a county, and to other men of knightly status, to raise troops for the monarch.

Common (land): 1. Land over which common rights applied (these might have been rights of pasture or of sowing arable land collectively in particular ways). 2. A term usually applied to areas of low-quality soil unsuitable for agriculture, but of value for pasturing livestock and providing a range of materials deriving from the local flora. Accessible to the whole community (hence, 'common'), but controlled by the manor and with fees payable for specific uses.

Common field: a large unenclosed area of arable land set out in individual strips and worked by the tenants in accordance with the various common rights appertaining.

Common pasture: an area of land (often too poor or difficult to cultivate) available for grazing.

Common of pasture: the right to graze livestock on ***common land***.

Common Pleas: a Westminster-based court that handled civil cases between subjects of the monarch.

Consolidation: the joining together of separate lands or estates to form larger units.

Convent: a body of clergy (male or female) living together in a community.

Conveyance: the process of transferring property from one person to another.

Copyhold: the holding of property under the rules of a manor, with a written copy of ***title*** in possession of the holder (this type of tenure evolving during the fifteenth century from ***villein tenure***). Copyholds of inheritance were, in practice, as secure as ***freehold***.

Coroner: a royal officer operating at county (or even hundredal) level, whose primary task was to hold inquiries into sudden, suspicious and unnatural deaths.

Court baron: a manorial lord's private, personal court, meeting at regular intervals, which enforced the manor's customs and procedures. Its business included property transfer, ***escheats***, dower arrangements, management of heathland and waste, and the respective rights of lord and tenants. It also appointed minor officers to assist with aspects of crop and animal husbandry, woodland practice and the maintenance of fences. In Lowestoft's case, by the end of the sixteenth century, many of its former activities had disappeared and it was largely concerned with property transactions and matters of complaint, meeting (on average) every four to six weeks.

Court leet: see ***Leet***.

Court rolls: records of manorial proceedings appertaining to the activities of lord and tenants.

Crayer: a small, single-masted vessel used extensively in coastal trading work, but which could also convert to fishing. It was also capable of river passage, with suitable depth of water available.

Crenellation: the construction of battlements on an existing building. This was a feature of the fourteenth and fifteenth centuries among the knightly class, as its members improved their dwellings, and became more of a declaration of status than of genuine defensive intention. Royal ***licence*** was required to carry it out.

Cure: a term for the *care* of souls in a parish.

Custom (of the manor): the local practices and rules of a particular manor controlling the tenants' activities.

Customary service: a feature of ***villein tenure***, whereby the tenant performed labour duties of a specified nature in return for holding the land granted him by the manorial lord.

Daughter house: a religious community of priory status which was under the direction and control of the parent establishment (monastery or abbey), which had either set it up or accepted responsibility for its supervision.

De vetito namio (plea of): a legal case concerning the distraint of goods or property, made legally or illegally.

Deacon: a member of the clergy who had not been ordained priest, but who assisted with parish duties.

Dedication: the naming of a church, usually in honour of a particular saint (or saints).

Default: failure to perform a specified legal requirement.

Defendant: the person against whom a case is brought in a court of law.

Deforciant: 1. The defendant in a case of landed dispossession. 2. Later on, the vendor in a sale of land or real estate.

Demesne: land held by a manorial lord for the direct supply and maintenance of his household. The manor's ***bond tenants*** performed labour service of various kinds upon it in return for their own holdings, often under the direction of a steward or bailiff. With the passage of time, monetary payments gradually replaced labour service (to the advantage of both lords and tenants) and demesne land was increasingly leased out, rather than worked by individual lords themselves, especially if they were ***absentees.***

Demise: to transfer/convey land or real estate by will or lease.

Devise: to leave landed property, by will, to a beneficiary.

Detention: occupation/possession of land or real estate (a term often used when the act was illegal).

Diocese: a large administrative and jurisdictional unit of the church comprised of scores of parishes spread across an area of the country transcending county boundaries, which was under the supervision of a bishop.

Dispensation: authorisation that a person should be allowed to do something that was not normally allowed under ecclesiastical law (given by ***popes***, ***archbishops*** and ***bishops***).

Disseise: to dispossess somebody of land or real estate, often with the use of force.

Distrain: to claim, and take, goods or money in payment of a debt.

Dogger: a bluff-bowed, two-masted North Sea fishing vessel used extensively in the Iceland cod voyages. Recorded carrying capacities are mainly in the range of fifteen to thirty-five ***tuns.***

Dower: the portion of an estate (usually, one-third) able to be claimed by a widow, usually for life or until she remarried.

Dowry: the money or property (or both) brought to a marriage by a bride, which could be ***entailed*** (with the agreement of both parties) to stay in her right and not pass to the husband.

Empark: to enclose land for hunting or visual amenity.

Enclosure: an enclosed (by fence or hedge) piece of land.

Enfeoff: 1. To put a tenant legally in possession of freehold land or real estate. 2. To appoint and empower trustees to administer property on behalf of a third party.

Enrolment: the recording of a conveyance or legal act in an official document (e.g. a Close Roll, Plea Roll etc.) – the term deriving from the fact that such records were kept on large sheets of rolled vellum or parchment. It also became applied to lesser transactions at manorial level. The practice began in the reign of King John with all documents leaving the court of ***Chancery.***

Entail: 1. To settle occupation of land or property on a specified heir, often with restriction imposed on the breaking-up of the estate. 2. To limit an estate's descent to a particular class of heirs.

Entrust (formerly, intrust): to place property in the hands of a person or persons, to be administered for the benefit of a third party or parties.

Entry: the taking possession of land or real estate.

Escheat: the reversion to the Crown (or to an individual lord) of an estate, following the death of a tenant without heirs. It also applied to an heir in his or her minority or in circumstances where the tenant had committed an offence resulting in forfeiture of the estate. Royal officers (***escheators***) were appointed in each county to collect the revenues from the ***sequestrated*** lands and pay them over to the Crown.

Esquire: the son of, or an attendant to, a knight or lord.

Estate: 1. A landholding and the appurtenances associated with it. 2. The personal wealth of an individual person, in terms of property and belongings. 3. The social level to which a person belonged (broadly synonymous with today's word 'class').

Estover: the right to take wood from common land for repairing houses or tools, or for use as fuel. It also extended to gorse and bracken for their specific uses.

Estreat: an extract, or copy, of some original legal decision – especially one relating to fines imposed for offences committed – which was then ***enrolled*** in the records of the particular court involved.

Exemption: legally granted immunity from the effects of a law or penalty.

Extent: a summary of the size, customs and value of a manor and its tenancies.

Eyre: a legal circuit of English shires, conducted by itinerant justices appointed by the Crown and handling both civil and criminal cases.

Fair: a periodic gathering of buyers and sellers of goods in a particular place and at a time designated, legally authorised by royal charter or established by ancient custom.

Fallows(s): cultivated land left unploughed and unsown (often grazed by sheep), to recover fertility.

Farkost: a two-masted trading vessel of greater size and sturdier build than a ***crayer***, suited to sea voyages of greater length. Also able to convert to fishing.

Farm: a lease of land, or of a particular resource (such as a ***fishery***), or of a jurisdictional privilege (such as a ***fair***), usually incurring a fixed annual rent for a specified period of time.

Farmed out: leased.

Fartill boat: a small, undecked inshore vessel, crewed by two, three or four men and propelled by oars. It was also used for ferrying work. The first word probably derives from the medieval word *fardel*, meaning 'pack' or 'small bundle' – a reference to the craft's limited carrying capacity.

Fealty: an obligation of fidelity on the part of a tenant to his (or her) lord, sworn by oath.

Fee: a landed estate, held in return for service to a superior.

Fee simple: freehold.

Feet of fines: records of decisions made regarding the holding of land and other real estate.

Felony: 1. An act which could result in a tenant having his property confiscated. 2. Crime of a more serious nature than misdemeanour and carrying the penalty of death.

Feoffee: someone who had been ***enfeoffed*** of land or who bore legal obligation in the process of transfer.

Feudal aid: a payment made by a tenant to his (or her) lord, in addition to the annual rent.

Fief(dom): an estate held by grant from someone of higher status in return for specified service of some kind (often of a military nature).

Fifteenths: part of a periodic national tax, confirmed by parliament and levied on rural populations, taking one-fifteenth of the value of movable goods or wages (town-dwellers, being generally more affluent, were assessed at one-tenth).

Fine: 1. The money paid to a manorial lord by an incoming tenant. 2. Money or service due to a lord from his tenants.

Fine rolls: Exchequer documents which record payments made to the monarch in return for privileges or favours granted. They also record the appointment of royal officials.

Fishery: 1. The act of capturing fish. 2. A particular freshwater or maritime location where fishing was conducted – the former often controlled by local ordinances.

Foldage: 1. The practice of feeding sheep within movable partitions (usually made of hurdles). 2. A manorial lord's right to have tenants' sheep graze on fallow ***demesne*** land in order to manure it.

Foreshore: the area of beach between low-water and high-water marks. It was part of the Crown Estate, unless otherwise stipulated or agreed.

Forestall: to sell goods on the way to market or before the official starting-time – an illegal act, contrary to the principles of fair trading.

Forest: 1. An extensive area of trees, but not necessarily densely wooded. 2. An extensive area consisting of trees and open countryside, primarily used for hunting by the monarch and his nobility. Strict laws were applied to forests' management and they were an important source of venison for both the royal household and aristocratic ones.

Forfeit: to lose the right to hold property after the committing of some illegal act.

Franchise: 1. A right or privilege. 2. An area in which a local lord exercised justice free from the authority of the county sheriff.

Frankpledge: an Anglo-Saxon system (originally) of local justice, whereby each individual member of a ***tithing-group*** was responsible for the good behaviour of the others. It continued to operate as a feature of local government right into the early modern period.

Freehold/free tenure: tenure of land or other real estate whose title could be upheld in the royal courts of common law. It was not subject to the ***custom of the manor*** or the will of the lord, and could be disposed of without encumbrance. An annual cash rent, with few or no labour services, was the usual payment made.

Freeman: a person able to access the courts of common law and/or free of the constraints of control by a manorial lord. The status was inherited through the male line or, in cases of bastardy, by process acknowledging that paternity could not be determined. Freemen usually held land by freehold tenure.

Free warren: a licence from the Crown enabling the grantee to hunt and take game from a specified area of land – one which was often in his own tenure.

Friars: members of four main religious orders (Augustinian, Carmelite, Dominican, Franciscan), whose purpose was to preach the Gospel and relieve human suffering. Originally, they were intended to move freely from place to place, living on charity, but they soon became organised into settled communities and accrued wealth via the bequests left to them by well-wishers.

Furlong: 1. The length of a furrow or strip in a common field. 2. A rectangular block of strips in a common field. 3. A length of 220 yards, originally reckoned to be the maximum distance that a plough-team could travel without deviation.

Gaol delivery: the conveying of prisoners accused of crime from their place of incarceration to the particular venue where their cases were to be heard.

Garb: 1. A sheaf of corn (especially wheat), as used in heraldry. 2. A sheaf, used as a term to define a proportion of the ***great tithes*** of grain payable to a parish church.

Gascon rolls: medieval records of the governance of English territories in south-western France.

Gavelacre: ploughing and/or reaping carried out by tenants in the service of their lord.

Geld: 1. Tax paid to the Crown by holders of land during the late Anglo-Saxon and Norman periods. 2. The sum of £1 levied on each ***hundred***, and of 10s levied on each ***half-hundred***, as its obligatory payment to the Crown.

Glebe: land which had been conveyed to a ***benefice*** by the donor for the benefit of the incumbent and parish church. Clergy were free to manage glebe land themselves or sub-let it to tenants.

Goings: strips of land set out in a common pasture, often with a specified number of beasts per strip.

Grange: land and buildings belonging to a religious house, located at some distance from it.

Grant: the authoritative conferring (often by the Crown) of a right or privilege.

Great boat: the two- or three-masted Lowestoft fishing vessel, used to catch herring and mackerel during the seventeenth and eighteenth centuries, and upwards of fifty feet long.

Great tithes: the most valuable tithes in a parish, usually of grain, hay and timber, from which an ecclesiastical or lay ***rector*** drew an income.

Grey friars: the Franciscans or *Friars Minor*, founded by St Francis of Assisi in 1210. The colour of the habit its members wore gave rise to the name.

Grove: a wood with minimal undergrowth, deriving from OE *grāf*. In the medieval and early modern periods it was the term applied to managed woodland, where coppicing and clearance were the standard means of producing the type(s) of timber required.

Guarantor: someone who stood surety (usually of a financial nature) for a person involved in a legal case.

Hagboat: a stoutly built single-masted vessel used for general carriage of goods and for military transport when required.

Half-hundred: an Anglo-Saxon and (later) Norman administrative unit within a ***shire***, theoretically made up of communities which had a combined total of fifty ***hides*** of arable land (6,000 acres) and fifty family groups. In practice, it was often of lesser size – especially in terms of acreage.

Half-mark: a monetary unit (not a coin) worth 6s 8d.

Hanaper: a department of the Court of Chancery, into which fees were paid for the signing and sealing of documents.

Headborough: 1. The chief-man of a ***tithing-group***, responsible for its being kept up to strength and for the general good conduct of its members. 2. The term sometimes used of a parish constable (this being a later development from the earlier meaning).

Heath: an area of poor, acidic soil characterised by certain plants, particularly heather (or ling), gorse, bracken and thorn. Although largely uncultivable during the Middle Ages, and offering only low-grade grazing for livestock, it provided an important amenity for local communities as a source of fuel and bedding. Common rights over heathland were strictly controlled by local manorial authorities.

Hide: the Anglo-Saxon term for a unit of 120 acres of arable land, reckoned as being the amount that one man could plough in a year with a full team of eight oxen. A greater thane's (or *thegn*'s) estate was usually estimated at five hides; men of lesser status held smaller areas.

Homage: 1. The pledge of loyalty made by a tenant to his lord (often on accession to an estate). 2. A term for the collective assembly of tenants attending a manorial court.

Honour: a grouping of ***knight's fees***, or of ***manors***, under one lord.

Household: in medieval legal terminology, the inmates of a house: family members and, in cases where applicable, servants also.

Hulk: a generic term for a large cargo vessel of some kind.

Hundred: an Anglo-Saxon administrative sub-division of a ***shire***, consisting (in theory, at least) of 100 family groups and/or 100 ***hides*** of cultivated land (12,000 acres). In practice, a number of hundreds were smaller than the official size, particularly in terms of the arable area.

Implead: to accuse, or sue, in a court of law.

Impropriation: the acquisition or annexation, by a lay body or person, of an ecclesiastical ***benefice*** and the ***great tithes*** attaching to it. See also ***Appropriation***.

In chief: the term used of land that was held directly from the Crown.

Incident: a privilege, burden or custom attaching to an office or an estate.

Incumbent: a person holding an office of some kind, with particular reference to a parish priest.

Indenture: a deed or contract made between two or more parties with the copies made on a single sheet of vellum or parchment, which was then cut with a wavy line along the divisions. The separate pieces then had to align with each other in order to prove authenticity.

Indult: a licence, or permission, granted by the pope, authorising that something could be done.

In fee: the holding of an estate according to due process of law.

Infeudation: the granting of an estate, to be held ***in fee***.

Inland: the ***demesne*** of a manor, used for the supply and maintenance of the lord's household.

In mercy: liable for the payment of a surety or fine required by a court, in the event of a case being lost or not pursued.

Inquest: a legal inquiry into some particular matter.

Inquisition: an ***inquest***.

Inquisition post mortem: an enquiry into the possessions, services and successors of a deceased person who had held land from the Crown.

Itinerant justices: see ***justices-in-eyre***.

Juror: 1. A man called upon to testify in a legal dispute (often about the ***title*** to land) or to give evidence at an ***inquisition***. 2. A member of the body chosen to hear evidence in a legal case and then deliver a verdict. 3. A member of the body chosen to present cases to a manorial or hundred court.

Justices-in-eyre: legal servants of the Crown, who travelled the country hearing both civil and criminal cases.

Justices of the Bench: 1. Lawyers serving in the court of ***King's Bench***. 2. A generic term used of lawyers engaged upon legal business generally.

Justiciar: a legal officer of the Crown, who had control of a law court of his own or who officiated in a shire court.

King's Bench: a court dealing with civil and criminal cases in which the monarch had an interest. It travelled with the king and court, but from c. 1400 onwards became permanently based in London.

Knight of the shire: a representative in parliament (in the Commons) of a particular county. The title later developed into the term MP.

Knight's fee: an area of land held from the Crown deemed to be sufficient for the support of a knight and his entourage, broadly varying between about 480 and 960 acres (four to eight ***carucates***). A payment of 100s was customarily paid to the crown upon entry to the estate and the holder was committed (in theory, at least) to 40 days' military service a year.

Knight's service: the military service due in return for holding an estate from the Crown (see above).

Lay fee: land held by secular tenants, as opposed to land held by the church.

Lay rector: a secular individual or organisation in control of the appointment made to a ***benefice*** and having also the privilege of collecting the ***great tithes*** attaching to it.

League: a variable measure of distance of one to three miles, probably best regarded as one-and-a-half miles during the late Anglo-Saxon and Norman periods.

Leet: 1. A collection of settlements forming a taxable unit for the purpose of hundredal ***geld*** assessment. 2. The six-monthly or annual meeting of the ***tithing-groups*** of a vill which, by the thirteenth century, was held as a court by the lord of the paramount [main] manor. This court dealt with petty criminal offences, including minor assaults, breaches of the peace, minor trading violations (such as infringing the assize of ale and bread), and local nuisance and public-order issues (e.g. highway encroachments, environmental pollution and gossiping). Lowestoft's annual assembly continued to function well into the eighteenth century, though with changes in emphasis concerning the business dealt with.

Liberate rolls: Chancery documents which authorised the Exchequer to pay salaries and pensions for Crown officials, to finance the cost of running the royal household and to meet other state expenses.

Liberty: 1. A right or privilege enjoyed by ***prescription*** or by ***grant***. 2. An area of land, or group of estates, whose lord held certain, specified privileges from the Crown (the county sheriff's authority was excluded and the lord dispensed justice).

Librate: 1. £1's worth of rent. 2. A piece of land with an annual rental value of £1.

Licence: legal authorisation or permission to do a particular, specified thing.

Living: an ecclesiastical ***benefice***.

Longshore: literally 'along (the) shore' and, therefore, close in to land. The term was of later origin and use than the medieval period.

Mainpernor: 1. A person standing surety for the appearance of a prisoner in court. 2. A guarantor.

Mainprise: 1. A writ issued to a ***sheriff*** authorising him to collect sureties for the appearance of defendants in legal cases. 2. The action of procuring the release of a prisoner by becoming guarantor of his/her appearance in court. 3. The act of standing surety for someone in a legal matter.

Manor: the lowest unit of estate landholding and administration, consisting of the lord's demesne land, freehold tenures and bond tenures, together with other resources, such as pasture, a mill and fisheries. It could also incorporate jurisdictional rights and privileges, such as the manor court, ***free warren*** and a ***fair***.

Manumission: the legal grant of release from ***serfdom***.

Mark: a monetary unit (not a coin) worth 13s 4d.

Market: a gathering of people for the sale and purchase of provisions and other goods, publicly displayed, at a stipulated time and place. Markets were usually established by royal grant.

Marriage-portion: a dowry.

Master: a title used of a priest to indicate that he had an MA university degree.

Mediety: a half-portion.

Merchet: a payment made by a ***bond tenant*** and a ***serf*** to his lord on the occasion of the marriage of a son or daughter (the term usually applied to the latter).

Messuage: a dwelling and the plot on which it stood.

Minor orders: the term given to clergy who were not priests in full, but who were either in training for the priesthood or whose permanent status stopped short of being deacon or priest.

Misdemeanour: an indictable legal offence of a less serious nature than ***felony***.

Moiety: half-portion or share. The term is usually associated with the holding of land or real estate.

Mort d'ancestor: a legal procedure established by the Assize of Northampton (1167), whereby manorial lords had to ensure that a tenant's heirs were admitted to property on his (or her) death. Cases of *mort d'ancestor* were often brought by heirs against relatives whom they believed had illegally dispossessed them.

Mortmain: a medieval French word (meaning 'dead hand') applied to the church's holding of land bequeathed to it by laymen, which could not then be subject to the usual fines imposed when tenants died or the property changed hands. The Crown, particularly, lost a good deal of revenue in this way. When Henry III revised *Magna Carta* in 1227 he prohibited the transfer of land to the church by individuals without the lord's permission in order to control the loss. Further legislation by Edward I in 1279 imposed penalties on the parties involved in causing land to become subject to mortmain.

Mother house: a monastery or nunnery that had subsidiary communities under its control.

Movable goods: household possessions or items of stock-in-trade.

Multure: payment made, in cash or kind, either to a manorial lord (who often owned the local mill) or to an independent miller for the grinding of corn.

Neif (naif): A ***serf*** or ***bondsman***.

Novel disseisin: a legal case in which complaint was made of recent dispossession of land or real estate – the first element of the term deriving from an Old French word now rendered as *nouvel*.

Nunnery: an enclosed community of female clergy living under a particular rule.

Occupy: to legally take possession of land or real estate.

Outlawry: the official declaration of a person being beyond the protection of the law of the land because he (or she) had absconded either before being brought to trial or after a guilty verdict had been passed. The term was also used for people who had failed to attend court sessions (usually four in number) designated to hear their cases.

Outlier: an estate that formed part of a ***manor*** but was detached from it by geographical distance.

Oyer and terminer: a Crown commission to itinerant justices authorising them to hear and determine criminal indictments and to administer the penalties due. The term derives from medieval French meaning 'To hear and bring to an end', with earlier origins in the Latin verbs *audire* and *terminare.*

Pannage: 1. The right to feed pigs in manorial woodland. 2. The payment made for this privilege.

Papal registers: collections of decrees, dispensations, grants and edicts relating to clergy and laity in the countries of Western Europe during the medieval period.

Paramount: appertaining to an overlord. Within the realm of England the term denotes superiority in terms of control below the level of royal authority itself.

Parcel: a piece of land.

Parclose: a wooden or stone screen separating a side-chapel from the rest of the church.

Pardon: free, or conditional, remission from the legal consequences of a crime.

Park: land that was enclosed for hunting or visual amenity.

Parliament rolls: the official records of the English parliament and its proceedings, recorded on large scrolls of vellum.

Parson: the holder of a ***benefice***, in full possession of all rights and dues (i.e. a ***rector***). The meaning of the word was later extended to include ***vicars*** also.

Patent rolls: Chancery records which cover royal grants and authorisations of many and various kinds. The word 'patent' derives from the Latin verb *patēre*, meaning 'to be open', or 'to be visible', the original grants being made by the Crown as open letters under the Great Seal.

Patron: a person, or agency, who held the right to make an appointment to a ***benefice***.

Pax: a silver tablet impressed or etched with an image of the Crucifixion, kissed at intervals during the mass by priest and people. Paxes were often treasured items of personal devotion.

Perpetual vicar: a vicar who held his post for life (if he so desired), this situation being either in the structure of an individual parish's ***advowson*** or in the wishes of its ***patron***. A perpetual vicar drew his income from the parish's ***small tithes***.

Petition: a formal request (usually in written form), seeking some particular legal process or outcome.

Piracy: an act (or acts) of robbery at sea, or on navigable rivers, or effected by assault from the sea on coastal areas by persons unauthorised.

Plaintiff: the party who brings a case against another person in court.

Plea: a legal action; a lawsuit.

Plenary remission: full forgiveness (of sin) granted by male clergy only.

Pluralism: the holding of more than one ***benefice*** by an incumbent.

Pone: a writ authorising the removal of a case from a petty court to the Court of Common Pleas. The word is the imperative form of the verb, taken from the Latin *ponere* (meaning 'to put' or 'to place') and is pronounced 'pō-ni'.

Port bailiff: a man charged with the conduct of maritime affairs in major coastal towns. There were four such officials in Great Yarmouth (none in Lowestoft) and they were among the most important of its civic heads.

Portage: 1. The act of carrying goods by land or sea. 2. The right of mariners to have an agreed amount of hold-space on board ship in which to carry goods of their own for sale abroad or at home. Sometimes this was granted in lieu of wages.

Pound: an enclosure for the retention of stray livestock which had been rounded up. It was usually a manorial facility and a *fine* was payable for the release of any animal(s) held.

Prebend: 1. The money granted to a member of a cathedral ***chapter***. 2. The land or tithes from which the income previously described was derived.

Preferment: appointment to an ecclesiastical post.

Prescription: the right to use the property or privileges of another party, such use being open, continuous and exclusive for an agreed period of time.

Presentation: the appointment of a priest to a parish. During Anglo-Saxon and Norman times the right of appointment was often vested in the local lord of the manor. However, as the medieval period wore on, religious institutions (especially dioceses, monasteries, priories and the like) tended to acquire ***advowsons*** by gift and bequest and thus became the controlling agencies.

Prise: 1. Something which was taken from a tenant by a lord for his (or her) own use. 2. Something requisitioned by the Crown for royal use.

Privilege: a right, under the law, to enjoy certain stipulated advantages over and above the common entitlements of other people.

Proof of title: legal establishment of the right to hold a particular piece of land or other real estate.

Province: an area of ecclesiastical administration (consisting of a number of individual ***dioceses***) under the control of an ***archbishop***. There were two in England: Canterbury and York.

Purpresture: an illegal encroachment of any kind, either on land held by another party or on any right or privilege granted.

Quarantena: the medieval Latin term for a ***furlong***, in the sense of it meaning a block of arable strips held by different tenants in a common field.

Querent: 1. The plaintiff in a case of landed dispossession. 2. Later on, the purchaser in a sale of land or real estate.

Quo warranto: a legal writ requiring a person or party to demonstrate and justify the authority granting a particular right or privilege held. The Latin phrase literally means 'by what right?'

Receiver: an official, servant or duly authorised agent who acted on behalf of the man (or woman) appointing him and collected monies due to that person.

Recognizance: 1. A legal obligation, whereby a person pledged himself or herself to perform some specific act or service. 2. A sum of money promised as a guarantee of such performance and subject to forfeit in the event of failure to carry it out.

Recorder: a lawyer appointed to have jurisdiction over civil and criminal cases in a city or borough.

Rector: 1. A parish priest who drew his income from all the tithes payable, including the *great* ones of grain, hay and timber. 2. A layman who (or institution which) appointed a parish incumbent and drew these same great tithes, leaving the lesser (or *small*) ones in the hands of the appointee as his payment for pastoral duties.

Re-enfeoffment: renewal of the terms of possession of a landed estate.

Reeve: a man elected by from among the ***bond tenants*** to serve as the manager of a manor for one year. The system of elected reeves was gradually replaced by the appointment of a professional farm manager, the ***bailiff***.

Regrate: to sell goods (at a profit) on the market where they had been purchased – an act generally made illegal and deemed contrary to the principles of fair trading.

Regular clergy: members of a monastic order. They were termed *regular* because they lived under the rule (Latin, *regula*) of their respective founders. Though mainly dwelling in closed communities, some of them (notably, Augustinians) were allowed to serve as parish priests.

Relief: 1. A payment made to a manorial lord by an incoming tenant on the latter's taking up occupation of land or real estate. 2. A payment made to the Crown by a new lord when a manor changed hands.

Rental: 1. A manorial rent-roll (i.e. a list of properties and the rents due from them). 2. The income deriving from the receipt of rents.

Requisition: to take supplies of food or other materials for official use (often military, but not exclusively so).

Right of wreck: the right of claiming salvage on maritime debris found on the foreshore (largely cargo and disabled or broken-up craft). The privilege was usually vested in the local lord of the manor, the lord of the hundred or half-hundred, or the Crown.

Royal protection: immunity from legal proceedings granted to a person while absent from home engaged upon royal business.

Safe conduct: authorisation by the monarch (sometimes authenticated by a document) that a person be free from arrest or molestation while travelling to and from a particular place or places.

Secular clergy: parish priests for the most part, and also some bishops of the medieval church, who functioned without being attached to any kind of monastic order.

Security: money paid over as a guarantee of performing a legal duty or process which had been undertaken (a ***recognizance***).

See: a ***diocese***.

Seigneurial/seigniorial: appertaining to manorial lordship.

Seised: to be in legal occupation of land or real estate (the term usually applied to freehold property).

Seisin: legal possession/occupation of freehold land or real estate.

Seize: to take possession of property, often after ***forfeiture***.

Selion: a ridge of land, with furrow on either side, used as a dividing mark in a common field.

Seneschal: a steward or governor acting on behalf of the sovereign or a major manorial lord.

Sequela: the family or household of a ***serf***. The word derives from the Latin verb *sequere*, 'to follow', and literally means 'followers'.

Sequestration: the taking (sometimes confiscation) of property or revenues from the owner/recipient for legal reasons.

Serf: a person who was personally unfree, a status inherited through the male line. Such people were liable for a range of restrictive dues to their manorial lord, which required them to obtain permission to marry and to leave the manor permanently. They were unable to make plea in the courts of common law and could not hold freehold land without their lord's permission. Around half of the population of England in 1300 was unfree. Serfs usually held land by bond tenure. Both ***villeins*** and ***bondsmen/bondswomen*** were serfs. The only means of their becoming legally free was by an act of ***manumission***, although many obtained *de facto* freedom by leaving the manor and not returning.

Serjeant: 1. A serving man or attendant. 2. A feudal tenant, of lesser status than a knight, holding land by military service. 3. A shortened form of *serjeant-at-law* (a specialist legal officer of the Crown).

Serjeant-at-arms: one of a body of men serving as the monarch's personal retinue, which was responsible for a wide range of legal and military activity.

Serjeanty: a form of tenure whereby the holder owed a specified personal service to a manorial lord (often the monarch). Such service was usually (but not exclusively) of a military nature.

Session: the sitting of a court of law.

Several/Severalty: a term indicating that a piece of land (of varying type) or some other resource (such as heath or fishery) had no common rights attached to it and was restricted in use to the landholder alone.

Sheriff: the Crown's representative in each county (literally, *shire-reeve*) and the main legal officer there until superseded by JPs during the fourteenth century. The office's duty also included the collection of revenues due to the monarch.

Shire: an administrative division of the old Anglo-Saxon kingdom, and of its post-Conquest successor, which eventually became the modern-day county.

Slave: the lowest level of labourer at Domesday, who was the direct possession of his (or her) lord. Slaves had no legal rights and were also sometimes landless. The word is not synonymous with ***serf***.

Small tithes: the produce of a parish, which yielded the one-tenth payment on income and assets due to the local priest from holders of land. Small tithes usually consisted of field-crops other than grain, livestock and poultry, and (in maritime parishes) a modest share of the profits from fishing.

Soc/soke: 1. An area/estate held by ***socage***. 2. A district under a specific local jurisdiction.

Socage: free tenure without the obligation of military service attached.

Sokeman (socman): 1. A ***freeman*** of some kind. 2. A superior type of ***villein***, who performed occasional, specified day-work for his lord in return for the land he held, but who had considerable autonomy in running his own enterprise.

Specialty: a special contract or agreement made between two parties.

Spiritualities: church income which derived from offerings and tithes.

Stetch/stitch: a ridge of ploughed land (of varying width) located in a ***common field***, with drainage furrows set on either side of it.

Stew: a fish-pond (usually artificially created), which produced freshwater species for the table.

Steward: a man who managed estates on behalf of the ***title-holder***.

Stint(land): grazing land set out in strips, often with a stipulated number of animals per division.

Sub-infeudation: the granting of a feudal estate by its holder to someone else (often of lesser status).

Sub-tenancy: the situation whereby land was occupied by someone leasing it from the person legally recognised as holder.

Subsidy (lay): a national tax, levied on the whole population for a particular purpose (often a war!).

Suffragan: an assistant bishop.

Supersedeas: a writ authorising stay of legal proceedings (the word's derivation is the Latin verb *supersedēre*, meaning 'to sit upon' or 'desist from').

Surety: security offered by one or other of the parties in a legal case – usually as a guarantee of his or her attendance in court. A monetary sum pledged by a relative was the commonest form.

Surrender: to give up possession or occupancy of property.

Tallage: 1. A tax levied by the Crown on towns and on ***royal demesne***. 2. A tax imposed by a manorial lord upon his (or her) ***bond tenants***.

Tallager: a collector of the national tax referred to immediately above.

Team: the eight oxen required to pull a heavy plough – a term much encountered in Domesday data.

Temporalities: material possessions of greater and lesser clergy, consisting of land and buildings.

Tenant: a person holding land or real estate, by whatever ***tenure*** applied.

Tenant-in-chief: a feudal tenant who held estates directly from the Crown.

Tenement: land, or other real estate, held by a ***tenant***.

Tenths: part of a periodic national tax, confirmed by parliament and levied on urban populations, taking one-tenth of the value of movable goods or wages (rural dwellers, being generally less affluent, were assessed at one-fifteenth).

Tenure: 1. The fact, or action, of holding a ***tenement***. 2. The condition(s) or service by which a tenement might be held.

Term: 1. A stipulated fixed period during which property might be held under certain specified conditions. 2. One of the four periods in the year (Hilary, Paschal, Trinity and Michaelmas), during which law courts sat and legal business was mainly conducted.

Testimony: evidence given by word of mouth at a legal enquiry or during a court case.

Thane/thegn: an Anglo-Saxon warrior who was part of the king's (or greater lord's) retinue and who owed military service in return for the land he held. Known earlier as a *gesith*.

Timber: trees grown for large-scale construction work (notably, that of houses and ships).

Tithe: a charge levied by the church on one-tenth of all agricultural and woodland produce in a parish as a means of maintaining the local priest (and, increasingly, as the medieval period wore on, to produce an income for the person or body who appointed him). The payment was made either in kind or commuted to an appropriate monetary value; it had its origins in Israelite practice during Old Testament times (see Numbers 18.26). See also ***great tithes*** and ***small tithes***.

Tithing-groups: a company of ten (sometimes twelve) households that stood surety for each other's good behaviour, the prime responsibility resting with the different family heads.

Title: the right to ***occupation*** of land or real estate.

Title-holder: the person who was legally entitled to ***occupation*** of land or real estate.

Tourn: the six-monthly Hundred Court, at Easter and Michaelmas, attended by the county sheriff (who was, literally, 'on tour'). It dealt with ***frankpledge*** procedure, review of ***tithing-group*** strength and minor criminal cases.

Trespass: a legal offence of some kind.

Trustee: a person to whom property is ***entrusted***, to be administered for the benefit of another.

Tunnage: the freight capacity of a sea-going vessel, primarily in terms of the amount of cargo it could carry. The tun was a cask of 252 gallons' capacity (seven standard barrels) and, thus, a craft of twenty tuns' burden was capable of carrying twenty such containers. It wouldn't have done so, however, as the tun was a static storage unit used mainly for wine and was too large to handle for loading. Its size was therefore used as an image of comparison for whatever goods were being transported, in terms of the space occupied in the hold. Weight had nothing whatsoever to do with the equation; nor have the modern terms *gross* and *net* tonnage – the former being the cubic area of *all space* below deck and the latter the *earning space* only: i.e. the storage hold(s).

Turbary: 1. An area where peat was dug (for fuel). 2. The right to dig peat. The word derives from OFr *tourbe*, meaning 'turf'.

Twentieth: a national tax, or ***subsidy***, levied on the population and assessed at 5 per cent of personal possessions and items of stock-in-trade.

Underwood: small trees or shrubs growing beneath larger trees being raised for ***timber***. They usually had a productive purpose of their own – e.g. ash, hazel or chestnut, coppiced for poles, handles and staves of different kinds.

Unjust disseisin: illegal dispossession of a person (or persons) from land or real estate.

Utrum: a writ authorising the holding of an ***assize*** to decide whether property was lay or ecclesiastical. The word is taken from Latin: *uter/utra/utrum*, meaning 'whether' or 'which of two'.

Varlet: a personal servant or attendant. The word had become a term of abuse by the time of Shakespeare and it also later transmuted into ***valet***: a 'gentleman's gentleman'.

Vicar: a parish priest who drew his income from a parish's ***small tithes*** only – the *great* ones being taken by the ***rector*** who had appointed him.

Vicar general: an archbishop's (or bishop's) deputy.

View of frankpledge: the right (and duty) of a manorial lord to take stock of the ***tithing-groups*** in his area of jurisdiction and of the county sheriff at the six-monthly hundredal ***tourn***.

Vigil: 1. The eve of a festival or holy day. 2. A devotional religious service observed at such a time.

Vill: a recognisable settlement, with its dwellings and defined lands.

Villan: The Domesday form of the word immediately below. This level of labourer was of more elevated status than either the ***bordar*** or ***slave***.

Villein: see ***bond tenant***. The term is often used interchangeably with ***serf***, so that a villein could be a tenant, an hereditary serf, or both.

Villein tenure: also known as unfree, customary or ***bond tenure***. The title to this land could not be pleaded in the royal courts of common law, but only in the manorial court of the lord from whom the land was held. Villein tenure was usually held for a rent package of labour services, renders in kind (such as poultry, eggs and grain) and a range of servile incidents (such as ***tallage*** and ***merchet***), rather than cash. These renders and incidents were either dropped or replaced with cash rents during the course of the late fourteenth and fifteenth centuries, as villein tenure evolved into ***copyholds***.

Virgate: an area of arable land one-quarter of a ***carucate*** in size (and, therefore, thirty acres).

Volumus: a royal authorisation issued on behalf of anyone sent abroad on Crown business, protecting him from any kind of legal action being brought in his absence. This was of particular significance where land or property might have been in dispute. Translated literally from Latin, the word means 'we wish' or 'it is our will', reflecting use of the royal plural.

Warland: 1. Land that was freely held and not subject to menial service as part of the conditions of tenure. 2. Non-manorial land.

Warrant: guarantee.

Waste: land of little use for agriculture (often located on the periphery of manors), but which was nevertheless of considerable importance to poorer tenants for the materials and uses it afforded. It was later known as *common*, because of its communal uses. The word is sometimes regarded as being broadly synonymous with the term ***heath***.

White canons: the Premonstratensians, a reformed order of Augustinians whose clergy wore white habits. The founder, St Norbert, established the first house at Prémontré, in northern France, in 1120. Among the later daughter-houses in England was Leiston Abbey, in Suffolk.

White friars: an order of clergy originating in the Holy Land during the late twelfth century whose base was situated on Mount Carmel. Their name derived from the colour of the habit worn.

White rent/white money: rent that was paid in silver coin. It was sometimes referred to as ***blanched***.

Wood: 1. An area of trees grown for particular practical purposes and managed accordingly. 2. The material deriving from smaller trees and shrubs growing below the larger specimens being raised to provide ***timber***.

Wreck of the sea: 1. Maritime debris found floating inshore or washed up on the beach. 2. The right to claim salvage rights on such material.

Writ: a written command or order issued by a court requiring that a legal process be carried out.

Yeoman: a small independent farmer who held his land freely and without encumbrance.

Bibliography

Primary sources

British Library

Additional MSS. 56070: a map of the local coastline (c. 1580).

Cottonian MSS. 1i/58/7950160, map of the local coastline (1540s).

Magdalen College Library

73/4, Akethorpe rental (1438–9).

151/19, Akethorpe account roll (1438–9).

FP 54, Akethorpe indenture (1455).

Akethorpe terrier (1843).

Norfolk Record Office

ATC/46, Archdeacon's visitation (1533).

PD 589/1, Lowestoft parish register (1561–1649).

PD 589/92, Revd. John Arrow's memorandum book.

PD 589/112, Lowestoft Town Book.

PD 589/80, Lowestoft tithe accounts (1698–1787).

TA 658, Lowestoft tithe map and apportionment (1842).

Norwich Consistory Court wills (register copies).

Suffolk Record Office (Ipswich)

Archdeaconry of Suffolk, and of Sudbury, wills (originals and register copies).

Suffolk Record Office (Lowestoft)

194/A10/71, Lowestoft rental (1545).

194/A10/4, Lowestoft manor court minute book (1582–5).

194/A10/5–22, Lowestoft manor court minute books (1616–1790).

194/A10/72, Lowestoft manor roll (1610).

194/A10/73, Lowestoft manor roll (1618).

454/1, Revd. John Tanner's listing of copyhold properties (1725).

454/2, Revd. John Tanner's Lowestoft court baron extracts (1720–25).

01/13/1/3, Lowestoft Settlement and Apprenticeship Book.

368: a map of the local coastlne (c. 1580) – a copy of BL Add. MSS. 56070.

The National Archives, Kew

E179/180/6, Lay Subsidy (1327) – Suffolk.

E179/180/92, Part 2, m 13, Alien Subsidy (April 1440).

E179/235/67, Alien Subsidy (March 1453).

E179/180/111, rot 3, Alien Subsidy (1483).
E179/180/184, Lay Subsidy (1524) – Suffolk.
E179/180/141, Lay Subsidy (1525) – Suffolk.
E179/182/359, Lay Subsidy (1568) – Suffolk.
Prob 11, Prerogative Court of Canterbury wills (register copies).
SC5/Suff/Chap/4, Lothingland Hundred Roll of 1274–5.
SP 1/80 f65v, Iceland fishing vessels' return (1533).
WAM 122261, Letters of denization.

Printed primary sources

Arts and Humanities Research Council, *Calendar of Fine Rolls, Henry III*, C60/22, 24, 27, 29, 30, 51, 53 and 67 (online resource).

Arts and Humanities Research Council (University of York), *England's Immigrants 1350–1550* (online resource, 2015).

Bailey, M. (ed.), *The Bailiffs' Minute Book of Dunwich, 1404–1434*, SRS 34 (Woodbridge, 1992).

Bliss, W.A. and Twemlow, J.A. (eds), *Calendar of Papal Registers Relating to Great Britain and Ireland*, vol. 6 (London, 1904).

Brewer, J.S (ed.), *Letters and Papers Foreign and Domestic, Henry VIII*, vols 1 and 4 (London, 1920 and 1875).

Brown, P. (ed.), *Domesday Book: Norfolk, Parts One and Two* (Chichester, 1984).

Brown, R. (ed.), *Calendar of State Papers Relating to English Affairs in the Archives of Venice*, vol. 1 (London, 1864).

Butcher, D. (ed.), *The Lowestoft Manor Roll of 1618* (Lowestoft, 2004).

Crump, C.G. and Trimmer, R.D. (eds), *Calendar of Charter Rolls*, vol. 3 (London, 1908).

Cunningham, W.R. (ed.), *Calendar of Charter Rolls*, vol. 6 (London, 1916).

Evans, D.L. (gen. ed.), *Calendar of Inquisitions Miscellaneous*, vol. 4 (London, 1957).

Gairdner, J. and Brodie, R.H. (eds), *Letters and Papers, Foreign and Domestic*, vols 10, 14(i), 15, 16, 17, 19(i) and 20(i) (London, 1887, 1894, 1896, 1898, 1900, 1903 and 1905).

Gallagher, E.J. (ed.), *The Civil Pleas of the Suffolk Eyre of 1240*, SRS 52 (Woodbridge, 2009).

Given-Wilson, C., et al. (eds), *Parliament Rolls of Medieval England* (Woodbridge, 2005). Also British History Online (digitised source).

Green, M.A.E. (ed.), *Calendar of State Papers Domestic, Elizabeth I, Addenda*, vol. 22 (London, 1871).

Hardy, T.D. (ed.), *Rotuli Litterarum Patentium*, vol. 1 (London, 1716).

Hervey, J.W.N. (ed.), *The Hundred Rolls and Extracts Therefrom: Made by Authority, Second Edward I, County of Suffolk, Lothingland* (Ipswich, 1902).

Hervey, S.H.A. (ed.), *Suffolk in 1327*, SGB 9 (Woodbridge, 1906).

—, *Suffolk in 1568*, SGB 12 (Bury St Edmunds, 1909).

—, *Suffolk in 1524*, SGB 10 (Woodbridge, 1910).

Illingworth, W. (gen. ed.), *Rotuli Hundredorum*, vol. 2 (London, 1818).

Kirby, J.L. (ed.), *Calendar of Signet Letters, Henry IV and Henry V* (London, 1978).

Knighton, C.S. (ed.), *Calendar of Inquisitions Miscellaneous*, vol. 8 (London, 1969).
Lemon, R. (ed.), *Calendar of State Papers Domestic, Elizabeth I*, vol. 17 (London, 1865).
Manship, H., *Great Yarmouthe, a Booke of the Foundacion and Antiquitye of the said Towne and of Diverse Specialle matters concerning the same* (a 1619 manuscript, edited and published in 1847 by C.J. Palmer).
Maxwell Lyte, H.C. (gen. ed.), *Calendar of Close Rolls, Edward II*, 1307–13 and 1318–23 (London, 1892 and 1895).
—, *Calendar of Close Rolls, Edward III*, vols 5, 6, 7, 9, 10, 11, 12, 13 and 14 (London, 1901, 1902, 1904, 1906, 1908, 1909, 1910, 1911 and 1913).
—, *Calendar of Close Rolls, Richard II*, vols 2 and 3 (London, 1920 and 1921).
—, *Calendar of Fine Rolls*, vols 2, 4, 5, 8 and 9 (London, 1912, 1913, 1915, 1924 and 1926).
—, *Calendar of Patent Rolls, Henry III*, vol. 2 (London, 1903).
—, *Calendar of Patent Rolls, Edward I*, vol. 1 (London, 1901).
—, *Calendar of Patent Rolls, Edward II*, vol. 1 (London, 1894).
—, *Calendar of Patent Rolls, Edward III*, vols 2, 3, 5, 6, 7, 9, 10, 12 and 14 (London, 1893, 1895, 1900, 1902, 1903, 1907, 1909, 1912 and 1913).
—, *Calendar of Patent Rolls, Richard II*, vols 1, 2, 3 and 6 (London, 1895, 1897, 1900 and 1909).
—, *Calendar of Patent Rolls, Henry IV*, vols 1, 2 and 3 (London, 1903, 1902 and 1907).
—, *Calendar of Patent Rolls, Henry V*, vol. 1 (London, 1910).
—, *Calendar of Patent Rolls, Henry VI*, vols 2, 3, 4 and 6 (London, 1907 *bis*, 1908 and 1910).
—, *Calendar of Patent Rolls, Edward IV (1467–77)* (London, 1900).
—, *Calendar of Patent Rolls, Edward IV, Edward V and Richard III (1476–85)* (London, 1901).
— (ed.), *Liber Feodorum*, vol. 1 (London, 1920).
Maxwell Lyte, H.C. and Stamp, A.E. (eds), *Calendar of Charter Rolls*, vol. 5 (London, 1916).
Rumble, A. (ed.), *Domesday Book: Suffolk, Parts One and Two* (Chichester, 1986).
Rye, W. (ed.), *A Calendar of the Feet of Fines for Suffolk* (Ipswich, 1900).
Sharpe, R.R. (ed.), *Calendar of Wills Proved and Enrolled in the Court of Husting, London*, part 2 (London, 1890).
Shaw, W.A. (ed.), *Calendar of Treasury Books*, vols 5, i and ii, and 6 (London, 1911 and 1913).
Stamp, A.E. (gen. ed.), *Calendar of Close Rolls, Henry III*, vol. 13 (London, 1938).
—, *Calendar of Close Rolls, Richard II*, vol. 6 (London, 1927).
—, *Calendar of Close Rolls Henry IV*, vols 2, 3 and 4 (London, 1929, 1931 and 1932).
—, *Calendar of Fine Rolls*, vol. 11 (London, 1929).
—, *Calendar of Inquisitions Miscellaneous*, vol. 3 (London, 1937).
Stevenson, J. (ed.), *Calendar of State Papers Foreign, Elizabeth I*, vol. 4 (London, 1866).
Twemlow, J.A. (ed.), *Calendar of Papal Registers Relating to Great Britain and Ireland*, vols 8, 11 12 and 13 (London, 1909, 1921, 1933 and 1955).
Webb, E.A. (ed.), *The Records of St. Bartholomew's Priory and St. Bartholomew the Great, West Smithfield*, vol. 1 (Oxford, 1921).
Williams, J.F. (ed.), *Bishop Redman's Visitation, 1597*, NRS 18 (Norwich, 1946).

Secondary literature

Abrams, P. and Wrigley, E.A. (eds), *Towns in Societies* (Cambridge, 1978).
Amor, N., 'Merchant adventurer or jack of all trades? The Suffolk clothier in the 1460s', *PSIA*, 40 (2004), 414–36.
—, *Late Medieval Ipswich: Trade and Industry* (Woodbridge, 2011).
Archer, R.E. and Walker, S. (eds), *Rulers and Ruled in Late Medieval England* (London, 1995).
Arts and Humanities Research Council, *The Lands of the Normans in England, 1204–1244* (University of Sheffield, 2007) – online resource.
Ashtor, E., *Levant Trade in the Middle Ages* (Princeton, 1983).
Bailey, M., *Medieval Suffolk* (Woodbridge, 2007).
—, 'The form, function and evolution of irregular field systems in Suffolk, c. 1300 to c. 1550', *AHR*, 57/1 (2009), 15–36.
—, 'Self-government in small towns in late medieval England', in B. Dodds and C.D. Liddy (eds), *Commercial Activity, Markets and Entrepreneurs in the Middle Ages* (Woodbridge, 2011), 107–28.
Banks, T.C., *The Dormant and Extinct Baronage of England*, vol. 2 (London, 1808).
Benedictow, O.J., *The Black Death, 1346–1353: The Complete History* (Woodbridge, 2004).
Blair, J., 'Small towns 600 to 1270', in D.M. Palliser (ed.), *The Cambridge Urban History of Britain*, vol. 1 (Cambridge, 2000), 245–70.
Bridbury, A.R., *England and the Salt Trade in the Later Middle Ages* (Oxford, 1955).
Britnell, R. and Hatcher, J. (eds), *Progress and Problems in Medieval England: Essays in Honour of Edward Miller* (Cambridge, 1996).
Brodt, B., 'East Anglia', in D.M. Palliser (ed.), *The Cambridge Urban History of Britain*, vol. 1 (Cambridge, 2000), 639–56.
Butcher, D., 'The development of pre-industrial Lowestoft, 1560–1730' (unpub. MPhil thesis, Univ. East Anglia, 1991).
—, *The Ocean's Gift* (Norwich, 1995).
—, 'The herring fisheries in the early modern period: Lowestoft as microcosm', in D.J. Starkey, C. Reid and N. Ashcroft (eds), *England's Sea Fisheries* (London, 2000), 54–63.
—, *Lowestoft, 1550–1750* (Woodbridge, 2008).
—, *Rigged for River and Sea* (Hull, 2008).
—, *The Island of Lothingland: a Domesday and Hundred Roll Handbook* (Lowestoft, 2012).
—, *Mutford Half-hundred: Domesday Analysis and Medieval Exploration* (Lowestoft, 2013).
Butcher, D. and Bunn, I., *Lowestoft Burning: The Fire of 1645* (Lowestoft, 2003).
Byng, G., 'Parish church building and the later medieval economy' (unpublished PhD thesis, University of Cambridge, 2014).
Cam, H.M., *The Hundred and the Hundred Rolls* (London, 1930 and 1963).
Campbell, B.M.S., *English Seigniorial Agriculture, 1250–1450* (Cambridge, 2006).
Campbell, B.M.S., Bartley, K.C. and Power, J.P., 'The demesne-farming systems of post Black Death England: a classification', *AHR*, 44/2 (1996), 131–79.
Campbell, J., 'Hundreds and leets: a survey with suggestions', in C. Harper-Bill (ed.), *Medieval East Anglia* (Woodbridge, 2005), 153–67.

Cautley, H.M., *Norfolk Churches* (Ipswich, 1949).

—, *Suffolk Churches and Their Treasures*, 3rd edn (Ipswich, 1954).

Childs, W., 'Fishing and fisheries in the Middle Ages: the eastern fisheries', in D.J. Starkey, C. Reid and N. Ashcroft (eds), *England's Sea Fisheries* (London, 2000), 19–23.

Collins, J., *Salt and Fishery, a Discourse Thereof* (London, 1682).

Copinger, W.A., *The Manors of Suffolk*, vol. 5 (Manchester, 1909).

Cornwall, J., 'English country towns in the 1520s', *EHR*, 2nd series 15 (1962), 54–69.

Davis, J., 'Market regulation in fifteenth-century England', in B. Dodds and C.D. Liddy (eds), *Commercial Activity, Markets and Entrepreneurs in the Middle Ages* (Woodbridge, 2011), 81–105.

Dodds, B. and Liddy, C.D. (eds), *Commercial Activity, Markets and Entrepreneurs in the Middle Ages* (Woodbridge, 2011).

Durbidge, P., 'A second limited excavation in the grounds of the John Wilde School, Lowestoft', LA&LHS *Annual Report*, 37 (Lowestoft, 2005), 21–43.

—, 'The earliest humans in northern Europe: artefacts from the Cromer Forest Bed Formations at Pakefield, Suffolk', in LA&LHS *Annual Report*, 38 (Lowestoft, 2006), 21–5.

—, *A Report on the Limited Excavation on the Site of No. 1 High Street* (Lowestoft, 2014).

Dyer, C., 'Small towns 1270–1540', in D.M. Palliser (ed.), *The Cambridge Urban History of Britain*, vol. 1 (Cambridge, 2000), 505–38.

—, 'Luxury goods in medieval England', in B. Dodds and C.D. Liddy (eds), *Commercial Activity, Markets and Entrepreneurs in the Middle Ages* (Woodbridge, 2011), 217–38.

Dymond, D. and Martin, E. (eds), *An Historical Atlas of Suffolk* (Ipswich, 1988).

Dymond, D. and Northeast, P., *A History of Suffolk* (Chichester, 1985).

Ecclestone, A.W., *Henry Manship's Great Yarmouth* (Yarmouth, 1971).

Ekwall, E. (ed.), *The Oxford Dictionary of English Place-Names*, 4th edn (Oxford, 1960).

Faith, R., *The English Peasantry and the Growth of Lordship* (Leicester, 1997).

Farnhill, K., *Guilds and the Parish Community in Late Medieval East Anglia* (York, 2001).

Fleet, K., *European and Islamic Trade in the Early Ottoman State* (Cambridge, 2006).

Gillingwater, E., *An Historical Account of the Ancient Town of Lowestoft* (London, 1790).

Gillingwater, I., *A History of Lowestoft and Lothingland*, 3 vols (c. 1800).

Godden, G.A., *The Illustrated Guide to Lowestoft Porcelain* (London, 1969).

Good, C. and Plouviez, J., *Archaeological Service Report: The Archaeology of the Suffolk Coast* (Bury St Edmunds, 2007).

Harper-Bill, C. (ed.), *Medieval East Anglia* (Woodbridge, 2005).

Hatcher, J., 'The great slump of the mid-fifteenth century', in R. Britnell and J. Hatcher (eds), *Progress and Problems in Medieval England: Essays in Honour of Edward Miller* (Cambridge, 1996), 237–72.

—, 'Unreal wages', in B. Dodds and C.D. Liddy (eds), *Commercial Activity, Markets and Entrepreneurs in the Middle Ages* (Woodbridge, 2011), 1–24.

Hewitt, E.M., 'Fisheries', in W. Page (ed.), *The Victoria County History of Suffolk*, vol. 2 (London, 1907), 289–300.

Hodgson, W.C., *The Herring and Its Fishery* (London, 1957).

Keene, D., 'Crisis management in London's food supply, 1250–1500', in B. Dodds and C.D. Liddy (eds), *Commercial Activity, Markets and Entrepreneurs in the Middle Ages* (Woodbridge, 2011), 45–62.

Kerridge, E., *Textile Manufacture in Early Modern England* (Manchester, 1985)
Kowaleski, M., 'Fishing and fisheries in the Middle Ages: the western fisheries', in D.J. Starkey, C. Reid and N. Ashcroft (eds), *England's Sea Fisheries* (London, 2000), 23–8.
—, 'Port towns: England and Wales 1300–1540', in D.M. Palliser (ed.), *The Cambridge Urban History of Britain*, vol. 1 (Cambridge, 2000), 467–94.
—, 'The shipmaster as entrepreneur in medieval England', in B. Dodds and C.D. Liddy (eds), *Commercial Activity, Markets and Entrepreneurs in the Middle Ages* (Woodbridge, 2011), 165–82.
Kurlansky, M., *Cod* (London, 1998).
Kussmaul, A., *Servants in Husbandry in Early Modern England* (Cambridge, 1981).
Langdon, J., 'Minimum wages and unemployment rates in medieval England: the case of Old Woodstock, Oxfordshire, 1256–1357', in B. Dodds and C.D. Liddy (eds), *Commercial Activity, Markets and Entrepreneurs in the Middle Ages* (Woodbridge, 2011), 25–44.
Lee, J., 'Grain shortages in late medieval towns', in B. Dodds and C.D. Liddy (eds), *Commercial Activity, Markets and Entrepreneurs in the Middle Ages* (Woodbridge, 2011), 63–80.
Lees, B.A., 'Introduction to the Suffolk Domesday', in W. Page (ed.), *The Victoria County History of Suffolk*, vol. 1 (London, 1911), 357–417.
Lees, H.D.W., *The Chronicles of a Suffolk Parish Church* (Lowestoft, 1948).
Letters, S. (ed.), *Gazetteer of Markets and Fairs in England and Wales to 1516*, vol. 2, List and Index Society, Special Series 33 (London, 2003) (online resource).
Michell, A.R., 'The port and town of Great Yarmouth and its social and economic relationship with its neighbours on both sides of the sea, 1550–1714' (unpub. PhD thesis, Univ. Cambridge, 1978).
Moorman, R.H., *A History of the Church in England*, 3rd edn (London, 1973).
Myers, A.R., *England in the Late Middle Ages*, rev. edn (London, 1963).
Northeast, P., 'Parish gilds', in D. Dymond and E. Martin (eds), *An Historical Atlas of Suffolk* (Ipswich, 1988), 58–9.
Oppenheim, M., 'Maritime history', in W. Page (ed.), *The Victoria County History of Suffolk*, vol. 2 (London, 1907), 199–246.
Page, W. (ed.), *The Victoria County History of Suffolk*, vols 1 and 2 (London, 1911 and 1907). Also available online.
Palliser, D.M. (ed.), *The Cambridge Urban History of Britain*, vol. 1 (Cambridge, 2000).
Peterson, J.W.M., 'Possible extension of Roman centuriation to Lothingland (Norfolk/Suffolk)', NAHRG *Annual Report*, 17 (Norwich, 2008), 57–60.
Phythian-Adams, C., 'Urban decay in late medieval England', in P. Abrams and E.A. Wrigley (eds), *Towns in Societies* (Cambridge, 1978), 159–85.
—, *Desolation of a City: Coventry and the Urban Crisis of the Late Middle Ages* (Cambridge, 1979).
Powell, M.L., *Lowestoft Through the Ages* (Lowestoft, 1950).
Raban, S., *A Second Domesday? The Hundred Rolls of 1279–80* (Oxford, 2004).
Rackham, O., *Woodlands* (London, 2006).
Reaney, P.H., *The Origin of English Place Names*, 8th imprint (London, 1985).

Reeve, R., 'A history of Lowestoft and Lothingland', 4 vols (unpub. manuscript of c. 1810 – SRO(L), 193/3/1, 2, 3 and 4).

Richmond, C., *The Paston Family in the Fifteenth Century: Fastolf's Will* (Cambridge, 1996).

Rigby, S.H. and Ewan, E., 'Government, power and authority, 1300–1540', in D.M. Palliser (ed.), *The Cambridge Urban History of Britain* (Cambridge, 2000), 291–312.

Roffe, D., *Decoding Domesday* (Woodbridge, 2007).

Saul, A.R., 'Great Yarmouth in the fourteenth century: a study in trade, society and politics' (unpub. PhD thesis, Univ. Oxford, 1975).

—, 'The herring industry at Great Yarmouth, c. 1280–1400', *Norfolk Archaeology*, 38 (1981), 33–43.

—, 'English towns in the late Middle Ages: the case of Great Yarmouth', *Journal of Medieval History*, 8 (1982), 75–88.

Sheail, J., 'The regional distribution of wealth in England as indicated by the 1524–5 Lay Subsidy' (unpub. PhD thesis, Univ. London, 1968).

—, *The Regional Distribution of Wealth in England as Indicated by the 1524–5 Lay Subsidy*, List and Index Society, Special Series 29 (London, 1997).

Smith, A., 'Aspects of the career of Sir John Fastolf, 1380–1459', in R.E. Archer and S. Walker (eds), *Rulers and Ruled in Late Medieval England* (London, 1995), 137–53.

Spufford, M., *Contrasting Communities* (Cambridge, 1974).

Starkey, D.J., Reid, C. and Ashcroft, N. (eds), *England's Sea Fisheries* (London, 2000).

Suckling, A.I., *The History and Antiquities of the County of Suffolk*, vol. 1 (London, 1846).

Thirsk, J. (ed.), *The Agrarian History of England and Wales*, vol. 4 (Cambridge, 1967).

Unger, R.W., 'The Netherlands herring fishery of the late Middle Ages: the false legend of Willem Beukels of Biervliet', *Viator*, 9 (1978), 335–56.

Van Niekerk, J.P., *The Development of Insurance Law in the Netherlands, 1500–1800*, vol. 1 (Cape Town, 1998).

Warner, P., *The Origins of Suffolk* (Manchester, 1996).

Williams, N., *The Maritime Trade of the East Anglian Ports, 1550–1590* (Oxford, 1988).

Woolgar, C., 'Take this penance now, and afterwards the fare will improve: seafood and late medieval diet', in D.J. Starkey, C. Reid and N. Ashcroft (eds), *England's Sea Fisheries* (London, 2000), 36–44.

Index of people

Numbered identical names give chronological order, without always indicating family ties.
The years cited usually relate to a particular event in the individual person's life.
Places of residence for people from outside the town are given, where known.
The terms Snr. and Jnr. derive from the sources and refer to father and son.
Occupations are appended where information has revealed them.

Abbeye, Simon de (Aberdeen merchant, 1370) 172
Adam(s), Henry (Lowestoft demesne tenant, 1274) 33, 38, 44
Aelmer (freeman, priest & lord of Akethorpe, 1066) 17, 23, 65, 190
Aethelstan (Gapton freeman, 1066) 17
Ager, Thomas (Lowestoft taxpayer, 1524) 233
Agnes, daughter of Selida (Akethorpe litigant, 1205–6) 65
Ailam, Andrew (Lowestoft ship's master, 1533) 293
Akethorpe, Edmund of (Lowestoft taxpayer, 1327) 62, 64, 291
Akethorpe, John of (brother of Stephen & litigant, 1240) 65
Akethorpe, Mabel of (mother of Robert & Richard, 1274) 65
Akethorpe, Richard of (brother of Robert & litigant, 1254) 65, 66
Akethorpe, Robert of (brother of Richard & litigant, 1254) 65, 66
Akethorpe, Stephen of (brother of John & litigant, 1240) 65
Akethorpe, William of (lord of that manor, c. 1190) 66
Akethorpe family 62, 76
Akle, John (citizen of Great Yarmouth, 1311) 164
Alan of Brittany, Count (Lothingland landholder, 1086) 17, 21
Aleyn, Henry (Lowestoft villeinage tenant, 1274) 33
Aleyn, John 1 (citizen of Yarmouth, 1308) 149, 164
Aleyn, John 2 (Lowestoft taxpayer, 1327) 62
Aleyn, family 63
Allcock, Richard (Lowestoft lesser tradesman, 1524) 233
Allen, Sir Ashurst (lord of the manor of Lowestoft, 1768) 300
Allen, Thomas (Lowestoft lesser merchant, 1525) 235
Allen, surname 236, 237, 238, 261
Ali (Dunston freeman, 1066) 17
Allin, Richard (gentleman & Lowestoft steward, 1726) 253 n.41
Alman, Henry (Lowestoft shipping-plunderer, 1343) 177
Alric (Corton freeman, 1066) 17
Alric (Lound freeman, 1066) 18
Alwold (Somerleyton freeman, 1066) 18
Ambrose, Saint (bishop & doctor of The Church, c. 337–97 A.D.) 213
Amor, Nicholas (Suffolk historian, 2011) 136, 254, 263, 265
Andrew, Robert (Akethorpe bailiff, 1438) 74
Andrew, Saint (disciple & church dedication) 24, 57, 191
Andrews, Avis (Lowestoft taxpayer, 1525) 235
Anne (Queen of England, 1702–14) 225
Annot, Thomas (Lowestoft merchant, 1524) 235, 238, 239, 249, 255, 269, 270, 293
Annot, surname 237, 238, 261
[Anon]. Bernard (French servant of John Goddard, 1524) 232

Gerald, John (Lowestoft taxpayer, 1327) 62, 291
Gerald (or Jerald), family 62, 63
Gerard, John (German weaver & continental incomer, 1436) 242
German, John (shipping-plunderer, 1343) 177
Gilbank, Robert (Lowestoft merchant & taxpayer, 1525) 235
Gilbank, Thomas (Lowestoft merchant, 1568) 250
Gilbank surname 238
Gillingwater, Edmund (barber, bookseller & antiquarian, 1790) 98, 125, 126 n.18, 186, 190, 211, 215, 216, 219, 222, 278, 300
Gillingwater, Isaac (brother of Edmund, Lowestoft barber & antiquarian, 1800) 117 n.6
Gilly, Thomas (Lowestoft taxpayer, 1327) 62, 64
Gleason, John (Vicar of Lowestoft, 1603–10) 222
Goddard, John (Lowestoft merchant, 1535) 207, 220, 231, 232
Goddard, surname 264
Gode, Richard (Lowestoft demesne & villeinage tenant, 1274) 34, 35
Gode, William (Lowestoft manor tenant, 1274) 38, 46
Godfrey, Thomas (gentleman & Lowestoft steward, 1680–1704) 253 n.41
Godwin (Browston freeman, 1066) 17
Godwin (Fritton freeman, 1066) 17
Goldwell, James (Bishop of Norwich, 1472–99) 219
Gooch, Richard (Lowestoft merchant, 1566) 225
Gopeld, Walter (Aberdeen merchant, 1370) 172
Goseford, John de (Lowestoft glebe tenant, 1306) 199
Gosenol, William (Lowestoft manor tenant, 1274) 38, 39
Gourneye [Gurney], Edmund (Norfolk J.P., 1369) 172
Gray, John (Newcastle merchant, 1352) 183
Grefyngk, Barnard (Lübeck merchant, 1476) 179
Gregory I [al. the Great], Saint (Pope, 590–604 A.D., & doctor of The Church) 210, 213
Gregory XII (Pope, 1406–15) 217
Gregory Nazianzen, Saint (bishop & doctor of The Church, c. 329–90 A.D.) 213 n.46
Grene, Henry (royal justice, 1353) 181, 182, 183, 184
Grene, John (Grantham merchant, 1398) 152
Grenehore, Robert de la (Hundred Roll victim, 1274) 52
Gretheved, William (Berwick or Newcastle merchant, 1352) 182
Groat, Philip (Lowestoft Guernsey servant, 1524) 234
Gronge, Harry (Lowestoft taxpayer, 1524) 233
Grudgefield, John (Lowestoft merchant, 1566) 225, 271
Grudgfilde, Thomas (Lowestoft ship's master, 1572) 296
Grudgfyld, John (Lowestoft ship's master, 1572) 296
Grym(e), Geoffrey (Lowestoft holder of salvaged timber & shipping plunderer, 1341) 171, 177
Grym. John (Lowestoft holder of salvaged timber, 1341) 171 – same man as either of the two below
Grym, John Jnr. (Lowestoft shipping-plunderer, 1343) 177
Grym, John Snr. (Lowestoft shipping-plunderer, 1343) 177
Grym, William 1 Lowestoft taxpayer, 1327) 62, 64 – possibly the same man, as below
Grym, William 2 (Lowestyoft shipping-plunderer, 1343) 177
Gryme, Henry (Suffolk customs searcher, 1383) 153, 166, 168
Grym(e) family 236
Gybbeson, William (continental incomer, 1440) 242
Gyrth Godwinson 16, 17, 18, 22, 274

Hadley, John (Lowestoft labourer-servant & taxpayer, 1524) 234
Haenyld, Thomas (Lowestoft villeinage tenant, 1274) 34, 38, 50, 292
Haenyld, family 62, 63
Hagenhild [Haenyld], Robert (Lowestoft taxpayer, 1327) 62
Hakenham, Roger de (commissioner, 1378) 185
Hakon (Flixton freemen, 1066) 17

Index of places

All localised names (streets, fields etc.) relate to Lowestoft, unless otherwise indicated.
References to English counties pre-date the boundary changes of 1891 and 1974.
Communities without geographical reference were all located in Suffolk.
Earlier names preceding those currently used are shown in italic font
Illustrations are indicated by bold type.

Index of subjects

Illustrations are indicated by bold type.